The Columbia Guide to Central African Literature in English Since 1945

The Columbia Guides to Literature Since 1945

The Columbia Guides to Literature Since 1945

The Columbia Guide to Central African Literature in English Since 1945

Adrian Roscoe

with Contributions by Anthony Chennells

Columbia University Press
New York

Columbia University Press
Publishers Since 1893
New York   Chichester, West Sussex

Copyright © 2008 Columbia University Press

Library of Congress Cataloging-in-Publication Data
Roscoe, Adrian A.
    The Columbia guide to Central African literature in English since 1945 / Adrian Roscoe.
        p. cm.—(The Columbia guides to literature since 1945)
    Includes bibliographical references and index.
    ISBN 978-0-231-13042-4 (cloth : alk paper)—ISBN 978-0-231-50379-2 (e-book)

    1. Zimbabwean literature (English)—History and criticism—Handbooks, manuals, etc.   2. Malawi
literature (English)—History and criticism—Handbooks, manuals, etc.   3. Zambian literature (English)—
History and criticism—Handbooks, manuals, etc.   4. Africa, Central—Intellectual life.   I. Title.
II. Series.

PR9390.5.R59 2007
820.9'96891—dc22   2007006783

Columbia University Press books are printed on permanent and durable acid-free paper.
This book is printed on paper with recycled content.

Printed in the United States of America

c 10 9 8 7 6 5 4 3 2 1

References to Internet Web sites (URLs) were accurate at the time of writing. Neither the author nor
Columbia University Press is responsible for URLs that may be expired or changed since the manuscript was
prepared.

*For those suffering misfortune
and those urgently portraying it*

Contents

Part III

Preface

This book reflects the growth of written literature in English since 1945 in the three Central African nations of Zimbabwe, Malawi, and Zambia, countries that share a common history as former British colonies. (Vernacular texts arising from the region's ancient oral traditions do not fall within the guide's compass.) The suggested baseline date of 1945 would be significant for an examination of modern literature from most parts of Africa. In the case of Central Africa, the end of World War II brought both imperial fatigue and broken British promises about freedom, which in turn revived liberation energies and ultimately produced both independence and a major upsurge in literary production.

Freedom arrived in the 1960s for Malawi and Zambia, but not until 1980 for Zimbabwe, and then only after a bloody war provoked by white settlers unable, or unwilling, to foresee the growing demand for freedom on the part of subjugated blacks. Central African literature from this period thus reflects colonial and postcolonial experience and in its responses naturally shares commonalities with writing across the continent. The introductory sections, therefore, and individual author entries, carry cross-continental allusion whenever literary and historical linkage seems illuminating. Because Central Africa, unlike, say, West Africa, was a site of classic settler colonialism, comparisons with such settler territories as Kenya, Uganda, and South Africa will arise most naturally. On the other hand, since a phenomenon like postcolonial disenchantment overleaps the boundaries of colonial taxonomy, allusion to this might reach in any direction across the continent. A related point is that, where comment on African writing once emphasized the West's shaping influence (Senegalese debts to Chateaubriand or Malawian echoes of Eliot), the connecting lines of fertilization are now distinctly African. A Zambian writer might reflect the influence of Uganda's Okot p'Bitek, a Zimbabwean writer the influence of South Africa's Es'kia Mphahlele.

A distinguishing feature of the *Columbia Guide to Central African Literature in English Since 1945* is its introductory focus on colonialism itself—its nature, origins, and varieties. This should need no apology. To investigate African literature without reference to colonialism would resemble, say, studying African Americans without allusion to slavery, or considering the Middle East without mention of the Ottomans. For Central Africa, then, this means not just colonialism but, precisely, British colonialism. This book asks—even if cannot clearly answer—what were British colonialism's motivating energies, how it could be legitimized, and how it differed from rival brands. Did it begin, as all modern projects and proposals must, with a neat statement of "aims and objectives" and bureaucratic confusion over how these terms might differ? Was there an identity of colonial impact, immediate and long-term, on all three Central African territories? And what characteristics is the new writing manifesting as colonialism recedes into history?

Central Africa has also produced a settlers' literature. With considerable success (witness Doris Lessing and Wilbur Smith) the white community, repeating Canadian,

Australian, New Zealand, and American experience, has made its own chronicle of the new lands, even while discouraging African literary expression. The *Guide* captures this white writing in a halting and eventually fading dialogue with its rapidly growing black partner.

The modalities of literary production also arise for scrutiny. Publishing houses, missionary and commercial printing presses, newspapers, journals, film, radio and television, school, college, and university curricula—these are all important. Relevant, too, are the weaponry of literary censorship and the relative health of the different genres. How well do the novel and drama fare? Do they match the short story's energy? And can they challenge the vitality of verse?

Core themes are perhaps predictable. One is the overarching struggle for freedom—achieved in Zimbabwe only after the loss of some thirty thousand lives in a guerilla war, and then perhaps twenty thousand more in a pointless civil conflict. Another is independence disillusion, echoing anterior experience in Africa East and West. But below these swirl related currents: an obsession (not always unqualified) with modern education as a precondition for liberation and postcolonial development; grinding poverty, seen starkly, for example, in Zambia's 1970s after the collapse of world copper prices; drought as an abiding fear in semiarid lands, and related cycles of feast and famine; joblessness in new cash economies that make rural life barely sustainable; catastrophic waste of talent when postcolonial leaders wallow in corruption and devise murderous strategies for survival. Meanwhile, an AIDS pandemic of mediaeval ferocity reaps swathes of the region's population, and writers, despite its sensitivities, are bravely addressing it. Amidst such misery it is unsurprising that alcoholism—everywhere—wreaks individual and social devastation. Much work, too, exudes an existential loneliness, jaggedly at odds with received impressions of societies classically collective and communal, if strikingly similar to the solitude of European romanticism during an age of similar social change.

With the departure of their founding presidents Kenneth Kaunda and Hastings Banda, Malawi and Zambia saw second political dawns and thus new challenges to their writers. Malawi's arrived after Banda's thirty-year effort to silence, murder, imprison, or exile a generation of writers and intellectuals. But, even in adversity, Central African writing constantly breathes an air of resilience. This, perhaps, is the heart of the matter. However brutal the oppression, deep the disappointment, or profound the trauma, the writing at least refutes George Orwell's apocalyptic image of the future as a boot stamped on a human face—forever. Individuals and groups astonishingly rebound. Sam Mpasu, Jack Mapanje, and Felix Mnthali live to describe the nightmare of Banda's jails, their human goodness unimpaired; Binwell Sinyangwe describes Zambia's harrowing poverty but still cultivates hope. Christine Nyamubaya survives the slaughter of Zimbabwe's Second Chimurenga and does rural work with Oxfam to build a radiant future.

The gaze of Central African literature thus shifts to successive issue-clusters, from colonial protest to postcolonial campaigns for social justice and political integrity, for education and economic empowerment, gender equity, participatory democracy, rural development, and environmental care—for delivery, often enough, on golden promises made as British flags were lowered. But while prophetically touching present and future, writers increasingly seek to chronicle the past. European colonialism, suggest Jack Goody and Walter Ong, exploited preliteracy—cultural conquest being harder in India with its written traditions than in a sub-Saharan Africa without them. Hence a movement, seen typically, but not exclusively, in Malawi's Mnthali and Steve Chimombo, Zimbabwe's Stanlake Samkange and Yvonne Vera, and Zambia's Dominic Mulaisho, to create an African literary-historical alternative to a white historiography in which the colonized was neither agent nor informer. Santayana's warning that those who do not know their history are condemned to repeat it is well understood.

Because this book seeks optimal coverage, it mingles established careers with careers nascent, midstream, or, like those of Dambudzo Marechera, Anthony Nazombe, and Zangaphee Chizese, tragically cut short. Sometimes a single anthology entry is used as a means of capturing this representational breadth. Non-African readers might well know of Charles Mungoshi, Dambudzo Marechera, and Jack Mapanje, but probably not the late Edison Mpina, Nozipo Maraire, Peter Kalitera, or Innocent Banda. It seemed important, also, given the global crises surrounding Central African liberation, and thus the shaping backdrop to the literature, to include key political figures and the structures with which they were identified: hence entries on Kenneth Kaunda, Hastings Banda, Ian Smith, Robert Mugabe, ZANU, ZAPU, and ZANLA.

Some barriers challenging Central African writers might surprise. To the list of familiar problems around health, drought, famine, war, misrule, and illiteracy, one must, for example, add physical obstacles to publication. There is no *Writers' and Artists' Yearbook* here, stiff with publishers and literary agents who know their tastes. Commercial houses, even if benign, seek profitable school texts rather than books of verse, fiction, and drama, which limits the circulation of creative work. Flora Veit-Wild's introduction to *Scrapiron Blues* (1994) mentions the effect this had on the brilliant young Marechera: "In 1983, he submitted 'Killwatch or Tony Fights Tonight' to Longman who rejected it because they were anxious 'about our ability to market non-educational books which is what we are best at.' In 1985, his novel 'Depth of Diamonds' was rejected by College Press in Harare and Heinemann in the United Kingdom. . . . This situation depressed him deeply and was compounded by his deteriorating health." Then colonial determination to control, direct, or ban literature reproduced itself as postcolonial instrumentation for driving writers into silence, self-censorship, or exile. Hence the chameleon as iconic symbol for Malawian writing during thirty years of Banda and his Censorship Board and initial Zimbabwean hesitation to censure Robert Mugabe's Matebeland massacres—committed *after* victory against the settler regime. Some writers still reside overseas. Zimbabwe's Yvonne Vera was an exile in Canada when she died in 2005; Chenjerai Hove writes in France, Jack Mapanje in Britain, Felix Mnthali in Botswana. Conditions, as they would be understood in most parts of the world, remain abnormal. Some writers (Malawi's Steve Chimombo is exemplary) resort to self-publishing, with all its technical complexities. But even commercial houses in Africa face distribution problems, as anyone in Europe or North America seeking a full range of Central African texts swiftly discovers.

The author entries, from A to Z, offer biographical detail, where available, and critical comment. Published works appear simply with title and date, their complete bibliographic profile appearing at the end of the volume. Entries close with suggestions for further reading, again if this is available.

Finally, a note on terminology: though not parallel with East Africa, West Africa, North Africa, and Central Africa, the southern part of the continent is called Southern Africa, to distinguish it from the nation of South Africa. I follow that usage here.

Acknowledgments

While my principal debt is to Central Africa's writers themselves, it was Bernth Lindfors who first suggested that I be invited to prepare this book. I must thank him here and trust that he will not find his faith misplaced. The task has proved more satisfying, though more challenging, than I could have imagined. It has thus required the help not simply of my wife and family—Janice, Julian, Wilma, Claire, and Jenny, and their spouses Beatriz, Coen, and Riccardo (the usual heroes and heroines in cases of writing survival), but of many others too: colleagues, former colleagues, librarians, booksellers, friends of authors, even authors themselves who on occasion have kindly posted personal copies of their work unavailable in the bookshops of Europe and America. Anthony Chennells I must especially thank for contributing his expert knowledge on Central Africa's white writing with chapters 6, 13, and 14 and the entries on N. H. Brettell and Doris Lessing in the section on authors and their works.

At Columbia University Press, Juree Sondker and Plaegian Alexander were constantly encouraging, as was outside editor Gregory McNamee. At Sultan Qaboos University, the Dean of Arts, Dr. Isam Ali Ahmed Al-Rawas, provided both a teaching post and congenial working conditions, enabling me, *inter alia*, to use with profligacy the outstanding editorial skills that my colleague Paul Scanlon had recently applied to his editions of *Joseph Andrews* and *Moll Flanders*. Luanga Kasanga, for his part, never hesitated to answer my desperate calls for his PC wizardry. My world literature students meanwhile kept me on my toes with the innocently profound questions of the neophyte. Others at Sultan Qaboos University to whom I am indebted include Janet Holst, Farooq Babrakzai, Charles Campbell, David Deller, Bill Sypher, Jamal En-Nehas, Jane Nineham, and Christopher Gray. In the United Kingdom, John Lwanda and David Kimble were helpful at important moments. From Central and Southern Africa, encouragement and help came from Es'kia Mphahlele, Felix Mnthali, Greenwell Matsika, Martin Ott, Lazarus Miti, Lucy Dlamini, Liz Gunner, Jo Nel, Sitwala Imenda, Kaela Mulenga, Hannelie Zulu, Sam Raditlhalo, and Ken and Lilian Mew.

On certain scholars I have leaned shamelessly. They include Rino Zhuwarara and Flora Veit-Wild for guidance on Zimbabwean writing and David Kerr, James Gibbs, and Chris Kamlongera for expertise on Central African drama. As a nonhistorian keen to illustrate an organic link between colonial historiography and the new African writing, I have needed urgent help from contributors to the *Oxford History of the British Empire*, and especially from Nicholas Canny, Anthony Pagden, N. A. M. Rodger, P. E. H. Hair, Robin Law, Hilary M. Beckles, Robin Winks, and Wm. Roger Louis. I very much hope they will feel that I have sufficiently acknowledged their assistance both here and in the body of the text. Timelines included on Malawi, Zambia, and Zimbabwe are based on those generously offered on the BBC's World News Web site.

Chronology of Major Political Events, 1944–2006

Malawi

1944   Nationalists establish the Nyasaland African Congress.

1953   23 October: Despite strong opposition from the Nyasaland African Congress and white liberal activists, Britain combines Nyasaland with Northern and Southern Rhodesia to form the Central African Federation.

1958   Dr. Hastings Kamuzu Banda, dubbed "the black messiah," denounces the Central African Federation and returns from an overseas stay of many years to lead the Nyasaland African Congress.

1959   Violent clashes between Nyasaland African Congress supporters and the colonial authorities lead to the banning of the organization. Its leaders, including Banda, are arrested, and a state of emergency is declared. The Malawi Congress Party is founded as a successor to the Nyasaland African Congress.

1960   Banda is released from Gwelo Prison, Southern Rhodesia, and attends talks in London with the British government on constitutional reform.

1961   Elections held for a new Legislative Assembly. Banda's Malawi Congress Party wins 94 percent of the vote.

1963   Nyasaland is granted self-government, and Banda is appointed prime minister.

1964   6 July: Nyasaland declares independence as the Republic of Malawi.

1965   6 July: Banda becomes president of the Republic of Malawi. The constitution establishes a one-party state. Opposition movements are suppressed and their leaders detained. Foreign governments and organizations raise concerns about human rights.

1971   Banda is declared president for life.

1975   Lilongwe replaces Zomba as Malawi's capital.

1978   The first elections since independence are held. All potential candidates must belong to the Malawi Congress Party and be approved by Banda. He excludes many by submitting them to an English test.

1980s   Several ministers and politicians are killed or charged with treason. Banda reshuffles his ministers regularly, preventing the emergence of a political rival.

1992   Catholic bishops publicly condemn Banda, sparking demonstrations. Many donor countries suspend aid over Malawi's human rights record.

1993   President Banda becomes seriously ill. Voters in a referendum reject the one-party state, paving the way for members of parties other than the Malawi Congress Party to hold office.

1994   In presidential and municipal elections, Bakili Muluzi, leader of the new United Democratic Front, is elected president. He immediately frees political prisoners and reestablishes freedom of speech and the press. Banda, meanwhile, announces his retirement from politics.

1997   Banda dies in hospital in South Africa, where he is being treated for a neurological disorder.

1999   President Muluzi is reelected for a second and final five-year term.

2000   The World Bank announces that it will cancel 50 percent of Malawi's foreign debt.

2002   Drought causes crops to fail across central Africa. Malawi's government is accused of worsening the crisis through mismanagement and corruption, including selling off national grain reserves before drought struck.

2001   September: the railway linking central Malawi and the Mozambican port of Nacala reopens after almost twenty years, giving access to the Indian Ocean coast.

2004   May: Malawi's government announces that it will provide antiretroviral drugs to AIDS sufferers free of charge. Bingu wa Mutharika, ruling party candidate, is declared the winner of the presidential election. Observers and opposition are critical of the conduct of the poll.

2005   January: Three ruling party officials are charged with treason after carrying guns to a meeting with President Mutharika. The president later pardons the trio.
        November: Agriculture minister says five million Malawians need food aid owing to regional drought.

2006   February: President Mutharika resigns from the ruling party over what he says is its hostility to his anticorruption campaign. He survives an impeachment motion backed by his former party. The speaker of parliament collapses and dies during angry exchanges over the motion.

Zambia

1944   The waning years of World War II bring discontentment at the way African troops are treated. Prewar promises of improved conditions are not kept, fueling the rise of liberation aspirations.

1953   The Federation of Rhodesia and Nyasaland, comprising Northern Rhodesia, Southern Rhodesia, and Nyasaland, is created. The new political entity is imposed on black citizens.

1960   The United Independence Party (UNIP) is formed by Kenneth Kaunda to campaign for independence and for the dissolution of the Federation, dominated by white-ruled Southern Rhodesia.

1962   Britain dissolves the Central African Federation. Nyasaland's Dr. Hastings Kamuzu Banda claims the credit.

1963   Northern Rhodesia is granted independence as Zambia, with Kaunda as president.

1970s   Key enterprises are nationalized, as is private land in an unsuccessful agricultural improvement program.

1972   Zambia becomes a one-party state, with UNIP as the only legal party.

1975   The Chinese-built Tan-Zam railway is opened, providing a link between the Copper Belt and the Tanzanian port of Dar es Salaam, reducing dependence for the country's exports on white-ruled Rhodesia and apartheid South Africa.

1976   Zambia declares support for the independence struggle in Rhodesia and becomes a target of Rhodesian bombing. Zambian help proves crucial to the transition of Rhodesia to independent Zimbabwe.

1990   Food riots break out.

1991   A multiparty constitution is adopted. The Movement for Multiparty Democracy (MMD) wins the election, and its leader, Frederick Chiluba, becomes president.

1996   A change to Zambia's constitution effectively bars Kaunda from future elections. Chiluba is reelected.

1997   Members of the military attempt a coup.

1999   A high court sentences fifty-nine soldiers to death after they are found guilty of treason for the failed 1997 coup.

2000   May: Fighting between Angolan forces and UNITA rebels spills over into Zambian territory.

        July: Environment Minister Ben Mwila is expelled from the MMD and dropped from the cabinet after announcing his intention to run for president in 2001.

        December: UN officials estimate that up to sixty thousand refugees, fleeing fighting in the Democratic Republic of Congo, have moved to Zambia in less than a week.

2001   May: Setback for governing MMD as senior members hive off to create the Forum for Democracy and Development. They oppose Chiluba's bid for a third term in office.

        July: Paul Tembo, former campaign manager for Chiluba, who joined the opposition, is murdered shortly before he is due to testify against three ministers in a high-level corruption case.

        July: The final summit of the Organization of African Unity (OAU) is held, and the African Union is inaugurated.

2002   January: Levy Mwanawasa is sworn in as president amid opposition protests over alleged fraud in the previous month's presidential elections.

        July: Parliament votes to remove ex-president Chiluba's immunity from prosecution on corruption charges.

        October: Zambia's government announces that it will not accept genetically modified maize to help alleviate the severe food shortages facing three million Zambians.

2003   February: Former president Chiluba is arrested and charged with corruption. He subsequently faces two long-running trials, which are dogged by adjournments and procedural problems.

        December: The Supreme Court affirms death sentences on forty-four soldiers for their role in 1997's failed coup. President Mwanawasa later commutes the sentences.

2004   September: Many charges of corruption against former President Frederick Chiluba are dropped, but within hours he is rearrested on six new counts.

2005   February: The Supreme Court rejects an opposition challenge to President Mwanawasa's 2001 election victory, but says that the ballot had flaws.

2006   Some economic optimism as world copper prices soar. General elections are held, and President Mwanawasa is reelected.

Zimbabwe

1945   The end of World War II brings disappointment to Southern Rhodesian blacks because of broken British promises of advancement as thanks for help with the war effort. There are suspicions about troops who did not return. White immigration increases from the ranks of British servicemen who had done wartime military training in the country. The economy takes off on the back of postwar global reconstruction needs. Black political parties appear, but the country's conditions closely resemble those of racially divided South Africa.

1953   Britain, at the urging of white settlers, creates the Federation of Rhodesia and Nyasaland (Southern Rhodesia, Northern Rhodesia, and Nyasaland), which is ruled from Salisbury. White settlers believe that creation of the Federation will help secure dominion status from Britain of the kind enjoyed by Canada, New Zealand, and Australia. There is opposition to the Federation among blacks in all three territories.

1963   Britain dissolves the Federation. Northern Rhodesia and Nyasaland move to independence as Zambia and Malawi.

1964   Ian Smith, of the segregationist Rhodesia Front, becomes prime minister and tries to persuade Britain to grant Rhodesia independence.

1965   Smith unilaterally declares independence under white minority rule, sparking international outrage and economic sanctions. Britain moves jet fighter squadrons to neighboring Zambia, though Prime Minister Wilson rejects the use of force. An oil blockade of the port of Beira in Mozambique begins.

1972   Guerilla war against white rule intensifies, with the rival Zimbabwe African National Union (ZANU) and Zimbabwe African People's Union (ZAPU) operating out of Zambia and Mozambique.

1978   Smith yields to pressure for a negotiated settlement. Elections for a transitional legislature are boycotted by the Patriotic Front, made up of ZANU and ZAPU. The new government of Zimbabwe-Rhodesia, led by Bishop Abel Muzorewa, fails to gain international acceptance. The guerilla war continues.

1979   British-brokered all-party talks at Lancaster House, London, lead to a peace agreement and new constitution, which guarantees white minority rights.

1980   Veteran liberation leader Robert Mugabe and his ZANU party win British-supervised independence elections. Mugabe becomes prime minister and includes ZAPU leader Joshua Nkomo in his cabinet. Independence on April 18 is internationally recognized.

1982   Mugabe sacks Nkomo, accusing him of preparing to overthrow the government. The North Korean–trained Fifth Brigade is deployed to crush a rebellion by pro-Nkomo ex-guerillas in Midlands and Matabele provinces. Government forces are accused of killing more than thirty thousand civilians over the next few years.

1987   Mugabe and Nkomo merge their parties to form ZANU-PF, ending the violence in the southern areas.

1987   Mugabe changes the constitution to become executive president.

1991   The Commonwealth adopts the Harare Declaration at its summit in Zimbabwe, reaffirming its aims of fostering international peace and security, democracy, freedom of the individual, and equal rights for all.

1998   Economic crisis accompanied by riots and strikes.

1999   Economic crisis persists. Zimbabwe's military involvement in the Democratic Republic of Congo's civil war becomes increasingly unpopular. The opposition Movement for Democratic Change (MDC), led by Morgan Tsvangirai, is formed.

2000   February: Squatters seize hundreds of white-owned farms in an ongoing and violent campaign to reclaim land they claim was stolen by settlers. Mugabe suffers defeat in a referendum on a draft constitution.

June: In parliamentary elections, ZANU-PF narrowly fights off a challenge from the MDC, but loses its power to change the constitution.

2001   May: Defense Minister Moven Mahachi is killed in a car crash, the second minister to die in this way in a month.

July: New Defense Minister Simba Makoni publicly acknowledges the economic crisis, saying that Zimbabwe's foreign reserves have run out and warning that the country faces serious food shortages. Most Western donors, including the World Bank and the IMF, cut aid because of Mugabe's land-seizure program. In October, visiting Commonwealth ministers say that the government has done little to honor commitments to end the crisis over the seizure of white-owned land.

2002   February: Parliament passes a law limiting media freedom. The European Union imposes sanctions on Zimbabwe and pulls out its election observers after the EU team leader is expelled.

March: Mugabe is reelected in presidential elections condemned as seriously flawed by the opposition MDC and foreign observers. The Commonwealth suspends Zimbabwe from its councils for a year after concluding that the elections were marred by high levels of violence.

April: a state of disaster is declared as worsening food shortages threaten famine. The government blames drought; the UN's World Food Program says disruption to agriculture is a contributing factor.

June: a forty-five-day countdown is announced for some 2,900 white farmers to leave their land under the terms of a land-acquisition law passed in May.

September: a Commonwealth committee—including the leaders of South Africa, Nigeria, and Australia—fails to agree on further sanctions against President Mugabe.

November: Agriculture Minister Joseph Made says that the land grab is over. He says that the government has seized thirty-five million acres of land from white farmers.

2003   March: A widely observed strike is followed by the arrests—and reported beatings—of hundreds of people. A BBC correspondent says the evidence points to a crackdown of "unprecedented brutality."

June: the leader of the opposition MDC, Morgan Tsvangirai, is arrested twice during a week of opposition protests. He is charged with treason, adding to an existing treason charge from 2002 over an alleged plot to kill President Mugabe.

November: Canaan Banana, Zimbabwe's first black president, dies in Britain at the age of sixty-seven.

December: Zimbabwe leaves the Commonwealth after the organization decides to extend suspension of the country indefinitely.

2004   March: Sixty-seven men alleged to be mercenaries planning a coup in Equatorial Guinea are detained and charged after their plane, arriving from South Africa, is impounded in Harare.

September: the leader of the accused mercenaries, British national Simon Mann, is sentenced to seven years in prison for attempting to buy guns. Meanwhile in South

Africa, Mark Thatcher, son of former Prime Minister Margaret Thatcher, is charged with involvement in the affair.

October: opposition leader Morgan Tsvangirei is acquitted of treason charges relating to an alleged plot to kill President Mugabe. He faces a separate treason charge.

2005   January: The government of the United States labels Zimbabwe one of the world's six "outposts of tyranny." Zimbabwe rejects the statement.

February: Information Minister Jonathan Moyo is sacked amid a succession struggle within the ruling party.

March: Pius Ncube, the Catholic archbishop of Matabeleland, urges a peaceful popular uprising to get rid of President Mugabe, accusing him of denying food aid to people who support the opposition. President Mugabe begins his Clear Out Rubbish campaign, destroying urban dwellings and affecting up to two million people, according to UN reports.

2006   The World Health Organization reports that life in Zimbabwe is shorter than anywhere else in the world, with neither men nor women expected to live to the age of forty. Archbishop Ncube attacks the government's performance.

September: Inflation exceeds 1,200 percent. Speaking during a visit to Malawi, President Mugabe urges reconciliation with his white citizens ("We must all live together") and offers to hand back some land to white farmers. Opposition demonstrations in support of a national strike are broken up.

Part I
History and Politics

1. Empire and Colonialism

In a recent history of the British Empire, N. A. M. Rodger writes, "If Empire, as Francis Xavier said, was little more than 'to conjugate the verb to rob in all its moods and tenses,' the English were the purest of imperialists."[1] Such comment, saintly or historiographic, is arresting. But modern scholarship, which prefers inconclusiveness to certainty, blunts its sharpness. For it shows that, beside Xavierian disgust, traceable through Swift, Orwell, and a Conrad who dismissed even Roman colonization as "robbery with violence, aggravated murder on a great scale," contrary comment runs, and sometimes from those felt to be loftily humanist. Edmund Spenser was a leading imperialist visionary, acquiring an estate in Ireland of twelve thousand acres on condition he develop it with Protestant English settlers—and experiencing early anticolonial protest when his mansion in Cork was torched. Michael Drayton was another enthusiast, his "Ode To the Virginia Voyage" urging pioneers to "Go, and subdue . . . Earth's only paradise," while lazy Britons "Lurk here at home, with shame." Bacon and Milton gave colonization a horticultural hue, calling it "plantation," Bacon writing an essay on the subject and Milton calling God the great Planter. Locke took much trouble to legitimize it and happily joined the Virginia Company. Macaulay's Whig optimism admitted no doubt. And while older Africans might reflect wistfully on colonial days, postcolonial eyebrows rise at the reentry of British troops into Sierra Leone, French troops into Ivory Coast, and American troops into Liberia.

Modern historical and literary scholarship (cooperative synergies become increasingly manifest) subverts easy assumption and casual generalization. As with democracy in the twentieth century, so now analysis of colonialism and imperialism in the twenty-first reveals polysemy in words long jingling unexamined in popular discourse. Would Gibbon's notions of empire resonate with those of Nyerere or Mandela? Would Conrad's perspective on colonialism chime with that of vendors in the souks of Zanzibar?

Conjugating colonization across its grammatical paradigm thus unearths complexity in a phenomenon ancient and modern. Calendared independence days, contemporary reminders of empire, are innumerable. Inquiry at any multiethnic gathering will reveal a majority who have been, or *feel*, colonized. Indians will recall the rule of the British, Brazilians that of the Portuguese, Bolivians of the Spanish, Ukrainians of the Russians, Ivorians of the French. Elderly voices may even recall double colonization—Bulgarians by Turks and Russians, South African blacks by Afrikaners and Englishmen. Cameroonians might even recall a triple colonization—German, French, and British.

Meaning and emotion reach farther. Populations even within imperial powers may feel colonized by compatriot groups: northerners by southerners, peasants by urbanites, tradesmen by professionals, a lower class by an upper class. In the ironically titled United Kingdom, Scots and Welsh, early victims of English expansion, feel sufficiently colonized to have recently demanded, and won, devolution, though in the case of Wales only partially so. Northern Ireland's Catholics still feel as much colonial subjects as Africans in the 1950s, and jokes about Cornish home rule reflect ambition that at one level is real. Northern England feels economically colonized by the south, and academically, too, with its redbrick universities beginning life as satellites of Oxford and Cambridge. In religion, the English Catholic writers Newman, Waugh, and Hopkins complained bitterly of Irish spiritual colonization and sought reconnection with the Catholicism of pre-Reformation England. As reformed poachers make the best gamekeepers, so the colonized can become colonizers too—witness a substantial contribution to Britain's burgeoning empire by the Scots, Welsh, and Irish.

A European imperialism that scrambled to possess Africa nursed ancient memories as colonial victim itself, bearing invader fingerprints on its language, law, and religion. Conrad's brooding overture to *Heart of Darkness* ("And this also . . . has been one of the dark places of the earth . . . marshes, forests, savages") conjures a colonized nation that later mounted its own imperial project, for which, says Anthony Pagden, Roman precedent provided inspiration and model.[2] With Roman Britain later becoming a classic settler colony of Anglo-Saxon, Dane, and Frenchman, expansion perhaps sank deep into the national DNA, as those treated with violence in childhood are said to grow up and inflict violence on others.

Precisely why nations expand and conquer is rarely a simple question. Yet it is prompted by every Roman grave in Chester or York, every Andalusian Arabic fresco, Maltese Roman mosaic, Zimbabwean Victorian villa, Cameroonian German botanical garden, and West African Portuguese fort. What impulse drives this determination to push out, subdue, and settle? What notions, rational or otherwise, caused Syrian legionaries to end their days in cloudy Britain or African levies to die in Burma? And how did rural communities in distant lands, isolated and unsuspecting, respond to bullying strangers determined to disrupt their private worlds?

These are germane questions when we read the poetry of Zimbabwe's Chenjerai Hove, the drama of Malawi's Steve Chimombo, or the fiction of Zambia's Lazarus Miti. Central African literature, it must be stressed, has emerged from the planning, management, and collapse of a global imperial project. In turn, that project's nineteenth-century African practice emerged from practice earlier and elsewhere, and especially in the Caribbean. British reaction to Roman control is, alas, little known; but an expanding corpus of literature and historiography captures Central Africa's response to British governance. In verse or prose, it registers group and personal reaction to colonial incursion and cultural change. Poets such as Chenjerai Hove, Felix Mnthali, Jack Mapanje, Musaemura Zimunya, and Steve Chimombo, and novelists such as Stanlake Samkange, Yvonne Vera, Shimmer Chinodya, Tsitsi Dangarembga, Charles Mungoshi, and Binwell Sinyangwe, portray multidimensional societies contesting a common colonial domination and shaping new grammars for life after its decease.

British imperialism is a site of scholarly contestation interdisciplinary in method and noisy in debate. Inherited simplicity no longer serves. Emerging complexity, perhaps naturally, demands explicatory theory, despite the perils of applying this to the humanities, and scholars such as Anthony Pagden and Niall Ferguson are making key contributions to its development. Indeed, yesterday's jingoism and pub-bar blather have yielded to an industry in which the *Oxford History of the British Empire* (1998) requires 156 international scholars and 3,500 pages even to begin mapping its subject's complexity.

It once sufficed to inform undergraduates that African literature in English responded to a colonialism that was fundamentally materialist. The distinguished scholar Salvador de Madariaga had pronounced that Britain's empire was at base economic, Spain's religious, and, intriguingly, France's intellectual—a Gallic solar system with Paris as center and sun.[3] Such categorical certainty will no longer do. The historian Hilary Beckles, for one, suggests that Spanish galleons were not actually built to carry Bibles, and Anthony Pagden notes that when envious Raleigh whispered to his queen that Spain's greatness grew from neither religion nor "sacks of Seville oranges" but from "Indian gold that disturbeth all the nations of Europe," there were zealous Protestant advisers listening, too.[4] Nor, if genuine, was France's lofty concern to assimilate, which later triggered a defiant negritude, unmixed with baser aims. Robert Harms's *The 'Diligent': A Voyage Through the World of the Slave Trade* shows via the journal of one Robert Durand that eighteenth-century Breton merchants were no high-minded savants living off the imagination but businessmen beavering for profit. Commercial calculation took total precedence over pity for the hapless cargo of *The Diligent*. Indeed, says Harms, Captain Durand "mentioned the African captives only twice during the entire 66 days of the middle passage, and then only to record deaths."[5]

Theory continues to multiply. Imperialism is seen alternately as the fruit of a capitalist high summer, as overseas expansion by an upper class struggling at home, as a national sleepwalking exercise, as a desire to protect vital trade routes, as distant intervention, becoming long-term, to prop up failed local regimes, and so on. All have their proponents.

2. British Imperialism

British imperialism created Zimbabwe, Malawi, and Zambia. And thus it shaped literary reaction. Around so complex a subject there is at least agreement on chronology. Nicholas Canny and his colleagues in the *Oxford History of the British Empire* depict England as a slow starter in the imperial game. While Portuguese caravels pushed south to the Gulf of Guinea, with Portugal operating sugar mills on São Tomé by 1460 and soon after commercially dominating Southeast Asia and the Pacific, and while Spain built a vast empire in the Americas, England's global vision stopped at Ulster. On the high seas beyond she confined herself to snapping enviously at the heels of Spanish treasure ships, as modern-day Mafiosi might nibble at the fat of Microsoft.[1]

This was still Little England. Its small ships were built for coastal trade, its pilots expert only on home ports and rivers. National consolidation rather than international expansion was paramount. But, as Canny shows, once expansionary fever struck, commerce and religion embraced. For, while bullion beckoned, before Catholic Europe English zealots were also flaunting a reformed Christianity—proof that God had smiled on a chosen people.

Before 1600, then, overseas territorial interest was minimal, despite minor stirrings with the 1562 establishment of an Anglo-French Huguenot colony in Florida. Then energetic Protestants such as Walsingham, Purchas, and the Hakluyts, failing to fire London merchants with enthusiasm for foreign projects, approached Elizabeth I, urging adventure that combined trade, colonization, and religion. Thus could England puncture Spanish pride and advance the cause of Protestant global rule. Did not England, after all, have a messianic duty to bring true religion to the world's pagans?[2]

Hence, England's first serious colonial venture, the 1585 plantation of Munster—significant as a settler experiment for later imperial governance—was also strongly religious. The blueprint envisaged introducing enough non-Catholic immigrants finally to convert all Ireland to a godly Protestantism—with results that continue to baffle the modern mind. Canny shows that, later, Bermuda's Berkeley Plantation promoters, also marrying God and Mammon, commissioned their agent "to erect and build a town called Barkley and to settle and plant our men and diverse other inhabitants there, to the honour of Almighty God, the enlarging of Christian religion, and to the augmentation and revenue of the general plantation in that country, and the particular good and profit of ourselves." John Winthrop, who dreamed of a colonist's life in Ireland but woke as a 1620 Plymouth plantation leader, felt so encircled by Catholics—French to the North, Spaniards to the South, and even Jesuits in Maryland—that he wanted a Protestants-only policy for New England. And when compatriots established the Providence Island colony off Nicaragua, it was essentially for attacking Spain's Catholic Empire. It failed when spiritual motive yielded to the same profit motive that, in Protestant eyes, so damned Spain.[3]

In Cromwell, the seventeenth century produced the perfect incarnation of religion and militarism. By this time, Anthony Pagden suggests, "Providentialism bulked as large in English discussion of Empire as ever it did in Spanish discourse."[4] Indeed, Cromwell's Western Design was "probably a device for exporting the Revolution of the Saints." The grim Ironside's Gaelic adventures are the small change of every schoolgirl's history. But Canny reminds us that his Western Design, producing the seizure of Jamaica from the Dutch, was the first deployment of the English state in the interests of transoceanic, as opposed to Irish, colonization. This stirred public interest in economic no less than in religious aspects of overseas possessions and changed English foreign policy for centuries. Protecting the few colonies secured during the early 1600s—Barbados, Virginia, New England, Providence, Jamaica—now became urgent, and it was also decided that enemy colonies could be seized by force.[5]

With the 1660 Restoration, crown and commerce made common cause. Merchants eyed territories they might seize for king, profit, or trade route protection. However, Canny's view that Nathaniel Cruch's *The English Empire in America* (1685) was purely a "commercial accounting and materialistic account," scarcely mentioning spirituality, suggests that imperial religious heat was already beginning to cool. More exciting than God, the Virginia Company of London was creating fortunes in tobacco to rival the sugar wealth of the Caribbean, where, by the end of the seventeenth century, drawing Africa into the imperial project, there were already some African slaves and a white population of 21,000. Thus, says Canny, "a new concept of Empire had been established: it involved the assertion of dominion over foreign places and peoples, the introduction of white, and also black, settlements in these areas and the monopolization of trade with these newly acquired possessions." Religion had lost its spark, and an inglorious African link had been established.

Business so fueled expansion that merchant trading companies, often bearing royal patents, litter seventeenth-century history like confetti. A frenzy of Silicon Valley proportions spread. Company names conjured exotic horizons and adventure (a serious study is needed that links colonialism with schoolboy reading). While, for our purpose, it anticipates colonial instrumentality in nineteenth-century Africa, the list is interesting in its own right. P. E. H. Hair and Robin Law tell us that it included the East India Company, the Royal Africa Company (by 1700 the biggest shipper of slaves to the Americas), the Virginia Company of London, the Providence Island Company, the Newfoundland Company, the Assada Company, the Company of Royal Adventurers Trading into Africa, the Muscovy Company, the Company of Adventurers of London Trading to Parts of Africa, the Company of Merchants Trading to Guinea, the Scottish Guinea Company, the Company of Royal Adventurers of England Trading into Africa, the Gambia Adventurers, the Royal African Company, and the Company of Scotland Trading to Africa and the Indies.[6] On companies of clerics sailing to convert Spanish colonials to Christianity, however, the record is silent. Yet the Elizabethan religious seedling eventually recovers, enjoys vigorous Victorian growth, and survives even the imperial sunset. Hence, on any objective assessment, Christian missionizing has made an unrivaled contribution to Africa's health, education, and, crucially, to the rise of its modern literature. Indeed, Zimbabwe's Ndabaningi Sithole, in *African Nationalism* and *Roots of a Revolution*, suggests that African nationalism and, ultimately, political freedom, were unthinkable without the modern schooling that Christianity brought. The list is long of writers in Malawi, Zimbabwe, and Zambia (as elsewhere across Africa) who are mission-educated. And it transcends mere coincidence that the first presidents of independent Malawi and Zambia were ardent Christians (one a less than model elder of the Church of Scotland) and that Zimbabwe's first black leaders as freedom dawned were both Christian clerics.

Yet while commercial energies rose, British colonial settlement beyond Ireland in the early seventeenth century still embraced only North America and the Caribbean. Afro-Asian trade beckoned, but not conquest or colonies. Long after their Portuguese allies, English merchants moved only slowly into West Africa, establishing factories at Whydah, Kormantin, Anomabu, Cape Coast, Sherbro, Winneba, Takoradi, and Dixcove.[7] Business was strictly by leave of local chiefs, and misbehavior courted deportation. Writing on early Euro-African encounters, Megan Vaughan asks who was using whom when she notes that between 1475 and 1540 the Portuguese shipped more than twelve thousand slaves from the Bight of Benin and São Tomé to the Gold Coast, not for onward carriage to the Americas, but for purchase by wealthy African chiefs.[8] And as late as 1752, Hair and Law remind us, the Board of Trade could observe, "In Africa we were only tenants of the soil which we held at the goodwill of the natives."

Though colonizing Africa did not appeal, slavery linked the continent to Britain's Caribbean empire. Crucially, too, patterns of governance among the West Indian planter class foreshadowed later practice in Central and Southern Africa. Growing spectacularly rich, Barbadian settlers, for example, soon coveted the rights and privileges of the aristocracy at home. Granted legislative assemblies, and flaunting a wealth many an English grandee could only envy, they created a confident, indeed impertinent, relationship with London. And fortunes could also be made elsewhere. Virginian prospects allured even transported convicts. The hero of Defoe's *Colonel Jack* (1722) insists that "in Virginia, the meanest, and most despicable Creature after his time of Servitude is expir'd, if he will but apply himself with Diligence and Industry to the Business of the Country, is sure (Life and Health suppos'd) both of living Well and growing Rich."[9]

Scholars agree that in North America, without the El Dorado that Raleigh conjured, land and agriculture assumed a defining place at the heart of settler colonialism. Ominous for the future experience of Central and Southern Africa, a conviction also arose that those blocking access to land must be swept aside. Hence, in New England and the Caribbean a species of apartheid emerged that Southern and Central African settlers would later imitate, with profound familiar implications. In contrast to Spanish and Portuguese practice, there was no miscegenation, merely a vertical distance between rulers and ruled. Partly for this, the Nigerian writer Chinua Achebe, with British experience in mind, could later write that in terms of human relationships, colonialism for the black race in Africa was a disaster.

3. *Legitimizing Empire*

The violence born of British privateers roaming the seas to pillage became a global enterprise, the object of philosophical enquiry, and even of legal justification—as highwaymen, dissatisfied with roadside spoils, might seize a victim's park and orchards and then find their crime sanctioned in jurisprudence.

Anthony Pagden explains this exercise in exculpation, and again the model is Spanish.[1] Though armed with five papal bulls allowing Ferdinand and Isabella's sailors to seize pretty much any lands they might find, Spain nevertheless asked its School of Salamanca to debate imperial legitimacy. The question was simple. How could Catholic Christians, in good conscience, conquer, say, American Indians entirely innocent of crime? Such moral delicacy triggered pious reflection in London, too; for if Satanic Spain was minded to pick over such matters, how much more a pure England proud in its new Protestant Christianity? Empire and religion converged once more. Claiming to save pagans for Christ, says Pagden, cleansed the nation's conscience. Hence *A True and Sincere Declaration of the Purposes and Ends of the Plantation Begun in Virginia* (1610) described such aims as "first to preach and baptize into Christian religion, and by propagation of that Gospel to recover out of the arms of the Devil, a number of poor and miserable souls wrapped up unto death, in almost invincible ignorance." English colonists, however, still found it difficult to answer Robert Gray's question in *A Good Speed to Virginia* (1609): "by what right or warrant can we enter into the land of these Savages, take away their rightful inheritance from them, and plant ourselves in their place, being unwronged or unprovoked by them?"

History now assisted religion. Though it is hard to imagine Drake's ruffians sitting down solemnly to ponder Cicero's dictum that "the best state never undertakes war except to keep faith or in defense of its safety," Pagden insists that the admired Roman model embraced moral and legal concerns as well as conquest and governance. "Every expansionist state," therefore, "was required to legitimate its actions by appeal to some law . . . of either supposedly natural or divine origin." It was understood, too, Pagden explains, that "in the terms accepted by every legal system of classical and Christian origin, acts of appropriation necessarily involved the denial of those rights which all men held by virtue of their condition as men." As urgent, say, as our modern need to justify cloning or genetically modified cultivation, the need to invalidate the natural rights of the conquered, and thus sanction robbery, challenged the age's finest minds.

Pagden argues that the Calvinist theory of revolution helped because it held that all property rights and sovereignty derive from God's grace. Without grace, there could be no rights. Thus, conveniently, the property, and even the persons, of graceless American Indians could be "forfeit to the first 'godly' person who came their way." Enter now John Locke, who, when not penning his great *Essay*, fathering Anglo-American liberalism, and indulging his hatred of Catholics, was busy with North American colonizing. Secretary to the grandly titled "Lords Proprietor of Carolina," he was also secretary to the Council of

Trade and Plantations and from 1696 to 1700 a member of the Board of Trade. Further, he had investments in the slaving Royal African Company and the Company of Merchant Adventurers to Trade with the Bahamas. Crude conquest naturally pricked the Lockeian conscience: hence his constitution for the Carolinas warned settlers that the "Indians' idolatry, ignorance or mistakes give us no right to expel or use them ill." The problem required special intellectual subtlety, for he wanted his countrymen to secure rights over land rather than people and thus, contrary to Spanish practice, as Pagden puts it, to "enforce a frontier between the Indian lands and the lands of the Crown"—a Caribbean arrangement that foreshadowed British practice in Africa.

Pagden cites two arguments by which Locke justified land theft. The first, in his *Second Treatise of Government* (1689), was that a man acquired ownership rights in a thing only when he had "mixed his Labour with [it]; and joined to it something that is his own." This, Pagden says, is a reprise of the Roman *res nullius* law whereby all "empty things," including unoccupied lands, remained humankind's common property until they were put to some use, generally agricultural. More used it in *Utopia*, and, significantly (empire and religion again embracing), John Donne told a merchant congregation in 1622: "A land never inhabited by any, or utterly derelicted and immemorially abandoned by the former inhabitants, becomes theirs that will possess it." Restrained by commercial, religious and natural law considerations, Locke now applied *res nullius* with consummate ingenuity. Thus America could be considered a kind of Eden, or, as he resoundingly phrased it, "In the beginning all the world was America." Its inhabitants were still in a state of nature and lacked civil institutions. Having not cultivated the land, they had no rights over it. They only ran "over the grass as do also foxes and wild beasts." By contrast, his English compatriots, in our modern phrase, had added value to "the vacant places of America." With logic that would have given Jonathan Swift apoplexy, Locke concluded that, since those who might resist European land seizure would be defying the natural law, they "might be destroyed as a Lyon or a Tyger, one of those wild Savage Beasts, with whom Men can have no Society nor Security."

For an understanding of Britain's nineteenth-century African (or, for that matter, Australasian), colonization, Pagden's account of *res nullius* is critical. From Kenya and Uganda to South Africa and the Rhodesias, this argument became a settler mantra of certitude and justification. Even during the imperial sunset, when colonial credos had jettisoned core arguments around health, education, or infrastructure, *res nullius* still dominated settler discourse—its exemplary form being one or other version of "But, honestly, there was absolutely nobody/nothing here." It can be heard to this day in a Southern Africa where scholarship shows the San people to have been living for 40,000 years, and where human settlement per se probably began 140,000 years ago. In countercolonial texts by a writer such as Zimbabwe's Yvonne Vera, these echoes of ancient reality are, understandably, powerfully present.

Locke's concern to legitimize raises a curious paradox. While globally robbing and pillaging, collecting colonies like shells from the seashore (Cook's eighteenth-century voyages are exemplary), the English displayed a mystical respect for written law and constitutional fig leaves—as used car dealers might flaunt copies of the Trade Descriptions Act. Legislation was sacrosanct, and the quicker it appeared the better. Ethical status meant little, inscription as statute everything—especially if cast in language to mesmerize. Servile respecters of law themselves, no matter how unjust, the English assumed that colonial subjects—West Indian slaves or Central African peasants—would be equally reverent; hence a settler reflex swiftly arose to seize some independence from London and begin legislating for local conditions. The practice loomed large in the American, Caribbean, and African colonies, as well as in Canada, Australia, and New Zealand. Ndabaningi Sithole's *Letters from Salisbury Prison* (1976) gives the merest glimpse of the extraordinary legal netting, endlessly extending itself to maintain dominance, that Rhodesian colonial authorities flung over Africans.

4. The British in Africa

Though British interest in Africa dates from the sixteenth century, initially, say P. E. H. Hair and Robin Law in *The Oxford History of the British Empire*, it was more maritime than territorial.[1] Shipping might briefly touch West Africa before crossing the Atlantic to Brazil. And despite Spanish or Portuguese practice, Britain showed little interest in slaves (the 1560s Hawkins voyages excepted). What trade there was, beginning under Elizabeth I, was material, not human, comprising commodities such as gold, redwood, hides, and gum, with the Guinea Company a key player and Senegal, Gambia, the Gold Coast, and Sierra Leone the main contact points. So minimal was slaving interest that, as late as 1620, Hair and Law tell us, a certain Jonson, offered slaves on the Gambia River, loftily replied, "We were a people who did not deale in any such commodities, neither did wee buy or sell one another, or any that had our own shapes." Yet by 1700 British Middle Passage dominance was unrivalled. Barbadian kith and kin wanted labor for sugar plantations, and that was enough. Religious scruple succumbed either to Lockeian argument or to the race for profit. Royalty grew so fevered that Charles II gave the Duke of York and Prince Rupert, via their Company of Royal Adventurers into Africa, a monopoly on Gulf of Guinea trading rights for a thousand years! Yet there was still no thought of plantation or colony. Expansion into the interior would begin only well into the nineteenth century.

British involvement in Southern and Central Africa began with equal indifference. Seizing the Cape from the Dutch in 1795 was for Napoleonic War strategy only. Yet, say Christopher Saunders and Iain Smith in the *Oxford History*, by the end of the next century, all hesitation gone, Britain ruled vast stretches of the southern part of the continent, taking in Bechuanaland, Basutoland, and Swaziland, all the so-called Boer Republics, and reaching beyond the Limpopo and Zambezi to what became the Rhodesias and Nyasaland.[2] As Jonathan Israel observes, "By the middle of the eighteenth century Britain was without any doubt the supreme maritime and colonial power and hub of global commerce" and was well placed now to build "the biggest empire the world had ever seen, in terms of territories, trade, and shipping."[3] Expansion first moved east across the Cape and then relentlessly north, with sufficient success to inspire, among much else, the legendary Cape to Cairo dream. With no significant opposition, British traders and missionaries (the revived religious linkage is noteworthy) were soon active well beyond the borders of Cape Colony.

Saunders and Smith report that, with more rigor than the Dutch, the British began seizing local KhoiKhoi land and making its owners labor on new white farms. Then in 1811 they cleared the Xhosa from the Zuurveld and handed it to five thousand white settlers. Such forced removal (Britain practiced it in Diego Garcia as recently as the 1970s), and discriminatory law of a kind framed earlier in the Caribbean, proved a model for twentieth-century Afrikaners. If, as the historian Arthur Keppel-Jones argues, apartheid went back to 1652 and the first hedge Van Riebeck planted at the Cape, then the British certainly kept the hedge well watered. Indeed, following conquest of the Zulus, the British divided their land into thirteen separate chiefdoms, providing an ideal blueprint for Verwoerd's Grand Apartheid and the ludicrous homelands of Bophutatswana, Venda, Lebowa, Transkei, and Ciskei. Defeating the Zulu, and then the Pedi or Northern Sotho, was prelude to crossing the Limpopo and thus to conquering the Matabele and Mashona.

The new arrogance of power—photographic evidence itself, in, say, James Ryan's *Picturing Empire* (1999), is arresting—imbued a line of imperial proconsuls with swashbuckling bravado. Independently decisive, they consolidated their colonial corners and soon created Caribbean-style legislatures in the Cape and Natal. Like gentrified versions of imperial dawn buccaneers, Sir Harry Smith, Lord Charles Somerset, Sir Bartle Frere, Sir Theophilus Shepstone, and Sir Alfred Milner routinely took decisions that London did not challenge. Hence, Saunders and Smith relate that Sir Harry Smith, in "the aftermath of the War of the Axe . . . brought on by land-hungry settlers in the eastern Cape . . . annexed more land and then succeeded in persuading the government in London that this would help to prevent future wars."[4] Sometimes resources, rather than land and conquest, tempted, as happened with the 1867 diamond discovery in Griqualand West. As our historians delicately put it, "Once it realized the scale of the discovery, the British government was concerned to take over the area in the interests of stability and control"! The 1886 gold discovery on the Rand, and then coal in Natal, prompted similar high-mindedness.

British expansion northward from a solid Cape foothold ensured that the colonial histories of Southern and Central Africa were inextricably linked. Plans for Central Africa, often improvised, arose from men ruling the south. But if Frere, Somerset, and Shepstone nursed dreams of crossing the Limpopo and Zambezi, the extraordinary Cecil Rhodes made it happen. With a fortune in diamonds and gold ("King Midas himself," quips David Cannadine, "could usefully have taken his correspondence course"), Rhodes was obsessed with Britain's imperial destiny and from 1890 held powerful positions in the Cape as crown agent and prime minister. None better than this complex figure illustrates how Britain's empire spawned personal fiefdoms built by Victoria's subjects able to manipulate London. A man of boyish dreams and patriotism, a liar and swindler, a ruthless speculator deaf to African aspirations and sensitivities, he seemed to manifest arrested adolescence. Schoolboy fiction and Oxford Greats had ravished his mind with the example of Greece and Rome and a subsequent determination to emulate it. Thomas Pakenham, in *The Scramble for Africa* (1991), says that Edward Fairfield, a Colonial Office official, found him "grotesque, impulsive, schoolboyish, humorous and almost clownish . . . not to be regarded as a serious person."[5] G. K. Chesterton dismissed him as cynically unprincipled. Cannadine wonders if he was mad. More delicately, Roland Oliver alludes to "the legend of the disinterested apostle of Empire." But the Rhodes dream—witness his last will and testament—exceeded even his wealth and conquests. This, with the overreach of a Marlowe, with the Maxim gun, and, as Niall Ferguson reminds us in *Empire: How Britain Made the Modern World* (2003), with huge financial backing from the Rothschilds, envisaged extending British rule throughout the world, occupying all Africa, the Holy Land, some Mediterranean islands, South America, and, the main prize, a recovered United States. Thus would God smile on Pax Britannica and all warfare cease. Chums like Lord Carnarvon and Sidney Shippard (this latter the humanitarian who wanted the Matabele to be "cut down by our rifles and machine guns like a cornfield by a reaping machine") would plot the project like boarding school prefects operating in Jesuitical secrecy. As

Cannadine puts it, facing this triune figure of "Caesar, Croesus and conquistador," there was little hope for the innocent subjects of Matabeleland and Mashonaland.[6]

Rhodes thought that northern expansion would reveal another Rand, but in any event lands that, under settlement, would join a white-dominated South Africa. Vestiges of his thinking survived until the Smith government in Rhodesia collapsed in 1980. And again, repeating a device by which Britain since the seventeenth century had delegated conquest powers to businessmen, Queen Victoria in 1889 granted a charter to Rhodes's British South Africa Company that sanctioned seizure of land for the crown not only north of the Limpopo but north of the Zambezi as well. A modern equivalent would see General Motors ruling Guam or, say, British Petroleum governing the Falklands, with an option on South Georgia. For Nyasaland, however, a separate protectorate from 1891, the commercial arrangement was slightly different.

Scholarship and literary text now chronicle a colonial misery no individual writer can fully describe. It is refreshing, however, to capture empire's sillier moments, as Pakenham's *The Scramble for Africa* does when picturing Rhodes's Pioneer Column preparing to cross from Bechuanaland into the land of a badly cheated Lobengula—a comic prologue, as it were, to the swelling act of the tragic imperial theme:

LORD METHUEN: Gentlemen, have you got maps?

THE OFFICERS: Yes, sir.

LORD METHUEN: And pencils?

THE OFFICERS: Yes, sir.

LORD METHUEN: Well, gentlemen, your destiny is Mount Hampden. You go to a place called Siboutsi. I do not know whether Siboutsi is a man or a mountain. Mr Selous, I understand, is of the opinion that it is a man; but we will pass that by. Then you get to Mount Hampden. Mr Selous is of the opinion that Mount Hampden is placed ten miles too far to the west. You'd better correct that: but perhaps, on second thoughts, better not. Because you might possibly be placing it ten miles too far to the east. Now good morning, gentlemen.[7]

The column's composition, says Pakenham, was equally vaudeville. Dreaming of gold and land (three thousand acres promised to all white participants), it comprised hundreds of Ngwato porters, "doctors, engineers, parsons, cricketers, butchers, bakers, unemployed miners, army deserters, even a Jesuit priest." What followed, especially the betrayed pact with Lobengula (he had agreed to accept just ten miners), reveals much about the morality of Rhodes and his colleagues Beit, Jameson, and Starr. Cannadine bluntly remarks, "The inadequate and unsupervised administration of what soon became known as Northern and Southern Rhodesia was one of the most shameful episodes in British Imperial history."[8] Stanlake Samkange has given a compelling African account of this fateful moment in his novel *On Trial for My Country* (1966). Open season was immediately declared on vast tracts of land and cattle and, by September 1890, a parade at the newly created Fort Salisbury marked the illegal annexation of Mashonaland into the British Empire.

Avarice apart, Rhodes wanted to extend the British South African sphere of influence rather than create new political entities. This point is important, because, though nominally discrete entities emerged in the Rhodesias and Nyasaland, their histories long remained bound to South Africa's, the political center remaining Cape Town and territorial significance diminishing in proportion to geographical distance. Historiography itself betrays this. Hence, for all its splendid coverage, the *Oxford History*'s narrative on Southern and Central Africa, provided by South African historians, grows thin to the point of anorexia as it crosses the Limpopo and Zambezi.

Meanwhile Englishmen and Afrikaners began farming the new Rhodesia's best land, applying labor relations and laws shaped long ago in the Caribbean, and taking time off to put down Matabele and Mashona revolts (1893–94 and 1896–97). Soon after Lobengula's final defeat, an area of ten thousand square miles was taken near his Bulawayo capital, and conquered villagers, with familiar modern results, were forced to work on new white farms. A ten-shilling hut tax in Mashonaland was equally traumatic. Those unable to pay also faced what amounted to forced labor. Others, in their thousands, pushed down to land at arid altitudes, were obliged to find work in the mines of South Africa. The history of this period, and especially the Chimurenga rebellions, is explored by such Zimbabwean writers as Yvonne Vera and Chenjerai Hove, with the prophetic figures of Nehanda and Chimunuka a focus of growing literary attention. The land question—colonialism's core issue—remains a running sore. Robert Mugabe, before independence, complained, "Half the land is in the hands of 250,000 settlers."

5. Nyasaland and Northern Rhodesia

The Lake Nyasa region (known between 1600 and 1800 as Maravi) had seen change long before Rhodes's column crossed the Limpopo. The Mozambique Yao had moved west and occupied the lakeshore, bringing Omani Arabic contacts and an interest in slavery. The Zulu *mfecane* that drove the Matabele north to Bulawayo, creating the kingdom of Mzilikazi and Lobengula, had also prompted the Nguni to trek to the Nyasa area and disturb the local Chewa and Tumbuka. The Portuguese, with exploratory knowledge and economic aims, saw Maravi as a potential bridge between Mozambique and their Angolan colony on the Atlantic. As rivalries in the African scramble intensified, Germany, serving a colonial apprenticeship in nearby Tanganyika, also grew covetous.

Nyasaland, some might say, was fortunate in its colonizers. Instead of Rhodes, Beit, Starr, Selous, and Jameson, they had Scottish missionaries, the saintly Joseph Booth, and the philanthropists Henderson, Laws, Maples, and the Moirs. Crucially, there was Livingstone. His dream of converting Africans to Christianity, commerce, and civilization (again the blend is noteworthy) fired many a European mind. Booth, for instance, a trade-union eccentric of British-Australian stock, from 1892 practiced what Livingstone had preached, wrote the prophetic *Africa for the African* (1897), and spoke of "the fragrance of the confidence inspired by such good men as Dr Livingstone." Though once more commercial instrumentation was chosen, the African Lakes Company ethos seemed more Salvation Army than British South African.

Surprisingly, the Livingstonian glow has survived modern iconoclasm. A man embracing the finest values of Scottish Presbyterianism, his epic journeys in Central Africa (1841–52 and 1858–63) stirred affection for the continent and a passionate desire to help. Even in training, Livingstone's profound hatred of slavery had caused him to weep while preaching on it, and he was described, without exaggeration, as "a man of sorrows acquainted with grief." Rob Mackenzie relates how in 1840 Livingstone attended a meeting of the Society for the Extinction of the Slave-Trade and for the Civilization of Africa, where a Wilberforce disciple had proposed that "Africans would only be saved from the slave-trade if they were woken up to the possibilities of selling their own produce. . . . Commerce and Christianity could achieve the miracle, not Christianity alone."[1] Religion, one notices, was once more entering colonial thinking. In response, Scotland's earnest son felt that Britain's slaving debt might be paid by way of the gospel. To endless setbacks—whether disease, family deaths, rivalries, an attack by six hundred Boers, or contempt from the explorer Burton—he responded with unshakeable faith.

Though sometimes depressive and uncompromising (his brother called him "the cursing Consul of Quillamane"), Livingstone felt only optimism about Africa's future, foresaw independence, and rejected all that might perpetuate subordination. His home popularity, however, fluctuated. Mackenzie tells us that, hearing in 1863 that the Zambezi Expedition was to be recalled after five years, *The Times* sneered, "We were promised cotton, sugar and indigo . . . and of course we got none. We were promised trade; and there is no trade. . . . We were promised converts, and not one has been made." But Livingstone's example created disciples and indirectly helped to soften the servile fate Rhodes planned for Nyasaland. A signal achievement, apart from stirring Britain finally to destroy local slaving, was favorable recall of Livingstone among Africans themselves. Mackenzie relates how Bishop Chauncey Maples met an old man in 1877 who showed him a ragged and muddy coat—given him ten years before by "a white man who treated black men as brothers and whose memory would be cherished along the Rovuma River . . . a man whose words were always gentle and whose manners were always kind, whom, as a leader it was a privilege to follow, and who knew the way to the heart of all men."[2]

Politically, if Rhodes created Rhodesia, Sir Harry Johnston created Nyasaland. A poorer but finer person, in dealings with Rhodes, who wanted the country for his British South Africa Company, he resembled an honest man desperate to escape the teeth of a loan shark. Colony making required money, and Johnston had none. Nor would the British Treasury help, no matter how loud Scottish missionaries bleated. Rhodes, however, a missionary-hater avid for land and minerals, had more money than he could count. His loans to nascent Nyasaland thus began a relationship that sorely challenged Johnstonian footwork until London eventually funded the colony and averted a British South African Company takeover.

Though both imperial believers, Rhodes and Johnston differed as an asset stripper might differ from Renaissance man. For Rhodes, Africa meant nothing but profit and power; for the diminutive Johnston, it meant everything to excite mind and imagination. No crude jingoist ("we are a nation of hypocrites, with philanthropy on our lips and a profit and loss account in our hearts"), and dubbed by enemies "the prancing proconsul of Quillimane," Johnston brought to Nyasaland unrivaled credentials. He knew North Africa well; had done fine work in the Niger Delta and Cameroon; had demonstrated skillful treaty making in East Africa, and possessed remarkable expertise in local languages. A large mind drove his talents in many directions.

Roland Oliver's definitive biography, *Sir Harry Johnston and the Scramble for Africa* (1957), portrays a man seriously underrated. With a mere secondary education, he became a painter, historian, botanist, explorer, ethnographer, administrator, imperial theorist, distinguished linguist, and novelist—indeed, author of some forty books. His scholarship alone should have secured him fame. For besides his *History and Description of the British Empire in Africa*, his *History and Colonization of Africa by Alien Races*, *The Uganda Protectorate*, *The River Congo*, and *The Common Sense of Foreign Policy*, he wrote the monumental *Comparative Study of the Bantu and Semi-Bantu Languages,* which at a stroke made him a world authority to rival Meinhof. Africa for Johnston was "the new world of the nineteenth century," marvelously rich in human potential.

Oliver also shows that Lord Salisbury's colonial policy at this time was essentially Johnston's and how a typical Johnston piece in *The Times* for August 1888 "outshone by many times any of the summaries of outstanding problems periodically prepared for ministers by officials of the Foreign Office. In its practical vision and comprehensive grasp it streamed far ahead of . . . Lugard, on the one hand, or Rhodes on the other."[3] Further, the Cape-to-Cairo dream, popularly credited to Rhodes, was in fact Johnston's, hatched during a walk with Lord Salisbury in the gardens at Hatfield.

Physically courageous, Johnston, together with Lugard and African Lakes employees, ended the region's slaving by defeating Mlozi at the northern end of Lake Nyasa. He then ran the colony virtually single-handed from his exquisite capital at Zomba. Quoting a letter from Johnston to Rhodes, Oliver pictures this tiny titan at work:

> I do not recall having spent one single day as a holiday during the two years and a half I have worked in Central Africa. Sundays and week-days, mornings and evenings, I am to be found either slaving at my desk, or tearing about the country on horseback, or trudging 20 miles a day on foot, or sweltering in boats, or being horribly sea-sick on Lake Nyasa steamers. I have to carry on in my office, myself, a most onerous correspondence in Swahili, which I have to write in the Arabic character, in Portuguese, in French, and in English. I have had to acquire a certain mastery over Hindustani to deal with the Indian troops. I have learnt three native languages besides Swahili in order to talk straight to the people. . . . One day I am working out a survey which has to be of scrupulous accuracy, and another day I am doing what a few years ago I never should have thought I should be called upon to do—undertaking the whole responsibility of directing military operations. I have even had myself taught to fire Maxim guns and seven pounder cannon, I, who detest loud noises and have a horror of explosives.[4]

So dire was Johnston's relationship with Rhodes that in later life he refused utterly to discuss it. Unafraid of berating Foreign Office officials, who scorned his social inferiority and envied his favor with Salisbury, Johnston would not be cowed by Rhodes either, despite needing his shilling. On one occasion, though perhaps prematurely, he accused him of insularity: "You only think of Africa south of the Zambezi: I not only consider our interests throughout Africa, but our imperial interests throughout the world."[5] And, unlike Rhodes, though no orthodox Christian, he admired missionaries, seeing their stations as growth points—rather as Anselm saw Benedictine monasteries as beacons of light during the Norman colonizing of England.

Though wanting settlement land, Johnston was no *res nullius* fanatic. He granted only leasehold tenure to non-Africans and was loath to diminish the role of traditional chiefs. And, while Rhodes repeatedly drew London's censure, he seemed to draw only golden opinion, such as this from Lord Cranborne: "He can be trusted to devise the measures which will be most likely to open up the resources of the country without leading to the exploitation of the natives." In Africa itself others agreed. Indeed, on Johnston's death in 1927, the Kabaka of Buganda (where he held his last African post) had a personal tribute engraved on his tomb: *Amazimage ku Buganda galaga nti Bungereza eyagala bona bekuma babere ne dembe*—"His faithfulness to Buganda shows that England wishes all whom she protects to be free."[6]

With such guiding spirits as Livingstone, Johnston, and Booth, little wonder that Nyasaland settlers were apt to argue a moral superiority to Southern and Northern Rhodesia. Yet the historical and literary record is not reassuring. The colonial authorities eventually banned the saintly Booth as subversive and hanged his pupil, the Reverend John Chilembwe, who led the Nyasaland Native Rising of 1915—a tragic event whose roots George Shepperson and Thomas Price locate in white estate abuses and contempt for African lives during World War I.[7] Ironically, among the few Europeans the rising targeted was a relative of Livingstone himself. Finally, for all Johnston's enlightenment, he imposed a Rhodesian-style hut tax, which produced a local forced-labor system called *thangata*. Villagers unable to pay faced the misery of work on distant estates and domestic disruption that became endemic in later decades. It also nourished Rhodes's view of Northern Rhodesia and Nyasaland as mere bottomless labor pools for his booming industries to the south.

Malawian writers now vigorously interrogate this period. Chimombo's panoramic novel *The Wrath of Napolo* (2000) finds nothing to praise in it. The late Edison Mpina's *Freedom Avenue* (1991) shows a colonial Nyasaland so poor (future President Banda fled it on foot) that villagers in their thousands trekked to racist Rhodesia as though to a land of milk and honey. Here employment was plentiful and diligence brought basic health care and training—for those who avoided politics.

What became Northern Rhodesia only slowly engaged Rhodes's attention. Believing Nyasaland to be mineral-rich, he needed time to manipulate Johnston and secure rights there. When Johnston's adroit diplomacy won full London funding, his fury was unbounded. He had arranged that Johnston, for a mere 15,000 pounds a year, would add to his responsibilities the vast lands to the west, a territory called merely the company's "sphere," as though without physical reality. In any case, if the Cape-to-Cairo dream still whispered, there was work enough in Salisbury to maintain full expansionist lungs. Though by 1905 a railway had been pushed across the Victoria Falls, this was principally a link to Katanga's copper mines in neighboring Congo. Commercial copper mining in the new Northern Rhodesia began only in 1920, a decade before its deposits were established as vast and inclusive of silver, gold, lead, zinc, talc, and iron ore. By this time, it had long become clear that Nyasaland could offer little beyond fish, tea, and coffee.

Yet evidence of mineral wealth west of Nyasaland dated back a thousand years. Copper ingots had been produced there as well as metal tools for Lake Nyasa people. As oriental objects were appearing at Great Zimbabwe in the fourteenth century, "Zambian" gold beads and iron bells were finding their way to east coast Arabs and down to sites in Southern Africa. Seventeenth-century Portuguese merchants exchanged cotton cloth for ivory and copper here, and in the nineteenth century began their lucrative trade in slaves.

Like Nyasaland, these western lands had seen migrations long before the "scramble for Africa." The Makololo had fled South Africa's Sotho area and taken over the Lozi kingdom in Barotseland, while to the north the Chewa had received the attention of the Zulu Nguni who had trekked into neighboring Nyasaland. During the 1860s and 1870s the Bemba and Lunda began the trade in slaves that so appalled Livingstone, who crossed the area three times between 1853 and his death in 1873. The trade mainly flowed east to the Yao and Arabs of Lake Nyasa and thence to the coast and Zanzibar.

When, with Portuguese, German, French, and German agreement, Rhodes's British South Africa Company took control of Northern Rhodesia, resistance came only from the belligerent Nguni. But they were no match for company troops. Nor did outbreaks of drought, locusts, smallpox, and rinderpest help to inspire opposition. Conquering largely by private treaty, the Company moved swiftly to secure its new possession and once more introduced a hated hut tax. The aftermath features in Kenneth Kaunda's *Black Government* (1966), *Zambia Shall Be Free* (1980), and *A Humanist in Africa* (1966), and in such novels as Binwell Sinyangwe's *Quills of Desire* and Lazarus Miti's *The Prodigal Husband*. Before quantifying mineral wealth, however, the Company saw its "sphere" much as it came to see Nyasaland—as a cheap labor supply for the farms and mines of Southern

Rhodesia and South Africa. By 1911, with Livingstone as its capital, Northern Rhodesia had a population of a million, with some 1,500 Europeans mining and farming. Like Nyasaland, it experienced the trauma of World War I, with 3,500 troops and 50,000 porters recruited for Britain's East African campaign—many never to return. And in a foreshadowing of liberation struggle, this stirred protest similar to John Chilembwe's in Nyasaland.

6. White Rhodesia

by Anthony Chennells

Southern Rhodesia was constitutionally unique among Britain's many African colonies. For thirty-three years, it was a chartered colony of the British South Africa Company, but in 1923 what was officially called "responsible government" replaced company rule, and governance devolved on the settlers. Southern Rhodesia might have been marked as British on imperial maps, but Whitehall was not involved in its administration, except for a few months at the end of 1979 and the beginning of 1980 when the governor and his staff presided over the elections for an independent Zimbabwe. There were other African chartered company territories; and responsible government, a stage toward full independence from London, was a late-nineteenth-century term that signaled Britain's approval of settler rule in the Cape and Natal and was granted in 1905 to the conquered Boer republics. But nowhere else in the empire did a chartered company colony make way for responsible government, and this curious constitutional progression was both consequence and cause of the discrete character of Southern Rhodesia and its settlers. Only by recalling these details can one understand the directions settler politics took in Southern Rhodesia after World War II.

When London allowed Cecil Rhodes's British South Africa Company to colonize the country north of the Limpopo, it was using company wealth to claim the interior as a British sphere of influence at no cost to the treasury. With the company in control, no other European power could harbor colonial ambitions on the Zambezi, and with the Limpopo as the southern boundary of the company's territories, the South African Republic was prevented from expanding northward. Because the Chimurenga risings in 1896 and 1897, now becoming a focus of literary interest, revealed administrative abuses by the company, a British resident commissioner was appointed to Salisbury. But this was to check company and settler racism, not to implement British policy on Rhodesia—since there was none. In a development seen elsewhere in Britain's colonies, eight years after the occupation, a legislative council of company officials and settlers was established on which, by 1907, settler representatives were in the majority. Rhodes's company has been described as a "great enterprise to marry capitalism to idealistic imperialism in Central Africa," but reconciling settler aspirations and company interests dominated the council's politics until the charter lapsed. White populism pitted itself against monopoly capital throughout much of Southern Rhodesia's history. But when settlers believed their rights were being sacrificed to those of blacks, the Colonial and later the Commonwealth Office became the enemy.

The referendum on responsible government confirmed that Salisbury, rather than London, directed Southern Rhodesia's future. For the overwhelmingly white electorate, the choice was whether Southern Rhodesia would become South Africa's fifth province or go it alone. The British South Africa Company, South African Prime Minister Jan Smuts, the great mining houses, the Argus Press, and the Colonial Office itself supported union with South Africa. Defiantly, the settlers asserted that Rhodesia was not an extension of white South Africa, nor were they British colonists with destinies plotted from London. From the start they had called themselves Rhodesians, and one day, such was their agenda, they would probably be as independent of imperial control as South Africa had become in 1910. Responsible government involved control of economic and, to an extent, political fortunes. Rhodesia was always responsible for defense, and its regiments fought in the Boer War and both world wars. With seventy years of defense autonomy, Rhodesian politicians liked to point out that since neither British money nor British casualties had ever been invested in the country, it had earned its right to independence.

Until the end of the Second World War, "the race problem" referred exclusively to Afrikaner and English-speaking rivalries. But Afrikaners within the Rhodesian white population did not press the most radical demands of Afrikaner nationalism—a complete rejection of empire. Indeed, until 1958 most Rhodesian settlers had South African origins and had emigrated partly in reaction to phases of Afrikaner nationalism. "Anti-Dutch" sentiment, which helped to swing the referendum, included fear that union would see Afrikaner "poor whites" trekking north and complicating white economic domination of blacks. The 1948 Nationalist Party victory, from which dates the word *apartheid*, was seen as divisive of whites, and provoked massive emigration northward. These émigrés, English speakers and Afrikaners alike, were not drawing nearer to Britain but seeking a space to reconfigure a white African identity free of Afrikaner supremacy. The most immediate model was the South African Union, independent of Britain yet imperially linked to other white-ruled states, known after 1931 as dominions. White Rhodesia, then, provided a space where Afrikaners and Britons could make common cause and put aside bitter divisions that separated South African whites. If Ian Smith's hard-line Rhodesia Front drew support from second- and third-generation white Rhodesians, Afrikaners, and immigrants from Britain and Europe, the liberal opposition, a quarter of the white electorate, also derived from those diverse groups.

The new nation's key exclusion, of course, was the vast black majority. Still, it would be an oversimplification to argue that whites defined their identity in an antagonistic relationship to blacks. Inherited from Cape Colony, the franchise held property and literacy rather than race as its key criteria, and a few black voters participated in all the elections after the one for responsible government. But, theoretically blind to racial difference, in practice the country's future was a white affair, with blacks' status reduced to the "Native Question." That so few black voters met the voting criteria for the post–World War II elections reflects vividly fifty years of inadequate educational and economic opportunity. Because tenure in reserves came under customary law, it did not qualify as property. Opportunities to buy land outside the reserves were thwarted by the Land Apportionment Act of 1931, which limited black ownership of land to special Native Purchase Areas designated for the purpose. Fear of economic competition from blacks was ongoing, especially from growers who could produce very cheaply; hence the Maize Control Acts in the 1920s and 1930s that denied black growers access to the lucrative export markets and Native Department policy that prevented blacks from becoming large-scale growers in the reserves by limiting their cultivable land. Meanwhile, the 1934 Industrial Conciliation Act prevented skilled blacks from competing with whites for jobs in urban areas, excluding them from apprenticeships and denying them training needed to compete in the newly industrialized society forming during the 1930s. Godfrey Huggins, who became prime minister in 1933 and dominated Rhodesian politics for the next twenty years, seeing eventual black influence on the vote, thought that black and white societies should develop separately—the so-called two-pyramid policy, an early version of South African apartheid. Although London could veto legislation directly affecting blacks, successive governments never did, oddly convinced that blacks were the beneficiaries of such blatantly discriminatory laws.

World War II shattered earlier patterns. Immigrants no longer sought permanent settlement but were a transient population of refugees from across Europe and British military men. White Rhodesians were suddenly exposed to a cosmopolitan gaze that registered them as provincial and regarded fifty years' progress as an achievement for which blacks had paid heavily. Young Rhodesians meeting these new arrivals, and others returning from war, began looking at the claims Rhodesians made about themselves and their society with a newly acquired cynicism. Segregation seemed impractical and unjust, and blacks deserved to share in the spectacular economic developments that marked the postwar period, especially as their labor had made it possible. Huggins began attending to these new voices. A pragmatist, by 1945 he knew that Britain's new Labour Government would find settler rationalizations for discriminatory legislation now less convincing. Indian and Pakistani independence suggested a new British skepticism at empire's assumption that a white presence presumed a civilizing mission. Many whites, however, remained as segregationist as they ever had been. In the 1946 election the segregationist (and oddly named) Liberal Party won nearly as many seats as Huggins's United Party, and he could govern only with the support of Labour representatives. The "Native Question" was now foregrounded. For the first time white political debate centered on the influence black voters should be allowed to have on Rhodesia's future. Black political advancement assumed an importance it had never had before. In short, until Zimbabwean independence made their ideologies irrelevant, segregationist, moderate, and liberal whites fought for control of Rhodesian politics.

While Huggins understood updated imperial ideology, white racism's victims were even more aware of it. By the mid-1930s, most reserves could not accommodate their black residents. The state thus reapportioned as reserves land in the Native Purchase Areas or proclaimed new reserves where poor soils, erratic rainfall, or tsetse flies made subsistence farming a seasonal gamble. The Land Apportionment Act designated urban areas as white. Legally, urban blacks were now temporary sojourners, and governments had no political reason to create facilities that a settled urban population required for a decent life. Squalid overcrowding in urban locations was no alternative to rural life, yet rural poverty made migration to the cities an economic necessity. Unsurprisingly, when industrial action first began, improved housing and higher wages headed the strikers' agenda. By demanding environments safe for women and children, black workers were claiming a place in Rhodesia's cities not merely as workers but also as families and implicitly as Rhodesian citizens. A 1945 railway strike signaled a new militancy and the rise of union and political organizations aimed at improving life for urban blacks. Joseph Bailey, an elected Bulawayo city council member, defended his involvement in the new movements by arguing, "Europeans and Africans are complementary, the one with the other, in the mutual aims and purposes as citizens in the Colony." Before the war, few whites would have entertained the idea.

Bulawayo was Rhodesia's industrial heartland, but even during the Khumalo kingdom's twilight, Ndebele workers had labored in South Africa's mines. After the 1893 company invasion, the Ndebele state's best land was alienated to white farmers and huge numbers were moved to areas unsuitable for agriculture. Work in industrial South Africa, an integral part of the Ndebele economy, brought migrants home with both money and political ideas developing within the black South African proletariat. Hence, by the end of the Second World War, Bulawayo workers had for sixty years heard the politics of capital and labor being articulated within a context of race. In April 1948, a general strike that started in Bulawayo and rapidly spread throughout the nation forced white awareness of rising black anger. Because strikers' anger targeted any black continuing to work, Bulawayo whites got their first measure of black discontent when groups entered their houses and forced their domestic workers to join them. If containing the strike was easy (strikers were locked into the locations where food and sometimes water quickly ran out), it showed that organized black labor as a political power could be ignored no longer. With customary realism, Huggins, responding to retribution calls, remarked, "We are witnessing the emergence of the proletariat and in this country it happens to be black." He also noted that white employers were entirely dependent on black labor. A segregationist vision of white Rhodesia dependent on its own human resources and excluding blacks had become for him a political and economic fantasy. Indeed, three years later, he was talking of the need to create "a native middle class," an astonishing mental leap forward for a man who had long mistrusted any black aspiring to a status other than peasant. The strike also had more tangible consequences. Government agreed to review urban wages and living conditions. Minimum industrial wages were introduced. Crucial were new housing schemes that addressed, however inadequately, black family problems in urban areas. New townships—the word replaced the old term "location" to denote areas set aside for blacks near "white" towns—showed government recognition that blacks had a permanent place in urban areas and thus within colonial modernity.

The 1948 strike did not decrease white intransigence, as might have been expected. In a manifesto for an election later in 1948, Huggins proposed that blacks be removed from the common voters' roll for twenty years and thus denied ballot-box power. Britain's Labour government was appalled at this cavalier disenfranchisement of blacks, and Huggins, faced with a possible British veto, withdrew the proposal. Instead, he raised the voting qualifications, which, in the short term, had the effect originally planned for.

His anxiety to placate London was driven partly by a larger ambition. Both Rhodesias were facing new prosperity. Immigrants were flooding into Southern Rhodesia, while in 1949 Northern Rhodesia's exports exceeded the value of Southern Rhodesia's. In 1953 they were more than double, since copper was in huge demand for postwar global reconstruction. With the north's mineral wealth and the south's diverse industrial, agricultural, and mining economy, the economic case for amalgamating the two territories had become indisputable, and now the right of the two territories to dominion status could be argued more strongly. If the term *amalgamation* suggests equality, Southern Rhodesia certainly did not see Northern Rhodesia as its equal, however lucrative the copper boom. Blacks in Northern Rhodesia and Nyasaland correctly interpreted federation when it finally came as an act of petty imperialism by Rhodesia's whites. Federation for blacks was a new helotry rather than a chance to be part of an enlightened British initiative to counterbalance apartheid. It is anachronistic that federation should have been achieved precisely when in Britain and Rhodesia whites had become more alert to black political aspirations. Britain was not, however, responding to black agendas but to South Africa's Nationalist Party victory, which made Pretoria's commitment to empire and commonwealth at best tenuous. In the early 1950s, Whitehall still believed that Britain's economic progress was inseparable from imperial strength. Empire would now comprise dominions formed from former colonies, but dominion status would no longer be reserved for colonies where whites formed a majority or, as in South Africa, where the betrayal of blacks was the price Britain had willingly paid to appease Boer hostility. A new British state in Central Africa would compensate for dubious loyalties in the south, and it would join the East African and West Indian federations and a Southeast Asian federation stretching from Malaya to Sarawak. Two contradictory motives thus underlay federation: British desire for a rich and loyal Commonwealth country characterized by racial tolerance, and Southern Rhodesian desire for enough economic power to demand dominion status and thus real independence from Britain. Colonized people's right to self-government may have become British policy, but for Rhodesia's whites, dominion status meant the continuing ability to limit black political power.

The unrealism surrounding federation stemmed from postwar optimism. Immigration increased the white population from 82,000 in 1946 to nearly 140,000 in 1951; by 1960 this had grown to 253,000. Only the eccentric far right spoke now about two pyramids, but the Land Apportionment Act was now recklessly used to secure space for a future white population. Between the end of World War II and federation, settlement areas were opened for whites that by 1980 had become some of Rhodesia's richest farming land. Few blacks could make the transition to new large-scale commercial agriculture, the state having locked them into a system of peasant production and subsistence farming. Though few immigrants actually took up land, agriculture joined with the mines to provide the impetus for Rhodesia's industrial expansion. If land segregation had been designed to create a prosperous white nation, this was realized by keeping agriculture and associated industries in the hands of white capitalists. Black labor's role in creating contemporary high living standards could be overlooked. Incompetent and undercapitalized white farmers also suffered and moved into the towns, but did not do badly there.

Postwar optimism produced organizations designed to remove social segregation. Organized by white liberals, many with distinguished war records, they ranged from the National Affairs Association and the Junior Chamber of Commerce to the slightly lunatic Capricorn Africa Society founded by aristocratic British immigrants dreaming of a British dominion stretching from the Limpopo to Ethiopia. Tolerance of white liberals, confident yet politically irrelevant, differentiated Rhodesia from South Africa, where, with communists and black nationalists, they were demonized as enemies of the Volk. The white liberals' agenda was paradoxical in that the federation they thought would moderate racism was seen by blacks in all three territories as Rhodesian racism's instrument to delay black rule indefinitely.

In 1953, nearly two-thirds of the whites-only voters accepted the federal constitution, whose preamble, crucially, provided the federation with the opportunity, "when the inhabitants . . . so desire, to go forward with confidence to attain full membership of the Commonwealth," the dominion status sought since 1923. How public opinion would be tested was not defined. The people of Northern Rhodesia and Nyasaland had their immediate future decided by their legislative councils, where official members were a majority. The wishes of Asians and blacks who feared white Rhodesia's power were ignored. A decade later, Britain dissolved the federation in response to massive black hostility.

When Huggins became federal prime minister in 1953, the humane Garfield Todd took over the leadership of the Rhodesia Party in Southern Rhodesia. Despite white distrust of especially Protestant missionaries, this New Zealand missionary was tolerated because a white majority wanted federation to work. Perhaps Federated Rhodesia could see blacks and citizenship as not mutually exclusive. Indeed, "African" now replaced "Native" in government documents, civil servants were instructed to refer to blacks as Mr. and Mrs., and the Land Apportionment Act was amended to allow hotels and clubs to apply for multiracial status. Hence came educational progress, too, as private white Anglican and Catholic schools began to accept black students. Uniquely among Rhodesian prime ministers, Todd had significant black support, but black leaders astutely recognized that his political constituency would allow few of their demands for change. Todd managed to pass a new franchise act that followed the federal franchise with two voters' rolls with different property and educational qualifications, and his government also scheduled new minimum wages for urban blacks that lifted living standards a little and briefly kept unrest to a minimum. A commission also recommended that the Land Apportionment Act be abolished.

But white reaction remained strong. Todd's mild reforms were too much even for his own cabinet, the majority of whom in 1958 resigned. Angry exchanges on minimum wages, the new franchise, and a proposal that interracial sex between white men and black women should be made illegal, as it was between black men and white women, clearly reflect white reaction. Edgar Whitehead, federal high commissioner—that is, ambassador—in Washington, replaced Todd, whose United Rhodesia Party failed to win a single seat in an election. When read nearly half a century on, the manifesto of the United Rhodesia Party is prophetic. It asked for the electorate's support because "Africans are becoming part of the machinery of the modern state which Europeans have established here," and legislation is required to give them "some voice and responsibility in its affairs." Some sign of white goodwill is needed to retain "their desire for co-operation and partnership" and without it, "they will be forced to become racialistic and hostile, and eventually a seed-bed of Communism." A final appeal echoed an older theme in Rhodesian politics. Rhodesians should use the election to confirm that they were different from and implicitly superior to South Africans. Are "white Rhodesians—as people overseas imagine them—like hard-line Afrikaner voters in the Union?" the manifesto asked.

Until the mid-1950s, London and Pretoria provided Rhodesia's international context. But globally empire was dying and new power realities emerging. British and French humiliation over the loss of the Suez Canal was pivotal. Rapid decolonization was in the air and on the ground. By 1960 France had freed most of its African colonies and, alarming to Central African whites, President Charles de Gaulle soon declared that even "French Algeria" had a right to independence. In the Gold Coast (1957) and Nigeria (1960), Britain was following suit. Nearer home, Belgium's abrupt Congo withdrawal poured Belgian refugees into Rhodesia. Fundamental ideological shift was dramatically shown, too, in 1960 when Harold Macmillan made his "wind of change" speech to an appalled South African Parliament. These changes increased Rhodesian black militancy and white determination to contain it. Under a 1959 State of Emergency, Whitehead arrested African National Congress (ANC) leaders and tried to co-opt black support for another constitution with the customary convoluted franchise requirements that ensured white voters indefinitely controlled election results. For the first time, however, a Declaration of Rights was entrenched in the constitution, which would have made new racist legislation impossible to pass.

Whites found the new constitution attractive because antidiscriminatory safeguards replaced Britain's right to veto legislation affecting blacks. It now seems extraordinary that the black middle class was expected to support a constitution continuing to curtail their political power. It shows the complex contemporary interplay of nationalist and white politics, however, that the delegates of the National Democratic Party (it had replaced the now banned ANC) initially accepted the constitution, a decision quickly reversed when the party leaders registered the hostility in the countryside. Their dilemma was clear. Joshua Nkomo, the delegation leader, knew well enough that South African apartheid was enticing for Rhodesian whites. But constitutionally Southern Rhodesia was federated with countries where blacks would soon control their territorial legislatures. Radical black and popular sentiment drew hope from the north; the more sober leadership looked with apprehension toward the south.

Whitehead achieved some reform. Racist clauses in the Industrial Conciliation Act were removed, blacks could become apprentices, integrated trade unions were allowed, and civil service promotional ceilings were removed. Crucially, in 1961 the Land Apportionment Act was abolished. Soon perhaps segregating white suburbs and black townships would also go. But these reforms were too late. By 1962, most of colonial Africa had become postcolonial. Northern Rhodesia and Nyasaland would soon follow. Rhodesian blacks were no longer satisfied with marginal concessions. The NDP enforced, sometimes violently, an election boycott and without the black vote moderate whites were powerless. Had blacks supported the new franchise in any numbers, the Rhodesia Front would not have gained power in 1962, and Zimbabwe's independence would probably have arrived without warfare.

The Rhodesia Front was the last and most important expression of white populism that had always strongly influenced Rhodesian politics. Black competition seriously threatened lower-income whites, who were therefore most suspicious of the policies of postwar liberalism. Industrialists, professionals, and large-scale farmers would be unaffected by the abolition of the Land Apportionment Act or the removal of racial barriers in government schools. Small-scale farmers and working-class whites had already given the Dominion Party a majority in the 1958 election, and in 1962 their fears translated into a massive Rhodesia Front victory. As in 1958, the franchise that privileged moderate candidates obscured the extent of white support for the Rhodesia Front. One detail shows that white populism at last controlled Rhodesian politics: no one in the new cabinet, including the prime minister, Winston Field, had ever held office before.

Two issues dominated Rhodesia Front politics: retaining the Land Apportionment Act and independence for Southern Rhodesia once Federation ended. White Rhodesian wariness of British governments now developed into an antagonism that grew until Zimbabwean independence, though it was never as vituperative as Robert Mugabe's references to Tony Blair's Labour government in the early 2000s. Britain allowed Nyasaland to secede from the federation in 1962, and Northern Rhodesia in 1963. Since this implied independence, Southern Rhodesian independence should have been an obvious consequence, too. Winston Field made this a condition of his attending the conference on the dissolution of the federation. What was promised him has been debated ever since. Nothing was committed to paper, and Ian Smith's version is probably correct. Britain's primary concern was swift dissolution, and R. A. Butler promised the Rhodesians independence in exchange for agreeing to the rest of the agenda. Ian Smith, who accompanied Field, writes in his memoir of Rhodesians for whom a word and a handshake were enough to seal an agreement, unlike the new breed of Britons whose word could be trusted only if was written, signed, and witnessed. Smith's account belongs to the discourse of Rhodesian populism that opposed its own straightforward honesty to the effete, devious, and amoral men who now ruled the United Kingdom. A more cynical account of the breakup of federation would observe that only someone naïve to the point of stupidity could have believed in the early 1960s, with apartheid execrated throughout the world, that Britain would give independence to a white-controlled African state. Even during the conference, the Northern Rhodesian delegation threatened to withdraw from the talks unless a postfederal Southern Rhodesian constitution provided universal suffrage, and the British government knew that it could expect a similarly hostile response to Rhodesian independence not only throughout Africa but in Asia as well. For Rhodesia there were two competing moralities, and at the end of 1963, when federation formally ended, white leaders were determined to claim a constitutional accommodation where Britain's newly discovered morality did not remove power from a white and responsible minority.

Black Rhodesian nationalists added their own confusion to events in 1963. From the early 1950s, radical black nationalism had remained united in a single organization that assumed different names as each successive party was banned. In 1963, its current incarnation was the Zimbabwe African People's Union (ZAPU) led by Joshua Nkomo, which had emerged from the banned National Democratic Party (NDP). In August 1963, Ndabaningi Sithole broke with ZAPU and formed the Zimbabwe African National Union (ZANU). Fighting between loyalists of the two groups continued for nearly a year both in the cities and countryside and ended only when most party leaders were detained and the parties banned. Most whites were indifferent to nationalist political issues and personnel, but black township violence was visible to everyone. For Smith the interparty fighting merely confirmed black inability to take power. In his memoir, he names the ANC and NDP only to recall their banning. Nkomo and Sithole are "nationalist leaders," but the parties they led are never mentioned until, in his account of the events of 1968, they become "terrorist organizations." Not once does he recall that these men and their parties once hoped for a constitution that would allow the majority of Rhodesians to take power peacefully.

Smith's preferred method was confrontation with Britain's devious liars, but when Field continued to negotiate with London, hoping that a Macmillan successor would be more pliable, Smith showed himself as devious as the British. Field had to go. In April 1964, behind Field's back, the Rhodesia Front caucus elected Smith as their leader, and Field resigned. Repeating Todd's ouster, an internal coup had again swung Rhodesian politics to the right. Smith's victory signaled the death of postwar liberalism. But if an election had been held, a majority might not have supported the Unilateral Declaration of Independence (UDI), the only issue in any election fought between Smith and Field. The electorate was never consulted about UDI, and in a general election of May 1965, Smith and his party explicitly claimed they were not seeking a UDI mandate, but instead only a convincing majority enabling them to "pursue vigorously the negotiations with the British government of the grant to Rhodesia of independence." This was an option moderates could support, and as a result the liberal opposition was annihilated. Because Smith was frightened that the voters would not support him on UDI, no referendum ever tested the electorate's opinion of the break with Britain.

If the common citizenship of black and white had been a growing preoccupation of postwar Rhodesian governments, Smith's government increasingly emphasized black and white differences and cynically used traditional leaders and gatherings (what he called "a tradition . . . of our country") rather than the ballot box to test black political opinions. In his first meeting with the Conservative government after becoming prime minister, Smith proposed a referendum on independence using the voters' roll (overwhelmingly white since the nationalists' boycott) and the opinion of "tribesmen," meaning traditional leaders, a constituency to manipulate. Smith's indaba in October 1964 gave unanimous support for full independence under the 1961 constitution. Faced with this invented tradition, the new Labour government under Harold Wilson remained true to its traditions of the ballot box and boycotted the event, while the nationalists became more vociferous in their demand, "One Man, One Vote."

Wilson's policy became clear—no Rhodesian independence under minority white rule—but was not spelled out until September 1965, and then only under pressure from African governments. Unimpeded progress to majority rule had to be guaranteed in the constitution; racial discrimination must be ended and the political status of blacks improved. Independence would be granted only with the consent of "the people of Rhodesia as a whole." This last demand alarmed the Rhodesia Front. Indaba outcomes could be guaranteed. All inclusive nonracial ballot-box exercises were a different matter. In October 1965, Smith flew to London, already determined on UDI, with Central African House of Lords ideas no Labour government could accept.

Sections of the British public, however, admired Smith. He cut a rather dashing figure on television and, after all, he had been an RAF fighter pilot in World War II. His image was that of a reasonable and moderate man merely implementing policies that until the Suez crisis would have been perfectly acceptable in Britain. Rhodesia was upholding Britain's own national traditions, while Britain was kowtowing to a Commonwealth dominated by Asia and Africa, the Organization of African Unity, and the Non-Aligned Movement—masks for Moscow's global ambitions. When Smith finally declared Rhodesia independent of Britain, he claimed that it was an anticommunist act of global significance.

Smith declared Rhodesia independent of Britain on November 11, 1965—a moment prepared since becoming prime minister. He shrewdly realized that kith-and-kin considerations would prevent Britain subduing its rebel colony by force—a move Wilson soon said was out of the question. Instead, sanctions and a naval blockade would be used to stop oil reaching Beira, a Mozambican coastal city, and being pumped to a Rhodesian refinery. Because Rhodesia's imports and exports passed through Mozambique and South Africa, Smith's first European visit as prime minister had been to Lisbon, where the dictator Salazar assured him of Portugal's support. So, too, apartheid South Africa, whose nationalist government had no desire to support sanctions that one day could be directed against itself. Despite sanctions, after initial post-UDI uncertainties the economy actually boomed, skillfully improvising import substitutions, and sanctions-busting became an industry on its own. Wilson's prediction of collapse within months proved ridiculous and politically naive. UDI (whose bizarre echo of the American Declaration of Independence only deepened a sense of provincialism) affirmed the white Rhodesian nationalism that had been shaping itself since charter days. Rhodesians were "a courageous people [whom] history has cast . . . in a heroic role" and who were refusing to allow their identity "to be shattered on the rocks of expediency," the word that Smith always used to describe any accommodation with the wishes of the Commonwealth or the OAU. White Commonwealth nations claimed new and sovereign identities (Canada, Australia, New Zealand) only when massive British migration swamped their indigenous populations. There were third and fourth generation whites with no other political identity than as Rhodesians (and after 1980 Zimbabweans), but a viable white Rhodesian nation needed white immigration on a scale unimaginable in the 1960s. If Smith's international stature among white conservatives was enormous, it did not translate into a flood of new settlers. More crucially, the white nation required a subservient black population that Smith could no longer ensure and that UDI had provoked into a new militancy. A Rhodesian nation based on racial exclusion was bound to fail, and when the Zimbabwean nation was born in 1980, it too claimed that it comprised courageous people who had played a heroic role in forming the nation; its empowering narratives, however, traced a history of resistance to white Rhodesians.

Petrol shortages and press censorship apart, the early UDI days showed more normality than crisis. Britain had instructed civil servants and the police to perform their routine duties—an astonishing instruction for servants of an illegal regime rebelling against the crown. By 1968 the white population was again increasing. In September of that year, the Rhodesian Appellate Division ruled that Smith's was the country's legal government. Britain claimed a sovereignty it was unable to exercise. With law, order, and finances in Rhodesian hands, the de facto must be recognized as de jure. Although two Supreme Court judges resigned, Wilson's response to UDI had been so inept that only a passionate legalist could see no merit in the Appellate Division's argument.

In 1968 and 1969, Wilson met Smith for talks on the British warships *Tiger* and *Fearless* in the Mediterranean, since, as a rebellious subject of the queen, Smith could not set foot in England. There was no agreement. Britain repeated its conditions: no constitutional change without a repudiation of UDI, consulting the people, and a return "to legality." Smith, heady with his rebellion's success, not only refused go back on independence but also already had determined to make the break with Britain final with a new constitution declaring Rhodesia a republic. Since 1890, there had been a legal possibility that blacks could one day assume power. The 1969 constitution allowed for "racial parity" at some vague future point, but that was as much as blacks could expect. It was a more obvious white supremacist document than any that Rhodesia had ever had, and two-thirds of the voters approved it in a June referendum. The republic was proclaimed on March 1, 1970, and a month later an election was held under the new republican constitution when, unsurprisingly, the Rhodesia Front won all the seats reserved for whites.

Smith's was a politics of gesture and his style cavalier. He could declare Rhodesian independence or a republic with fanfare one day and gain electoral support, and within months begin negotiating for yet another constitutional scheme. Soon after the referendum on the republic, a new British Conservative government raised Rhodesian Front optimism. Alec Douglas Home, the new foreign secretary, seemed so sympathetic that by November 1971 a new constitution had been agreed upon. The foundation of the 1969 republican constitution was that "Europeans must surrender any belief in permanent European domination and Africans must surrender any belief in ultimate African domination." A year later, the Smith-Home constitution envisaged some future time when educated blacks could command a majority in the lower house, though because this was so remote in time no whites needed feel alarm. The extent of British concessions can be measured by Home's agreeing to accept as the basis for negotiation the republican constitution, which, as far as the British were concerned, had been arrived at illegally. A previous condition, however, remained: the people must validate any new constitution.

What followed marked a turning point in Rhodesian history. Smith now agreed that black opinion should be tested not through the ballot box, but through a commission whose members would tour Rhodesia. His "experts in this field" had assured him that blacks would agree and not be intimidated by "communists and extremists"—the nationalist leaders. The experts Smith refers to were officials in what once had been the Native Department and was now the Department of African Affairs. At the time of the Pearce Commission, the Secretary for African Affairs, as the Chief Native Commissioner was now known, was Hostes Nicolle, a confirmed segregationist, who dangerously claimed to know the "African Mind." He guaranteed black acquiescence or boasted that his department could manage any meeting between the commissioners and blacks to give an impression of acquiescence. Such advice explains Smith's abiding delusion that blacks had no political opinions unless they were expressed through their traditional leaders. His whole political life assumed that blacks were incapable of intelligent participation in a parliamentary democracy. The Pearce Commission decided to use impressionistic testing methods; without a voter roll they could do nothing else. Instead of indabas, commissioners would tour the country testing opinion at mass rallies. For Smith, hopelessly out of touch with black opinion, it was a disastrous exercise. The exiled and imprisoned nationalist leadership had created a body called the African National Council comprising leaders still free and living in the country. Using the grassroots organization of both ZANU and the People's Caretaker Council, as ZAPU was now called, the council arranged that wherever the commissioners went, in town or country, they met crowds shouting their opposition to the constitution. Required to reach a determination from impressions, the commission was obliged to find "that the majority of Africans rejected the Proposals." It noted how greatly Smith's government was mistrusted and contextualized this historically: "Apprehension for the future stemmed from resentment at what they felt to be the humiliations of the past and at the limitations of policy on land, education and personal advancement." Smith called the exercise "a farce" and an "absolute fraud"; the commission "had seen less than 5 per cent of our black people" but claimed to know "the views of 100%." Inasmuch as Smith's experts in internal affairs had never consulted the opinion of anything like 5 percent of those it claimed to represent, and inasmuch as every constitution Smith had negotiated was designed to silence black voices, this comment sought the wrong target. His fulminations and the anthropological lore of internal affairs could not hide the fact that the nationalist leadership controlled mass movements vociferous in their opposition to his Rhodesia Front and his Rhodesia. The black majority did not look to traditional leadership to represent their views, but to political parties shaped within colonial modernity.

The Pearce Commission reported in May 1972. In December the Liberation War began in earnest. The years from UDI to Pearce had seen guerilla incursions, but with Mozambican and South African support, only Zambia's border allowed guerilla access, and the Zambezi Valley was relatively easy to defend. More professional than internal affairs, with its fantasies of contented and primitive "tribesmen," Rhodesian military intelligence had scrutinized factionalism within the nationalist movements and knew well the bitter rivalry between ZANU and the PCC. All white, "coloured," and Asian males had to perform national service. Together with the police, the air force, and regular army (comprising black and white regiments), the Rhodesian military was as professional as any force in Africa. The guerilla movements for now were more inconvenience than threat.

This changed at the end of 1972. ZANLA, the armed wing of ZANU, had infiltrated the Tribal Trust Lands in the northeast, set up bases in the mountains of the Zambezi Valley escarpment, and attacked farms in the Centenary area. Soon after ZAPU forces launched attacks in Matabeleland, and until Zimbabwean independence Rhodesia was in a state of war. Throughout 1973, the situation's gravity was played down, though the call-up length was extended and the upper age limit steadily raised until in 1978 it reached sixty. Censorship and patriotic rhetoric failed to conceal the situation's gravity because most white families had members involved militarily. Emigration restarted, the white population from its 1973 peak of just over 300,000 having declined ever since. In April 1974, Portugal's anticolonial coup changed the balance of white power in the region. Within months, the Portuguese army no longer patrolling Rhodesia's eastern border, a thousand miles of the Rhodesia-Mozambique border were opened to ZANLA infiltration, stretching the Rhodesian army to its limit. South Africa had never officially recognized Rhodesia's independence, though unofficially its support had made UDI possible. Mozambican and Angolan independence left South African whites perilously isolated, forcing Pretoria to rethink its regional alliances. With Mozambique and Angola almost independent, Rhodesia's status illegal, and an escalating war often involving cross-border attacks into Zambia and Mozambique, unwelcome attention was focusing on Pretoria's support for Smith. If Rhodesia must be sacrificed to serve South African interests, John Vorster's government was willing to perform that ritual. Hence a détente with Zambia using Rhodesia as a bargaining chip. In August 1974, at President Kenneth Kaunda's request, and without informing Smith, Vorster withdrew the South African police helping to patrol the Zambezi and for six months, for days at a time, withheld ammunition. Nothing more forcibly reminded Rhodesia of power realities in the region. The decision to remain separate from South Africa made in the referendum over fifty years before now returned to haunt Rhodesians. With Portugal gone, Pretoria now moved with desperate speed to get a Rhodesian settlement. In one bizarre move, in August 1974, a number of railway carriages were placed on the Victoria Falls Bridge, where Smith could confer with the nationalist leaders without either crossing international borders. But Smith was not yet desperate enough to meet the nationalists' basic demands. He hoped that what he saw as their extreme positions would persuade Pretoria as well as Kaunda (cosponsor of the conference) that accommodation with such fanatics was impossible. But increasingly both Zambians and South Africans saw Smith as the fanatic and détente remained South African policy. Indeed, in November 1974 Pretoria forced Smith to release the leaders of the two principal nationalist parties, some of whom had been in detention since 1962 and who, once released, crossed the borders and joined their comrades in exile.

China, the Soviet Union, the German Democratic Republic, and other African and Eastern Bloc countries supported the nationalist armies. Cash and humanitarian support came from Scandinavia, West Germany, and the Netherlands. Unfortunately, the presence of the released leaders in Zambia and Mozambique increased the internal nationalist tension that had been prevalent since the early 1960s. Factionalism based on regionalism, class, and ethnicity erupted in fighting in both Zambia and Mozambique.

In March 1975, Herbert Chitepo, the ZANU external chairman, was assassinated, with an OAU commission blaming a powerful faction in ZANU. Several ZANU leaders were subsequently detained in Zambia. In 1976, to address factionalism, ZANU and ZAPU formed an alliance called the Patriotic Front and the guerrilla armies fought under this title until Zimbabwean independence. Zambia's detention of ZANU leaders worked to Robert Mugabe's advantage. In 1977, at Chimoio in Mozambique, he was elected ZANU president and commander-in-chief of ZANLA. He succeeded in unifying the squabbling party, and the Patriotic Front now became a much more effective fighting force.

Political pressures on Smith continued to build. In late 1975, the South Africans attacked independent Angola but were shocked to be driven back by Angolan forces stiffened by Cuban and Soviet support. With Mozambique and Angola as Soviet spheres of influence, such wars were no longer local conflicts without external repercussions. And now American attention became fixed on the region with more concentration than at any time before or since. Secretary of State Henry Kissinger agreed to help Pretoria regain international acceptability if it could reconcile itself to its African neighbors. An obvious way was by withdrawing support from Rhodesia. With Rhodesian attacks into Mozambique increasing during 1976, Vorster, according to Smith, demanded that these should now be cleared with Pretoria—evidence enough that Rhodesia's independence and sovereignty were an illusion. Furthermore, the war kept Rhodesia under the international spotlight. White emigration increased. Smith's options were running out. Early in 1976, he started negotiations with Joshua Nkomo, a man increasingly isolated within the Patriotic Front by the ZANU leadership. When these got nowhere, he announced that he was bringing blacks into his cabinet. In September 1976, at a meeting with Kissinger and Smith, Vorster made his position absolutely clear: Rhodesia could no longer rely on South Africa financially or militarily. Three days later, Smith broadcast to Rhodesia announcing that a conference would be held to set up an interim government leading to majority rule within two years.

Nearly eleven years before, Smith had defiantly declared Rhodesia independent of Britain, and, after the HMS *Fearless* talks, had notoriously proclaimed there would be no majority rule in a thousand years. Now black rule was only two short years away. He called his memoir *The Great Betrayal*, not blaming Britain, the old enemy, but Pretoria, whose "deceit and treachery" in cutting Rhodesia's lifeline forced him to accept whatever South Africa demanded. With Washington involved, the survival of the white Rhodesian nation was of minimal consequence to either the South Africans or the Americans, who had other concerns. Majority rule was inevitable. The Rhodesia Front caucus agreed, according to Smith, that "the only responsible course was . . . to rescue the maximum from the tragedy that was about to unfold." The Kissinger proposals, discussed in Geneva for over two months from the end of October 1977, found Mugabe and Nkomo reluctant to accept what Vorster and Kissinger had imposed on Smith. If Smith had rejected all the earlier proposals that might have gained black support and given him international recognition, it was now the nationalists' turn to obstruct what had been agreed upon, arguing, quite correctly, that they had never been consulted.

Not once, however, as he retreated from one entrenched position after another, did Smith admit that UDI had been an absurd blunder. Even now one can only speculate on why he did not anticipate that an illegal action to promote a cause internationally perceived as immoral was bound to fail. He certainly believed that Rhodesia had a moral right to the same independence that the partners of Federation had been given, and Britain also agreed with this. There was a great difference, however, between granting independence to African countries on the basis of universal suffrage and licensing 200,000 whites to control the lives of ten times as many blacks. Smith believed that UDI would offer a saving stability and stanch white emigration—as important to him as it had been to all Rhodesian prime ministers. As late as 1976, he warned Kissinger and Vorster that their proposals would involve "a mass exodus of [white] skills, expertise and investment, with resultant disaster." There could be no white Rhodesian nation if whites chose to leave. He also hoped that UDI would be a seven-day wonder, remembered only by the relevant department in Whitehall. That was singularly naive. Black voices may have been subdued in Rhodesia, but they spoke loudly throughout the continent. Smith used continental chaos to confirm that he had taken the sensible course. But illegalities and corruption in numerous African regimes were unimportant. Creating and maintaining conditions in which a white nation could prosper was Smith's goal, and he tried to pursue this without considering the moral and political international contexts of the 1960s.

Without South African backing, the war effort became futile. Whites began to question their future. If emigration expressed doubts UDI was supposed to have allayed, in March 1977 twelve Rhodesia Front caucus members resigned over what they regarded as Smith's accommodation with Kissinger and Pretoria. As with several previous Rhodesian prime ministers, the dissidents now represented Smith as a dangerous liberal. Atypically, however, their revolt received little electoral support. With majority rule inevitable, and South African support gone, the time for internal squabbling had passed. In his New Year's speech for 1978, Smith acknowledged for the first time that his principal political objective was to retain white confidence and keep whites in the country. It showed how far he had traveled from his portentous 1965 demand that the nation be allowed to realize its historic destiny. By nation he of course meant whites, now showing minimal commitment to their history by simply leaving. At the end of 1977, he sought no more than "safeguards which will ensure that a future Government will not be able to abuse its power by resorting to actions which are dishonest or immoral." A "justiceable Bill of Rights to protect the rights and freedoms of individuals" would prevent such an abuse of power—a curious expectation from the man who for fourteen years had governed under a state of emergency and who had, with UDI, thrown all constitutions aside.

Smith was left now with the Pretoria agreement that Kissinger had negotiated and Vorster guaranteed. But war and international pressure had made the terms even of this agreement (especially on whites retaining security and defense control for two years) no longer acceptable to either London or Washington. An Anglo-American team, led by British Foreign Secretary David Owen and U.S. Ambassador to the United Nations Andrew Young, that arrived in September 1977 offered new terms. These left Smith with the sole option of opening negotiations with the many nationalists disaffected with their new leadership or marginalized by internal power struggles. Rhodesia Front delegates thus met Abel Muzorewa, who had led internal opposition to the Pearce Commission in 1972 and who had his own political ambitions; Ndabaningi Sithole, principal victim of Mugabe's rise to power; James Chikerema, veteran nationalist with unrivalled liberation credentials, who had formed a rival group to ZANU and fallen out of favor with Mugabe. Together with these and two traditional chiefs an internal settlement was hammered out. When Muzorewa's delegation showed signs of marching out in protest at Smith's inflexibility, South Africa's General Magnus Malan threatened to remove vital military equipment from Rhodesia unless Muzorewa's objections were met. This threat carried larger implications. Pretoria clearly meant to carry apartheid to its logical conclusion. Whites would continue to rule only in those parts of South Africa set aside for whites. Zimbabwe-Rhodesia would thus be just another Bantustan within the grand apartheid system. Since no nation in the world believed in the fictional independence of the Bantustans, why Pretoria believed that Europe or the United States would accept a Zimbabwe-Rhodesia Bantustan as evidence of the apartheid project's seriousness is as mysterious now as it was then. In March 1978, Smith, Muzorewa, and Chief Chirau signed the settlement, which created Zimbabwe-Rhodesia, mandated "one man, one vote," and abolished everything Rhodesians claimed they had been fighting for. In May 1979, Muzorewa's United African National Council won an election, the Rhodesian parliament was dissolved, and Muzorewa became Prime Minister on June 1, 1979. Ninety years of white rule had ended. But since Britain had not agreed to the Zimbabwe-Rhodesia constitution, the new dispensation was as illegal as UDI had been fourteen years before.

Like Smith's republic, Muzorewa's Zimbabwe-Rhodesia needed international recognition. But this was not forthcoming. Washington refused to lift sanctions. Muzorewa failed to convince anyone who had not been party to the internal settlement that his regime legally represented the people. Even Pretoria hesitated. Smith claims that white presence in the Zimbabwe-Rhodesia cabinet called into question Pretoria's preferred models of Bantustan governments where whites played no public political role. Meanwhile the war continued. For six years caught between the Rhodesian army and the forces of the Patriotic Front, rural people now faced the private militias of Sithole and Muzorewa, the latter quickly obtaining a reputation for brutality unmatched by any other combatants. How far the Muzorewa regime ever had popular support is difficult to determine, but with the war daily more violent, whatever hopes the people placed on it quickly turned to disillusionment.

Margaret Thatcher became the British prime minister in May 1979. Though the Rhodesia Front could no more trust Conservative than Labour administrations, Smith knew he was unlikely to get anyone more sympathetic in Downing Street. But, whatever her private sympathies, Thatcher found no support for the Muzorewa arrangement at the 1979 Lusaka Commonwealth Conference and seemed determined to end all involvement in Zimbabwe-Rhodesia. Smith could now only rescue whatever he could from the ruins of his grand design. Sanctions remained. Pretoria was ready to pressurize Muzorewa as much as it had Smith to end the war. Thatcher now proposed the historic Lancaster House Conference for September, where all sides could hammer out a new constitution. The various delegations, including Muzorewa and Smith, attended. Meanwhile the undefeated Zimbabwe-Rhodesia army, on the eve of the conference, and presumably on Muzorewa's orders, launched a major attack on Mozambican bridges and railway lines that directly affected the conference outcome. Mozambique's Samora Machel with increased urgency pressed Mugabe to agree to a settlement. In elections the following year Mugabe was able to argue that Muzorewa had shown himself only too willing to kill his own people. With Muzorewa leading the government delegation at Lancaster House, Smith was sidelined. A constitution was voted on with only his opposing vote. Even David Smith, minister of finance in the last Rhodesia Front administration and one of the two whites with voting powers, voted with Muzorewa. Smith's hopes rose briefly when Mugabe tried to backtrack, but Machel's threatening to deny access to Patriotic Front bases in Mozambique quickly brought Mugabe back into line.

A constitution had finally been agreed on in which parliamentary power had passed from white minority to black majority. In a hundred-seat parliament, whites were guaranteed only twenty seats, and then only for seven years before a constitutional review. By insisting on a racially divided voter's role, the Rhodesia Front showed itself still unable to think outside racial categories, and in independent Zimbabwe's first years whites featured as a discrete community with its own electoral privileges. The constitutions of the previous quarter of a century had all been preoccupied with race and manipulated voting patterns to prevent blacks exercising their majority power. With specially reserved seats, this pattern had now been turned against the whites, though their rapidly dwindling ranks gave them more representation than their numbers warranted. The agreement now required a return to British rule. London thus assumed a direct control over the country that it had never exercised in the previous ninety years. The British governor was to oversee the cease-fire and organize elections for an independent Zimbabwe.

The last important decision of the Zimbabwe-Rhodesia parliament was to agree to implement the Lancaster House agreement. At the end of November the Government of National Unity, as the Muzorewa regime was called, voted itself out of office. Cease-fire arrangements involved guerillas handing in their arms at assembly points around the country supervised by peacekeeping soldiers from various Commonwealth countries. The Rhodesia Front's last hope of influencing the first Zimbabwean parliament was that the black vote would be so split among Muzorewa, Sithole, Nkomo, and Mugabe that Smith's party could use its twenty white seats to form a coalition against Mugabe, seen as the most extreme of the black politicians. This seemed not improbable, since Mugabe had refused to contest the election as part of the Patriotic Front, preferring to enter parliament at the head of his own party, ZANU (PF). It was a calculated gamble, for Nkomo was certain to win most Ndebele votes, and Mugabe could not be sure he commanded a Shona majority. Indeed, intelligence convinced London and Pretoria that Sithole and Muzorewa had enough support to win over a third of parliamentary seats. Thus, if Mugabe could not in fact gather enough support, a new government of national unity could emerge, which Smith would be invited to join. The March 4 results showed success for Mugabe's gamble, his party taking fifty-seven seats. Nkomo had taken twenty, Muzorewa only three, and Sithole none. If Muzorewa had commanded any support in 1979 (assuming the results had not been rigged) this had dissipated, voters now clearly identifying him with Ian Smith and with responsibility for the closing violence of the Liberation War. Smith and Sithole both claimed massive rigging and intimidation, but Mugabe's victory was so complete that even with some voter coercion, and even though it was not a result London had hoped for, the British governor was able to pronounce that the outcome represented the wishes of the people of Zimbabwe. On April 18, 1980, Zimbabwe became an independent republic.

After independence about 100,000 whites chose to stay, many of them professional people or productive farmers and businessmen. Their presence promoted economic stability and progress during the new dispensation's first decade. Smith retained a following among them. When last they voted for their twenty-three reserved seats in the 1985 general election, the Conservative Alliance of Zimbabwe, the final incarnation of the Rhodesia Front, won a majority of the white votes. Mugabe saw this as spurning his reconciliation gestures, although it was another fifteen years before he decided to target whites as a community, and then only when his own power was threatened and whites became a scapegoat for his growing unpopularity.

7. Historiography and Literature

An age of taxonomic meltdown brings historical writing and literature ever closer. History greets literature when touched by aesthetic creativity; literature meets history when marked by period, culture, or ideology. Of the former, Pliny and Livy are familiar examples, as are Gibbon and Macaulay. In a continent where (pace Walter Ong's *Orality and Literacy*) literary redefinition has become obligatory, the link becomes seminal. Africans seeking to diagnose continental plight, to discover, in Chinua Achebe's phrase, "when the rain began to beat us," face, beyond the limits of local orality, history as conventionally conceived in the West. When that version denies a people's memory, and when strangers inscribe it while ignoring internal sources, African authors seek to set the record straight. Avoiding European archives—unless, like Stanlake Samkange, they are professional historians—they will consult oral tradition and write, as the Madagascan poet Rabemananjara once said, "with one ear bent to the sleeping centuries down the dark road of time."[1]

Especially in work by Ndabaningi Sithole (*African Nationalism*, 1959), Stanlake Samkange (*On Trial for My Country*, 1966), and Lawrence Vambe (*An Ill-Fated People: Zimbabwe Before and After Rhodes*, 1972; *From Rhodesia to Zimbabwe*, 1976), Zimbabwe has witnessed a determined effort, involving literary tools, to correct the historical record—to let Africans say what happened when Rhodes and his Pioneers conquered their land. Echoing continental practice elsewhere, they use the colonialist's language, religion, and cherished rational argumentation against him, and, in the case of Samkange, archival documentation, too.

More recently, Zimbabwe has seen deliberate collaboration between literature and conventional historiography. Terence Ranger has described his 1993 reaction to the late Yvonne Vera's novel *Nehanda*, which explores the first African rebellion against Rhodes's settlers of the 1890s. Astonished by Vera's "obviously deliberate refusal to draw upon works of history or anthropology," he was deeply impressed by the result, a work he called "an extraordinary feat of imagination." This novel, he says, "discards the techniques of male historiography. There are no public narratives; no events."[2] Thus began a professional dialogue probing history's nature as conceived in both Western and African terms. The relationship, he believes, has already generated mutual influence. A social history he is writing on Bulawayo "is a conscious response to the challenge of Vera's novel *Butterfly Burning*." His narrative will be a 'real' history, "but one that reads like a novel." In response, her last novel, *The Stone Virgins* (2002) "represents a development, or at least a change, in Vera's engagement with history," with one character a professional historian. Illustrating Vera's imaginative freedom, Ranger notes that this novel reaches back far beyond the 1890s, the title's virgins being prehistoric rock paintings of San women in the Matopos Hills, which echo hauntingly for Vera. A character touching the painted women says:

Forty thousand years gather in my memory like a wild wind. It is true, everything else in Gulati rots except the rocks. On the rocks history is steady, it cannot be tilted forwards or backwards. It is not a refrain. History fades into the chaos of the hills but it does not vanish. In Gulati I travel four hundred years, then ten thousand years, twenty more. The rocks split open, time sifts and I confess that I am among the travelers who steal shelter from the dead.[3]

Others, too, feel duty-bound to place on record memory and witness of the colonially voiceless by enfolding history in literature. Vera's compatriot, the brilliant Dambudzo Marechera, worked into his pathbreaking "House of Hunger" a version of Lobengula's letter to Queen Victoria, with its doom-laden message of betrayal by Rhodes, Rudd, and Jameson:

> A document was prepared and presented to me for signature. I asked what it contained, and was told that in it were my words and the words of those men. I put my hand to it. About three months afterwards I heard from other sources that I had given, by that document, the right to all the minerals in my country. I called a meeting of my indunas, and also of the white men, and demanded a copy of that document. It was proved to me that I had signed away the mineral rights of my whole country to Rudd and his friends.[4]

Echoing a practice seen initially in Chinua Achebe's West African classic *Things Fall Apart* and in the early novels of East African Ngugi wa Thiong'o, Central African writers busy with history include Zimbabwe's Shimmer Chinodya, Freedom Nyamubaya, George Mujajati, Thomas Bvuma, Tafataona Mahoso, and Albert Chimedza; Malawi's Jack Mapanje, Steve Chimombo, Edison Mpina, Dede Kamkondo, David Rubadiri, and Felix Mnthali; and Zambia's Andreya Masiye, Binwell Sinyangwe, and Dominic Mulaisho. Steve Chimombo's *The Wrath of Napolo* (2000), for example, uses the historical sinking of the steamer *Viphya* as fictional pivot for a critique of Malawian colonial and postcolonial history, one character remarking: "The *Maravi* story is the history of [Malawi], in both time and space. The ship sailed from south to north and west to east, touching almost all the districts of the country. On board, it carried all the races or tribes." For his part, Zimbabwe's Chenjerai Hove in *Palaver Finish* (2002) baldly asserts literature's superiority as a historiographical instrument:

> As a writer, I have developed certain principles, from experience. If I go to a new country, I do not want to read its history from history books. I want to know who the country's important writers are. *The Violent Land*, by Jorge Amado, gave me more history of Brazil than I would ever get from history texts. The true history of Zimbabwe is found in the heartbeat of Zimbabwe's writers. . . . The land, for example, which is now being used as an election campaign gimmick, was written about many years ago by Charles Mungoshi in his great novel, *Waiting for the Rain*.[5]

Fear that if Africans do not control historical discourse others will continue doing so informs the texts themselves. Achebe scorns the British colonial official who writes *The Primitive Tribes of the Lower Niger* during tragedy in Umuofia, and Ngugi scorns an official doing the same ethnological work in Kenya. Anxiety about this control also informs Felix Mnthali's manifesto in his verse collection *When Sunset Comes to Sapitwa* (1980):

And a voice said to me

. . .

Write and erase all this
In the waters of the lake
Before historians disturb what was
While inventing what was not.[6]

Mnthali, novelist and poet, agrees with Joseph Conrad's view that creative writing, fiction especially, is clearer than reality and that its collective truth challenges the arrogance of "documentary history." Postmodernism usefully reemphasizes textual provenance, asking who is writing, to whom, about whom, and from whose point of view. (It would certainly note that my introductory reflections on empire depend heavily on scholars overwhelmingly European and male.) It also reminds us that colonialism meant not only losing your land and freedom but also your voice. Hence colonial historiography became largely an inscription of the voiced discussing the voiceless.

That said, an outline of British imperial historiography is sufficiently complex to merit a complete volume in the *Oxford History* (1998). Meticulously edited by Yale's Robin Winks, the text maps shifting academic fashion and professional civil war. It also moves from Gibbonian sweep, with its irony and certitude, on to pioneering Ranke and waspish Strachey, and down to postmodern psychosis. But it firmly establishes that, for over a century, British involvement in Central and Southern Africa was merely the story of white settlers and their struggles with London—a narrative of frontier expansion, land seizure, and dialogue with the Colonial Office. Until the second half of the twentieth century, African people, except as tiresome extras, rarely featured narratively, and almost never *in propria persona*. Those writing the texts included Coupland and Seely, Curtis and Mansergh, Acton and Egerton, Namier and Woolf. Focus and orientation, we learn, began to shift with Gallagher and Robinson's *Africa and the Victorians*, continuing with Flint and Ranger, Fage and Oliver, Shepperson and Webster, Omer-Cooper and Linden, Pagden and Judd, McCracken, Keppel-Jones, and Vaughan. In the postcolonial phase, African historiography, in topic anyway, began creeping from center to periphery, from rulers to ruled. But as recently as 1999 George Shepperson's foreword to D. D. Phiri's *Let Us Die for Africa: An African Perspective on the Life and Death of John Chilembwe of Nyasaland*, states, "The African viewpoint has still to be properly integrated into general historical writing about modern times."[7]

Early practice was perhaps inevitable. Professional historians do not grow like daisies in a meadow. Nor, ideology aside, could colonial policy privilege historians over farmers and tradesmen. However, at a time of West African historiographical progress, with the emergence of Kenneth Dike and Cheikh Anta Diop, and East African too with Bethwell Ogot and Gideon Were, Southern and Central African black historians remained distinctly rare. Besides those of European origin writing on this area—Ranger, Rotberg, Saunders, Bundy, Marks, De Kiewiet, Stuart, Van Jaarsfeld, Guy, Channock, Linden, Van Onselen, McCracken, and Vail—it is hard to find African names beyond Trepido, Nzula, Molema, Phiri, Zeleza, and the hugely productive Bhebe, though the work of Sithole, Samkange, and Vambe recalls a time before Rhodes. Understandable for Malawi and Zambia (impoverished countries with new universities), it does not excuse South Africa and Rhodesia, comparatively wealthy countries with older, well-resourced universities.

Rino Zhuwarara's *Introduction to Zimbabwean Literature in English* (2001) accuses the Rhodesian colonial government of strenuously directing African scholars into technical areas for reasons political as much as developmental.[8]

In Southern and Central Africa, white historians taught mainly white students, whom, because in colonial thought excellence must lie at the center, they sent as postgraduates to Oxbridge or London. Even then, such students seeking "African" topics met opposition from British gatekeepers. Wm. Roger Louis tells us that in the 1960s Sir Geoffrey Elton "opposed the expansion of the Cambridge curriculum into 'Third World' studies," or, as he put it, "into bits of history from Mexico to Malawi." Hugh Trevor-Roper, though contradicted by Roland Oliver and John Fage, denied that Africa had any history at all before the arrival of whites, but offered only "the unrewarding gyrations of barbarous tribes."[9] Even when exceptions occurred, men like Dike and Ogot faced prejudice against oral sources, the most authentic channels of their own history. Yet, as Shepperson remarks in comments on his own and Phiri's account of John Chilembwe's revolt against Nyasaland's British plantocracy, Phiri had access to "African oral evidence which eluded us."[10]

8. Independence

Literature celebrates diversity. Yet this guide takes into account three different countries and sees them as an entity called Central Africa, as though they, and their literary output, are homogeneous. Fortunately, commonality can be identified even beside divergence. The region was already seen as a political entity in the 1890s, when the term British Central Africa first became current. Much later, in 1953, the Colonial Office, with settler urging, detected a coherence so strong that it created the ill-starred Central African Federation of Rhodesia and Nyasaland, with Salisbury as its capital—a decision whose unintended consequence was acceleration of African strategies for independence.

There is also geographic coherence. The three countries are subtropical and landlocked. In all three, despite varying soil and altitude, erratic precipitation has historically fostered the creation of rain shrines and their associated cults.[1] Writers reflect broadly similar landscapes of mountain and plain, lake and valley, mopane and brachystygia woodland. Zimbabwe's Musaemura Zimunya recalls the Vumba Mountains of his childhood; Felix Mnthali, Legson Kayira, and Lupenga Mphande the hills and lake of northern Malawi; Jack Mapanje and Steve Chimombo the Shire Highlands; and Edison Mpina the Mulanje Mountain area near Mozambique. Binwell Sinyangwe and Dominic Mulaisho reflect a similar topography in Zambia. Linguistic relationship is evident in major regional languages such as Chinyanja, Bemba, Shona, Ndebele, Lomwe, and Tumbuka, all classified as Bantu.

Yet similarity does not minimize diversity. Sir Harry Johnston and Scottish missionaries kept Nyasaland safe from British South Africa Company control; Cecil Rhodes's treatment of Northern Rhodesia was diluted by initial ignorance of the country's mineral wealth, the need for Southern Rhodesian consolidation, and subtle change in the zeitgeist. In particular, Southern Rhodesia's economic dominance and large settler population caused political divergence—and thus a distinctive literary response to it. When Hastings Banda and Kenneth Kaunda destroyed the Central African Federation (with Banda assuming sole credit), Nyasaland and Northern Rhodesia moved swiftly to independence in 1964 as Malawi and Zambia. By contrast, Southern Rhodesia became independent only in 1980, after a liberation war costing some thirty thousand lives and triggered by Prime Minister Smith's 1965 Unilateral Declaration of Independence. The victory of Robert Mugabe and Joshua Nkomo's guerilla armies in Zimbabwe foreshadowed the end of white rule in South Africa, and, with the installation of Nelson Mandela's government in 1994, the end of Africa's long chapter of European colonialism.

The Liberation War, which profoundly disturbed Zimbabwe's national psyche, receives treatment of varying intensity in the work of Shimmer Chinodya, Yvonne Vera, Chenjerai Hove, Freedom Nyamubaya, Tafataona Mahoso, Thomas Bvuma, George Mujajati, Stanley Nyamfukudza, and Hopewell Seyaseya. Indeed few writers ignore it. With an extraordinary mixture of *Boys' Own* naiveté, culpable ignorance, racial arrogance, and contempt for Harold Macmillan's warning about "the winds of change," Ian Smith's regime believed it could stem the floodtide of decolonization, vowing that Africans would not rule for a thousand years. The conviction was that while South Africa remained white-ruled, so could Rhodesia. Meanwhile, Kaunda's Zambia became a frontline state in a conflict involving not just Rhodesia but also South Africa as the African National Congress, growing desperate in its struggle against apartheid, moved beyond the republic's borders to assist in the battle against both Salisbury and Pretoria. David Kerr writes, "In foreign policy, Zambia supported liberation movements such as the African National Congress (ANC) of South Africa, the Front for the Liberation of Mozambique (FRELIMO) and both the Popular Movement for the Liberation of Angola (MPLA) and UNITA, the South West African People's Organization (SWAPO) of Namibia and the Zimbabwean African People's Union (ZAPU) of Zimbabwe."[2] Zambia paid a crippling price for its altruism at a time when falling copper prices were ravaging its own economy, leading to the stringent Structural Adjustment Program inflicted by the International Monetary Fund in the 1990s. The resulting misery is powerfully evoked in Binwell Sinyangwe's novel *A Cowrie of Hope* (2000).

Malawi behaved differently. Presiding over one of the world's poorest countries, Banda chose pragmatism over idealism and retained links with both South Africa and Rhodesia. In return, Pretoria supported Malawi economically, supplied technical expertise, continued accepting miners under the hated WENELA scheme, advised Banda's Special Branch on terror tactics, and largely funded the new capital at Lilongwe. Malawi became a pariah state within Africa (one of the few countries South Africans could visit), its relations with even Zambia souring as Banda grew increasingly autocratic. He jailed writers and intellectuals without charge or drove them into exile, and he used his Young Pioneers and Special Branch to harass suspected opponents. Few families escaped their attention. Like Zimbabwe's guerilla war and its subsequent civil strife, such oppression devastated national morale. Via a system of complex figurative allusion, it informs the poetry of Mnthali and Mapanje, Chipasula and Mphande, Chimombo and Chiseze, the prose of Lipenga and Zeleza, Kayira and Kamkondo. More recent coverage, as Malawian literature seeks post-Banda directions, appears in Sam Mpasu's *Nobody's Friend* (1995) and *Political Prisoner 74/6* (1995), in Chimombo's novel *The Wrath of Napolo* (2000), and in Mapanje's *The Chattering Wagtails of Mikuyu Prison* (1993), *Skipping Without Ropes* (1998), *Last of the Sweet Bananas* (2004), and *Gathering Seaweed: African Prison Writing* (2002).

Not least among Central African commonalities is the corrosive disappointment of freedom. Its literary reflection recalls earlier West African experience, especially Wole Soyinka's, whose work scholars have likened to the Jacobean gloom of post-Renaissance England. Central African Literature, then, arises against this regional background of shared and divergent experience. The early period saw missionary-nurtured writing growing in all three countries and also work from small local presses such as Mambo and College in Rhodesia and Hetherwick and Montfort in Malawi. Journals emerged, too, as witness Malawi's *Odi* and *Outlook*, and Zimbabwe's nonracial *Two Tone*, where some of the country's new poetry first appeared. Alongside the biennial *Poetry in Rhodesia*, the influential Mopani Poets series flourished, in which, in 1979, Musaemara Zimunya had work published while still in exile. Each Rhodesia had a state Literature Bureau of dubious intent. Independent Malawi lacked one but compensated by creating a Censorship Board of stupefying obtuseness. Across the region English writing developed slowly, though vernacular literature, especially in the Rhodesias, grew swiftly, encouraged by Literature Bureaus designed on South African lines. Creative writing conferences held at Salisbury's Ranche House College into the mid-1970s (the 1964 event attracted Wilbur Smith, a native of Northern Rhodesia), focused almost entirely on vernacular work. Contemporary opportunities for publishing in English are much improved, but Steve Chimombo's magazine *Wasi Writer* reminds us that although in Malawi there are some fifteen publishing houses, creative writers are increasingly turning to self-publishing. Newspapers, journals, and radio provide better outlets, with Chimombo listing for local writers the following: *The African, Baobab, Baraza, Bonanza, Daily Times, Denga, Entry, Flavour, Impact, The Journal of Humanities, Moni, Malawi News, Nyala, Odi, Odini, Outlook, Police Magazine, Quest, Religion in Malawi, Tizame, Zed Magazine, Malawi Broadcasting Corporation*, and *This is Malawi*.[3]

The language question needs comment, especially the curious fact that, during the colonial period, state authorities appeared remarkably progressive by encouraging the publication of vernacular writing. Was this not precisely what West African champions of negritude such as Senghor and the Diops had urged in the 1930s and '40s—a return to roots across all African art and culture? And did it not therefore predate Ngugi wa Thiongo's high-profile campaign later for literature in African languages? Given that South African polity extended north of the Limpopo in most matters, this was more redirection and safety valve than high-mindedness—a strategy in fact to confine Africans within their own culture. A version, in other words, of South Africa's infamous apartheid and Bantustan policy so loathed by that country's black intelligentsia. Freedom to write and publish in any language was what aspiring writers wanted.

Central African literature thus reflects history's shadowing passage over a region once seen as a colonial entity and now comprising independent republics. It also shows sociopolitical experience creating untypical writing profiles. Though still in its early stages, it displays, for example, careers dramatically telescoping the natural growth of authors working in normal conditions. Frank Chipasula's experience is exemplary. Within a few short years, under the pressure of Banda's tyranny, a wrenching shift is seen from the innocence of his first verse volume, *Visions and Reflections* (1972), to the coruscating bitterness of his 1986 *Nightwatcher* collection. Legson Kayira is an example in prose. Where a dreamy pastoralism touches novels on colonial Malawi, like *Jingala* (1969), *The Civil Servant* (1971), and *The Looming Shadow* (1968), his only novel on the Banda years, *The Detainee* (1974), suddenly becomes as satirically strident as Chipasula's *Nightwatcher*.

Independence chronologies are also significant. While Malawian poets such as Mnthali, Mapanje, and Chimombo were already beginning to register postcolonial pain, many Rhodesian writers, in exile like their South African colleagues, could still only dream of a future independence. The Pretoria-Salisbury axis looked permanent enough to cause despondency and even suicide. However, though it is tempting to speak neatly about preliberation optimism and postliberation disillusion, Flora Veit-Wild's view that the postcolonial gloom seen in East and West African writing was visible even before Zimbabwean liberation applies with some truth to writing across the entire region.[4] Certainly Malawi's freedom icons, *kwacha* (dawn) and *tambala* (rooster), as seen in the new currency, receive swift subversion in, for example, early poems collected in Felix Mnthali's anthology *When Sunset Comes to Sapitwa* (1980).

Meanwhile, Southern Rhodesia's material dominance was double-edged. On one hand, it proved a magnet for those, like the hero of Mpina's *Freedom Avenue* (1991), who sought escape from the poverty of a subsistence economy. It also produced the cross-nationality of such writers as Mnthali and Seyaseya—one a Malawian with Rhodesian roots, the other a Rhodesian with Mozambican roots. On the other hand, the Rhodesian model was predicated on a racism that restrained black cultural and artistic aspirations. While white writers (Doris Lessing and Wilbur Smith, for example) developed international reputations, black writers faced multiple barriers. Rino Zhuwarara, in his *Introduction to Zimbabwean Literature in English* (2001), cites a bibliography compiled by Anthony Chennells and colleagues that lists nearly four hundred novels by white writers published between 1890 and 1977. By contrast, says Zhuwarara, "the first serious creative work written by Zimbabweans had to be published in London and South Africa." Solomon Mutswairo had his Shona novel *Feso* published in South Africa in 1956. Herbert Chitepo's epic Shona poem *Soko Risina Musor* (1958) was published in London.[5] And in an egregious example of colonial absurdity, Kadhani and Zimunya, in their excellent introduction to *And Now the Poets Speak* (1981), report that Charles Mungoshi's *Coming of the Dry Season* was banned because one of its short stories might "bring the police into disrepute"! The travails of black Rhodesian writers also emerge starkly from *Pen Point: Tales for Sundown*, a publication of the Salisbury Writers' Club. Among twenty-three pieces not a single black author appears, and this in 1972, decades after modern literature's emergence across most of Africa, and despite the effort of such local figures as Arthur Shearly Cripps, Ken Mew, Anthony Chennells, Tim McCloughlin, and Ray Brown. Ironically, *Pen Point* says that Writers' Club aims are "straightforward: to promote and encourage all writers . . . the emphasis is on stories for the enjoyment of 'Everyman.' We think we have achieved our aim." Meanwhile, in the 1960s and '70s, small but free Malawi, even under Banda's oppression, was already producing significant work in verse, drama, and fiction. Indeed, as late as 1990, Heinemann's *New Poetry from Africa* (selected by Adewale Maja-Pearce) included only two Zimbabwean poets—Chenjerai Hove and Musaemura Zimunya—while Malawi's representation was much greater, with Frank Chipasula alone appearing with more entries than even Nobel laureate Wole Soyinka. Significantly, and again despite censorship, Malawi's Writers' Workshop regularly attracted up to sixty participants when its counterpart at University College Rhodesia could draw only a handful. Colonial state policies and black energies engaged in the struggle would be natural explanations. Since independence, however, Zimbabwe has seen a volcanic upsurge of writing that makes it by far now the most prolific of all three countries.

The dynamics of literary influence on Central Africa are also important. Fortunately, neither state control nor censorship totally prevented exposure to the great movements of the twentieth century. Many writers indeed could tap into three broad traditions: their ancient oral heritage, the literature of newly free Africa, and modernist, Marxist, and existentialist writing from the West. While their memories cherished a corpus of revered and age-old oral praise songs, prayers, myths and legends, they read Soyinka and Achebe, Ngugi and Ekwensi, Armah and Laye. Then they turned to Pound and Eliot, Joyce and Sartre, Camus and Mann. Malawians and Zambians did this more freely than Zimbabweans, however, who, especially under the Rhodesian Front government (1963–1979), felt seriously cut off from outside influence. This caused some of the angst and gloom of Zimbabwean writing. Zhuwarara, in his *Introduction to Zimbabwean Literature in English*, quotes Kizito

Muchemwa: "We felt left out, culturally and politically, from the mainstream of beliefs and thoughts current in free independent black Africa. The isolation from the rest of Africa, the lack of any fruitful contact, has had adverse effects." Zhuwarara adds, "Aspiring writers inside the country had to rely on the strengths and suffer from the weaknesses of a more or less marooned and beleaguered cultural context. This partially explains the cultural anomie and neurosis found in Mungoshi's fiction and poetry, and some of the nihilistic aspects of Marechera's artistic vision."[6]

Part II

Genres

9. Verse

It is a truism that modern African verse matured more swiftly than prose. The reasons are unclear, and the phenomenon is in any case global. Perhaps written poetry arises more readily from oral tradition than prose. Perhaps oral verse's mnemonic aims and mechanisms grip mind and memory tighter than the tropes and themes of oral prose, thus permitting an easier extension into writing. Perhaps, more mundanely, poetry's dimensions demand less effort than prose's wider canvas. Perhaps verse's rootedness in communal praise, prayer, and song is also a convenience for writers hurrying to address social groups wrestling with colonial and postcolonial trauma. One might also ask if the oral poetic tradition feels more attunable to contemporary comment than a prose tradition dominated by fantasy and fable. On the other hand, perhaps colonial education simply privileged poetry over prose, verse anthologies offering a cheaper choice than a collected Dickens or George Eliot.

Whatever the reasons, Central Africa's settler colonialism, more damaging than its nonsettler variety in, say, West Africa, retarded the flowering of a modern written tradition. This was especially true of Rhodesia. Rino Zhuwarara, in his *Introduction to Zimbabwean Literature in English*, is eloquent on the corrosive effects of white rule. It disturbed the national psyche by seizing the land, with all that this means for spiritual and cultural identity, by imposing an alien religious and economic system, urbanization, modern schooling, and (never to be underestimated), a racial arrogance that often denied even humanity to the other.[1]

Significantly, *Two Tone*, originally styled *A Quarterly of Rhodesian Poetry*, later a promoter of black writing, carried in its December 1974 issue, among thirteen whites, only one black poet, M. C. Munzabwa. As late as 1981, the Mopani Poets series, while arranging first publication of Charles Mungoshi's *The Milkman Doesn't Only Deliver Milk*, carried the discouraging notice "Submission of manuscripts is by invitation only"—a cultural parallel to "Right of admission reserved" notices still seen as apartheid reminders across Central and Southern Africa. At this time literary Central Africa was conscious of lagging behind East Africa, just as East Africa had in earlier decades lagged behind West Africa. But perhaps the delay was in some ways propitious, creating reservoirs brimming with material ready for production when times became propitious.

Beyond Rhodesia, strong external influences arose, whether from wider Africa's new burgeoning literature or from the rest of the world. In Malawi, while clearly admiring Wole Soyinka, Steve Chimombo found T. S. Eliot equally infectious ("I almost worship him"). Edison Mpina read widely in Octavio Paz, Pablo Neruda, Allen Ginsburg, Louis Simpson, and Marvin Bell. But even in colonial Zimbabwe, and despite Kizito Muchemwa's representative lament, Musaemura Zimunya reports that one of his schoolteachers, Toby Moyana, introduced him to the negritude poets Senghor and the Diops, as well as to Eliot, whose "The Hollow Men" he saw as symbolizing Africans' contemporary helplessness. Chenjerai Hove, meanwhile, found inspiration in Wilfred Owen and David Rubadiri. Influences on Albert Chimedza, who typifies a bold independence in Zimbabwe's new writing, were, in one regard, surprisingly eclectic. He cites Gabriel Okara, Wally Serote, Christopher Okigbo, and Ama Ata Aidoo alongside Bob Dylan, Pink Floyd, and Frank Zappa; but then he says, "Concerning the older writers it is undeniable that they are the architects of African literature but I can't relate to most of them. I and quite a few of my contemporaries are a new breed of African." He gives short shrift even to Okot p'Bitek's classic *Song of Lawino*, saying, "No, there's too much purpose in that sort of thing."[2] Such deep wells of influence might explain both the speed with which the new poetry has matured since independence and its bold boundary expansion. One remarkable instance is how the new writers (Freedom T. Nyamubaya and Thomas Sukutai Bvuma are just two examples) will venture into areas of personal intimacy hitherto taboo in African literary practice. As Flora Veit-Wild seems to suggest in her *Patterns of Poetry in Zimbabwe* (1988), external influence from across the continent might also explain the shadows of disillusion surrounding the dawn of independence. From the pens of Ngugi wa Thiong'o in the East or Soyinka and Ayi Kwei Armah in the West, the warnings had sounded.

One might suppose that protest broadly motivated the new poetry—protest against colonialism, where it still existed; protest against the bloodshed of liberation warfare; protest against a betrayed independence. But impulse varied. Felix Mnthali, as noted, wrote a poetic manifesto blending the urge to delight and comfort with a determination simply to set down the truth before it could be falsified. For others, psychological survival was central. Introducing his collection *Of Chameleons and Gods* (1981), Malawi's Jack Mapanje writes, "The verse in this volume spans some ten turbulent years in which I have been attempting to find a voice or voices as a way of preserving some sanity."[3] Steve Chimombo's nightmarish poetry, also written during the Banda years, reveals a similar reaching for psychological firm ground: "atomized reflections reveal skeletons / smuggling skullfuls of teeth crawling / nearer to gnaw at an insulated mind." On the other hand, Edison Mpina, another victim of the Banda regime, in his *Raw Pieces* (1986) and *Malawi Poetry Today* (1986) was driven by a refreshing desire to challenge the theoretical foundations on which Malawi's new verse was growing: the young shoots, he argued, had been planted in academe's tidy garden instead of in rural soil. Frank Chipasula, author of Malawi's first verse collection, *Visions and Reflections* (1972), wanted his work to be "utilized for the reconstruction of the society." In Zimbabwe, where white oppression would have been the obvious stimulus, Chenjerai Hove simply told Flora Veit-Wild, "When I was a little boy, I was very quiet, and poetry made me relate to myself, made me communicate with myself, try to understand myself and try to express myself. And this is still so. I always saw poetry as a medium to expose what is in me."[4] Veit-Wild also reveals that mere student rivalry got Musaemura Zimunya started, while Charles Mungoshi saw verse only as an effective way to improve his prose: "When I was writing [poetry] I was trying to condense meaning in a few lines, it was an exercise for my prose writing. I keep on cutting to get the utmost concentration." More recently, the Liberation War in Zimbabwe has clearly become a powerful catalyst. Zhuwarara reminds us of the stunning upsurge of poetry that the war's end produced. Mudereri Kadhani and Musaemura Zimunya describe it, too, in the introduction to their anthology *And Now the Poets Speak: Poems Inspired by the Struggle for Zimbabwe* (1981):

From towns and villages, schools and assembly points; from Zimbabwe, Mozam-
bique, England, Romania, Azania and America; in Shona, English and Sindebele;
from blacks and from whites; in type-written scripts and hardly legible scrawls;
from academics, workers, politicians, students, guerillas, and school pupils: sub-
missions began to flow in. First a trickle, then in a deluge. . . . We were humbled to
the stature of little boys who had opened a floodgate.[5]

This collection, a parallel to Alec Pongweni's *Songs That Won the Liberation War*
(1982), concerns itself with both the war and ideas for peace. The editors write: "In the first
part, the poets portray our historical experience of colonial domination, rampage, im-
prisonment and the blood that flowed. Parallel with this preoccupation runs a second
concern: suggesting ideas for the creation of a morally superior alternative."[6]

The editors were also proud to use as their opening offering a piece by Carlos Chombo,
Thomas Sukuta Bvuma's pen name, which struck the right note for the volume:

The Real Poetry
Was carved by centuries
Of chains and whips
It was written in the red streams
Resisting the violence of
"Effective Occupation"

Since then, as with Malawian prison poetry, Zimbabwean war poetry has become a
burgeoning category, as though implying delayed psychological effect. This can be seen in
Bvuma's *Every Stone That Turns* (1999) and Nyamubaya's *On the Road Again* (1986) and
Dusk of Dawn (1995). Tafataona Mahoso's *Footprints About the Bantustan* (1989), while ex-
amining the war, sets it within a context of historical capitalism and Cold War antago-
nism. The work of these, and many others, also reflects postwar disenchantment, which,
with the massacres in Matabeleland, descended all too soon after the independence eu-
phoria Kadhani and Zimunya capture. This and economic chaos have since been com-
pounded across Central Africa by the ravages of AIDS, killing, it is said, up to 240 victims
a day in Malawi alone. It is to the credit of writers in all three countries that they are now
aggressively addressing this problem against a cultural background far from conducive to
the airing of deeply private experience. To illustrate, an impressive feature of Clement
Chihota's *Before the Next Song and Other Poems* (1999) is both its serious concern for the
country's youth and its refusal to embrace pessimism. An artful poem on AIDS called
"Horns" vividly personifies symptoms, but prepares us with a jeu d'esprit called "Danger-
ous Disease," which carries a nice touch of defeated expectation. It is not the anticipated
AIDS that emerges but a disease

Called economic lechery,
Caused by a retro-virus
First discovered
By an African scientist
In wild Western monkeys

While Zimbabwe's poets wrestle with the disappointing aftermath of the liberation
struggle and Zambia's with the experience of decades of poverty, Malawian poets must

now find new subjects for their work after the downfall and death of Hastings Kamuzu Banda and the arrival of multiparty democracy. A useful recipe from South Africa's renowned writer and scholar Njabulo Ndebele might be seen in the title of his post-apartheid collection of essays *South African Literature and Culture: Celebration of the Ordinary* (1994).

10. Prose

A common view in the 1970s was that the quantity of Central African prose in English was pitifully small. This meant not just novels and short stories but also journalism, biography, historiography, essays, and criticism. By contrast, the statistics for vernacular prose are startling. For Zimbabwe, George Kahari, a leading vernacular literary scholar, calculates that among the Shona alone, vernacular writing since 1945 has far outpaced its English equivalent. Citing what he classifies as romances and novels, he lists for the 1956–60 period eight publications and for the period 1961–70 fifteen. Between 1971 and 1980 (notable for the Liberation War) the number suddenly rises to an astonishing forty-eight publications and for the 1981–84 period forty-one.[1]

The argument that prose traditions globally emerge more slowly than poetry is persuasive, but it does not account for Central African prose arising more slowly than prose in West or East Africa. The same can be said about arguments from audience size and literacy rates, which after the Second World War probably differed little across Britain's African empire. Are we perhaps back to the differences between settler and nonsettler colonialism? With no large settler population, West Africa had to shake off fewer cultural and psychological fetters than Central and Southern Africa, or even East Africa, a site of classic but lighter settler colonialism. The account of obstacles facing Central African writers in Zhuwarara's *Introduction to Zimbabwean Literature in English* (1982) and Kadhani and Zimunya's *And Now the Poet Speaks* (1981) is relevant here. We are also back to the chronologies of liberation, with Malawi and Zambia securing independence long before guerilla warfare delivered it to Zimbabwe.

In Malawi, early novels came with Aubrey Kachingwe's *No Easy Task* (1966), David Rubadiri's *No Bride Price* (1967), and from the country's most internationally published writer, Legson Kayira, *The Looming Shadow* (1968), *Jingala* (1969), *The Civil Servant* (1971), and *The Detainee* (1974). Significantly, these were early postindependence publications. Prose productivity has since increased though not dramatically. In 1974, Sam Mpasu's *Nobody's Friend* appeared, which brought him imprisonment, its title a suspected reference to Hastings Banda. Steve Chimombo, a writer of marked fertility, published his short novel *The Basket Girl* in 1990, and in 2000 *The Wrath of Napolo*, at six hundred pages Central Africa's longest novel to date. Tito Banda was the first to appear in the pioneering Malawi Writers Series with his novel *Sekani's Solution* (1979), which was followed in the same series by Dede Kamkondo's *Children of the Lake* (1987) and Edison Mpina's *The Low Road to Death* (1999) and *Freedom Avenue* (1999). Paul Zeleza's *Smouldering Charcoal* appeared in 1992, and Felix Mnthali's *Yoranivyoto* in 1998. Malawi's first thriller emerged in 2002 when Sambalikagwa Mvona published *The Special Document*; the same year brought George Kayange's *Gone for a Walk*, a nicely crafted novella on AIDS and cross-culturalism. Steve Chimombo's *Wasi Writer* ("a magazine for the modern writer . . . for everyone involved in the business of writing"), reporting on the growth of self-publishing in Malawi, draws attention to the career of Aubrey Kalitera, a man of enormous writing and entrepreneurial energy, who, within the space of three years, printed and published nine vernacular novels and two magazines, selling more than a thousand copies of each. *Wasi Writer* claims that the readership for self-published products is "obviously the literate population living mostly in the urban areas. Aubrey Kalitera's salesmen plied the trade in Blantyre, Zomba, and Lilongwe. . . . The author tramped from office to office selling his novels. Lecturers, secretaries, executives, students etc. are all among the consumers catered for." Kalitera himself, who set up his own shrewdly named Power Pen Books, told Bernth Lindfors in *Kulankula* (1989), "I was able to generate an income of something like a thousand kwacha a month. . . . I was surviving on the power of writing. . . . If there are three novelists in black Africa who live wholly by their writing, I am one of them."[2]

Zimbabwe's war diminished literary energies; its aftermath brought weariness and then paralyzing disbelief at the Matabeleland massacres inflicted by the new government on its own people. Prewar and postwar chronology charts a fluctuating prose output. Ndabaningi Sithole's novel *Busi* (1959) appeared serialized in the magazine *African Parade*, and *The Polygamist* in 1972. Stanlake Samkange's *On Trial for My Country* was published in 1966 and *The Mourned One* in 1975. This was the same year in which Charles Mungoshi published his acclaimed *Waiting for the Rain*. Dambudzo Marechera's novella *House of Hunger*, which won the *Guardian* fiction prize, appeared in 1978. So did Stanlake Samkange's *Year of the Uprising* and Solomon Mutsvairo's *Mapondera: Soldier of Zimbabwe*. Stanley Nyamfukudza's *The Non-Believer's Journey* came out in 1980, and Irene Mahamba's novella *Woman in Struggle* in 1984. Shimmer Chinodya published his *Dew in the Morning* in 1982, *Farai's Girls* in 1984, and *Harvest of Thorns* in 1989. Tsitsi Dangarembga's *Nervous Conditions,* a pioneering feminist novel, appeared to international acclaim in 1988. In that year also Chenjerai Hove brought out his novel *Bones*, then in 1991 *Shadows*, and in 1996 *Ancestors*. George Mujajati's short poetic novel *Victory*, encompassing war and disillusion, appeared in 1993, and Violet Kala's *Waste Not Your Tears* in 1994. Alex Kanengoni published his *Echoing Silences* in 1997. Among the past decade's most remarkable events was the emergence of the late Yvonne Vera, whose mystical voice and deeply poetic prose took the critical world by storm. *Nehanda* appeared in 1993, *Without a Name* in 1994, *Under the Tongue* in 1996, *Butterfly Burning* in 1998, and *The Stone Virgins* in 2002. The 2002 Berlin Conference on African Literature honored her with a special session on her work, and in 2003 Robert Muponde and Mandi Taruvinga brought out a substantial collection of essays, *Sign and Taboo: Perspectives on the Poetic Fiction of Yvonne Vera*.

Zambian novels are rare. Dominic Mulaisho published his first, *The Tongue of the Dumb*, in 1971 and *The Smoke That Thunders* in 1979. Lazarus Miti published *The Father*, a bildungsroman, in 1989, and *The Prodigal Husband* in 1999. Binwell Sinyangwe, in a short career, has published *Quills of Desire* (1993) and *A Cowrie of Hope* (2000), both powerful accounts of Zambian life in the 1990s, when drought, economic collapse, and AIDS ravaged the nation, leaving its weakest people exposed to hunger, multiform abuse, and demoralization. Sitwala Imenda's *Unmarried Wife* (1994), which probes the problem of Christian men taking a second wife, is set in South Africa.

That the short story is healthier than the novel is clear from its greater quantity and consistent quality. Again the reasons are debatable. Though the short story, as conceived in Western scholarship, is a modern written form distinct from such traditional oral forms as myth, fable, folktale, and legend, one can imagine aspirant writers familiar with the latter wanting to attempt the former—even perhaps seeing it as apprenticeship for a novel. The canvas is similarly small, with an economy of theme, setting, and characterization. Considerations of audience and economic status also arise. Those used to tradition's smaller dimensions can move to the short story with relative ease. By contrast, the West's fashionable and rather expensive blockbuster novel is unlikely to appeal in lands economically poor, where daily survival is a consuming problem, where electric light might be nonexistent, intermittent, or expensive, and where even paraffin for lamps might be unaffordable. Such an audience finds the price of even a short novel prohibitive, whereas the short story can be read in a comparatively cheap newspaper or journal or heard free on the radio. The region's political history suggests another reason. South African writer Es'kia Mphahlele (and his experience was echoed by Alex La Guma's) used to link his literary choices to racism's daily onslaught of petty hate, obstruction and contempt:

> I am now more convinced than ever before in my belief that I wrote short fiction in South Africa because the distance between the ever-present stimulus and anger was so short, the anger screamed for an outlet with such a burning urgency, that I had to find a prose medium that would get me to the focal point with only a few eloquent movements. The short story was such a medium. Indeed it came to one as reflex. Outside South Africa, in the bigger world of bigger ideas and in situations that demand a larger variety of emotional responses, one's reflexes take on a different quality, a greater complexity.[3]

Since experience in the Rhodesias (less so in Nyasaland) included a northerly extension of South African racism, it is unsurprising to find a similar writing decision here. And Mphahlele's comments provoke further thought. For instance, whereas the novel likes to treat a handful of core issues, Africa's writers daily face a bewildering complexity of major problems calling for attention. A short story collection is one way forward. The economics of literary production are also relevant—and Zimbabwe in particular has commendably moved to printing texts on the cheapest paper available. Thus, individual readers or, more crucially, school and college authorities, might well choose over a novel a smaller volume of short stories by a single author, or better, a multiauthor collection. What is clear, anyway, is that the quantity of short story collections, either from individual or multiple authors, is growing apace.

Significantly, when Malawi's Montfort Press wanted to encourage local literature, its second publication (following a book of myths and legends) was a collection of short stories by Paul Zeleza, *Night of Darkness and Other Stories* (1976). Ken Lipenga's collection *Waiting for a Turn* soon followed. In 1993 Moira Chimombo edited a collection of twelve stories called *Relationships*, directly confronting such current issues as teenage pregnancy, abortion, marital infidelity, and AIDS. In 2002 Alfred Msadala edited a collection of fifteen stories by different authors, *Neighbour's Wife and Other Stories,* in which the AIDS pandemic also features. And in 2003, the Malawi Writers Union, with Norwegian financial help, published *Modern Stories from Malawi*, containing work by no less than forty writers. It was collected and edited by Sambalikagwa Mvona.

In Zimbabwe, Fwanyanga Mulikita's collection *Point of No Return* appeared in 1968, and Charles Mungoshi's *Coming of the Dry Season* in 1972 (it later reappeared as *The Setting Sun and the Rolling World*). Dambudzo Marechera issued his collection *The House of*

Hunger in 1978, Stanley Nyamfukudza his *Aftermaths* in 1983, and Stephen Mpofu his *Shadows on the Horizon* in 1984. Stanley Nyamfukudza published his *If God Was a Woman* in 1991. In 1992, Yvonne Vera appeared with her first collection of short stories, *Why Don't You Carve Other Animals.* And in 1993 Alex Kanengoni published his *Effortless Tears.* Dambudzo Marechera's *Scrapiron Blues,* edited by Flora Veit-Wild, emerged post-humously in 1994. Charles Mungoshi published his *Walking Still* in 1997, and Shimmer Chinodya his *Can We Talk* in 1998. A collection compiled and edited by Clement Chihota and Robert Muponde, *No More Plastic Balls,* appeared in 2000, and Virginia Phiri's *Desperate* in 2002.

Among contributors to history and biography, Ndabaningi Sithole in 1959 published *African Nationalism,* in 1968 *Roots of a Revolution: Scenes from Zimbabwe's Struggle,* and in 1977 *Frelimo Militant.* The autobiography of Zambian dramatist Andreya Masiye, *Singing for Freedom,* appeared in 1977 and D. N. Beach's *The Shona and Zimbabwe, 900–1850* in 1980. Ngwabi Bhebe and Terence Ranger, among many other publications, brought out their two-volume collection *Soldiers in Zimbabwe's Liberation War* in 1995, and Bhebe's *The ZAPU and ZANU Guerilla Warfare and the Evangelical Lutheran Church in Zimbabwe* in 1999. Among the most prolific authors in this field is Malawi's D. D. Phiri. In addition to his history of his own people's trek from South Africa, *From Nguni to Ngoni* (1982), he has written biographies of John Chilembwe, Clements Kadalie, and, in Longman's Malawians to Remember series, those of Inkosi Gomani II, James Frederick Sangala, Charles Chidongo Chinula, and Dunduzu Kaluli Chisiza. In 1995, Sam Mpasu, a politician fortunate to survive Banda's detention cells, published his *Political Prisoner 3/75,* a prose narrative to complement prison verse by such writers as Jack Mapanje, Felix Mnthali, and Ken Kalonde. Though Banda, a man of some scholarship, wrote nothing, Zambia's Kenneth Kaunda has published *Black Government* (1960), *Dominion Status for Central Africa?* (1963), *A Humanist in Africa* (1966), *Letters to My Children* (1974), *Zambia Shall Be Free* (1980), and *Kaunda on Violence* (1980). More recently, Banda's successor in Malawi, Bakili Muluzi, has written his autobiographical *Mau Anga: The Voice of a Democrat* (2002). In Zimbabwe, Joshua Nkomo's autobiography *The Story of My Life* appeared in 1984 and Ian Smith's memoir *The Great Betrayal* in 1997.

There has been no regional *Black Orpheus* or *Transition* to reflect on Central African writing. Instead, criticism has appeared in small journals such as *Odi, Kalulu,* and *The Journal of Humanities,* in newspapers and magazines, and on radio. Published studies include George Kahari's *The Search for Zimbabwean Identity* (1980), Tim McLoughlin and M. Mhonyera's *Criticism of Zimbabwean and Other Poetry* (1981), Musaemura Zimunya's *Those Years of Drought and Hunger: The Birth of African Fiction in Zimbabwe* (1982), Rudo Gaidzanwa's *Images of Women in Zimbabwean Literature* (1985), and Ranga Zinyemba's *Zimbabwean Drama: A Study of Shona and English Plays* (1986). Flora Veit-Wild's *Patterns of Poetry in Zimbabwe* appeared in 1988, her *Dambudzo Marechera* in 1988, and *Teachers, Preachers, Non-Believers: A Social History of Zimbabwean Literature* in 1992. Emmanuel Ngara and Andrew Morrison brought out their collection *Literature, Language and the Nation* in 1989 and Ngara his *Teaching Literature in Africa* in 1984, *Art and Ideology in the African Novel* in 1985, and *New Writing from Southern Africa* in 1996. David Kerr's *African Popular Theatre* appeared in 1995, and *Dance, Media Entertainment & Popular Theatre in South East Africa* in 1998. Anthony Chennells and Flora Veit-Wild brought out *Emerging*

Perspectives on Dambudzo Marechera in 1999 and Ken Kalonde *A Special Guide to the Anthology of Malawian Literature for Junior Secondary* in 2000. In the same year, Steve and Moira Chimombo's *Culture and Democracy* appeared. In 2001 Francis Moto's *Trends in Malawian Literature* emerged, and Robert Muponde and Mandi Taruvinga's collection *Perspectives on the Poetic Fiction of Yvonne Vera* was published in 2003.

11. Drama

Newcomers to African literature might assume that prose fiction and verse command its heights while drama lives quietly in the valleys. Aware of novels by Chinua Achebe and Ngugi wa Thiong'o, Es'kia Mphahlele and Alex La Guma, or poetry by Léopold Sédar Senghor, Christopher Okigbo, and Dennis Brutus, they might be able to name no dramatist beyond Nigerian Nobel Prize laureate Wole Soyinka. Few African plays appear in their local bookshops. But even within Africa the public will know its novelists and poets better than its dramatists. Appearance, however, masks reality. Across the continent, and certainly within Central Africa, there are more dramatists than those internationally known, more plays than those published, and more dramatic experiments than reach London's West End or Broadway.

Drama's complex roots in religious experience, and here within a continent profoundly spiritual, cannot be overstressed. So too its group-based nature and participatory form among populations still overwhelmingly agrarian and village-based. Its inclusiveness is unrivalled. Not only can it address and call into participation an entire village community; it can also employ beyond speech the arts of dancing, singing, and drumming; and, beyond these, skills in weaving, dressmaking, and mask carving. Further, while drama remains splendidly inclusive even when scripted, reading verse and prose are distinctly exclusive. Alongside community-embracing drama, then, its sister forms seem exclusive almost to the point of divisiveness. And while illiteracy attracts neither funds nor votes, we await a scholarly study to demonstrate that nothing more than literacy—not colonialism, capitalism, famine, drought, or globalization—has contributed so effectively to the steady erosion of African rural life. Because reading is a solitary activity—enough in itself to stir anxiety in collective cultures—it is, then, in a radically obvious sense, antisocial. Who can read the latest novel by Sinyangwe or Chimombo and at the same time weed village fields, fetch water, or carry home the firewood? Reading drives its practitioners to the social fringe, where lie witchcraft and magic (ancient links between which and reading would repay investigation). Its high status disrupts patterns of respect and authority in family relationships, setting literate child against illiterate parent and vice versa. In the by now classic "educational" journey from home to village school, from village school to remote boarding school, and thence to distant university and city, what chance has rural life of retaining new skills and refreshing its vitality?

Nor should we mistake African drama's low exposure internationally for paucity, since it can live without texts. In any case, within Africa the economies of book production are adverse. In an age when publishing decisions descend to accountants, the demand for drama texts in societies low on literacy can hardly be high. Impoverished schools may possess no books at all. And yet, as pathbreaking work by David Kerr, Chris Kamlongera, and James Gibbs shows, because governments now see drama as a convenient instrument for national development (and electoral success), it can also boast material advantage.

Whether to campaign against slash-and-burn cultivation, overfishing, deforestation, and water pollution, or to promote breastfeeding, mosquito nets, and pit latrines, government enthusiasm for drama is rising. Indeed, as readers construe these comments, traveling theater groups across Malawi, Zimbabwe, and Zambia will be performing on riverbanks and in village squares, remote school halls, and mission gardens, teaching about safe sex, AIDS, cheap fertilizers, and improved hygiene. While evidence grows that governments are seeing school and college poetry and fiction courses as unaffordable, funding theater for development (or state propaganda) is another matter.

For drama scholars Africa is an unrivalled research field. Here, as current affairs, they can find every growth stage the form has undergone. Processions to springs and wells; dramatization within prose narratives; magic rites; rituals for hunting, sickness, infertility, rain and health; sacrificial and scapegoat ceremonies to cleanse collective guilt; protean mask and dance forms for spirit possession; ancestor evocation and gender strife; scripted drama in theaters purpose-built or open air; studio theater; drama for radio and television—African dramatic diversity is astonishing. The continent also cherishes flexibility and innovation, scorning rules that pin the wings of creativity. Nineteenth-century West Africa saw the emerging Concert Party and Yoruba Folk Opera pouring protodramatic phenomena into crucibles of inventiveness to create modern forms. But West Africa is not alone. The South African dramatist Mothobi Mutloatse could have been speaking for African colleagues everywhere—indeed, was reflecting anterior experience elsewhere—when describing new dramatic shape for the post-apartheid era:

> We're involved in an exciting art form that I can only call PROEMDRA—PROSE, POEM and DRAMA. We are going to pee, spit, and shit on literary convention. We are going to kick and pull and push and drag literature into the form we prefer. We're going to experiment and probe and not give a damn what the critics have to say. Because we are in search of our true selves—undergoing self-discovery as a people.[1]

West African pronouncements lacked the desperation of this 1990s quest for self-discovery (nonsettler colonialism left local culture more oxygenated) but it resonates in the heavier colonialism of East, Central, and southern Africa. Precisely because settler colonialism was so damaging and needed force to remove it (witness Kenya's Mau Mau uprising and the bloody struggles in Zimbabwe and South Africa), traditional cultural forms needed urgent resurrection for deployment in battle.

In Malawi, after random growth in the schools, modern drama, as in Uganda, Kenya, Tanzania, and Zambia, found focus in the university. The early work of Trevor Whittock, John Linstrum, and David Kerr was consolidated and extended by James Gibbs, Mupa Shumba, and Chris Kamlongera. The arrival of Gibbs and his Ghanaian playwright wife Patience Addo brought international expertise and theater scholarship. A leading authority on Soyinka, and with experience in Ghana and Sudan, Gibbs achieved swift results. Joined soon after his arrival by Mupa Shumba, fresh from postgraduate studies in West African drama (and the man who, with Linstrum, had founded the Travelling Theatre in 1969), he fashioned effective instruments to foster local talent. Theater workshops, courses in practical drama, a remodeled Travelling Theatre, use of the new Malawian Writers Series, construction of an open-air theater in the shadow of Zomba Plateau—to these must be added an insistence on pace and punctuality in all productions, care over detail, and, what was often neglected elsewhere, the urgency of critical reflection at every step. Gibbs and Shumba had a flair for flysheet reviews, each performance causing a paper storm as students, teachers, and members of the public rushed into print to do battle with banner and manifesto. Willing to keep a mind open to influence from all parts of the continent and beyond, and reluctant to impose one chosen doctrine, they encouraged a wide-ranging approach. Anything with dramatic potential became material for their actors, whether poems by Soyinka and Okot p'Bitek, moral tales from Chaucer and Hans Christian Andersen, or, crucially, local myths and legends. While the standard Western repertoire got adequate coverage, the broad push was toward plays written, produced, and acted by Malawians.

James Ngombe's *The Banana Tree* and *Beauty of the Dawn*; Joe Mosiwa's *Who Will Marry Our Daughter?*; Innocent Banda's *The Lean Years*, *Lord Have Mercy*, *Cracks*, and *The First Rehearsal*; Chris Kamlongera's *Love Potion* and *Graveyards*; and Bayani Ngulube's *Phuma-Uhambe* all imaginatively employed local material and local approaches. They appeared in James Gibbs's pioneering collection *Nine Malawian Plays* in 1976. Ngulube's play questioned "the values of the Ngoni/Tumbuka tradition of banishment." Mosiwa's, built on a theme of social ambition, used to superb effect a Narrator-Chorus device and visits to Cloud, Sun, and Wind. Instead of a stale exercise in the struggle between tradition and modernity, Mosiwa offered a complex fight in which a kind of modernity won out on completely traditional terms. The most ambitious play from this period, Steve Chimombo's *The Rainmaker*, used both the material of Malawi's ancient M'bona legends and the M'bona cult's surviving mask convention.

Conventional opinion suggests a West African advantage over East and Central Africa in its move into modern drama—the form more easily flourishing in old settled communities with their cults and fraternities than among nomadic and transhumant peoples. But David Kerr's magisterial studies *African Popular Theatre* (1995) and *Dance, Media Entertainment and Popular Theatre in South East Africa* (1998) reveal Central African drama as vital and varied. Whether scripted or unscripted (mostly the latter), in English or the vernaculars (again mostly the latter), in rural village or city center, on radio or television, drama emerges as an instrument for social survival, for cultural affirmation, for opposition to oppression, and for creating new grammars for postcolonial life.

And just as new dramatic forms grafted themselves onto traditional theatrical practice in West Africa (hence the Egungun and Oro masquerade drama among Nigeria's Yoruba), so the Beni dance became an East and Central African parallel, some of its stylized features, it is suggested, borrowed from white military tradition and Omani Arabs. It is now traceable through Zambia, Malawi, and Zimbabwe to South Africa, where it is especially popular with the large indigenous Zionist Christian Church. Kerr personally saw it employed in Malawi during the 1990s campaign against Banda's one-party state. Using the research findings of Matthew Schoffeleers, Kerr also shows how Gule wa Mkulu, the central dance of Malawi's ancient Nyau hunting cult, has been employed for defensive cultural purposes—against invasion by missionaries or Arab slavers and against the powerful status of women in Chewa culture.[2]

In colonial Rhodesia, the struggle against Ian Smith's Rhodesia Front required tradition to harness its most potent strengths. George Kahari tells us that this partly involved traditional Shona narrative drama, while Kerr cites a Shona possession ritual called Bira, used in the first uprising against white domination in the 1890s. The 1970s guerilla war revitalized Bira so that peasants and fighters could draw spiritual confidence and inspiration from it. Alec Pongweni has studied the songs that sustained morale among the freedom fighters and, quoting him, Kerr suggests how the following kind of song could be used in a more formalized dramatic setting:

We cry to you Nehanda our guardian angel
Yes, you are that to us
Yes, you are that to us.
Please guide our steps in this struggle
Until we return to a liberated Zimbabwe

Another example of resistance theater was the Pungwe. Kerr quotes Ross Kidd as saying that this "was highly participatory—villagers and fighters acted out and danced their commitments and built up their morale through collective music-making."[3]

The shift into scripted drama across the region owes much to the work of a small band of skilled and inspiring individuals with a flair for teaching, organization, and critical reflection. In Malawi and Zambia, open-air arenas were constructed and traveling theaters formed similar to those of Nairobi, Ibadan, and Makerere. National school drama competitions rivaled soccer leagues in popularity. Preeminently, this was the work of David Kerr, James Gibbs, John Linstrum, Andrew Horn, Chris Kamlongera, Michael Etherton, Fay Chung, Tamakloe, Mupa Shumba, Dickson Mwansa, Mike Nambote, and Ross Kidd. Kerr, Chung, Etherton, Mwansa, and Horn were involved in the influential Chikwakwa Theatre at the University of Zambia and its associated Travelling Theatre—projects that moved local drama well ahead of productivity in its sister literary forms. "The idea of the Chikwakwa Theatre," wrote Michael Etherton, "was to develop, through self-help, a theater place that would allow an expansion of the traditional performing arts into drama in which the spoken words developed the action. Or put the other way round, the theater was meant to develop a style of drama that used the dances, songs and music of the rural areas and the urban townships, the masks and the fabulous costumes, the artifacts, the fires, and the lamps of traditional story-telling."[4] If, as Bob Leshoiai argues, drama in Tanzania supported the political thinking of Nyerere's Ujamaa, it did the same for Kenneth Kaunda's national philosophy of humanism, while attacking racism in Rhodesia and South Africa. Thus Godfrey Kasoma's plays *The Long Arms of the Law* and *The Fools Marry* deal with township life, and his *Black Mamba* dramatizes the rise of Kaunda and his UNIP party during colonial days. Echoing Kenyan struggles against the colonial dominance of Nairobi's Donovan Maule Theatre, Kerr has written, "Chikwakwa contributed much towards a Zambian dramaturgy which was opposed to the urban neo-colonial theater dominated by expatriates. In contrast to the typical Western form of drama . . . the Chikwakwa enthusiasts helped build an indigenous Zambian dramaturgy using mime, dance, Zambian languages, simple symbolic props and décor, episodic plots, a thrust or in-the-round stage and a participatory audience."[5] He further remarks that, despite the weaknesses shared by all university traveling theaters (transient students and staff and the bourgeois ambitions of students escaping rural backgrounds), Chikwakwa fed into a genuinely popular theater beyond the university by way of "workshops, cultural societies and community theatres."

Though much created drama in the region remains unscripted, plays with published texts constitute a growing list. In Malawi, in addition to those mentioned earlier, Desmond

Dudwe Phiri has written *The Chief's Bride*. The past decade witnessed the spectacular emergence of the late Du Chisiza Jr., leader of the Wakhumbata Ensemble Theatre, whose plays include *Diandra and the Priest*, *Pumashakile*, *Check It Out*, *De Summer Blow*, *Misidi Burning*, *Papa's Empire*, *Storm on the Litada*, *Democracy Boulevard*, and *Barefoot in the Heart*. Kamlongera has meanwhile established himself as the leading authority on theater for development in Malawi, to which David Kerr has also returned after distinguished work in Botswana during the latter years of the Banda regime.

Kerr tells us that by far the most prolific dramatist throughout Central Africa is Zambia's Stephen Chifunyise, author of many unscripted works and of plays for television. They include *Mabusisi*, *Blood*, *The District Governor Visits a Village*, *Because of Principles*, *Organized Disorganization*, *Thorn in Our Flesh*, *Solo and Mutsiai*, *The Returned Ones*, *Mr Polera*, *Vultures*, and *I Resign*. His *Temporary Market* appeared in 1993, and his *May Day, May Day* was performed by Harare's Dzivare Sekwa Group in 1993. His work also appears in a collected volume, *Medicine for Love and Other Plays* (1984). Zambia's Godfrey Kasoma is the author of *The Long Arms of the Law*, *The Fools Marry*, the *Black Mamba* trilogy, and *The Poisoned Cultural Meat*. Masauto Phiri has written *Soweto Flowers Will Grow*, *Nightfall*, and *Kuta*. Mulikita Fwanyanga's work includes *Shaka Zulu* and *Homecoming*. Whitney Lukuku has written *Drown in a Drink*. And Andreya Masiye (who, Kerr tells us, had many radio scripts burned by the colonial authorities during the Central African Federation years) has written *The Lands of Kazembe* and Darius Lungu *The Man in the Street*.

Though the list for Zimbabwe is shorter, it includes George Mujajati's *Children of God*, *The Rain of My Blood*, and *The Wretched Ones*; Basil Diki's *The Tribe of Graves*; and Bertha Msora's *I Will Wait* (1984). Independence, however, has stimulated so strong a dramatic flowering that estimates suggest there are a hundred theater companies active there, with the same creative mix of word, dance, and song that has developed across the continent. In Bulawayo, for example, Amakhosi Productions, founded by Cont Mhlanga, energetically organizes workshops and an annual three-week festival, and Mhlanga himself is now responsible for a highly popular television soap opera, *Sinjalo*.

12. Children's Literature

As sensitive monitors of cultural tradition, African writers constantly reflect the complexities of colonialism. The pathology of decolonization is also complex. Fighting to regain land and freedom might eventually seem simple compared with healing lesions scarring psyche and soul, as acute pneumonia yields quicker to drugs than the neuroses of posttraumatic stress. While, broadly, politicians have dealt with the former, writers and artists—humanities activists—are dealing with the latter. Evidence from across the continent shows them continuing long after the furling of colonial flags. As Robert July reminds us in *An African Voice: The Role of the Humanities in African Independence* (1987), education, in its broadest sense, remains a major battleground. Systems and syllabus need patient reconstruction to set upright the inverted pedagogic principle of moving from known to unknown—as, for example, Central Africans studying Birmingham before Bulawayo or Cinderella before Kalulu the Hare.

Modern Central African writers, then, in Chinua Achebe's words, are teaching Africa "to regain its belief in itself and put away the complexes of the years of denigration and self-denigration." Indeed, Samuel Ajayi Crowther, in similar vein, even before his consecration as first Bishop of the Niger in 1864, had been urging the need for vernacular preaching and published grammars in Yoruba, Nupe, and Igbo. Edward Blyden, in 1872, had written a blueprint for a university where an African could be "tutored in his own history, languages, and customs . . . hear his own songs and learn his own traditions, taught by Africans who knew and respected an indigenous culture." Ghana's first president, Kwame Nkrumah, said in the 1950s that his people should "study the history, culture and institutions, languages and arts of Ghana and of Africa in new African-centered ways—in entire freedom from the propositions and presuppositions of the colonial epoch." Given these West African responses, more effort was needed from Central Africa, a classic site of stifling settler colonization.

The centrality of primary education, neglected during free Africa's race to establish secondary and tertiary systems (primary teachers suffered the lowest status and lowest pay) dawned on creative writers rather slowly. In West Africa, Cyprian Ekwensi, Amos Tutuola, Christina Ama Ata Aidoo, and Nigeria's first president, Alhaji Sir Abubakar Tafawa Balewa, began producing children's texts rooted in local landscapes, oral traditions, and values. In East Africa, work began with Grace Ogot, Pamela Ogot, and Onyango Ogutu. Central African authors, in prose and verse, have been following suit. They include, in Zimbabwe, Clement Mapfumo Chihota (*Before the Next Song and Other Poems*, 1999), Violet Kala (*Waste Not Your Tears*, 1994), Patricia Chater (*Crossing the Boundary Fence*, 1988, and *Streetwise*, 2004), and Shimmer Chinodya (*A Child of War*, 1985, and *Tale of Tamari*, 2004). In Zambia, there is Sitwala Imenda (*My Grandfather's God*, 2004; *Mind Over Matter*, 2004; and *Dancing Mice and Other African Folktales*, 2004), Beatrice Bwalya Erlwanger (*Tales from Kasama*, 2000), Brian Zanji (*Stories from Zambia*, 2000), K. Kangende (*Zambian*

Myths and Legends of the Wild, 2001), and Friday Sinyiza (*True Love Is Scarce*, 2001). Malawians writing for children include Steve Chimombo (*Caves of Nazimbuli*, 1990; *Child of Clay*, 1992; *Operation Kalulu*, 1994; and *The Bird Boy's Song*, 2002), Moira Chimombo (who edited *Blood Relationships*, 1993), Desmond Dudwa Phiri (*Diniwe in Dreamland*, 2001), Joseph Alexander K. Banda (*Calling Dr. Kalulu*, 1993), Dede Kamkondo (*Innocent Boy*, 1976; *The Children of the Lake*, 1987; *Sivo and the Cruel Thief*, 1989), George Kanyanga (*Gone for a Walk*, 2002), Mike Sambalikagwa Mvona (*Sun at Njuli*, 2001; *The Special Document*, 2002), and Ken Kalonde (*Smiles Round Africa*, 1996).

Their aims and themes? A priority of carrying into print oral tradition narratives and values remains evident. But a writer such as Zambia's Imenda, a professor of chemistry and dean of education, brings a measure of scientific analysis to the task of marrying the best of tradition with the best of modernity. Elsewhere concern shifts rapidly to the terrifying realities of modern life—even if this sets new writing at radical odds with the discursive obliqueness of traditional culture. Thus, while Malawi's Steve Chimombo and Zambia's Brian Zanji and Bwalya Erlwanger offer engaging folk material, others are either abandoning fantasy or blending it with scarifying realism. Within a conventional oral structure, Dudwa Phiri builds a text around folklore, world history, ecology, and gender equality. Joseph Banda's hare, Dr. Kalulu, works in a modern hospital. Dede Kamkondo's children face both opportunities and perils within urban life. But the HIV-AIDS pandemic, reaping old and young in biblical numbers, has shocked writers into a startlingly new awareness. In an edenic setting, George Kanyange has a young Malawian describe the AIDS crisis to a visiting New Zealand girl, sketching its slaughter while preaching premarital chastity. Clement Chihota's verse urges the young to cherish their rural environment and examine carefully the horrific details of developing HIV. Violet Kala makes an opening paragraph portray a young couple in bed after unprotected sex—the youth knowing he has AIDS—and proceeds to record ensuing misery. Shimmer Chinodya highlights the pitiful situation of AIDS orphans within a modern scene of hunger, rising prices, and glue-sniffing street children.

Despite rising productivity in this area of Central African writing, evidence only increases to show that imported texts from the West still overwhelm Afro-centered reading matter.

13. White Rhodesian Poetry

by Anthony Chennells

John Snelling edited the first anthology of Rhodesian poetry in 1938 to commemorate the fifty years since the British South Africa Company had been formed to colonize Mashonaland. The tone of *Rhodesian Verse, 1888–1938* is less triumphalist than that anniversary might lead one to expect, and Arthur Shearly Cripps, a bitter critic of both company and settler rule, is the poet who is most widely represented. Snelling would have had no problem in finding material for his collection if quantity were his only criterion. Rhodesia had an astonishing number of weekly, monthly, and quarterly publications directed to constituencies as diverse as the railway unions, farmers, unskilled workers, different churches and the Jewish communities, police, and territorial forces. Looking through less specialized journals, it seems that every possible point of view in Rhodesian politics commanded its own publication. All of these regularly published verse, most of it facetious and sentimental doggerel. *New Rhodesia*, which offered lively commentary on contemporary affairs and appeared from 1938 to 1954, was much more discriminating in what it accepted, and several of Doris Lessing's first published poems appeared in its pages. This proliferation of journals continued after the war, and in 1950 Snelling had enough new material to compile a second selection, *A New Anthology of Rhodesian Verse*. Immediately after the war, *Labour Front* provided a platform for white radicalism; Cripps, who in his later years had become deeply involved in the Rhodesian branches of the Communist-influenced South African Industrial and Commercial Union, published some of his last poems in this journal. After federation, the *Central African Examiner* provided a voice for the left that was no longer concerned with labor issues. The preoccupation of white Southern Rhodesian unions with black and white labor forming a united front against capital had long ceased to interest organized black labor in Northern Rhodesia. Instead, the progressive whites on the *Examiner* recognized that they should engage with race, franchise, and nationhood and discover how far the federal project could be wrested from Rhodesian whites and mining capitalists. Much of the poetry published in the *Examiner* was satiric, often cleverly subverting the claims of the federal and Southern Rhodesian establishment. It closed when the censorship laws put in place after the Unilateral Declaration of Independence (UDI) made radical journalism impossible.

In 1952, the first journal devoted entirely to poetry appeared as the *Poetry Review Salisbury*, which, after the first three numbers, became *Rhodesian Poetry* and appeared sometimes annually and sometimes biennially until Zimbabwean independence. In the 1970s it published both new poems as well as republishing the best poetry that had appeared in the previous year or two, much of which originally appeared in *Two Tone*. This was a quarterly that was begun in 1964 and continued to appear regularly until 1981. *Two Tone*, as its name suggests, set out to publish the work of both black and white poets, and its early issues contained translations from Shona and Ndebele originals. The founders of *Two Tone* were Phillipa Berlyn and Olive Robertson, both stalwarts of the Rhodesia Front; Robertson was to become a senator in the upper house established under the 1969 constitution. The political allegiance of these two women warns against easy generalizations about white attitudes to blacks. When *Two Tone* was founded, UDI was less than a year away. Berlyn, who spoke fluent Shona, believed that an independent Rhodesia must accommodate both black and white and that *Two Tone* should be a space where poets from different races could at least listen to one another. Several black poets who used English as their medium began to publish in *Two Tone* (although some preferred to publish in *Parade*), and writers who were to achieve considerable fame, such as Dambudzo Marechera, Shimmer Chinodya, and Musaemura Zimunya, published their early work in the quarterly. Some of the poems of John Eppel, who is Zimbabwe's best-known white writer, first appeared in *Two Tone*. Although Berlyn and Robertson censored what was offered them—on one occasion Robertson reported a contributor to his headmaster for possible "terrorist" sympathies—guest editors sometimes accepted work by black writers that subverted the vision of the journal's founders, namely, that blacks and whites shared a common national loyalty. One of Henry Pote's contributions, "To a White Child," mournfully registers that the child addressed by the poem will one day be taught to mistrust and despise him, and the title of one of Kizito Muchemwa's best-known poems, "Tourists," refers to his fellow whites. This was certainly not a metaphor Berlyn and Robertson would have chosen for white Rhodesians.

A confidence that poetry from Rhodesia could be read without embarrassment in an international context inspired Colin and Olan Style to found *Chirimo* in 1968. Expensively produced, and subtitled "an international review of Rhodesian and International Poetry," *Chirimo* appeared thrice yearly between 1968 and 1970. This ambitious project could not be sustained, since few international poets and scholars chose to identify with the cultural productions of a pariah state, especially after 1969, when Rhodesia declared itself a republic. The work of the Styles was not entirely lost, however. In 1986 they edited the *Mambo Book of Zimbabwean Poetry in English*, which remains the fullest record of Zimbabwean poetry and has never been surpassed in the breadth of its coverage. The year 1968 also saw another anthology, D. E. Borrell's *Poetry in Rhodesia: 75 Years*, which included several poems from Spicer's anthologies, together with poems that had appeared since 1950. This was the first anthology that gave biographical details of the contributors and annotated local references that helped to make the poems accessible to readers who were not Rhodesian.

In retrospect, this burst of publishing can be attributed to the apparent success of UDI, and from the point of view of the whites who controlled the publications it was an attempt to capture the sensibility of the new nation. Once the war started in earnest in 1972 and white emigration increased, the poets become increasingly less confident of their own identity, and more and more frequently poems in *Two Tone* and *Rhodesian Poetry* are about the experiences of the war. Often the war is seen as gratuitous violence intruding without justification into the seasonal harmonies of a peaceful and enlightened land. Phillipa Berlyn, who as a journalist was allowed into areas normally restricted to white civilians, describes her fear of land mines in "Border Roads":

And then, I remember there are still
—thank Heaven—rainbows
in quiet places;
bush without ambush,

tracks that lead somewhere
other than bloodied death

D. E. Borrell, who with her husband Hugh Finn tirelessly promoted poetry in Rhode-
sia, captures her sense of being implicated in both sides of the struggle in "Frontiers,"
written from a farm on the Mozambique-Rhodesia border:

Someone is out there:
In the dying light
Hair-prickle warns
Self will meet self.
Smell brute in this dark.

John Eppel, who, like all young white men, was repeatedly called up during the last
years of the war, recalls in "Spoils of War" looking at the bodies of guerrillas killed during
a contact:

Sarge tells me to save my tears
for the civilians these gooks have slaughtered.
But I am not thinking of them, and I
cannot explain that I am being purged
of my Rhodesianism. That ugly
word with its jagged edge is opening
me. . . . I move to the past tense.

That was, of course, one possible response to the war, but a possibility only for a man
who was to become a willing Zimbabwean.

In 1977, the Poetry Society of Rhodesia devised the Mopani Poets Series. Local critics
edited and selected the best works of individual Rhodesian poets, and these were pub-
lished as substantial pamphlets. Hugh Finn's *Sunbathers and Other Poems*, N. H. Bretell's
Season and Pretext: Poems (both 1977), D. E. Borrell's *A Patch of Sky*, and Musaemura
Zimunya's *Zimbabwe Ruins* (both 1979); after Zimbabwean independence, Charles Mun-
goshi's *The Milkman Doesn't Only Deliver Milk* and Colin Style's *Musical Saw* (both 1981)
make up the series.

Several Rhodesian poets published selections of their poems and these range from vol-
umes published at the author's expense to selections of the work of writers of the stature of
N. H. Brettell. *Bronze Frieze: Poems, Mostly Rhodesian* was published by Oxford Univer-
sity Press in 1950 and prompted Douglas Livingstone's remark that Brettell was the best
poet writing in the region. Normally thought of as a South African poet, Livingstone was
the author of *Outposts* (1960) and *Sjambok and Other Poems from Africa* (1964), which
contained many poems that he wrote when he was working for the federal government in
Salisbury. Throughout his life, he retained contacts with the writers he had known in
Rhodesia. Noelline Barrie published a selection of her poems in *A Book of Verse from Rho-
desia* (1957). She later ran successful poetry clubs for schoolchildren in Highfield with
Borrell and selected their work from the whole country, which was published in annual
anthologies during the 1970s. Throughout the 1930s and 1940s, Hylda Richards, who
wrote under the pseudonym T, published humorous verses, and during those years her
annual collections became something of a Rhodesian institution. A selection was published

in 1958 with the title *Hurrah for the Life of a Farmer*. Richards sets out to amuse, and her jaunty meters register with good-humored irony the perseverance with which farmers faced the hardships on many farms in the 1930s. What little interest her verses retain lies in the skill with which she also conveys her anxieties and insecurities as a farmer's wife. Other selections include Olive Robertson's *The Mighty Turtle* (1965) and a later volume in which she collaborated with Phillipa Berlyn, *Two Voices* (1974). Colin Style's *Baobab Street* was published in 1977. Style is the most interesting of this group; his poetry is often unashamedly nostalgic for the Zimbabwean veldt, disappearing with new developments, and for Rhodesia itself. In "The Cemetery," the lives, the achievements, and the culture of Rhodesia that will soon be only a memory become as detached from the present as a San rock painting:

> The soil is fine:
> it mingles with my sweat and stains red in my sandal,
> muddy itching ochre seeping into mind
> while in their crevices and caves the rock-imprinted impala
> restlessly stir.

Throughout the best of the poetry written after the Second World War, there is an attempt by white writers to move away from registering Rhodesia as exotic and making it instead a part of one's familiar experience. The best of the writers were well-read in English and American poetry and, like their metropolitan counterparts, recognize poetry in whatever materials are at hand and make a poetic diction out of colloquial English that sometimes is local in origin. There is, however, an insistence on belonging in the more polemical nationalists that is shrill in proportion to its own lack of conviction. Eppel, with customary witty economy and irreverence to both nationalisms, summed up the mood of some white poets in "Emigrant's Dream":

> I was sliding into bliss
> when Zimbabwe burped and spewed
> me out.

The better poets manage simultaneously to register that, however deep their involvement with Rhodesia, their hold on it is at best tentative. Finn, in "Archaeological Site," describes bones that

> can say nothing,
> These bones, nothing of man; for they are nothing.

The poem moves on to describe potsherds and rock paintings and the charcoal of a cooking fire:

> All these have voices
> To speak of man, whose animal hand lies here
> Humanly still beneath his sleeping skull.

As another product of human imagination, the poem itself takes its place among the paintings and the artifacts signifying human industry and creativity. Finn sensed that Rhodesia would be remembered not by a rhetoric that claimed for Rhodesians an identity that would endure for a thousand years, but by what Rhodesians created and understood.

In the last years of Rhodesia, a Rhodesian poetry that encompassed the work of black and white writers was seen by many black writers to be inappropriate. This was most dramatically signaled in 1978, when Kizito Muchemwa edited *Zimbabwean Poetry in English: An Anthology,* which contained only the work of black writers. The title is significant because, at that date, to give anyone or anything a Zimbabwean as opposed to a Rhodesian identity was regarded as subversive, although in fact the anthology was never banned. It did, however, anticipate the extraordinary flourishing of Zimbabwean fiction and poetry in English written by blacks in the twenty years after independence.

14. White Rhodesian Fiction

by Anthony Chennells

In *A History of Rhodesia*, Robert Blake observes that Southern Rhodesia was "a cultural desert; neither literature, music, nor the visual arts flourished in its arid soil." The book appeared in 1977, and the following year the first complete bibliography of Rhodesian literature in English was published. It ran to nearly three hundred pages and listed hundreds of short stories, thousands of poems, and more than three hundred novels, most of which were published in London. Blake knew the merit that metropolitan publication accords a literary work. Southern Rhodesia's white population reached its peak of about 300,000 in 1973, having stood at the end of World War II at 80,000. Blake would recognize in those figures the population of a prosperous English market town or a small English industrial city. From 1961, Salisbury, where half of those whites lived, had a national gallery that displayed the work of local artists alongside magnificent work from other parts of the continent; from the mid-1950s, both Salisbury and Bulawayo had symphony orchestras with professional conductors; and there was a full-time director of the theater in Salisbury where professional actors worked alongside amateurs. Of course, much of this cultural production was provincial: the poetry doggerel, the short stories and novels, the love and adventure stories of the veldt, the paintings, daubs, and plays recycling work from London's West End or New York's Broadway. But there was also work of quality, and nowhere in England did towns and cities with equivalent populations exhibit such a variety and mass of creative talent. Side by side with these cultural settler institutions, Shona music had been drawing on Western music from the 1930s to create a new sound, and after independence a Zimbabwean music that had developed from these early experiments acquired an international reputation, as did the stone sculptures from the National Gallery School. Before Zimbabwean independence, blacks had also written poems, novels and short stories in English, and the first generation of novelists and poets had published work in Ndebele and Shona. Some of the Shona poems had been translated into English and had appeared in local periodicals, and an anthology of poetry in English written by blacks appeared in 1978. Rhodesia was not Blake's cultural desert; still, whites were almost completely unaware of the musical revolution that was taking place around them, and it was only in the late 1960s that white writers began to read the work of some of their black contemporaries in translation. The stone sculpture was of its nature more visible, but, as with avant-garde art anywhere, only an educated minority appreciated and bought it. White Rhodesians missed the opportunity of producing a new art that was informed by the cultural traditions of their adopted country.

Rhodesia was always a nation in the making, even if it never achieved nationhood. Nations require narratives that construct their discrete identity by contributing to a collective memory, and the accounts by British hunters, missionaries, and travelers in the interior showed in books and articles how whites were beginning to take imaginative possession of the country from the late 1860s. The most widely read romance of the nineteenth century was Henry Rider Haggard's *King Solomon's Mines*. Haggard had worked with the colonial leader Shepstone during the first British occupation of the Transvaal, and reports about the Ndebele kingdom and rumors that had filtered down to Pretoria about Great Zimbabwe provided the inspiration for the forgotten mines in Kukuanaland. In 1885, Haggard was content to leave the Kukuana in splendid and savage isolation. By 1889, he had met Cecil Rhodes. In *Allan's Wife*, a settler farm repopulates an ancient, ruined settlement and gives shape to the wilderness, thus anticipating the need to bring Africa under white control. Many early Rhodesian novels that are inspired by Great Zimbabwe and the Ndebele use this later version of Haggard's romance formulas, and the presence of white men ensures the domination of wild nature and the containment of savage people. Histories and novels saw the occupation of Mashonaland, the invasion of Matabeleland, and the suppression of the Risings of 1896 and 1897 as episodes in an epic struggle in which the heroism of a few whites lays the foundations for a new nation. Where white women are present in early novels, their function is to become mothers of the next generation of Rhodesians. Of the early writers in the twentieth century, Gertrude Page and Cynthia Stockley are the best known and most prolific, and sales of their books ran into the millions. A Rhodesia that is exotic to European eyes and provides a chance to liberate individuals from stifling conformity makes way in their later work for a country that is the familiar reality of its settlers who have the task of developing it for future generations. Once black resistance was overcome, blacks largely disappear from the literature of the first thirty years except as servants and farmworkers in the novels, although in the poems there are occasional invocations of black lives lived out in self-indulgent and occasionally idyllic stasis. Only in novels of the 1930s is a second rising imagined; this was possibly an expression of white insecurity as closed mines, falling commodity prices, and large-scale white unemployment evidenced the effects of the Great Depression. As the 1931 Land Apportionment Act was implemented, people were shifted from land designated as "white" into the reserves, which, especially in the Midlands, were unable to support any additional increase in population. The poverty of the reserves and the squalor of the urban locations made it difficult to write of blacks living in idyllic contentment under white rule and the fictional risings can be read as a guilty acknowledgement of the social and economic reality of most black lives.

In the first anthology of Rhodesian verse published in 1938 there is little evidence of formal innovation, but rather an attempt to use the less adventurous conventions of early-twentieth-century English poetry to explore and convey aspects of settler self-awareness, which inevitably involved the tug of loyalties between the old country and the new. The most widely represented poet in the anthology is Arthur Shearly Cripps, who for more than thirty years had attacked the British South Africa Company and settler governments in his novels, short stories and poems and rejected the stereotypes settler racism had created about blacks. Cripps's prominence in the anthology is evidence that Rhodesians of this period were not as incapable of self-criticism as they are sometimes represented as having been. As early as 1940, Blanche Longden's *Who Begins to Live* creates a protagonist, Perdita Wayne, whose name suggests that life on a Rhodesian farm that provides the bare necessities of life is a slow attrition of a young woman's British inheritance. Perdita realizes that insofar as her life has a purpose it is to reject her Rhodesian identity by recovering England for herself. Perdita anticipates Martha Quest in Doris Lessing's "Children of Violence" series, who similarly longs only to escape from Rhodesia to England. The first two volumes of Lessing's series, *Martha Quest* (1952) and *A Proper Marriage* (1954), which are set in the 1920s and 1930s, confirm that Rhodesians were surprisingly diverse. Martha's estrangement from her fellow settlers on neighboring farms is mitigated as she discovers that there are other people who recognize like her that Rhodesia's complacent provincial culture—it is called Zambezia in the series—not only reproduces second-rate English attitudes but is also closed to the ferment of new ideas that are creating a new world in Europe. More than any other novels, Lessing's *A Ripple from the Storm* (1958) and *Landlocked* (1965) within the series show the impact on Rhodesia's cultural isolation of the Royal Air Force training camps and the first waves of refugees fleeing from Nazism. The RAF provided a new publishing outlet for local writers, and some of Lessing's early poems and short stories appeared in the various journals that were produced in the RAF training camps.

Immigrants coming into Rhodesia after the Second World War were entering into a society that possessed both histories and fictions that made possible national self-description and self-definition, although the narratives were sufficiently diverse to allow these to be contested. Mary Cathcart Borer's *Distant Hills* (1951) traces a trek from South Africa that endures attacks by Ndebele and laagers until finally they arrive "where one day houses and shops, churches and schools would be built: in the future birthplace of their children and grandchildren." In Mollie Chappell's *The House on the Kopje* (1953), English immigrants learn from their hosts of their pioneer past and one of the English women sees children as "children of a New World" who possess "vitality, self-possession, good manners." Great Zimbabwe, as the relic of a failed imperialism, is sometimes brought in as an admonition of what may happen if whites fail to keep blacks in an appropriately subservient position. A woman refugee from Hungary, who has married a white Rhodesian in Elizabeth Fenton's *Rhodesian Rhapsody* (1958), is told that the ancient civilization collapsed because the original settlers "must have intermarried with the adjoining tribes, and so acquired a Negroid appearance and Negroid brains." Rhodesians are determined that this will not happen again, and they will prove worthy of the men who fought in the 1890s. The immigrant bride ponders on the "heroism and sacrifice there has been to make this Africa a continent worth living in." The immigrant has to prove herself worthy of this heroic heritage. That Rhodesia preserved what was best in British culture is an idea that appears frequently in these postwar novels. If socialist Britain has made the British passive, in Rhodesia they will rediscover their self-reliance. In Wilson MacArthur's *The Valley of Hidden Gold* (1962), an English youth who wants to become a Rhodesian is treated to the usual stories of the pioneers and the battles of the 1890s. In the 1930s, white men worked on the roads rather than take government money. The young man is reminded that no good comes to a country inhabited by people who "encourage that sort of gutless attitude." That Rhodesians had built the country from nothing remained an important perception throughout Rhodesia's ninety years. In Daniel Carney's *The Whispering Death* (1969), a young Englishman who has married the daughter of a pioneer family is tested for the firmness of purpose Rhodesia once had and in the years following the unilateral declaration of independence (UDI) requires more than ever. "How can a man from another country," the young man is asked, "who buys his house from another man and then owns an acre of land—but who never had to fight for it, or make the bricks, or hew the wood to build it—understand me or how I feel?" In 1969, the question was a Rhodesian nationalist question directed to anyone who denied Rhodesia its right to independence. Such novels are invariably silent, however, on who actually dug the clay and cut the trees.

The nationalist voice becomes more strident when Rhodesia's dominion status began to seem a political possibility. Often the stridency is directed towards a decadent Britain. In Clarke Mackinnon's *Leopard Valley* (1963), the fact of Britain's decline does not require debate. A rural Rhodesian community realizes that Britain is a country gone to pot. "The Welfare State. Teddy Boys. The Prejudice against the Colony. Bias on the BBC." It is a splendidly random list of everything that seemed to threaten middle-class British certainties in the postwar period, offered here as a basis for Rhodesia's independence. Once Smith declared Rhodesia unilaterally independent of Britain, white Rhodesian populism, mistrustful alike of Britain and big business, which was often South African, is expressed in several novels. W. A. Ballinger's *Call It Rhodesia* makes an advocate of Responsible Government say in the 1920s, "We didn't make [this country] for the people down in the Cape. We didn't make it for the fat-bottomed Board of Directors in London. We made it for ourselves. We didn't say: 'Call it North Transvaal . . . New London or New Britain. . . .' We said then 'Call it Rhodesia.'" The anti-British sentiments are anachronistic and belong to the 1960s rather than to the 1922 campaign that successfully prevented Rhodesia from joining South Africa and that emphasized Rhodesia's British identity. Lessing is more accurate in showing how Rhodesians' sense of their difference developed over time. "Few of [the settlers] had not been brought up with the words Home and England continually in their mouths, even if they had not been born there," she observes in *A Proper Marriage*. They eagerly anticipate the arrival of the RAF because "it was their own people they were expecting—and more: themselves, at one remove, and dignified by responsibility and danger." In fact, the first details of the RAF are mechanics who to Lessing's settlers have "a look of incompleteness. . . . They could not own these ancestors; their cousins from home were a race of dwarfs, several inches shorter than themselves." Instead of admiring the achievements of a mere fifty years, the settlers sense a criticism of their provincialism and resent the men's nostalgia for England because, as Lessing notes, "the Colonial's England is not the England that these men longed for." In *Landlocked*, the capital city is held momentarily in an English gaze. Martha Quest's mother during the victory parade at the end of the war looks with distaste at "this little town, this shallow little town, that was set so stark and direct on the African soil—it would not feed her, nourish her. . . . And the troops would have black faces, or at least some of them would be black." But for younger settlers in the novel, Zambesia is their familiar reality. The Sports Club in *Martha Quest* stands as a metonym for the whole country. Young whites protest at any attempt to exclude whites who are in menial jobs. "It might be said that this club had come into existence simply as a protest against everything Europe stood for. There were no divisions here, no barriers, at least none that could be put into words; the most junior clerk from the railways, the youngest typist, were on Christian name terms with their bosses and mingled easily with the sons of Cabinet ministers." This egalitarianism takes it for granted that blacks are simply excluded, of course. In William Rayner's *The Reapers* (1961), Rhodesians are "colonial Bourbons," Salisbury, "a city built on boom . . . and ignorant assurance" and "an improbable dream . . . a bubble afloat in an ocean of bush." In the first four novels of "Children of Violence," Lessing glances toward other egalitarian possibilities. A famous epiphany in *Martha Quest* envisions arising out of "harsh scrub and stunted trees, a noble city" where children without sense of difference of color or degree play among "white pillars and tall trees." Later in the novel, Martha senses the futility of claiming a single political destiny for the country when "each group, community, clan, colour, strove and fought away from one another in a sickness of dissolution" and she experiences "the effort of imagination needed to destroy the words *black, white, nation, race*," which leaves her exhausted and with aching head.

In "Children of Violence," Lessing's whites are defiant of British conventions and the authority of the settler state, but it is only a small and deviant group that refuses to conform to the prevailing racism. In her first published novel, *The Grass Is Singing* (1950), new arrivals are expected to accept white Rhodesian attitudes on race or get out. Lessing's autobiography records that her first novel was part of a much longer novel that told the story of a newly arrived Englishman, Tony Marston, being transformed into a Rhodesian. His learning to respond correctly to the murder of Mary Turner was one episode in this process. Ann Mary Fielding's *The Noxious Weed* (1951) is one of the few novels, apart from Lessing's, that shows how difficult this process of adjustment could be. Daphne Berys, who has immigrated with her husband and children to make a fortune from tobacco, finds in Rhodesia only an "an aridness of landscape—and soul." She finds herself growing apart from her son, Ben, who finds in the raw country a challenge that England would never have provided him with. "He loved, in the scorching heat, to take the tractor up to the virgin land and feel its great teeth dragging the heart out of the stubborn soil," a sentence that suggests something of the ambiguous relationship between settlers and soil. When Ben beats a laborer who has allowed a curing barn to catch fire, he knows that Rhodesia has given him "a savage strength" and acknowledges that a harsh country demands in turn a harshness of its settlers. Other responses than Ben's violence to what was still called the "native question" were possible. In *A Proper Marriage*, Mr. Player, the head of the company that "controls half of the minerals on the central plateau," casually remarks that "the whole legal system as affecting the Africans was ridiculously out of date and should be radically overhauled." The young Martha thinks of such a remark as so radical that she would expect it only from the small progressive group she has come in contact with. In fact, Player values blacks as a source of cheap labor and objects to settler politics only because they make blacks more incompetent and discontented than they need be. In Lessing's novella *A Home for the Highland Cattle*, she again traces how a postwar English immigrant first resists white racism, registering her servant as a person, and feeling contempt for her white neighbors' obsession with blacks. Only at the end of the story have blacks become for her as they are for other settlers, almost invisible, and when they intrude on her consciousness are contained within the clichés of racial stereotypes.

Postwar blacks were not willing to remain passive, allowing themselves to be regarded with loathing or contempt and treated with casual brutality. *The Grass Is Singing* registers this change in the murder of Mary Turner. The brutal act allows Moses an agency that no other black has in the novel, even if after the murder he waits passively for his inevitable arrest. Both Lessing in *Landlocked* and Peter Gibbs in *Stronger Than Armies* (1953) describe the general strike of 1948. With the streets of Rhodesia's towns suddenly emptied of blacks, whites joke to one another that "it seems like a real white man's country at last." Lessing notes how the strike momentarily confirms white fears about "the kaffirs rising and throwing the whites into the sea; of murders, bloodbaths, throat-slittings, rape and arson," and when whites patrol the streets they are living out "heroic fantasies." Gibbs makes one of the strike leaders emphasize white dependence on black labor, a dependence that generations of whites tried to ignore. "One day when the Africans will not work the white people will not have food, they will not have their houses clean, their trains will not go, their motors will be still." When a delegation of strikers meets the cabinet, Gibbs remarks that "characteristically, none of [the ministers] gave any thought to what Muntambo had told them about his people. All that concerned them was whether the natives would take any action." For a novel published in 1953, *Stronger Than Armies* is singularly prescient. The violence of the reprisals by the whites gives blacks a deeper political understanding. A strike leader says, "They will use their guns to frighten us into submission. That is why one day we must have guns too." Near the end of the novel the inevitability of violent confrontation is emphasized. In the locations, the strikers are saying, "There is only one thing the white man understands, and that is strength." At the other end of the city, the white men were saying, "the nigger only understands force." *Landlocked* similarly recognizes in the strike the first stirrings of a modern and militant nationalism.

As the Federation exposed Rhodesia to black militancy in Northern Rhodesia and Nyasaland, some novelists argued that some black political aspirations should be accommodated, although only Lessing and Gibbs register the extent to which the political initiatives have shifted to black politicians. In Clark Mackinnon's *Lost Hyena* (1962), a gas-station attendant is seen as a pathetic figure in a place of "petrol pumps and . . . Coca-Cola bottles and the wistful longing for a paler skin." Rhodesia has given him access to "schools, a university, hospitals and clinics, a higher standard of life and the chance to vote," but this surge of benevolence is as qualified as the various franchises that were made available for blacks in the 1950s and early 1960s. Such a man should not try "to dream in the white man's idiom [or] . . . to forget his place, though it was no fault of his own that, simple, backward, lazy, kindhearted, he had been press-ganged into the twentieth century mess." From the first decade of the settler invasion, there were always novelists who pondered whether their presence had improved the quality of black lives. Mackinnon is certain that without the whites his gas-station attendant would have known only "the kraal with the dirt and the ignorance, the slave-raids and the tribal cruelty." Joyce Collin-Smith's *The Scorpion on the Stone* (1954) offers another version of the impact settlers have had on Africa. A settler remarks that blacks "infiltrate our civilization and live sordid lives in squalor and filth." This is partly the fault of whites themselves. Once blacks were "simple childlike people living blameless tribal lives" and there are parts of the country where this idyll can still be glimpsed but they are "the last outposts of a civilisation dying beneath the indifferent hand of the white men." In Mackinnon's *Leopard Valley*, sentiment that most whites in the early 1960s would have seen as liberal accommodation is put into the mouth of General Milton-Powell, a leading tobacco grower. He argues that the choice is "either you use strong-arm stuff, or you woo. I'd be just as ready to use strong-arm stuff, but the time has arrived to woo." *Leopard Valley* was published during the violence that followed the split of the Zimbabwe African People's Union (ZAPU) into warring factions and when the process of decolonization had been completed in much of Africa. Mackinnon's central character knows that there are young blacks only too willing "to challenge [the white man] with his own ideals of freedom and quality and common justice." Despite this liberal gesture, the colonists' terror that their surveillance of the colonized blacks has failed continually surfaces. An apparently loyal employee turning against his master is explained in racial terms: "Then suddenly the dark blood throbbing to a different rhythm—a massacre. Look at Kenya. Look at the Congo. . . . Civilization's long chain held the whiteman, but their people [i.e., the blacks] were free—from justice, from God, from the cry on the lonely hill." Having vilified missionaries for seventy years for filling the minds of blacks with inappropriate aspirations, the settlers are now carping at them for failing to use Christianity as an efficient policing tool. Only in the early 1960s do whites routinely imply that blacks are ungrateful for what has been achieved for them. Ronald Leavis's *Hippodile* (1961), which deals boldly with interracial sex, provides an exchange between Steve Hind, who is in love with a black woman, and a young black nationalist. According to Steve, without the settlers blacks would still "be sitting under a banana tree, hoping for the best." "It would have been my banana tree on my land," is the reply.

Sex between the races is not as frequent a theme in the novels as one might expect, given white hysteria on the subject and the probability that Todd's attempt to decriminalize interracial sex was one reason that his cabinet turned against him. In the prewar novels, sex between white men and black women is regarded as undesirable as it is inevitable, and women authors are more vociferous on the subject than their male counterparts. Sex between black men and white women is always rape and even then occurs very infrequently in the novels. Rather unexpectedly, a former Chief Native Commissioner, Charles Bullock, wrote the first postwar novel that deals with the subject in any detail. *Rina* (1948) is a historical novel mainly set before the Company invasion of Mashonaland. Robert Marston, a young hunter traveling north of the Limpopo, meets and falls in love with an apparently white girl who has been brought up among local people. When he discovers that Rina's mother is of partly African origin, he realizes that he cannot marry her. In exploring the competing demands of love and "the crime against posterity" that "hybridisation" entails, the novel successfully conveys the pain of someone bewildered by whether his reactions are an irrational prejudice or may have the support of science. Marston's experience sixty years before is given a contemporary relevance when his godson, Adrian Vintcent, tells him that he has fallen in love with a South African woman who refuses to marry him when she discovers that he has African ancestry. Marston relates the story of Rina in order to help the younger man make a decision. Looking at the loneliness of his godfather—for Marston has never loved another since he left Rina—Adrian determines to persuade his fiancée to marry him. But Marston, and indeed the novel, remains unconvinced that this is the wisest choice. We must wait until science authoritatively proclaims that when whites marry people of color they inherit or do not inherit "a barbaric mentality and emotional nature." The whole novel moves uneasily between romance and realism, mysticism and science and the refusal to conclude the debate embodies and reveals interracial sex as both desirable and the ultimate transgression. *Hippodile* similarly uses the prejudices of an earlier period in Rhodesia's history to speak about sex across the color bar in contemporary Rhodesia. Steve Hinde, a young commercial traveler, falls in love with a black woman, Denise Ndube, who has just returned from completing her degree in London. The two encounter the anger not only of the whites but also of blacks who drive Denise from her rural village. A white farmer who sees them together asks Steve what he is doing with his woman in daylight and accuses him of being an immigrant who doesn't know how to treat blacks. Steve's employer, Holtzberger, implies that interracial sex was common enough in the past when he warns that "what happened for two-and-sixpence, fifty years ago isn't like what it would be with Ndube's daughter straight from London back to the kraal here!" Holtzberger recalls with shame how, fifty years before, a black man was lynched after being unjustly accused of touching a white woman and how he had helped to pull the rope "to show that although a Jew, he could be like the others." In Lessing's novellas *Leopard George* and *The Anthill*, other whites tacitly accept the fact of interracial sex between white men and black women as long as it is surrounded by silence. Sex between a black man and a white woman is a different matter, upsetting both racial and gender orders of power, which is one of the reasons why *The Grass Is Singing* was found to be so deeply offensive in Rhodesia. *The Grass Is Singing* and *Hippodile* are exceptional in not feeling obliged to offer some psychological explanation why whites are attracted to blacks or to develop a scientific theory to explain why such attraction should be resisted. As late as 1963, Ada Patterson Kuhn in *Black Heritage* can write of a man of mixed race having "from his father . . . inherited his sharp wits, fine build and natural graces, while showing the cunning, unscrupulous mind of a half-caste." This mishmash of theories covered up a deeper fear that Lessing speaks of *In the Grass Is Singing*: " 'white civilization' . . . will never, never admit that a white person, and most particularly a white woman, can have a human relationship whether for good or evil, with a black person. For once it admits that, it crashes and nothing can save it."

In his autobiography, Ian Smith denies that UDI made the Liberation War inevitable. But only after 1965 do the novelists dwell almost exclusively on military confrontations between black and white. The central character in Rayner's *The Reapers* remarks that a representative settler "could not regard the black man as dangerous because he could not believe in his full humanity." But that was in 1961. After 1965 blacks asserted their humanity through militant nationalist parties, and blacks were consequently accorded a visibility in the novels that they had not had before. If Rhodesia's declaration of independence confirmed that Rhodesia was indeed a new nation, its right to exist was being challenged by Rhodesian blacks as soon as it was proclaimed. Initially whites are assured of their military superiority. When the possibility of an invasion from the north is discussed in Ballinger's *Call It Rhodesia*, the whites do not doubt their strength for a moment. "It's not guns, it's the man behind the guns," a politician says, and one member of his audience reflects that liberalism "is sweet surrender. . . . The world belonged to the strong. The future, God help us, belonged to her and her breed." Twelve years later in Emily Dibbs's *Spotted Soldiers*, the war is almost over and now we are told that the guerrillas "operated like phantoms, stealing down the mountains during the nights, and then melting away again before daylight. The farmers were goaded to fury, and [the soldiers] became progressively more fatigued and frustrated as the attacks intensified." Referring to the guerrillas as melting phantoms continues to deny blacks their full humanity but whites, impotent in their fury, fatigued and frustrated, no longer embody strength and her breed.

Dealing with nationalist organizations that are contemplating military action is Merna Wilson's *Explosion* (1966), where nationalist politics are played out in the compound of a mine. The novel, published after UDI, shows no awareness that the militancy of the black nationalist parties was an informed and intelligent change of tactics. Instead, the nationalist leader is power-hungry and cynically changes his recruiting methods to suit the people he is dealing with. The wrath of the "witch-doctor" will be used against less educated men, while a student at university is promised a scholarship to Moscow. The nationalists have power not because they have popular support but because, as the principal nationalist says, "We are dealing with a world that is all on our side! . . . Whatever we tell these fools [in Europe], they will believe so long as we appeal to their idealism." Throughout Rhodesian literature there is resentment that people outside will not accept that only Rhodesian whites know how to deal with the blacks they live among. *Explosion* expresses

Smith's claim that UDI seized the initiative from British politicians who knew nothing about Africa, an ignorance that he was later to extend to South Africa's leaders. Wilson's novel differs from its many predecessors only in that one of the consequences of Britain's naïveté is that the black leaders can confidently predict that the streets in Rhodesia's towns will run with the blood of both whites and blacks who do not cooperate.

In 1967, John Gordon Davis published *Hold My Hand I'm Dying*, which became an international best-seller. Davis worked for the attorney general's office and had been one of the prosecutors in the trial of ZAPU cadres who had been trained in the Soviet Union and subsequently infiltrated Rhodesia. As a result, Davis was not blinkered by the heavy censorship after UDI, and he is unusually aware of how far both the nationalist parties had committed themselves to an armed struggle. His principal character, a government official called Mahoney, who deals specifically with the black population, understands enough of the realities of African politics to exclaim, "What the bloody white Rhodesian can't realize is that the *wog is going to rule Rhodesia*." The only future for whites will be to create "a middle-class of munts, who are conservative and suburban and reasonable." As the derogatory terms "wog" and "munt" suggest, Mahoney has a total contempt for blacks unless they are in the remotest parts of the Zambezi valley, untouched by Western technology. At the end of the novel when the fighting has begun, he looks at "wogs jabbering in the bus and picking their noses and spitting, black and woolly-headed and ignorant and primitive," and he realizes, "I love Africans . . . but I do not want to be ruled by them." Throughout Rhodesia's history, white novelists and poets celebrate the primitive; sometimes, as in *Hold My Hand I'm Dying*, Rhodesia has allowed the writers to return to fundamental values that European technology and urbanization have obscured. Mahoney can relate to people he thinks of as primitive, but in a world controlled by extremists, whether they are Marxists or black nationalists, white power must be guaranteed. "Moderation," Mahoney reflects, "is compromise, and, therefore, moderation is weakness. . . . That is the tragedy, that is why there was UDI. . . . You are forced to choose between black and white. . . . The Rhodesians have made a stand. Now they must fight for it."

Smith claimed that he had declared Rhodesia independent from Britain in order to defend the values of Western Christian civilization. He and his rebels, earnest, dressed in suits and largely urban, were improbable agents for a contemporary pastoral that discovered in nature the fundamentals of humanity that decadent Britain had lost sight of, although Smith also argued that UDI preserved all that was best in British values. John Gordon Davis was not the only novelist who saw in UDI an attempt to recover fundamental strengths. Alan Burgess's *The Word for Love* (1968) is set after UDI, although this may have been an afterthought as the political details belong to the early 1960s and the violence in the novel is based on the violence following on the split within ZAPU. A police inspector, Bill Field, whose wife is unable to have children, allows himself to be seduced by a "rain goddess," who acts as a medium between the spirit world and the living community to guarantee its continuing life. In transgressing settler conventions concerning interracial sex and adultery, Field is responding to our basic urge to let our lives reproduce the seasonal cycles of birth, fruition, and death. The novel is played out against nationalist agitation, and it suggests that both nationalism and Western marriage conventions are artificial impositions on an Africa whose identity is more accurately represented through the "rain goddess" than through the nationalist politician. A cynical reading of Burgess's and Davis's novels would see in their celebration of the primitive the recognition that

Rhodesia's security forces can more easily control people untouched by modernity than when they have been given different aspirations by modern political parties armed with modern weapons and revolutionary Western ideologies.

Rhodesian novelists were slow in recognizing that Rhodesian whites were fighting a modern anticolonial revolution. This is borne out by Daniel Carney's *The Whispering Death* (1969) where the guerrilla band is lead by an albino claiming to be the spirit of the last Ndebele king, Lobengula. The ZAPU split of 1962 soon developed along ethnic lines, and in 1969 it was improbable that the Shona would look to Lobengula as a spirit of contemporary resistance. The novel is not interested in ethnicity but in why blacks have not reported the guerrilla presence to the police. Carney's protagonist remarks that if such a man "could perform a few tricks, hold a few impressive ceremonies, he might be able to sway them or at least terrify them so much that they wouldn't hand him over." Carney's blacks are the savages of two centuries of imperial writing, able to be beguiled by tricks and ceremonies, and the whites are past masters of both.

The Zimbabwe Liberation War began in December 1972. Although there were random incursions over the previous six years, they were poorly coordinated and never constituted a sustained campaign. Peter Stiff was a superintendent in the British South Africa Police, and since Zimbabwean independence, writing from South Africa, he has become an important popular historian of the war. His novel *The Rain Goddess* (1973) shows that he was aware of the extent and organization of Zimbabwean African National Liberation Army (ZANLA) incursions into northeastern Rhodesia during 1972. He also perhaps knew that both Rhodesia's Ministry of Internal Affairs and the Zimbabwe African National Union (ZANU) recognized the importance of winning the loyalty of traditional religious leaders. The rain goddess of the title supports the regime and regards the guerrillas as agents of violence and death who will bring drought to the land. The novel works from the assumption that no rational blacks would align themselves with the guerrillas and that a reversion to atavistic savagery would be needed before the rural people turned against the whites. When the cynical nationalist leader orders that a village be burned because it has been indifferent to the nationalist cause, the mob obeys, "Their eyes glazed with savage excitement, each man hypnotized by violence." The young man who is to become the principal guerrilla in the novel is, however, persuaded to leave Rhodesia with the promise that he will be trained as a doctor. At UDI, only two government schools provided the classes that gave young blacks the education needed to enter the University College of Rhodesia, although mission and private nonracial schools allowed the children of blacks to gain the necessary qualifications. Neither Wilson's nor Swift's novel recognizes that while young whites could be educated to the highest level if they wished, the majority of blacks dropped from the system because there were no places for them in the upper levels of secondary schools and the thwarted ambitions of tens of thousands of young blacks laid the foundations of discontent on which nationalism was erected. Neither novel addresses the contradiction that if a desire for education is a motive for crossing the border, blacks are not submitting to a savage irrationality in joining a nationalist party.

Only with Michael Hartmann's *Game for Vultures* (1976) are blacks who oppose white rule seen for the first time as men making a rational choice rather than as people who have regressed into savagery from the benefits of Rhodesia's civilization. Marungu, looking for work, is mocked by a group of white women having tea: "Dismissed as a minor, amusing diversion, sinking with humiliation he had left. Right then he would have cut every white

throat in Rhodesia." Hartmann's novel refuses to confirm other Rhodesian beliefs. Al-
though most white Rhodesians lived in towns and cities, the Rhodesian man hardened by
life in the bush was a fictional convention shaped over eighty years. Hartmann allows a
Cabinet minister to look down at Salisbury's rush-hour traffic and observe, "There's our
army down there. . . . Men who spend eleven months of the year pushing pens and one
month pushing themselves through some of the dirtiest country in the world." Through-
out the war, the whites in the Security Forces largely consisted of conscripts. A police re-
servist is described as "an old man trying to relive the lost days of his youth by dressing up
and guarding a lonely mission station." Marungu, who is about to attack the mission,
imagines him thinking, "I've fought Hitler and hell, I'm still good enough to show a few
munts the wrong end of a rifle." Not only does *Game for Vultures* question Rhodesian ste-
reotypes, but Hartmann is also the first novelist who recognizes that this is a civil war
rather than savagery flinging itself against civilization. Peter Swansey, the principal white
character, fights for the Rhodesian army and has a colored wife. Her brother is a black na-
tionalist guerrilla. Swansey's brother is a sanctions buster who supplies the Rhodesian
army with weapons. By localizing within a family the conflict of loyalties that the war
provoked, Hartmann allows the conflict a complexity so that it becomes more than a con-
frontation between black and white or Christianity and communism or civilization and
savagery. Black nationalism in the novel, however, is never more than a response to white
racism; *Game for Vultures* makes no attempt to show that Rhodesia had created a political
system designed to maintain and reinforce the political privilege and economic power of
whites, a structure that black nationalists saw as not only unjust and exploitative but also
anachronistic in the Africa of the 1970s. Nationalism created its own agenda and its claim
to control Zimbabwean modernity was a claim that no white novelist recognized as a
right. William Rayner had a chance to give his war this character. In *The Reapers*, he had
shown that the frustration of nationalist ambitions would lead inevitably to armed insur-
rection. Fifteen years later, in *The Day of Chaminuka*, he had the chance to trace the path
the revolution had taken. The later novel, like *Game for Vultures*, has his two principal
characters representing Rhodesian and black nationalist points of view and the guerrillas
are people with a serious political understanding of Rhodesia, competently organized and
idealistic. But the real battle in the novel is fought between a guerrilla commander and a
dissident who claims to be possessed by the spirit of Chaminuka, a leading Shona spirit,
who preys on the superstitious fears of peasants using all the paraphernalia and rituals
of a Shona medium. Rayner's representative of white Rhodesia is a farmer who ritually
dances on his lawn in order to assert a virile authority over his laborers and who, as it
turns out, is the father of the guerrilla commander. Both the farmer and the dissident are
representative of no one in particular and in any case are killed. The guerrilla commander
continues the war, the novel implying that the nationalists are unlikely to be diverted
from their course.

Hartmann's text remained unique in white-authored novels about the war, although af-
ter independence T. O. McLoughlin's *Kurima* (1985) examines the conflict of loyalties for
white Rhodesians during the war and Bruce Moore-King's *White Man Black War* (1988)
develops with considerable skill the way in which whites were conditioned into believing in
the justness of their cause. As the end of Rhodesia became inevitable and the war became
more violent, the novelists registered its progress with even more brutal realism. Robert
Early's *A Time of Madness* sets out to justify white violence that was responding to a violence

that could be expected from savages. A missionary priest reflects that "a thousand years of savage, pagan existence could not be wiped out at one stroke" and that "many generations of dedicated men" such as himself were needed "to eliminate the fears and superstitions which were fundamental to the tribal African's make-up." The priest is killed in his attempt to be one of those dedicated generations, but his presence in Africa has no effect one way or another. Rhodesia's real enemies are not savages who in the end can be contained as they always have been. A more lethal combination is savagery, which has become a tool in the expansionist strategies of the Soviet Union. *A Time of Madness* expresses a fundamental belief of Smith and the Rhodesia Front. The Liberation War was not a local phenomenon that could be understood as a part of the historical and political processes of Rhodesia and more recently of the decolonization of Africa. Instead, it was fostered and was now being conducted by the sinister forces of international communism. *A Time of Madness* not only details the bush war with attacks on farms and pursuit of guerrilla groups by the army but also shows agents from Eastern Europe operating in Salisbury nightclubs and hotels at the Victoria Falls. In these parts of the novel, Early is writing out of a twenty-year tradition of spy novels that the Cold War engendered. Soldiers' secrets are coaxed out of them in a brothel equipped with listening devices and closed-circuit television. All that Rhodesia has against the might of the Soviet Union is the fellowship of strong men forged in the bush. In contrast, the Eastern European agents are decadent and the guerrillas are their puppets. Without their communist masters, the only initiative they are capable of is brutality and their only ideologies are those forged by ethnic rivalries. Even in the luxurious flat in Lusaka that Soviet money has made available to him, the guerilla commander employs the highly metaphorical language that nineteenth-century authors assumed that savages used, inasmuch as they were incapable of abstract thought: "They are the white sheep bleating at the scent of a leopard in the wind" is a sample.

When *The Whispering Death* was published, South African economic and political pressure had made Rhodesia's end inevitable. Two novels published in 1978 and 1979 reach into fantasy as a means of ensuring Rhodesia's survival. British gold hidden in the Sahara during the Second World War is the object of a treasure hunt in Lloyd Burton's *The Yellow Mountain*. It will be used to finance an elaborate electronic fence along Rhodesia's eastern border to prevent further incursions, but the Rhodesians have to compete in the search with an American oil company, the British Treasury, Eastern Bloc intelligence officials, and the corrupt local police. The Rhodesians are, of course, successful. They have taken on some of the powerful forces in the world and have emerged victorious, if victory is to retire behind a fence. Peter Armstrong's *Operation Zambezi* (1979) is a fictional reconstruction of the Rhodesian Air Force raids into Zambia in October 1978, but historic raids are forgotten in an elaborate plot in which the Soviet ambassador to Zambia is kidnapped, drugged, and hypnotized so that when he returns to Lusaka he withdraws Soviet aid from ZAPU and offers it to ZANU instead. This change of allegiance is designed to confuse everyone, including the Chinese who supported ZANU.

The Rhodesian war attracted several writers who were not Rhodesian, the best known of whom was Wilbur Smith. Smith was born in Zambia and lived briefly in Rhodesia in the early 1960s. *The Sunbird* (1972) draws an elaborate parallel between the destruction of an ancient city whose ruins are discovered on the Rhodesia-Botswana border and the contemporary nationalist forces that are now trying to destroy Rhodesia. Africa is inherently savage and the guerrilla leader who is also an academic shows that his apparent sophistication cloaks the primitive. Behind the "impassive mask" of his face "a chained ferocity glowers through eye slits. . . . There is a dark satanical presence about him, despite the white shirt and dark business suit he wears." Although he is a doctrinaire Marxist-Leninist, he has been initiated into tribal mysteries by his "witchdoctor" grandfather and is liable to lapse into a trance as the spirit of his grandfather possesses him. The war in Laurens van der Post's *A Story Like the Wind* (1972) shows a Chinese communist and leaders of the "World Council of Christian Churches" manipulating black nationalism for their own sinister or naïve purposes. Van der Post sees all three as attacking Africa's primitivism and the novel affirms our need "to allow the flow of a primitive world . . . to help thaw the frozen imagination of our civilised system so that some sort of spirit can come again to the hearts of men." Insofar as Rhodesia is represented at all, it is through a great farm, Hunter's Drift, which is a curious mixture of feudal settlement, socialist commune, and reservation, and is destroyed at the end of the novel. In the last years of the Liberation War, Wilbur Smith once again wrote about Rhodesia; in a quartet he traced the country's colonial history through a single family, the Ballantynes. Recognizable figures from the country's colonial past are all Ballantynes. The first two novels in the series, *A Falcon Flies* (1980) and *Men of Men* (1981), were probably written before Zimbabwean independence and are plotted as imperial romances in which whites bring Africa under their control. At the end of *The Angels Weep* (1982), the last Ballantyne is leaving a country that black rule has made uninhabitable. In *The Leopard Hunts in Darkness* (1984), he has returned in order to support the Ndebele in the ethnic-based civil war that has broken out.

As this survey implies, Rhodesian novels were never a private literature, if private literature means to record interpersonal relationships and take for granted the larger social context. The writers are always explaining and appropriating the country for themselves and their characters, considering how far black aspirations can be accommodated, and finally spelling out the need to defend Rhodesia against the various forces that seek to destroy it. White Rhodesian fiction is a nationalist literature.

Part III
Authors and Works, A–Z

A

And Now the Poets Speak (1981). This landmark collection arose from the liberation struggle in Zimbabwe. Compiled and edited by Mudereri Kadhani and Musaemura Zimunya and published by Mambo Press, it divides into eight sections: "The Heritage," The Colonial Scourge," "Black Man's Burden," "Chains, Shackles and Gaols," "The Clouds Gather," "The Storm," "Tribute," and "And the People Celebrate." It lists among its many contributors Zimunya and Kadhani themselves, along with Carlos Chombo, Kizito Muchemwa, Chenjerai Hove, Samuel Chimsoro, Toby Moyana, Charles Mungoshi, Alexander Kanengoni, Eddison Zvobgo, Solomon Mahaka, Colleen Samupindi, Canaan Banana, Samurai D. Seyaseya, John Gambanga, Pathisa Nyati, Emmanuel Ngara, Geoffrey Ndhlala, Hopewell Seyaseya, Elisha Chakanyuka, Violet Moyo, Wanda Kawadza, Nemi Tichapedza, Killian Mwanaka, and Nicodem Huchu. In what the editors call a "commendation" rather than an introduction, they describe the flood-tide response that met their call for contributions. It came from "towns and villages, schools and assembly points; from Zimbabwe, Mozambique, England, Romania, Azania and America; in Shona, English and Ndebele; from blacks and from whites; in type-written scripts and in hardly legible scrawls; from academics, workers, politicians, students, guerillas and school pupils." Crucially, they said, the text looked not only back to colonialism and the devastating war it produced but also forward to the kind of settlement that would best bring peace to the new Zimbabwe.

Further reading: Rino Zhuwarara, *Introduction to Zimbabwean Literature in English* (Harare, 2001).

B

Banana, Canaan (1936–2003). Independent Zimbabwe's first black president (1980–87). Born in Esiphezini, in Matabeleland, of a Malawian migrant worker father and a Zimbabwean mother, he trained as a teacher and was also ordained a Methodist minister in 1966. Religion led to politics. A founding member and vice president of Rhodesia's African National Council (1972–73), he represented it at the United Nations (1973–75). His radicalism provoked the colonial government, which constantly detained him and banned his publications. He was appointed national president in 1980 (Joshua Nkomo had rejected the post as decorative); subsequent achievements included peace for his own Matabeleland—ravaged by Robert Mugabe's Fifth Brigade, which left some twenty thousand dead. He also reconciled political rivals Mugabe and Nkomo, which produced the Zimbabwe African National Union–Patriotic Front (ZANU-PF). In 1989 he led a World Council of Churches mission to apartheid South Africa, and until 1999 was the Organization of African Unity's envoy to war-torn Liberia. His career was besmirched in 2000 by a conviction for homosexual assault, costing him popularity, priesthood, and the religious studies chair at the University of Zimbabwe. He died of cancer in London on November 10, 2003.

Banana's books include *The Church in the Struggle for Zimbabwe* (1996), *The Politics of Repression and Resistance Face to Face with Combat Theology* (1966), and *The Gospel According to the Ghetto* (1980). His poetry, included in Kadhani and Zimunya's independence anthology *And Now the Poets Speak* (1981), reveals rhythmic vitality, Bible-inspired imagery, and a preacher's way with rhetoric. Famous for recasting part of the Paternoster as "Teach us to demand our share of the gold / And forgive us our docility," he did much the same with the Credo:

> I believe in a colour blind God,
> Maker of technicolour people,
> Who created the Universe
> And provided abundant resources
> For equitable distribution among his
>   people.

It ends:

> I believe in the spirit of
>   Reconciliation,
> The united body of the dispossessed;
> The communion of the suffering
>   masses,
> The power that overcomes the
>   dehumanizing forces of men.
> The resurrection of personhood,
>   justice, and equality,
> And the final triumph of
>   Brotherhood.

Banana's commitment to national solidarity should not be undervalued when Shona-Ndebele ethnic rivalry caused such slaughter. Nationhood as a "sacramental state of being" suffuses "Together," whose lines repeatedly attack tribalism and individualism. "The *phovo* [poor person] out of the nation is like a fish out of water," and

> The lives laid down in lonely spots
> And the crimson blood shed on
>   thirsty land
> Cry out against fragmentation.

Banda, Hastings Kamuzu (1906–97). President of Malawi (1966–94). Born at Kasungu in what was then Nyasaland, at seventeen he literally walked away from the colony to South Africa to get an education. Later, he studied at the Wilberforce Academy in Ohio, the University of Indiana, and Nashville's Meharry Medical College, graduating in 1937. After practicing medicine in Britain and Ghana, in 1958, when he was sixty, he was invited home by the Nyasaland African National Congress to spearhead its independence movement. Exuding a confidence born of learning in classics and medicine, his oratory brought him instant fame and swift imprisonment.

Autocratic leanings emerged within weeks of independence in 1964. Dismissing ministers who dared to question his policies, he crushed Henry Chipembere's armed revolt in 1965 and Yatuta Chisiza's in 1967. Behind a mantra of "Peace and calm, law and order," he drove young talent into exile or detention. Nor were his threats to feed enemies to crocodiles empty. Banda's Special Branch and Young Pioneers combined to intimidate an entire nation. Favorite targets were Jehovah's Witnesses (who refused to carry Malawi Congress Party cards), writers, and university academics. Felix Mnthali, Jack Mapanje, Edison Mpina, and Sam Mpasu were four authors among many imprisoned without charge. In Banda's looking-glass world, ministers would be peremptorily sacked (even collectively) and dispatched to their villages. He arrested the able but sick Aleke Banda (no relation, but suspected of seeing himself as a successor), and in 1977 he hanged Albert Nqumayo, secretary general of his own Malawi Congress Party. Most cruelly, he enjoyed seeing the aged and dignified Orton Chirwa die, shackled in leg irons in prison. In 1983 several ministers, including the popular Dick Matenje, died in a car crash so clearly stage-managed as to add the coinage "accidental-ized" to the local lexicon.

Banda was an elder of the Church of Scotland, and his anticommunism brought him Western support but few African friends. Unblushingly maintaining links with apartheid South Africa and colonial Rhodesia, he also succored the right-wing Renamo movement that wrought havoc in neighboring Mozambique.

When human rights replaced Cold War hysteria, Banda became increasingly exposed. Aid was stopped. The new era of faxes and email saw a 1991 pastoral letter from the Catholic hierarchy raise alarm across the world about a rumored move against the bishops themselves. Yielding to international pressure, this self-styled president for life agreed to a referendum on multiparty democracy in 1993, lost an election in 1994, and handed power to Bakili Muluzi. Out of office, he was arrested and tried for the 1983 ministerial killings but won acquittal from a nation inclined to forgiveness.

Malawian literature grew to maturity during Banda's thirty-year rule, figuratively reflecting its horrors. For their part, incarcerated writers created a new category of prison literature. Debate will continue about Banda's achievements. Unlike Zambia's Kenneth Kaunda, he wisely emphasized agriculture—but unwisely emphasized estate farming. He had a Victorian way with crime and corruption and encouraged good university standards. Yet his fear of African intellectuals was pathological; as a medical doctor, he left hospitals woefully underfunded; and many went homeless while he built himself palaces he did not need.

Further reading: Philip Short, *Banda* (London, 1974); T. D. Williams, *Malawi: The Politics of Despair* (New York, 1978); John Lloyd Lwanda, *Kamuzu Banda of Malawi: A Study in Promise, Power and Paralysis* (Glasgow, 1993); Emily Mkamanga, *Suffering in Silence: Malawi Women's 30 Year Dance with Dr Banda* (Glasgow, 2000).

Banda, Innocent (b. ca. 1950). Malawian poet and dramatist. Born in Malawi's Central Region, educated at Zomba Catholic Secondary School, the University of Malawi, and the University of Wales, he has held academic posts in Malawi, Zimbabwe, and the United States. A private writer whose work was shaped by Banda-era pressures, his early writing announced a spiritual lyricism emphasizing the poet's role as a force for good. Hence in "Bright Like the Sun":

> Like the wind
> that haunts the world, I wish I could
>   walk
> Night and day
> mourning for the unloved
> Souls of the world.

> And

> I will lean my head
> against the old baobab
> to hear the echo of creation.

The verse often achieves effects of stark beauty:

> For the kingdom is for children
> Only those who meet God
> In a raindrop
> *Kyrie eleison.*

Exposure to the University of Malawi Writers' Workshop and anger at political oppression eventually produced a stronger statement. Hence:

Allow me
One more curse
Through this God-fearing mouth
For, trying to forgive
I choked close to death.

He has also turned his energies to drama. The Malawi Broadcasting Corporation accepted radio plays from him, and dramatic ferment at the university stimulated such pieces as *The Lean Years*, *Lord Have Mercy*, *Cracks*, and *The First Rehearsal*.

Further reading: Martin Banham, ed., *A History of Theatre in Africa* (Cambridge, 2004); Adrian Roscoe, *Uhuru's Fire: African Literature East to South* (London, 1977).

Borrell, D. E. (b. 1928). Zimbabwean poet. She was born in Hetton, County Durham, England, and educated at Durham University, where she graduated with honors in English. She emigrated to what was then Rhodesia in 1956, working as a lecturer, teacher, editor, and freelance writer while energetically promoting local writing with her husband, the poet Hugh Finn. Her work appeared locally and in Britain and America. Her collection *A Patch of Sky* was published in 1979 in a double volume of the Mopani Poets series with Musaemura Zimunya's *Zimbabwe Ruins*. At a moment close to Zimbabwe's independence, editors Anthony Chennells and Hugh Finn wrote, "We are pleased, in our first double-volume, to publish the work of a white and a black poet together, at a time when this seems singularly appropriate."

Chennells's preface praises Borrell for not trying to "contain the problems of human existence in a few stanzas," for an objectivity that results in her not "detailing experiences so intensely personal that I cannot make them part of my own life," and for not struggling "to contain an African experience within a sensibility and diction shaped by an English tradition." He praises her candor and humor, too, her unpretentious language and concreteness of imagery. The two worlds she inescapably must capture, immediate Africa and remembered northern England, receive, he suggests, an honest and pragmatic humanity that privileges both and holds them together as, for her, a unified experience.

This balance is widely evident. Thus, she can write an amusing inner monologue of a Durham alderman embarrassed at having to preside at a piano recital by John Clegg:

'Ow long does this go on? What a
    draught!
Might blow the blighter's bleedin'
    music down
But no such luck

and paint the African grave and church of poet-priest contemporary Arthur Shearly Cripps, where all is sad ruin:

Wrecked columns,
The church's rain-washed floors,
White fragments of a shattered saint,
Wall sliding to earth—

And she captures the misery of apartheid's hapless "Coloured" victims as portrayed in Athol Fugard's play *Boesman and Lena*:

We are the white man's trash,
Carrying our lives on the platform of
    our heads,
Bumming from nowhere to
    nowhere.

Not given to strident rhetoric, she can make delicate feminist points, as she does in "Above Grasmere," where, while recalling Wordsworth's life in those parts, the emphasis falls lightly on his sister Dorothy and the "fertile notebook / of their lives" that the poet was to use so richly. Best is a hint that while William and Samuel did their famous walking, there was poor "Dorothy far behind." In "If I Have to Leave" she writes that, should the liberation struggle drive her back to England, it is the laughter, optimism, collegiality, and companionship of African women she will treasure most:

> If I have to leave,
> I shall take from Africa this
>   strength,
> This strange bond of women.

Further reading: Anthony Chennells and Hugh Finn, eds., *A Patch of Sky* and *Zimbabwe Ruins* (Salisbury, 1979).

Brettell, N. H. (1908–91). Zimbabwean poet. Born in Worcestershire, England, Brettell studied English at the University of Birmingham and in 1930 emigrated to Rhodesia, where he worked in rural schools, often as headmaster, until his retirement. When his house at Nyanga was attacked and destroyed during the Liberation War, he and his wife moved to Kadoma, where he died in 1991. His first volume of poetry, *Bronze Frieze*, was published by Oxford University Press in 1950, and *Season and Pretext* provided the first volume in the Mopani Poets Series. The autobiography *Side-gate and Stile* (1981) begins with his Worcestershire childhood and then recalls the different ways in which the country that was to be his home for over sixty years slowly revealed itself to him. One of his first postings was to the Chivhu district, where he got to know and admire Arthur Shearly Cripps. Indeed, "Threnody in Spring," the opening piece in his collection *Season and Pretext*, pays warm tribute to the career and writing of this distinguished poet-priest. Unlike the older poet, however, who famously wrote Mashonaland as Arcadia, Brettell allows

Zimbabwe some autonomy, even while the poetry acknowledges that he is mediating what he sees through a sensibility shaped by the English canon, European music, and influences as exotic to Africa as Chinese poetry and painting. He was an acute observer of black lives, which he registered with respect even while noting how much had been stifled by dispossession and poverty. He often wrote about animals and birds, and his poems always allow them an existence that is independent of the response to them that his poems construct. This refusal of anthropomorphism makes his poetry refreshingly unsentimental, and as a result he is able to write about suffering as easily as beauty. In "Wind and an Eagle Owl," he finds a stick to kill a hopelessly wounded bird, but he knows that the bird sees his compassion as entirely inimical:

> With pity brimming like a cup
> I come deliverer in disguise:
> Your great beak gaped in savage
>   grin,
> Your great stare narrowed to a frith
> Of gleaming horror and surprise—
> And oh the walls of hatred in
> Your wildwood eyes, your wildwood
>   eyes.

In "Eavesdropper," he offers a meditation on death that also celebrates life as it can be heard in the sounds of rural Zimbabwe:

> But someone is done with sense
> And cannot hear
> The thronging neighbours
> Ripple the valleys' flagons brimmed
>   with dark,
> With loo, halloo, and longspun
>   quivering answer
> Lifted on lilt of wind. . . .

Unlike most Rhodesian poets, Brettell wrote little about politics, skeptical perhaps of the certainties in which politicians have to indulge. At the beginning of the Liberation War he visits Cripps's church, which fell into ruin after the poet died. He observes,

> Only weed, bird, saint, complete
>   their purposes.
> The stepping stones stand dry,
>   Arcady's further off,
> Further than ever.

But he was perfectly aware of the increasing rancor of the voices of both black and white nationalism. In "The Cabbage Seller," he describes an encounter with a child selling vegetables that his class has grown who is not yet alert to Rhodesian racism and the tension of the times. The innocence cannot last, and his delight in the boy dims into an impression of what he may become:

> . . . demagogue, advocate,
> Climbing the rungs each brief
>   occasion brings
> Not now the blue and green, but
>   black and white,
> Black silk, white bands, white smile,
>   and cobra-black
> The oiled eloquence that slides and
>   stings;
> On the night's rostrum, the spot-
>   lights on you fawning,
> Will you in pause of your intent
>   attack
> —Flint-edged polemic slash down all
>   the weed—
> Give a thought for me, acquaintance
>   of your morning,
> Old brassica whose fancies run to
>   seed?

Perhaps Brettell's instinctive poeticity did not fully realize itself. Memorable imagery can arise from microscopic observation (hence of the white harrier: "Down soft as deceit, flint eye, and hooks of steel / Honed by the wind to rip through snarl or squeal"); concrete and abstract creatively blend; confidence in stanza and rhyme underpins a sensual response to season and landscape. But there is verbal overkill, too, annoyingly arcane diction (raising audience questions), rhythmic awkwardness, a perilous preference for opacity over simplicity and clarity. He is at his best when, in, say, "Wind and an Eagle Owl," "Song for Severn," "The White Harrier," and "Chalton Mill," he gives up the struggle for complexity.

Although Brettell is widely anthologized, he deserves a more substantial reputation than he has. There was little room for white writers in Zimbabwe in the decade immediately after independence, and Brettell's genius was the principal casualty.

Bvuma, Thomas Sukutai (b. 1954). Zimbabwean poet and journalist. Born in Marondera, he attended St. Augustine's Secondary School and, after interrupting study at the national university, he left to fight in the Liberation War. From 1979 to 1981 he studied linguistics and literature and wrote verse at Mozambique's Eduardo Mondlane University. He returned home in 1982 to join Zimbabwe's Ministry of Information, an appointment taking him as attaché to embassies in Maputo, London, and Washington. After earning a master's degree in media studies at the University of Oslo, he joined the national newspaper *The Herald* as deputy editor.

Bvuma's verse appears mainly in his collection *Every Stone That Turns* (1999). But he received special notice in Mudereri Kadhani and Musaemura Zimunya's anthology *And Now the Poets Speak: Poems Inspired by the Struggle for Zimbabwe* (1981), which used his piece "Poetry" as a "choric prelude" honoring Africa's anticolonial struggle as a whole:

> The Real Poetry
> Was carved by centuries

Of chains and whips
It was written in the red streams
Resisting the violence of
"Effective Occupation"
It was engraved in killings in
    Katanga
In the betrayals of Mau-Mau,
In the countless anti-peoples coups
Its beat was the bones in Bissau
Its metaphors massacres in
    Mozambique
Its alliterations agony in Angola
Its form and zenith
Fighting in Zimbabwe . . .

Using his pen name Carlos Chombo, the editors compared Bvuma with Angola's Agostinho Neto: "In this and other of his poetry, we have found the power of the intellect, control of rhythm and style well combined and married to idea, action and reflection." Bvuma's own collection creates an inner and outer life. Bush war tragedies counterpoint an interior life of solitude, remembered childhood pain, and a haunting rural beloved who first inspired his muse. He creates vignettes of life as a child, a guerilla, civil servant, journalist, and editor—and an aching wish in readers that he might find his long-lost love.

The typical statement is lyrical and *in propria persona*. Line and stanza are short, punctuation minimal, the diction common core, and the tone, if occasionally ironic, generally phlegmatic. There are few literary allusions or debts. To a dead uncle who mistreated him in childhood he says,

I am your tough boy
No tears and no smiles
Cold flesh and livid soul.

Yet the soldier-poet who fights in filth ("I marvelled at how a louse could grow / so fat on my starved skin") is all emotional turmoil. Initially materialistic, contemptuous of a mud-walled home, "Crowned com-

ically with conical grass caps," he yearns now for the old homestead—symbolic of the values he is defending. He yearns, too, for his enigmatic love, a woman named Yeukai, whose imposed sublimation made him a warrior-poet. The final poem, "You Will Never Know," addresses her, though she cannot read and lacks friends who can:

But it was you that frustrated
my youthful desires and sent me
    writing.

The struggle to subdue words, he says, became an exercise in sexual sublimation, and when they "finally surrendered" in the deep watches of the night,

The satisfaction was to the soul
Equal to the carnal orgasm you
    denied me.

A consequence of the Liberation War was the destruction of ancestral indirection and propriety in Zimbabwean literary discourse. Hence the explicitness here ("We Surrendered Our Balls," "Grabbing the Bull," "Warming Another Man's Groin"). In "Private Affair," bush defecation, graphically pictured, accompanies the wry hope that "the revolution / would not socialize shitting." Ornateness rarely tempts, and an overall tact protects the verse from mere rhetoric even with such topics as the lowering of colonial flags and post-struggle disenchantment.

"Marrow" laments the war's resulting dog-eat-doggery based on clan ("everyone pissing and shitting on those below"), an economic order turning freedom fighters into beggars, an Africa still "obscene on her back" being raped by the developed world, and an international brand of justice that demanded execution for the Nuremburg Nazis but forgiveness for Zimbabwe's white settlers.

As for the poet's own victory spoils, he owns no mansion in Harare's suburbs or even a slum-dweller's three-roomed shack. He possesses neither a Mercedes nor one of the capital's clapped-out Morris Minors. This "son owns no sod of soil" and will die simply as another "unknown soldier." Politicians meanwhile, finding him "liberation-struggle fodder," will use him for "slogans and votes."

Chihota, Clement Mapfumo (b. ca. 1950). Zimbabwean poet. After posts at Murewa High School and teachers' colleges in Nyadire and Seke, he became head of applied linguistics at the University of Zimbabwe's College of Distance Education. In addition to his academic text *Language, Literature and Communication*, he has published a verse collection, *Before the Next Song and Other Poems* (1999), which reflects experimentation, social concern, and enterprise. Chihota and Stanley Tichapondwa jointly compiled this six-section anthology, aimed judiciously at a high school and college readership.

The text offers verse (plus commentaries by Tichapondwa) strong on subject range and morality. Its Afrocentricity is never parochial, its influences eclectic. Tichapondwa links the poetry to Gambia's Lenrie Peters, Sierra Leone's Awoonor-Williams, Nigeria's Soyinka, Zimbabwe's own Muchemwa and Zimunya, and to British romanticism. There is Keatsian kinesthesia in "Song of the Savannah Dove" and metaphysical wit in "Horns," "War and Peace," "African Tears," and "Dangerous Disease."

Yet this is not servile imitation and his nature poems ("Song of the Savannah Dove," "When the Rain Fell," "The Land of the Sun") serve no empty aesthetic, but foreground issues he believes youth must address: the environment, wildlife protection, rural deprivation. Further, when such concerns arise—they also include drunkenness and AIDS, colonialism and economic dependency—the tone is never drearily didactic.

The AIDS problem is an example. "Dangerous Disease" first uses defeated expectation to turn a deadly subject into an anti-Western joke. Persuaded that the poem will discuss the new scourge, we find instead a sickness

> Called economic lechery,
> Caused by a retro-virus
> First discovered
> By an African Scientist
> In wild Western monkeys.

The tone darkens with "Horns," a five-section poem whose persona grimly lists AIDS' key symptoms: "Horns growing in my groins.... Horns swelling in my armpits and my neck.... Horns whistling in my lungs.... Horns burgeoning in my brain ... this barbed wire cough ... this dirigible diarrhoea ... this cancer of the skin." No traditional warrior, says the speaker, could defeat such multilateral opposition, especially when "herpes, night-chills and fever come in as "spear bearers" for the major assailants. With oral-style personification, the poem asks,

> Is T.B. such a coward
> It needed the company of diarrhoea
> Before going out to hunt?
> Is diarrhoea such a sycophant
> It needed to be led by cancer
> Before agreeing to go?
> Is cancer such a dunce
> It had to call dementia
> Before moving out of camp?

Yet those fearing death from AIDS are reassured. All nature detests death:

The tree groans and cracks
before it falls . . .
Fishes of the sea
fight the rising net
with their bare faces . . .
The headless chicken
sprints away from death
after it is already dead.

It might anyway be all a divine canard:

Perhaps God created us all
Death-fearing creatures
Then sentenced us to die.

But avoiding AIDS is best. Hence the minatory "Before the Night Song." Adam, drunk in the Wine and Wench bar, finds his Eve and when he takes her to a taxi "to circumnavigate the night," a dirge, ominously, "filters(s) / from the East / of tomorrow."

But Chihota mainly meets crisis with pragmatism, not zeitgeist gloom. If yesterday's colonialism demands rational analysis (his "War and Peace" sees it as oxymoronic), and if the continent gets Donne-like treatment in "African Tears Are Everywhere" (its central conceit being that all the world's seas contain African tears), the pivotal message is sanguine. AIDS *can* be overcome (abstinence one solution); so too the curse of alcoholism, gender inequalities, and rural despondency. As to complaints about Africa's economic plight, "Dangerous Inertia" calls them "the mumblings / of a man in his sleep" and rejects the culture of dependency.

Chihota, then, shares the no-nonsense optimism of his compatriot poet Freedom Nyamubaya. He urges wholesome morality on the young. Pedagogic flair also drives him to fire their literary interests and even to expand their vocabulary. Words like "shadufs," "loquat," "remotont," "sussurations," "primogeniture," and "plasmolysed," which the watchful Tichapondwa might

have red-inked, will certainly send students scurrying for their dictionaries.

Chimedza, Albert (b. 1955). Zimbabwean poet. Born in Harare, he left the country when the Rhodesian Front's 1965 Unilateral Declaration of Independence triggered the Liberation War. He was thus largely educated in Zambia, when that country was a frontline state struggling against Rhodesia and apartheid South Africa. In 1980, with independence won, he joined the Zimbabwe Broadcasting Company as a television producer and director. He was later a public relations officer for Anglo-American before joining the film industry. Unlike the withdrawn Hopewell Seyasaya, with whom he wrote the anthology *Counterpoint* (1984), Chimedza is boldly outspoken. Impatience with literary orthodoxy makes him very much the Taban Lo Liyong of Central Africa. And, like Liyong, who whimsically called his first book *The Last Word*, Chimedza titles his debut work in *Counterpoint Goodbye Scallywag (. . . and all the rest of you)*. His closing lines end a career only just begun:

I am the jagged edge of a broken
     bourbon glass
I won't mince my words
A spade is a spade and the truth the
     truth
That is all
I cleaned my slate and it's time to go
That is all.

The text's enigmatic epigraph seems to reveal a painful sense of class division:

You de kid in de 'ouse
At de top o' de 'ill
An' us is de kids in de 'uts
Surroundin' an' always below.

Chimedza told Flora Veit-Wild that his years abroad freed him from Rhodesian insularities. However, though admiring Ghana's Ayi Kwei Armah and Ama Ata Aidoo, Nigeria's Okigbo and Okara, and Cameroon's Oyono, he says that "music, lyrics influenced me generally more than any particular writing." And, in a species of literary sacrilege, he disparages East Africa's Okot p'Bitek, saying young Africans like him have moved on from Okot's kind of verse. Important instead were Bob Dylan, Pink Floyd, and Frank Zappa, "who all combined music and poetry in search of a new consciousness." The result is jaunty verse, stylistic whimsy, and a modernist freedom. He can range widely, speak fearlessly, and capture the crackle of throwaway comment.

His return home in 1980 brought disillusion: a glimpsed chasm between political image and reality, materialism among the black commercial elite, and hypocrisy across the civil service. Expecting utopian change, he found pragmatic self-interest but no socialist revolution. After all, he says bitterly, like people anywhere, "the average black man in Zimbabwe just wants a house, a car and to be promoted quickly."

Hence a verse acidly critical of bourgeois life, Christianity, and Western education's destruction of human community. But the venom finds self-direction too:

Am I the scallywag
Slinking along the wall
Or the creep
Slithering in the goo? . . .
I'm the sulking sullen voice
Misguidedly quietened but knowing
   the bleeding truth.

The fruits of the Liberation War he lists with disgust:

We balance that delicate freedom
In champagne glasses as we strut
   around
Hands in our pockets

Wine very definitely in our heads
And very vile vermin in our mouths
As we make our names out of very
   real victories
And losses that cost good lives
While we were saving our own.

At times a Prufrockian voice breaks in:

I shall ride a camel the wrong way
   round
I shall look at my watch as I traverse
   the desert sands
I shall approach an oasis and then
   drink palm wine
After which I shall bury my head in
   a sand dune.

Chimedza's stimulating contribution to *Counterpoint* is enough to make readers regret his exchanging pen for camera.

Further reading: Flora Veit-Wild, *Patterns of Poetry in Zimbabwe* (Gweru, 1988).

Chimombo, Steve (b. 1945). Malawian poet, novelist, short-story writer, and dramatist. Born in Zomba, he attended Zomba Catholic Secondary School, the University of Malawi (his early work appeared in its Writers' Workshop), the Universities of Leeds and Wales and, finally, Columbia, where he took a doctorate. He retired from the University of Malawi's chair of English in 2002. His country's most prolific writer, he created from the oral heritage a mythic framework within which he could shape an ironic response to life under Banda's tyranny. He wrote Malawi's first full-length play, *The Rainmaker* (1978), and sequels *The Harvests* and *The Locusts*. A Chichewa-language play, *Wachiona Ndani?*, appeared in 1983, and a short-story collection, *Flight of the Python*, in 1985. Other work includes children's books featuring the animal folk hero Kalulu, the nation's first *Directory of Writing*, and *Wasi Writer*, a journal for aspiring authors. His first anthology, *Napolo Poems* (1987), was followed by a novella, *The Basket Girl* (1990), a retold tale, *Child of Clay* (1993), and an epic poem, *Napolo and the Python* (1994). *Breaking the Beadstrings* (1995) preceded *The 'Vipya' Poem* (1996), *Epic of the Forest Creatures* (2005), and *The Hyena Wears Darkness* (2006).

Chimombo's play *The Rainmaker*, dramatizing the life and early death of M'bona, a Christlike figure hunted down by enemies seeking his key vulnerability, became a classic virtually overnight. As with the poetry, Chimombo uses traditional cultural material, in this case ancient M'bona legends and surviving M'bona cult practice. The play appeared in 1975 soon after a drama conference at which Matthew Schoffeleers, a leading authority on Central African anthropology, highlighted the Nyau cult's protodramatic features—rather as Molly Mahood had done with East Africa's Agikuyu and Nyakyusa dances in the 1960s. He urged their use for creating a distinctively modern Malawian theater. Arising from hunting rituals, and undergoing significant change during nineteenth-century warfare between the Chewa and Ngoni, Nyau performances last for several days and follow a clear cyclical pattern. As with equivalents in East, West, and South Africa, they have absorbed some Christian influences and work in both tragic and comic modes. Nyau, Schoffeleers argues, "is a genuine form of theatre and since most genuinely creative work is rooted in the culture and the past, we have a duty to take up Nyau where it [is] uncorrupted and develop it from there." Chimombo's play seemed an inspired response to this call. This is powerful poetic drama, strong on pity and suspense, its resonances sometimes elusive, but its overall impact heavy and menacing. It uses a chorus of spirits from the past called the Matsano who are given their own memorable verse:

Fractured elongations of circles
Ride the ripples of the pool
And multiply in the crest
Only to die on the mossy banks
Of oblivion.

Chimombo's verse has won BBC and Penguin awards. Before the *Napolo* collection (nominated for the 1987 Commonwealth Poetry Prize), it had featured in anthologies and in such journals as *Odi*, *The Malahat Review*, and *The London Magazine*. His lines from "Chaosis," heard in the early 1970s at the Writers' Workshop, announced a bold new talent fusing concrete and abstract experience to foreshadow the psychological mode he was about to create:

atomized elongations reveal
    skeletons
smuggling skullfulls of teeth
    crawling
to gnaw at an insulated mind
traversing the same bloodied
    pathways
that lead to the walls where
    watchdogs
prowl and snap at betrayed shadows.

Thus began Chimombo's defense against the Banda terror that scarred Malawi's first thirty years of independence. Though avoiding the humiliation of physical detention suffered by his contemporaries, his was a psychological prison of relentless rumor, threat, and nightmare. Driven to inner life poetics, he created a second-order mythic world within which to interrogate the Banda phenomenon. Security would lie in blending local lore with modernist fluidity (Eliot was an acknowledged mentor), and adding irony for indirection and ambiguity. Banda emerged as Napolo, a multivalent figure dominating Chimombo's best verse as much as Ogun dominates Soyinka's, and described in the *Napolo Poems* preface as "the mythical subterranean serpent residing under mountains and associated with landslides, earthquakes, and floods." Napolo's cyclical visitations are replete with paradox, his predilections both insanely destructive and creative. Visits during drought will bring rain on the one hand and slaughter on the other.

"Beggar Woman" symbolically sketches Napolo's misdemeanors. The woman mourns a life of ceaseless misery and can only anticipate its end:

> And will the lice
> having intimations of my death flee
>   from my body
> like rats abandon a sinking ship
> or fleas a dying hedgehog?

Given her situation in history, the creatures sucking her blood are black and white:

> The black ones claim my head,
> The light-skinned ones my body.
> The glinting patches, the bloody
>   splotches,
> The skeletons are all signs of their
>   progress.

She rages with incomprehension. Why should she be victimized and not the rich and powerful? Yet she has struggled:

> I have peeled, scraped, and wiped off
> Blotched carcasses, mangled corpses,
> Raged at the giant blobs of blood,
> The smear of lice juice on black skin.

"Four Ways of Dying," a verse colloquy, employs beast fable and allegory. Because only martyrdom can destroy Napolo, a call goes out for volunteers. (This is nicely ironic: Malawian independence having arisen from martyrs' blood, a second dawn seems mooted.) Responses from Crab, Mole, Chameleon, and Kalilombe reflect the nation's disparate reaction. Crab, shell-protected and skilled at walking sideways and backward, is wondrously equipped for evasion. He will

> Avoid
> direct action on public matters,
> confrontation,
> commitment.

Chameleon, powerfully ambivalent folklorically, and implicated in creation, chooses camouflage for survival. He will only act when absolutely necessary:

> Until I have exhausted my wardrobe,
> Lost my dye to a transparent
>   nothingness,
> Free of reflection, true to my image,
> I'll match my colors with yours.

Far from embracing martyrdom, he will

> snake my tongue out to your fears,
> bare my teeth to puncture your
>   hopes,
> tread warily past your nightmares,
> curl my tail round your sanctuaries,
> clasp my pincer legs on your veins,
> to listen to your heartbeat.

Mole chooses subterranean evasion, a dreamer's life in a species of living death:

> Wormlike I build in the entrails of
>   the earth,
> fashion intricate passages and halls,
> tunnel utopias and underground
>   Edens,
> substitute surface with subterranean
>   vision,
> level upon level of meaning of
>   existence,
> to die in a catacomb of my own
>   making.

The hero is Kalilombe, possibly Chameleon under his vernacular name. He shares Napolo's dual nature, perhaps representing the human ego and id. Here he symbolizes creativity, artistic solitude, and fecundity, even martyrdom itself—recalling a major creation myth that has him falling from a tree and dying as he pours from his innards a stream of creatures that swim, fly, and walk, including man himself. He will die now in a supreme act of democratic sacrifice.

The Basket Girl began as a short story that eventually grew into a novella, allowing for a setting shift from Mandania (Malawi) to New York and a postmodern experiment with plural narrators. Wina is first the shy daughter of a Mandanian prostitute and later a solo mother in New York. She returns to Africa to marry Bona, the novella's second narrator, but not before an exercise contrasting American and African culture.

Like Mnthali's *Yoranivyoto* and much Zimbabwean work, *The Wrath of Napolo* dissects colonial and postcolonial history to rectify European historiography. It exploits historical event—the sinking of the lake steamer *Vipya* in 1946 with the loss of more than two hundred lives. A post-Banda document needing no camouflage, it is part history, part detective thriller, and part sociopolitical analysis. Revisiting the disaster illuminates colonial attitudes and exhumes the lives of forgotten village victims. The ship's owners stand accused of a cover-up and of threatening investigators' lives; the white captain is an incompetent who set sail in a storm; black lives were ignored to privilege white passenger safety. The story is well told, its censure evenhanded. Malawians themselves are vilified for accepting colonialism, their supine adoption of westernism, and what the novel calls a pervading mediocrity. Though Chimombo has a distinguished record of rooting modern art in tradition, as he does with his satirical verse account of postcolonial politics in *Epic of the Forest Creatures*, he can boldly censure traditional practice. *Breaking the Beadstrings*, blurbed as "the longest poem on women's liberation in the world," examines aspects of bead wearing

and tattooing that work against women's "self-love, self-respect, self-determination," while his novella *The Hyena Wears Darkness* pillories old practices that spread AIDS—in particular *kuchotsa fumbi*, which involves "the ritual deflowering" of girls at initiation ceremonies, and *kusudzula*, "the sexual cleansing of the widow or widower" by a dead spouse's relative.

Further reading: Martin Banham, ed., *A History of Theatre in Africa* (Cambridge, 2004); Anthony Nazombe, "The Role of Myth in the Poetry of Steve Chimombo," in *New Writing from Southern Africa*, ed. Emmanuel Ngara (London, 1996); Emmanuel Ngara, *Ideology and Form in African Poetry* (London, 1990); Alfred Msadala, *One Steve Chimombo* (Blantyre, 1996); Adrian Roscoe, *Uhuru's Fire: African Literature East to South* (London, 1977).

Chimsoro, Samuel (b. 1949). Zimbabwean poet and novelist. Born in Mrewa in Southern Rhodesia, but educated in East Africa, he is chief technician at Bulawayo's National University of Science and Technology. He joins a writing minority with a scientific background, working in Shona as well as English (he has written science fiction in the vernacular). His verse collection *Smoke and Flames* appeared in 1978 and captured colonial-period anger. His novel *Nothing Is Impossible* (1983) is admired for optimism during a time of political disenchantment. A vernacular verse collection, *Dama Rekutanga*, appeared in 1990.

Kadhani and Zimunya honored Chimsoro in *And Now the Poets Speak* (1981) by including fourteen entries by him—the most by any poet. Passionately committed, the verse is sometimes insufficiently realized, its imagery and meaning unclear. Chimsoro is at his best in a poem like "The Curfew Breakers," with its emphatic infinitives—"to talk in the sun," "to sweep the streets," "to turn to moonlight," "to sleep," "to wake up in the morning." Less compelling are poems such as "Home Coming" and "Take Heed," where imagery around the repeated word "Freedom" confuses with its mix of concrete and abstract ("Landscape of human rights / With blisters of tombs"). Similarly, in "Corrigenda," the lines "The murmuring majority / Tired of / Meaningful memoranda" and "The integral of inhumanity" do not sink anchors in the memory. Liberation euphoria, however, lets him begin "On Independence Day" with the refreshingly plain statement "We are now free to bear / Children rather than raise soldiers / Even if blood groups may differ." One might hope from Chimsoro a greater use of his scientific expertise as a source of poetic statement.

Chinodya, Shimmer (b. 1957). Zimbabwean novelist, short-story writer, and poet. Born in Gweru, he was educated at Goromonzi High School, the University of Zimbabwe, and the University of Iowa, where he took a master's degree in creative writing. His books include *Dew in the Morning* (1982), *Farai's Girls* (1984), *Harvest of Thorns* (1989), and *Can We Talk* (1998). Several poems appeared in T. O. McLoughlin's *New Writing in Rhodesia* (1976). Under the pen name B. Chirasa, he has written children's books, including *A Child of War* (1985) and *Tale of Tamari* (2004). He won the Commonwealth Writers' Prize for Africa in 1990 and from 1995 to 1997 was a distinguished visiting professor at New York's St. Lawrence University.

Dew in the Morning, published when Chinodya was only twenty-three, drew praise from Doris Lessing and announced the arrival of a serious writer, maturely unassertive, yet refusing to plough old furrows. While contemporaries foregrounded colonialism and struggle, Chinodya allowed these only background space, privileging instead rural life. Racialism, implicitly, is passé: the new imperative is the nation's heartbeat, which is rural and agrarian. City life may proceed textually in the margins.

Land recovery is dawning after colonial darkness—hence the title. The Mamambos reconnect with the soil after decades as townies—opening a farm in a remote community still steeped in tradition. Outsiders become insiders as they integrate into country life—even a skepticism about witchcraft yielding to honest doubt. In precolonial echo, in this autonomous domain the village headman apportions land with reference to neither white nor black authority.

Long a townie himself, Chinodya explores the complex texture of country life, but he will not romanticize rusticity. Cameo portraits candidly blend the contradictions of human personality. Urban solitude cannot match country collectiveness, but villages hardly offer nirvana. In lockstep with solidarity march envy, jealousy, poison, theft, promiscuity, financial irresponsibility, and the same alcoholism ravaging the towns. Furthermore, patriarchy rules this world untouched by Dr. Greer. Characters convince precisely because they can be at once industrious and ambitious, yet alcoholic, dishonest, and venal. Village scenes celebrate the communal diversity seen in the work of a painter like Malawi's George Chilinda, because people engage Chinodya more than ideology. Indeed he indulges a painter's relish for physical portrayal—bad teeth, rough skin, bandy legs, weepy eyes, tattered clothing. By contrast, the smart Mamambos are hybrid rustics; only mother is village-based, while father works in town to oversee the children's schooling.

Relationships—especially as they emerge in dialogue—are drawn sensitively. The fluctuating friendship between Godi and Jairos's daughter Lulu, with its delicate teasing on the one hand and Godi's hesitant urban ways on the other, are especially fine. So, too, the well-crafted dialogue between Godi's mother, paragon of wholesome values, and her worker Remoni. He is a picaresque figure whose easy accommodation of domestic correctness and titanic work rates, alongside drunkenness, sexual profligacy, and vaulting arrogance, makes him seriously menacing.

With the Mamambo children, bred to revere education and now being taught never again to abandon the land, two parts of Chinodya's vision fall into place.

Sexual maturation, a thematic strand of *Dew*, becomes central in *Farai's Girls*, described by Greenwell Matsika as a bildungsroman. Schoolboy Farai, expelled for marching against conscription, sees peers leaving for war, but opts for study and libido. A list of girls takes center stage. But maturing Farai feels heartless, his women mere trophies unable to fill the vacuum: he needs "an anchor to his drifting soul." When Vongai, fellow churchgoer, complains that, like the others, she is only serving her time, his moral position clarifies and they reunite on Independence Day—the young man now ready for freedom's responsibilities. He can admit too that he is celebrating victory in a war where, ironically, the girls got nearer the front than he did.

The eleven short stories in *Can We Talk* mark further growth—perhaps propelled by Iowa Workshop exposure. Chinodya can beam his skills more widely. He shifts styles to suit the young, as in "Hoffman Street," the middle-aged married, as in "Can We Talk," the sensitive adolescent, as in "Going to See Mr B.V," Zimbabwean whites as well as blacks, as in "Among the Dead," and the North American world as in "Snow." Concisely disciplined, this last piece offers a brio alliterative performance with one-word impressions, as in "French-fries, fritters, frankfurters, fish, fillet, farina, falafels, figs, fennel, flax, fanta, fruitbread." Also, as a part-time poet, he happily stitches verse into prose in "Can We Talk."

Two stories deserve special mention. "Among the Dead" links to the opening of *Farai's Girls*. It probes psychological nuance across the racial divide, surface narrative proceeding over an undercurrent of growth—of nation toward freedom, of student toward university and authorship, of teacher toward retirement and death. Chinodya reaches beyond politics and prejudice. Reconciliation will move Zimbabwe from racist colonialism into a wholesome independence. The story explores two solitudes, of oppressed and oppressor.

The narrator, a lonely schoolboy with a novel in draft, meets a supportive white teacher. "Mission teachers in those days," says the text, "were regarded as liberals" and Melbury, a solitary layman among clerics, having long dreamed of independence, is now, as it dawns, ending his career. A moment of becoming, of moral growth and of collapsing stereotype, occurs when the narrator says: "I had never thought the whites could be lonely. In fact I had never thought about them at all, except as our oppressors." Later, a published author, he meets the retired Melbury, who is visiting from London, hands him his novel, and receives fulsome praise. Disturbed that a white man who taught him for only one term could affect him so, he wants to reply, but a chaotic life prevents him.

The title story, "Can We Talk"—not a question—is the collection's longest. Its close climaxes Chinodya's growth with an explosive blend of Swiftian misanthropy and lists ("I hate men and women," "I need friends. I hate friends"), modernist fluidity, postmodern oxymoron, ironic juggling with form and narrative, existential angst and ennui, postcolonial disillusion, and midlife marital cynicism. Partly the confessional hate dialogue of a middle-aged couple, she is a "successful" churchgoing mother and career woman, he, an artist, "totally amoral. Selfish. Irresponsible." Paragraphs repeatedly begin with "I hate," followed by a litany of lamentation.

Yet all is not as it seems. The male speaker is the overall narrator, despite the woman seeming to speak on her own account. His repeated complaint that the world is "full of lonely unspeaking couples" who miss the catharsis of talk ("We were both raised on the culture of not talking") is made ironic by his overwhelming discourse dominance. But this *is* therapeutic, he says, because it moves toward confessed sin, reconciliation, and healing. It also reveals that his alcohol abuse (that pervasive motif of Central African literature) arises from the loneliness of a silent marriage whose mistaken cure is flight to fellow drinkers with the same problem.

Paradoxically—oxymoron flourishes here—all this talk, and talk about talk, happens in writing, as therapeutic, the narrator tells his wife, as having sex with her. Writing the story has let him "switch out" of his life for weeks. The narrating husband is a writer himself. And he admits to an affair with one Alice precisely because "She had read my books . . . and could say, 'Why did Godi or Farai or Benjamin do this on page so-and-so?'"—references of course to Chinodya's own novels. Further self-reference occurs when, in a poem hymning early married arcadia, he yearns "For my dew in the morning days / For my Hoffman Street days."

Amid gloom reminiscent of his contemporary Marechera, we hear meanwhile that life is full of fatigue, AIDS, bad government, betrayed political vision, abused tradition. A favorite bar stands next to the main cemetery:

We are dying like flies. But we live on, clinging to the frayed edges of our lives with our pathetic claws. We live on, pretending things are OK. We live on, hiding our despair behind tired smiles.

It is all a far cry from Farai's youthful optimism, awakening sexuality, and dreams of authorship.

Further reading: Rosemary Moyana, "Literature and Liberation . . . the Second Phase: Shimmer Chinodya's *Harvest of Thorns*," in *New Writing from Southern Africa*, ed. Emmanuel Ngara (London, 1996); Rino Zhuwarara, *Introduction to Zimbabwean Literature in English* (Harare, 2001); Musaemura Zimunya, *Those Years of Drought and Hunger* (Gweru, 1982); Greenwell Matsika, "Shimmer Chinodya," in *The Routledge Encyclopaedia of Post-Colonial Literatures in English*, ed. Eugene Benson and L. C. Connolly (London, 2005).

Chipamaunga, Edmund (b. 1938). Zimbabwean novelist. He was born in Chivhu. After education at Daramombe Primary, St. Mary's Secondary School, St. Augustine's High School, and the University of Rhodesia, he held headmasterships and at independence was appointed Zimbabwe's Ambassador Extraordinary and Plenipotentiary to the United States and Kenya. There are two novels, *A Fighter for Freedom* (1983) and *Chains of Freedom* (1997), the first featuring the bush war and the second postcolonial disenchantment.

A single family symbolizes the dysfunction colonialism inflicted on ancestral Zimbabwe. Husband and father Gari is a headmaster in whom colonial education has killed any capacity to love and replaced it with arrogance and individualism ("His education has assisted him in his search for self-destruction and self disrespect," "a mind taken over by foreign elements"). Brought low by chasing false gods, he is redeemed by love springing from tradition. The struggle to repair his broken family parallels the war fought to repair the broken nation as a whole. The two are linked when Gari's hated son Tinashe learns traditional humanism from his Uncle Roro and becomes a heroic leader in the Liberation War. If the book is about the Second Chimurenga, it is also about its causes within the complex pathology of colonial society: its arrogance, prejudice, stupendous parochialism, and a fatal refusal to share, especially where land is concerned. But the book urges optimism and tolerance of the other. Colonialism has not totally extinguished the fire of traditional life. It lives on in the social beauty of Uncle Roro's village community, which transforms young Tinashe and where chauvinism and patriarchy are absent. Expressing this humanity are whites like Farmer George, whose land is worked on a shared basis. This farm and Roro's village are part ashram and part rehabilitation center for Rhodesia's sick society. Gari learns to love his wife and son and a shift from an abiding obsession with Tennysonian verse to local black poetry signals his transformation. The struggle's basic motivation is conversion rather than killing.

The novel's fundamental seriousness is sometimes undermined by strained credulity and excessive detail. But the book usefully recalls the role of freedom songs and spirit medium activity in the prosecution of the war and how Ian Smith's absurd Unilateral Declaration of Independence in 1965 intensified a freedom struggle that had already begun in 1962. An engaging point arises when Farmer George, an Irish Catholic, suggests that colonial rule is very Protestant and that Irish Catholics will have a natural affinity for Africans facing an old foe of the Irish—a notion not entirely new across the continent.

Chipasula, Frank (b. 1949). Malawian poet. Born in Luanshya, Zambia, he attended Malosa Anglican Secondary School, Malawi, whose training he cherished. As a University of Malawi undergraduate, he achieved distinction as the first Malawian to have a verse collection published, *Visions and Reflections* (1972). It appeared in Zambia, however, where he had fled during intensifying government oppression of northern Malawians, including his own family. Zambia produced rapid literary and sociopolitical growth. Taking a principled stand against apartheid South Africa and white Rhodesia, it was a hotbed of frontline activity, including bombing, assassinations, intrigue, and world media attention. After graduate work at Yale and Brown, Chipasula currently teaches black studies at the University of Nebraska. *Visions and Reflections* was followed by *O Earth, Wait for Me* (1984), an edited volume, *When My Brothers Come Home: Poems from Central and Southern Africa* (1985), *Nightwatcher, Nightsong* (1986), *Whispers in the Wings* (1991), and *The Heinemann Book of African Women's Poetry* (1995), edited with his wife Stella.

Youthful idealism and candor inform *Reflections*. It exudes a salad-days mood of early independence with recollections of a defeated colonialism, the excitement of literary exposure, and a passionate desire to do something noble for his country ("Let's all help acquire / Freedom for all Africa! / Brother and sister, freedom's / our birthright!"). This abruptly yields, however, to the stridently tragic tones in *Nightwatcher, Nightsong*. Anthony Nazombe explained to Bernth Lindfors that Chipasula had by now come under the influence of African American and South American writers. Hence the grating key shift between, say, these lines from *Reflections*:

Straw is used for weaving
Hats, mats and baskets,
Simple but beautiful.
African Art, simple Art!
Wonderful Art!

and these from "Dusk" in *Nightwatcher,*
where the horrors of Banda's jails receive
full-throated vent:

> Nightwatcher:
> Fast falls the night unfurling its vile
>   veil
> Showering its soot into our eyes
>   plunging us into deep darkness
> Extinguishing the fiery flame of the
>   spent sun
> The sharp shrilling shrieks of the
>   first detainees
> Herded into dark catacombs of
>   Mikuyu and Chingwe's hole
> Drown in the maenadic frenzy of the
>   ululating chorus bitches
> . . .
> Then death goes hunting through
>   men's huts with sharp knives.

Banda's rule now receives sustained
onslaught—its materialist order devoid of
spiritual light, conspicuous consumption,
cruelty toward a poor and gentle people, its
fostering of human greed, its sexual license
among the elite, and cynical waste of ur-
gently needed talent. At its best, the verse
transmutes horrific realism into the stuff of
fantasy and nightmare. Macabre imagery
pictures Banda descending from a "lofty
throne of polished bones," bathing in hu-
man blood, drunk from the "bitter cham-
pagne of tears from battered babies," and
drinking from "a chalice of polished hu-
man skulls." Beloved Malawi has become
"This ceased engine abandoned at the road-
side of history . . . this discarded peanut
shell, its oily seed chewed by others." But
Chipasula can also summon optimism and
energy to contemplate a new dawn. The
agents of good will awake. Indeed,

> The old year has folded his mats and
>   gone limping away
> Sulking into the thickets of dark-
>   ness, graying to the skin.

Malawi's lake will rise and dance, the
poet will bathe in it, a "bloody violent light"
will pour forth, and "delayed day" will
shout its "first victory cry rending the
shrouded sky."

One waits to see how Chipasula's verse—
favorably reviewed in *Time*, honored in
Adewale Maja-Pearce's 1991 collection *New
Poetry from Africa* (his twelve poems out-
numbering even Nobel laureate Wole Soy-
inka's), and now promoting the cause of
Africa's women poets—responds to the
post-Banda years and the new democratic
order.

Further reading: Anthony Nazombe,
"Poetry and Liberation in Central and
Southern Africa," in *Literature, Language
and the Nation*, ed. Emmanuel Ngara and
Andrew Morrison (Harare, 1989), 50–64;
Adrian Roscoe and Mpalive-Hangson
Msiska, *The Quiet Chameleon: Modern Po-
etry from Central Africa* (London, 1992);
Adrian Roscoe, *Uhuru's Fire: African Liter-
ature East to South* (London, 1977).

Chipembere, Henry Blasius Masauko
(1930–1975). Malawian politician and biog-
rapher. Born at a mission station near Nk-
hotakota, where his father served as an
Anglican priest, he led a nationalist group
that fought to destroy the white-imposed
Central African Federation and secure
Nyasaland's independence. His colleagues
included Kanyama Chiume, Orton and
Vera Chirwa, Rose Chibambo, and Dun-
duzu Kaluli Chisiza. Inspired by Booker T.
Washington and Marcus Garvey, among
others, though lacking a figurehead of Ke-
nyatta's or Nkrumah's stature, they brought
home Hastings Banda, using his lofty edu-
cation and Baptist-style oratory to electri-
fying effect. But by the time Nyasaland
became independent Malawi in 1964, Ban-
da's despotic instincts had emerged. Disil-
lusioned democrats left his first cabinet, and
in 1965 a failed rebellion by Chipembere

caused him to flee into Tanzania. Later, in the United States (his earlier education having taken him to Nyasaland's Blantyre Secondary School, Rhodesia's Goromonzi High School, and South Africa's Fort Hare University College), he began a master's program in political science at UCLA. Three years' teaching in Tanzania preceded return to America for doctoral studies, an assistant professorship in history at California State University, and initial work on a memoir. Robert Rotberg edited the unfinished manuscript and arranged its publication in 2001 as *Hero of the Nation: Chipembere of Malawi, an Autobiography.* The text carries illuminating comment on the birth of Nyasaland nationalism, resentment of the Central African Federation, British colonial arrogance, early signs of Banda's quirkiness, and Nyasaland's marginalized Muslim community.

Further reading: Robert I. Rotberg, *The Rise of Nationalism in Central Africa: The Making of Malawi and Zambia, 1873–1964* (Cambridge, Mass., 1965).

Chisiza, Du, Jr. (1963–1999). Malawian dramatist. Born in Karonga, he held a degree in acting from the Philadelphia College of Fine and Performing Arts. Author of four play collections—*Du Chisiza Jr's Classics* (1990), *Barefoot in the Heart and Other Plays* (1992), *Democracy Boulevard and Other Plays* (1998), and *De Summer Blow and Other Plays* (1998)—his emergence was sudden and his rise meteoric. Writer, actor, producer, director, composer, dancer, drummer, choreographer, stage designer, and makeup artist, he rose on a tide of opposition that finally ended Banda's thirty-year autocracy. With his Wakhumbata Ensemble Theatre, Malawi's first full-time professional drama group, he sought to accelerate political change and articulate it dramatically. English-medium drama, after such progenitors as Steve Chimombo,

Innocent Banda, Chris Kamlongera, David Kerr, James Gibbs, Mupa Shumba, and John Linstrum, had assumed a sunset glow, yielding place to vernacular theater. Chisiza created a second dawn—bold, dynamic, experimental. Like its Amakhosi counterpart in Zimbabwe, his company reenergized the form, soon staging more than forty productions and training a hundred and fifty actors.

Chisiza, then, signposted a post-Banda literary direction. His *Papa's Empire* contemptuously dismisses the former president as part of a relentless smashing of old taboos on communication; a systematic exercise in iconoclasm at once entertaining, deconstructively analytical, and didactically therapeutic. Brash youth insolently demystifies aged iconic bogeyman, revealing hidden levers and pulleys, and proving ultimate nakedness. If Banda allowed talk about nothing, Chisiza insists on talk about everything. And with calculated shocking effect. This is theater for national rehabilitation, a prescription part psychodrama, part exorcism, and part regression therapy. Each play brandishes for scorn key components of Banda's oppression, addressing the psychic nuances of audiences listening with a sense of sacrilege as taboo subjects are kicked airily around the stage. In play after play—*Misidi Burning, Papa's Empire, Storm on Litada, Dianda and the Priest, Pumashakile, Check It Out*—Chisiza confronts past traumas (at one level seeking to get history right), addresses a changing present, and plans a path to national health.

The plays carry their cargo lightly, avoid thematic or emotional overload, and codeswitch into Chichewa and Chitumbuka where necessary, their scoffing outspokenness conjuring a powerful sense of Banda's ghost cringing in the wings.

Where Malawian literature had been a site of enforced caution and camouflage—witness Jack Mapanje's favorite chameleon metaphor—Chisiza, a true child of American confidence, is all blunt realism. Indirection and silence are now taboo. Names can be named. Banda's old enemies, like Chipembere, Dunduza Chisiza, Bwanausi, Chirwa, Kanyame and Chiume, can be invoked and praised. Landmarks in Banda's decline can be dramatically reenacted. The Catholic hierarchy's pastoral letter, with its punishing attack on governmental abuse, is one. The brutal murder of Banda's colleagues Sangala, Matenje, Gadama, and Chiwanga, falsely described as dying in a road accident, is another.

But Chisiza has satiric targets beyond Banda. Materialist clerics, patriarchy and incest, gender inequity, drugs (and ministerial profits from them), tall-poppy prejudice ("If you're successful it's a crime"), jealousy, sexual irresponsibility around AIDS, tribal and regional factionalism threatening the new multiparty democracy—they all come into his sights.

Chisiza liked character conflict, play within play, a clipped American register ("she doesn't dig you," "yeah . . . a guy from Burundi," "check it out," "you are one hell of a brother"), and fun with assonance and double consonance ("living and bountiful loving," "index" and "appendix," "lowly and slowly," "no bumps and no humps"). Meanwhile, Malawi's newly prolific media (*Democracy Boulevard* mentions the two solitary papers of Banda's time) registered the Chisiza phenomenon, their effusions adorning his volume's jackets: "Theatre Genius," "Theatre Maestro," "Multi-Talented Theatre Mega-Star," "Stage Artist par excellence," "Theatre Wizard." In the *Independent*, the writer Mike Kamwendo concluded, "He is a culture, a phenomenon, Malawi's first true superstar." Amid cyclical drought and hunger, Malawi had something to celebrate as its literature underwent revitalization. Chisiza's tragically early death struck a serious blow at Malawian theater arts.

Further reading: Martin Banham, ed., *A History of Theatre in Africa* (Cambridge, 2004); Alfred Msadala, *Destined For Great Things* (Blantyre, 1999); the review pages of the following Malawian publications: *The Nation*, *The Saturday Nation*, *The Democrat*, *The Weekly Chronicle*, *The Weekly News*, *The Mirror*, *Scope*, *The Enquirer*, *The Business Telegraph*, *The Star*, *Malawi News*, *Quest*, *The Independent*.

Chiume, W. Kanyama (b. 1929). Malawian novelist and politician. Born in colonial Nyasaland and educated in South Africa and Uganda, he rose to prominence in the 1950s when opposing the white-imposed Central African Federation. With young activists Chipembere, Chisiza, and Chirwa, he organized African political structures (becoming publicity secretary to the Nyasaland African Congress and a member of the Federation's Legislative Council of Nyasaland) before inviting home Banda to spearhead the drive for secession from the Federation and eventual independence. With colleagues, he suffered the wrath of an abruptly transformed Banda and fled the country soon after independence. In exile for some thirty years (his name damned in Banda's every public speech), he returned in the 1990s to help vote out his old friend and foe. *Kwacha: An Autobiography* was published in Kenya in 1975 and his novel *The African Deluge* in 1978.

An earlier work, *Nyasaland Speaks: An Appeal to the British People*, was published by the Union of Democratic Control in 1959, when Chiume had fled to London during a state of emergency and detention of activists, including Banda himself. The document gave Britons a succinct history of their colony and an African conviction that the imposed Federation could only mean Nyasas sharing the servitude of blacks living under Southern Rhodesia's whites. Poignantly, the pamphlet sports a smiling picture of Banda and an 1866 quotation from John Bright on freedom and nonviolence.

Wanting *The African Deluge* to symbolize racial plight as it relates to slavery, Chiume uses a composite setting that blurs rather than clarifies. The appellations Inkosi and Bayettia, the fictitious land's name, suggests Zululand in South Africa. But there is enough West African reference ("dash," for example, whisky and brandy as slave payment) to unsettle this idea. Bayettia's ancient university hints at Timbuktu, though the book's coastal slave markets could lie either West or East. Nor does a shift of scene to Britain to capture slave trade politics help much. Perhaps the author's predicament was to blame. Banda's repression was at its height. The Cold War promised no early end to it. With South Africa's dreaded Bureau of State Security teaching Banda's Special Branch to assassinate opponents, Chiume's family was perpetually at risk. Also, watching fratricidal dissension within Rhodesia and South Africa, Chiume was perhaps urging continental solidarity (lack of which had initially allowed slavery to take hold), which emerges as the novel's central theme.

Hesitation disappears with the slave trade focus. Those complicit are European, Arabic, and Bayettian. Horrific detail of one particular group of slaves, sold by their fellows and led by Professor Zungaro, a teacher of dialectics at the national university, receives graphic treatment. A whiff of allegory arises, with Bayettia, its betrayals and inland geography, sounding unsurprisingly like the Malawi Chiume had left.

Brutality continues on America's plantations, the slaves' destination, where, except for the Quakers, Christianity receives a mauling. The Professor morally and politically guides his compatriots, whose decency before inhumanity converts a plantation owner's wife to their cause, symbolizing, presumably, the start of the long road to Selma, Martin Luther King Jr., and emancipation.

Chizeze, Zangaphee (b. ca. 1956; d. 1998?). Malawian poet whose early death adds tragically to a cohort of writers and intellectuals who lost their lives, directly or indirectly, through the tyranny of Banda. Educated at the University of Malawi, Chizeze belonged to a student generation whose enthusiasm sustained the University's Writers' Workshop in the 1970s and 1980s and who have since distinguished themselves in literature and scholarship.

Chizeze's cheerful brilliance flared within Banda's encircling gloom. When nonconformity was perilous, he was refreshingly maverick, articulate, amusing, and boldly opinionated in the way academics want students to be. He was unafraid to ask awkward questions—safe within Writers' Workshop discussion but risky among informers in public lecture halls. His healthy contempt for colonialism prefigured similar animus for its sequel. On his inevitable arrest by the Special Branch, he joined a swelling group of the nation's intelligentsia whom Banda locked away to rot.

Chizeze's undergraduate contemporary, the late Anthony Nazombe, before his own death in 2004, included several of his poems in *Operations and Tears: A New Anthology of Malawian Poetry*. "To Vince Johns" shows Chizeze thanking his West Indian law teacher for smuggling messages into Zomba's Mikuyu Detention Centre, whose proximity to the university Banda himself must have approved. These are messages that "arise from the abyss / of the past / into the mist of the future." They are much appreciated, but anyway there is no repining, no bewailing of an undeserved lot. The poet is typically jaunty, his incarceration merely investment in a better future:

MESSAGES
not of wailing
& cringing
& whimpering
messages
of the price of struggle
& the imminence of the inevitable
La Luta Continua

"On the Road to Blantyre" shows Chizeze, freed from detention, enjoying Malawi's landscape south of Zomba, with its "blue mountains," "circles of hills," and veils of afternoon rain. But a hillside gouged for granite and a view of Zomba's old hospital and prison recall darker concerns:

a crumbling hospital
of a colonial capital
stands
like an aged mourner
facing a state penitentiary.

"Referendum" is tonally more somber. It refers to the early 1990s plebiscite on multiparty democracy forced on Banda by a withdrawal of aid from international donors impatient for human rights reform. It foreshadows the Banda regime's fall, but laments that the awaited change has taken too long. Weariness shrouds both nation and poet. More reflective verse is now heard. Gone is the fear that stalked the land for thirty years, but there is "the anger / of a relentless drought / and the vengeance / of storms unchained." The poet's early brio has gone, and so has the people's. There is now

Only the endless toil
Of men too tired to rest
And the grief of millions
Too hungry to eat;

Chizeze's early death, like so many across Central and Southern Africa, cut short a talented life, prevented the full blossoming of a literary career, and deprived his young Malawi of much-needed intellectual and professional energy.

Further reading: "Zangaphee Chizeze and Edge Kanyongolo," *Index on Censorship* (1984), 42–43; Wisdom Kamkondo, "In Passing" and Zangaphee Chizeze: Some Upstarts in the SCR," *The Muse* 16.

Cripps, Arthur Shearly (1869–1952). Zimbabwean poet and novelist. Born in Tunbridge Wells, England, and educated at Charterhouse and Oxford, where he studied modern history, he is seen as Zimbabwe's first English-language writer of significance, as a progressive missionary, and as an astute analyst of Rhodes's colonial creation. Ordained in 1893, he went to Rhodesia in 1901 to work with the Society for the Propagation of the Gospel. If unable to reject empire in principle, he immediately pinpointed land theft as the nub of settler colonialism, tirelessly campaigning on land issues. And, while reviling other injustices, like the hut tax, forced labor, segregation, racism in secular and church life, settler greed, and "our barbed-wire Pass Law"—none discouraged by Rhodes's Chartered Company—he fostered the rise of African nationalism. Historically, he suggests how British imperialism, blending faith and commerce in its Elizabethan dawn, and then neglecting the former by noon, reunited these elements in the late afternoon. Meanwhile, during an exhausting clerical life, Cripps wrote profusely. There were eight novels: *The Brooding Earth: A Story of Mashonaland* (1911); *Bay-Tree Country: A Story of Mashonaland* (1913); *A Martyr's Servant: The Tale of John Kent, AD 1553–1563* (1915); *A Martyr's Heir: The Tale of John Kent, AD 1553–1563* (1916); *Africans All* (1928); *Chaminuka: The Man Whom God Taught* (1928); *Lion Man: An Easter Tale* 1928); and *Saint Perpetua: Martyr of Africa* (1928). Three sets of short stories were *Magic Casements* (1905); *Faery*

Lands Forlorn (1910); and *Cinderella in the South* (1918). Verse volumes were *Primavera* (1890); *Titania and Other Poems* (1900); *An Ode in Celebration of the Proposed Quadrupling of the Hut-Tax, in This Year of Grace and Dearth, 1903* (1903); *Lyra Evangelistica: Missionary Verses of Mashonaland* (1909); *Pilgrimage of Grace: Verses on a Mission* (1912); *Pilgrim's Joy: Verses* (1916); *Lake and War: African Land and Water Verses* (1917); *A Million Acres* (1918); *Judas Maccabeus* (1926); *Some Essex Verses* (1930); *Carols of Christmastide from Africa* (1935); and *Africa: Verses* (1939).

A priest of the lonely road and the wild places, where he loved to celebrate the liturgy, his physical life of journeying mirrored precisely the spirituality that gave his calling and writing their core, tone, and metaphoric framework. John the Baptist (he "appears" in his story "Locusts and Wild Honey") inspired his love of the wilderness, St. Francis his service to the poor, Tolstoy a faith to survive pain.

Providing an indispensable guide to Cripps, A. J. Chennells, G. R. Brown, and L. B. Rix discuss his writing's strengths and weaknesses. Intensification triumphs over development; diction can be stilted and archaic; British romantic imagery does injustice to the African landscape (Rix calls Keats "a seductive incubus"); idealizing Africa as Arcadia denies an African complexity; the pure Christian vision carries disruptive implications of which Cripps seems unaware; his supernaturalism often damages his realism; he hesitates, despite supporting African aspirations, to portray Africans themselves. On the other hand, Cripps is applauded for driving values and message through the barrier of received Oxonian discourse to state a common humanity at odds with crass settler racism and materialism. And if his ear was poor, his eye captured vividly Africa's landscapes, dawns, and dusks. Rix also reminds us that Cripps's work preserves "a

feature of the early days of Rhodesia too often forgotten—the liberal idealism that mingled with, and actively tried to soften, the harsh impact of the Occupation. Cripps is the father not only of Rhodesian verse, but of a long tradition of radical moral opposition to the new white-dominated society." One might add that, aware perhaps of colonial romanticism's sirens, Cripps's debt to a Keats or Arnold, because so candid, prevents them seeming to sweat hidden behind the msasa tree. As for the African portrayal hesitation (he tries hard with the prophet Chaminuka), this might spring from either the humility of accepted limitation or contempt for the common settler boast, "I really know the African."

Acknowledged literary allegiances are common. Keats, "our singing shepherd," is important (hence an Africanized prose version of "The Eve of St Agnes" and a sonnet "On Keats's Nile Sonnet"). Shelley and Tennyson are also present, with an occasional hint of Herbert and Theocritus. There is even mention of Burke and Mill, and he had apparently read Olive Schreiner. Unsurprisingly, Arnold's "Scholar Gipsy," with its hymnal of rural Oxfordshire, powerfully infects him: indeed, his alma mater and her shaping influence remained a lifelong obsession—a pole at one end of a magnet pulling him either home or to Africa. In such stories as "The Open Way," "A Change of Colour" (where a white man adopts African disguise to understand oppression), "The Scales of Passion: A Friend's Story," "Fuel of Fire," "The Place of Pilgrimage," Man's Airy Notions," all narrated in a relaxed manner reminiscent of the South African writer H. E. Bosman, the central characters are all Oxonian, often painters, writers, and sculptors coming into a settler society that Cripps calls philistine.

Despite a secure status, Cripps remains in some ways hard to define. A Christian pilgrim in the received sense, he lacks the bleak austerity of a Bunyan. With a gift for metaphor and symbolism, he does not reach Blakeian mystical heights. He learns from Keats's sensibility, yet lacks his negative capability. His rhapsodic flights over God's creation might bracket him with Teilhard de Chardin, but without the science. Hopkins provides an interesting comparison. The Jesuit poet and Cripps were both exiled Oxonians eternally enamored of their alma mater; both were ascetic and solitary from a High Anglican background and worshipful of God in nature. And both imitated Keats. It is tempting to rearrange history and imagine Hopkins as Cripps's missionary neighbor (the early Jesuit presence in Rhodesia was seminal) also hymning Africa's landscapes and people, and perhaps feeling happier far than in his Dublin exile.

Meanwhile, N. H. Brettell, often called Cripps's successor, wrote his generous "Threnody in Spring" as a memorial to him. Its vernal imagery stresses the new growth, earthly and spiritual, that the devoted priest and poet of Mashonaland had achieved:

> You chose the time well to die:
> Our air still tingles with the latest
>   frost;
> Now, where the dead leaf falls, the
>   new blade shoots,
> With furtive fingering to the hidden
>   springs
> To bring life bravely up.
> . . .
> Among the gaunt stones of your
>   lonely home
> See, the first frail msasa shakes its
>   fronds
> In shreds of tender hope.

Further reading: G. R. Brown, A. J. Chennells, and L. B. Rix, *Arthur Shearly Cripps: A Selection of His Prose and Verse* (Gwelo, 1976); D. Jenkins, *They Led the Way in Central Africa* (London, 1967); D. V. Steere, *God's Irregular: Arthur Shearly Cripps, a Rhodesian Epic* (London, 1973).

Dangarembga, Tsitsi (b. 1959). Zimbabwean novelist and short-story writer. Born at Mutoko, in the Eastern Highlands, she left for Britain at the age of two, returning home at eight when Ian Smith's Unilateral Declaration of Independence had dramatically increased international tensions. She completed her secondary education—like one of her protagonists—at a convent mainly for whites. This was sufficiently rigorous to ensure admission to Cambridge in 1977 to study medicine, but the university's racism (Wole Soyinka had also felt it) and anxieties about the Liberation War brought her home in 1980. At the national university, she now studied psychology, wrote short stories and a play, *She No Longer Weeps*, and then left to study film in Berlin. She is best known for her novel *Nervous Conditions* (1988), rejected by Zimbabwean publishers; two films, *Everyone's Child* (1996) and *Neria* (on AIDS and legal injustice respectively); and a short story, "The Letter" (1990).

Seen as a classic to match Chinua Achebe's *Things Fall Apart*, by 2002 *Nervous Conditions* had already stimulated wide admiration. Not, one suspects, because she was a pioneering black Central African woman novelist, nor that its famous opening ("I was not sorry when my brother died") heralded an outspoken feminism complete with breakdown and anorexia; still less that it explored the dilemmas attendant on living in and between two worlds, the poverty-to-privilege miracles of modern education, and similar tropes.

Instead, sheer literary power drew readers to see how, relentlessly, female ambition meets the subtly twinned pressures of Western education and iron-fisted patriarchy. The social and psychological pain of Rhodesian colonialism found its ideal diagnostician in Dangarembga. A darting intelligence, trained in psychology and medicine, marks the text's every chapter, probing and lancing, testing and prescribing, ordering and balancing, tactfully omitting and excluding, mingling the tragic and comic, the peasant and bourgeois. Dangarembga's spacious prose allows pauses, reflection, second thoughts, and deftly inserted qualifiers. Tambudzai, the narrator, explores inner and outer worlds, her own and those of others, lighting on paradox and irony that stir life deep in the narrative structures. Always alert, always exquisitely sensitive, she pulls us on, with the pronominal "you" a constant marker for self-persuasive narrative and reader-directed rhetoric.

Tambu's candor, her sense of sin and constant pleas of *mea culpa*, create a text at once honest and intensely cerebral. Her case-arguing and storytelling emerge in abundant verbs of reflection and ratiocination: think, talk over, perceive, analyze, reason, discuss, examine, realize, discuss matters rationally, define a position, delimit an issue, look into, draw conclusions, consider the consequences, explain, go over the facts, stop and consider, set one's mind on, think your way out.... The novel becomes a vortex of relentless rationalizing.

If education is a conventional theme, its treatment is not. Schooling dreams were especially heady in Southern Rhodesia, where, as in Kenya and South Africa, white schools possessed a material splendor scarcely imaginable to black students. Their ivied buildings, manicured grounds, pools, golf courses, rifle ranges, fine libraries, and facilities for tennis, squash, soccer, rugby, fives, and hockey mesmerized impoverished blacks like Tambu. (In 1968, University College Nairobi's library housed fewer volumes than that of the nearby Prince of Wales School.) Dangarembga captures a dream the more intoxicating because such bastions, now privileging a handful of blacks such as Tambu, loomed as spoils of victory in the Liberation War.

Educational access was more open for boys than girls, and this fact provides the plot's springs and its powerful opening. But access brings problems too complex even for Tambu's relentless analysis. There is constant talk of cultural hybridity and identity. Tambu begins to sympathize with her mother's view that education (this "Englishness") is murdering her children. In a compelling breakdown scene, her educated cousin Nyasha screams, "They've trapped us. They've trapped us." Whites had long denied blacks a good education. But when education is finally achieved, it seems more poisoned chalice than golden fleece—rather as Senghor and Césaire found French assimilation in the 1930s.

Further reading: Flora Veit-Wild, "Women Write About the Things That Move Them: A Conversation with Tsitsi Dangarembga," in *Moving Beyond Boundaries*, ed. Carole Boyce Davies (New York, 1995), 27–31; Anthony Chennells, "Authorizing Women, Women's Authoring: Tsitsi Dangarembga's *Nervous Conditions*," in *New Writing from Southern Africa*, ed. Emmanuel Ngara (London, 1996); Liz Gunner, "Tsitsi Dangarembga," in *Encyclopaedia of Post-Colonial Literatures in English*, ed. Eugene Benson and L. W. Connolly (London, 2001), 329; Jacqueline Bardolph, "The Tears of Childhood of Tsitsi Dangarembga," *Commonwealth Essays and Studies* 13, vol. 1 (1990): 37–47; Rino Zhuwarara, *Introduction to Zimbabwean Literature in English* (Harare, 2001); Charles Sugnet, "*Nervous Conditions*: Dangarembga's Feminist Reinvention of Fanon," in *The Politics of (M)Othering: Womanhood, Identity, and Resistance in African Literature*, ed. Obioma Nnameka (London,

1997), 33–49; Sally McWilliams, "Tsitsi Dangarembga's *Nervous Conditions*: At the Crossroads of Feminism and Post-Colonialism," *World Literatures Written in English* 31, no. 1 (1991): 103–112.

Diki, Basil (b. 1971). Zimbabwean playwright. Born in Kadoma and educated at Rimuka High School and Sanyati Baptist School, he then trained as a quality assessor. Now a writer and actor, he works with Rimuka Performing Arts, a pioneering drama group, and organizes theater workshops.

His *Tribe of Graves* (2000) reenacts the Rosvi people's initial contact with whites, especially missionaries, and thus joins a regional effort to correct the historical record. An apparently slight acquaintance with global literary traditions gives this work a decided freshness.

While censuring missionary cultural damage and moral contradiction, the play seeks judgmental balance. Pre-Christian Rosvi unity and success included a capacity for slaughter and enemy skulls as status symbols. Christianity's more pacific message, though to Rosvi taste rather effeminate, at first resonates well. Nor does traditional culture entirely lack Western-style individualism and ambition. Hence the elder Duri's "singularity"—he is an independent thinker who kills off three missionaries (Father Raymond, his wife, and Johns); the king, Mbano, whose throne he usurps; and ex-traditional medium Gondo, one of Christianity's first converts. If modernity can create confusion, so can tradition.

A preference for extended oratory over brisk dialogue creates a lengthy text, but Diki knows what satisfies a local audience and length creates space for vigorous analysis. Hence he interpolates modern issues into an historical setting: gender struggle and feminist debate, tribal democracy, Christian celibacy, miscegenation (the missionary Johns

is in love with Yemurai), regicide, slavery, abortion (Yemurai aborts Johns's baby), apologetics (objections to a joyless hellfire Christianity), and gerontocracy (revolutionary Duri wants to liberate Rosvi youth).

Diki's style generates memorable touches: white ants and weevils are metaphoric of European subversion, and the epilogue is visually startling: a stage bare but for rubble, bones, and mainly cross-bearing graves. A year after the play's events, brother has turned against brother—forgetting oracular "wisdom" which long ago warned that whites should not be killed. On balance, the text privileges not so much white Christians over the traditional Rosvi but key components in the Christian message.

Eavesdropping: A Collection of Short Stories on Everyday Problems (2000). The editor was Monde A. Sifuniso, an Oxford Brookes University graduate in publishing and current president of the Zambia Women Writers Association, who featured in an earlier ZWWA volume, *The Heart of a Woman* (1997). Published with assistance from UNESCO, *Eavesdropping* features six women writers—Lungowe Sifuniso Chabala, Milumbe Haimbe, Florence Chunga, Mulenga Kapwepwe, the editor herself—and two males, Cheela F. E. Chilala and Samuel Kasankha.

Sifuniso's introduction, in which she laments a limited response to her call for texts, mentions themes old and new. Poverty, chronic debt, glacial bureaucracy, patriarchy, marital childlessness, sexual abuse, and stressed tradition appear in Kasankha's "Good People Live Here," Chabala's "Shattered Dreams," Sifuniso's "The Choice of Name," Haimbe's "Groundnuts and Maize,"

Chunga's "Free of Shame," and Chilala's "The Blind Alley." Unexpectedly, Kasankha's "Just Absurd" examines homosexuality and his "Glorious Apartheid" contemporary African-Asian racism. Sifuniso admires Kasankha (she includes four of his stories) seeing him as a key commentator on life during the years 1972–91. If the outsider's view of Zambia during this period was benign (the country at least lacked a racial war and Malawi's despotism), Kasankha paints a grim reality: chronic shortages, empty shops, paramilitary police, terrified silence, rampaging crime, a voiceless poor, and indifferent elites. His wryly titled "Peace in the City" even attacks Kaunda's national philosophy. As Humanism Week opens, Mr. T. T. Sakala, model citizen, husband and father, has his house ransacked by gangsters wielding crowbars, sticks, and pickaxes; his wife is sexually abused and then, inexplicably, he himself is beaten to death by thuggish policemen.

Florence Chunga's "Free of Shame" explores a perennial theme—marital childlessness and in-law interference ("Bearing children is a duty that must be fulfilled. . . . A woman without a child is like a tree without fruit. It should be cut down")—but even its predictable denouement (husband not wife is infertile), detracts nothing from the story's suspense and impact.

Mulunga Kapwepwe's "The Fury of a Cobra" is, says Sifuniso, "a biographical account of the murder of Kapwepwe's great-great-grandmother." A highly poetic narrative, it ranks high among modern renderings of oral history. Nor can one find elsewhere in Central African writing so vivid a first-hand account of Ngoni destruction wrought while these warlike people fled north from Chaka Zulu into modern Zambia, Malawi, and Zimbabwe.

English Poetry and Short Stories (1998). This blandly titled collection by members of

the Zimbabwe Women's Writers group seems faceless: it mentions no editors or publishing house, offers no introduction or biographies. The project's communality is stressed, for the ZWW group is marked by nothing if not solidarity. Yet this understated identity and textual slimness belie both content weight and variety. Fifty-two women authors (forty-six in verse, six in prose) speak out on pregnancy and motherhood, prostitution, widowhood, senescence, sexual abuse, murder, street children, drought and hunger, feminist solidarity, tradition, and even nonchauvinist best practice. Their compelling candor is pervasive. The featured writers are Tawona Mtshiya, Chiedza Musengezi, Sonia Gomez, Shumba Sikhumbuziwe, Gladys Moyo, Tsvutayi Tawainga, Maureen Mataranyika, Egely Donadi, Trecy Mutendereki, Stella Changar, Precity Mabuya, Grace Mafu, Shumirai Mugambi, Soneni Lisa Makhalima, Colette Mutangadura, Hazel Edna Mudokwenyu, Tibelelo M. Silayigwane, Pumla Dzvona, Perpetual Kabunze, Spiwe N. Mahachi, Viviene Kernohan, Zandile Makahamadze, S. Changara, Collete Mutangadura, Sydia Gweshe, Patience Chiyangwa, Mary Sandasi, Kudzai Mudungwe, Mary Olivia Tandon, Barbara Makhalisa, Shumirai Makasi, Virginia Phiri, Bekezela Ncube, Sibusiwe Sibanda, Ama Asantewe Ababio, Elsworth Benhura, Priscilla Adams, Audrey Achihota, Beauty Ncube, Emelda Tshuma, Mrs. P. Kabunze, E. G. Andrea, Ayala, Lady Tash, and Zaida Maria Anna Bhika.

Precity Mabuya's "I Am Always There" notes that women have now conquered most social and professional peaks but must still tell males, "Do not look at me with a despising eye." Ama Asantewe Ababio's "How Sweet Your Sugar" attacks rapacious sugar daddies, "waiting like a shark / Wits sharpened / Tongue oiled," to prey on innocent maidens and then "spit them out" into a life of dishonor. This often means the prostitution in Egely Donadi's "Woman for Sale," which, poverty-driven, incurs a fate resembling "toilet paper" to be "flushed away." Male betrayal underlies Priscilla Adams's poignant "My Plea," whose speaker, one more victim of male mendacity and now dying of AIDS, pleads not to be abandoned. Four times she cries "Stay," while shivering with the disease whose "virus floods me like a river." Her futile cri de coeur is,

> When all the world has gone its way,
> Please stay!

The grief-stricken speaker in Tsvutayi Tawainga's "The Time Bomb" is also an AIDS victim. Forewarned, her life would have been different. But, as she puts it, "time is already up for me." Her parents will suffer, her lover will find another, her children will be orphans remembering only a sick, never a happy, mother. Grace Mafu's rhyming "Street Kid" embraces the plight of a street child, the product of evils suffered by women throughout the poems. His parents are both dead, and he has no more tears left.

The verse gives tradition a broadly negative press. Chiedza Musengezi's "Try Again" shows a good marriage buckling under traditional pressure. Swift pregnancies produce three girls with diminishing joy among the in-laws, who want a boy. When she finally produces a son who is clearly unwell, she is accused of witchcraft, of not wanting to expand the clan, and is driven back to her mother. In "The African Widow," Sydia Gweshe laments the notorious traditional practice across Central Africa by which a widow loses all her possessions to her in-laws. On the other hand, the speaker in Chiedza Musengezi's "When I'm Old" deplores the idea of ending up penned in a modern old people's home where "they'll scrub me squeaky-clean," preferring a dignified ending at home in her traditional hut among her chickens and snuff bottles.

Male physical and verbal abuse is pervasive, and Perpetual Kabunze's speaker in "Charged with Murder," after a surfeit of both kinds, has retaliated and will plead self-defense to a murder charge. By contrast, in "Not Equal Rights: Just a Little Bit More Love" Mrs. P. Kabunze celebrates a husband who, when she returns weary from work, has tidied the house beautifully and has a meal under way in the kitchen.

The prose comprises more fragments than fully fledged short stories. Sibongile Mnkandla's "Observations" takes a satirical look at being the only black at a church-related card-making party—a young mind among old whites registering delicately nuanced racism. Elsworth Benhura's pioneering piece "Just a Ray of Hope" shows a couple choosing adoption when in-laws nearly destroy their marriage, and it recommends the practice, despite its alienness to African tradition. Pat F. Dobah's "And I'll Comfort You" returns to AIDS and male treachery. A husband has cruelly left his wife for a younger woman, scorning his wife's inferior physical attributes. But now that he is back again, dying of AIDS, it gives her no joy, no sense of revenge. She grants him "the assurance and love he ached for." The piece ends as she covers his face in death and goes to tell the children their father is dead.

Eppel, John (b. 1947). Zimbabwean poet and novelist. He was educated at South Africa's University of Natal and at University College, Rhodesia. His undergraduate studies began in troubled times. South Africa was still an apartheid state, and Rhodesia's Ian Smith had proclaimed his Unilateral Declaration of Independence, which effectively triggered the Liberation War that cost so many lives. He is the author of two books of verse, *Spoils of War* (1989) and *Sonata for Matabeleland* (1995), and three novels, *D. G .G. Berry's Great North Road* (1992), *Hatchings* (1993), and *The Giraffe Man* (1994). His work, which has received wide critical acclaim and prizes, marks him as a regional writer, in the best sense of that term, in that it focuses relentlessly on the Matabeleland area of south Zimbabwe. The critic Anthony Chennells praises him for his excellent eye, his satiric view of nationalisms, whether black or white, and his readiness to identify with the new Zimbabwe. His evocation of and strong identification with the African landscape are such that he shows no trace of the colonial romanticism that imitated British models seen in, say, some of the settler poetry of Australia, Canada, and New Zealand—and this despite his deep immersion in the Western literary canon.

Further reading: Douglas Killam and Ruth Rowe, eds., *The Companion to African Literatures* (Oxford: James Currey 2000).

Finn, Hugh (b. 1925). Zimbabwean poet. Born in Port Elizabeth, South Africa, and a chemistry graduate of Rhodes University, he settled and taught for many years in Rhodesia, at the same time achieving recognition as a poet, his work appearing internationally in anthologies published in England, the United States, and Canada, and in such journals as *Atlantic Monthly*, *New Coin*, and the *Dalhousie Review*. With his wife, the poet D. E. Borrell, he was energetic in encouraging local writing. His collection *The Sunbathers and Other Poems* (edited by Vernon Crawford) appeared in the Mopani Series in 1977.

A pleasing diversity marks the form, content and mood of Finn's work. When bored with *in propria persona* statement he can happily shift viewpoint and hand the narrative voice to, say, a eucalyptus tree, as he does in "Mary and the Voices" and in "The Eucalyptus Speaks," a clever piece avoiding mawkishness over farewells and alienation. Some of his best work comprises sonnets (especially his "Four Prayers for Seasons in the Western Cape") and narrative verse, as in "Encounter," whose nostalgic irony portrays a pupil sincerely ambitious for a medical career met later in life as a clerk. He is also happy in haiku:

Marble's but chilly
Immortality beside
This brief warmth of blood.

and

In here the mind's cold
Awareness: there, the leaves, bright
With unthinking joys.

In "Kind Kittok" he translates an amusing medieval Scots poem by Dunbar, and "Flick-Knife Afternoon" is a brave exercise in Anglo-Saxon alliteration, beginning:

In this slum of a season . the winds
    are stropping
Knives for the night . renewing
    their knuckle-
Dusters for the deadly . treacheries
    of the dark;

A man of religious faith, never moving far from the shadows of mortality, he can, however, balance a gift for the solemnly poignant and elegiac with freewheeling comic irreverence, as in "After a Surfeit of Tennyson":

The splendour palls of castle walls
And snowy summits merely bore me
When Alfred shakes across the lakes
His tinsel-gay Victorian glory.

Blow, damn, and blow! Set his torn
　pages flying;
Alfred needs a little gentle guying,
　guying, guying.
O hark, O hear! A modern ear
Finds Alfred rather heavy going;
Too sweet by far his verses are—
Like streams of treacle slowly
　flowing . . .

His collegiality appears in "To N. H. B,"
in which he prods his poet-friend Brettell
into renewed effort on hearing that he is to
write no more. The two make an interest-
ing comparison: the first-class-honors
graduate in English blurring his poetic
statement with verbosity and complexity,
and the man of science delighting in a style
at its best precise, open, and simple.

Further reading: *The Sunbathers and
Other Poems*, ed. Veronica Crawford (Salis-
bury, 1977).

**The Heart of a Woman: Short Stories from
Zambia** (1997). This substantial collection
of fourteen stories, published by the Zam-
bia Women's Writers Association, was ed-
ited by Norah Mumba and Monde Sifuniso.
Their introduction suggests a rationale
based partly on concern for the predica-
ment of Zambian writing overall, partly on
the urgency of addressing the dire condi-
tion of gender relations.

Educational books, the editors complain,
form the core of Zambian publishing, be-
cause profitably prescribable for school and
college. Because the creative writing market
is too small to sustain local publishers, a
flood of imported Western literature con-
tinues. But the ZWWA urges the impor-
tance of "culture" for producing rounded
citizens ("a person denied music and litera-
ture is not a complete person") and com-
plains that this not being widely realized is
"the tragedy of our society." Anxious to fill
a serious gap, *The Heart of a Woman* will

pioneer its efforts. This has been possible,
however, only with grants from InterPares
of Canada, channeled through the South-
ern Africa Women's Initiative.

Though no themes were listed in the call
for material, submissions overwhelmingly
reflect bad gender relations. Violence and
abuse abound. The editors note that females
in eleven stories are abuse victims—a point
stressed even in two male submissions.
Only two texts feature domestic harmony.
This anthology and counterparts from
Zimbabwe and Malawi show literary dis-
course shifting focus from anticolonial and
postcolonial protest to chauvinism and pa-
triarchy, among other matters. A depress-
ing pattern emerges. Initial joy with a
plausible man, and dreams of serene do-
mesticity, yield to gloom—signaled by
variations of "Then the rumours started."
The man comes home late. Then later.
Sometimes not at all. Suspicion precedes
accusation, violence, hospitalization, and
even death. For Norah Mumba this is dese-
cration of the heart of a woman, which, in
her title story, she calls "a nest of purity,
with the capacity to hold in limitless quan-
tity the most undefiled feelings."

Given literary production's sociology,
the volume predictably depicts city rather
than village life—thus a middle-class world
of university and college education, profes-
sionalism, posh hotels, exclusive boutiques,
supermarkets, executive gatherings, mar-
keting strategies, international phone calls,
clubs and preprandial drinks, nannies, and
maids. A rural text, however, might not re-
flect significantly different gender relations.

Neither Mumba's nor Sifuniso's view of
men is totally bleak. Mumba's title story, in-
sisting that prostitution usually means the
girl next door facing penury, also features a
caring male. Leya, a young prostitute and
mother, meets affluent Michael whose hu-
manity creates loving happiness. An es-
tranged wife's reappearance, and what looks

like murder, intervenes, though the relationship has emboldened a now pregnant Leya to ensure access to provision in Michael's will. (Like her compatriot Tsitsi V. Himuyanga-Phiri, Mumba is much concerned about widows' rights and helped to bring into law Zambia's 1989 Intestate Succession Bill.) In "Waiting," a waitress in sleazy Joe's Restaurant reports on gender strife. She overhears women employees complaining of blocked promotion for withholding sexual favors. Overheard, too, is the formulaic patter of a Don Juan who brings successive women into the restaurant for food and seduction. Even an embarrassing public beating by a ditched conquest does not inhibit this man from calling over the waitress narrator and restarting his seduction lines. "Come Back Nancy" examines male psychological fragility. Narrator Ben, single and shy, meets Nancy. They fall in love, plan marriage, and buy wedding clothes. But Nancy is found at home overdosed and dying from an attempted abortion. Relatives reveal a tragic background. Raped at seventeen by her father's friend, she killed the resulting baby while postnatally depressed and was sent to a psychiatric ward. On their planned wedding day, Ben will don his new suit, visit the cemetery, and "deliver a beautiful bouquet of flowers to my bride." Mumba's narrative offers a rare positive male portrayal and optimism about happier gender relations.

Monde Sifuniso, ex-teacher turned publisher, also offers nuanced understanding of male psychology. In "Getting to Know Andrew," Omega, hearing Andrew as a conference speaker, classifies him instantly as a chauvinist poseur of cultivated shabbiness. She leaves his talk and is devastated later when her friend Anne decides to marry him. He flirts unsuccessfully with Omega and when a rejected lover beats up both of them, his acute embarrassment stirs sympathy and some seeds of affection.

Her neatly symmetrical "Beijing, Beijing" revolves around a Women's Rights Conference in China. With Jack Zulu's wife gone to the conference, he plans time with his mistress, only to find her gone to China too. The sisterhood has nimbly outwitted the chauvinists.

In Dorothy Makasa's "No More Pain," Shimbi tells her story for self-therapy and to empower others to reveal the awful secrets patriarchy teaches them to die with. Her taped tale will also augment women activists' database. At twenty-two, dreaming of marriage and domesticity, social worker Shimbi meets engineer Ben, who confounds appearance by soon becoming an alcoholic ruffian. All self-blame, Shimbi recalls patriarchy's advice: always be subservient, hide your problems, and never mention your qualifications. She loses a baby through violence and returns home. Her parents send her back, whereupon Ben the Barbarian now attacks her with a knife. She departs, finds friends kinder than husbands, and after more brutality from Ben, develops courage enough to file for divorce, open a police docket, and defy her parents.

"The Initiate," by Muyapekwa Liengamuwa, moves from Lusaka to the Barotse Plain and from urban realism to rural fantasy. Sepo, a headmaster's daughter, eerily recalls her grandmother rising from the grave and inducting her into witchcraft. Women are comprehensively inferior to men, says grandma, so seize supernatural power and make them fear you. It is a compelling explanation of witchcraft. Now thirty-five, Sepo uses her power in modern boardrooms to exploit men's underlying fear of women that they disguise as hatred and superiority.

Susan Chitabanta, in "A Lie to a Liar," conjures another pocket hell created by a sexually predatory husband. A remark that "he got sick because he still had to hunt for women even after marriage" might suggest that he is also an AIDS carrier, this being a problem the volume, given its publication date, strangely does not foreground.

"A Hug from Uncle Peter" by Cheela Chilala, using an omniscient viewpoint and the first-person voice of a poor nine-year-old, gains poignancy from its lack of sentimentality. Mabvuto (literally "problem") is a beggar, his life dominated by hunger. Born to a sixteen-year-old prostitute, he often asks about his father and dreams of one day meeting him in a village, when, so to speak, all will be well and all manner of things will be well. ("When I meet him will be the happiest day of my life . . . our suffering will be over.") Meanwhile, he has many "uncles," his mother's clients. Begging on Lusaka's Cairo Road, he sees dapper Uncle Peter and recalls a hug from him and a promise of help at any time. Following him into his office aglow with expectation brings only a kick in the groin and ejection. He concludes, "At the door I turned and looked back. Uncle Peter was still standing there looking at me with hate in his eyes. For a brief moment I felt like waving to him goodbye. But I could not. I turned and walked out. I did not want to see Uncle Peter again."

An admirer of Nadine Gordimer, Malele Dodia sets "Family Ties" in the confined urban spaces of Lusaka, where Angela and Shelley, waitress and teacher, share drab accommodation. Shelley's boyfriend James finds a curious snake charm in her purse, which takes us to secret societies, witchcraft, protection rackets, the murder of two women carrying narcotics over the Tanzanian border (the chief suspect Angela's relative Ken, a businessmen shot by a border patrolman), and a drugs racket stretching from East Africa to India.

Mbuyu Nalumango offers a well-told story, with tight prose, good dialogue, and a feel for metaphor ("There was no morning dew . . . only dried out grass in front of us"). In "Demons of Love," Busie and Chiko

marry and enjoy initial bliss. "Then come the rumours." She sticks by him, is beaten, and twice hospitalized for her trouble. Still she returns for more. Then, in swift succession, Claudia, Mary, Josephine, Benhilda all ring to say that they have Chiko's babies and need support. Benhilda goes one better by bringing her baby and handing it to Busie, who now shoots Chiko and gets a seven-year sentence. Her crime has freed her to deliver a strong message: "Never again would I allow myself to be used and abused by a man. I wished I could yell to all the women out there to stop shedding tears and fight for their sanity."

Felicitas Chinanda's "On the Other Side of the Fence" is a warning against drugs. Lusford, recently bound in bed in Chainama Mental Hospital, began as a healthy schoolboy, a soccer player and cross-country runner. But he became antisocial, led a school gang, earned the nickname Lucifer, smoked cannabis, and, when his boarding school faced food shortages, plundered neighboring village fields. He escapes from hospital and becomes a thieving vagrant, until an uncle returns him to Chainama. Treatment will be "long and difficult."

Nakatiwa Mulikita's "Women Alone" returns to the book's thematic core. Rona's Jeff has left her and her children to marry another woman. Rejecting the guerilla warfare of maintenance demands, Rona, junior partner in an accounting firm, decides to support herself. To her friends whose husbands are equally wayward her message is simple: when marriage failure stares you in the face, don't fight it. Accept it, but, crucially, "leave some happiness and energy for your children and, most importantly, for yourself." She is tough enough to ridicule men's assumptions that women, especially women alone, always and automatically need them and that women really cannot be happy in one another's company. We see her in a smart hotel telling two arrogant male predators where to get off. Happy, confident, salaried, she can run her life alone.

The late Gaur Radebe, a South African refugee in Zambia, contributes "Don't Marry Her," adding wry male-perspective prejudice to a collection heavy on gloom. Since God gives women as an unsolicited gift, men can surely do what they like with them. In any case, women are both a nuisance (it would be nice if we could be born without them) and too silly for their own good. Why on earth do they let themselves be abused and keep coming back for more? A wife loses all her front teeth but swears to the court that her husband is not cruel. Another, via abuse, loses a baby and her husband's affection but blames herself. She is incurable, eventually loses house and home, wanders abroad, is committed to a mental asylum, and dies. The narrator, who has resolutely remained single, ends his exercise in humor with the hope that when humanity gets to the moon, women will stay behind on the earth.

Himunyanga-Phiri, Tsitsi V. (b. ca. 1950). Zambian novelist. She can best be understood as a Central African Mary Wollstonecraft. Partner in a prominent Lusaka law firm, she holds a master's degree in community systems and development and a doctorate in social development and public policy analysis, both degrees focusing on women's needs. She is also founder and principal shareholder in the H-P Development Company, whose core activities empower women in the areas of law, finance, management, and business.

The Legacy, a novel published in 1992, directly reflects her professional concerns, its aim solely to challenge any strand in tradition that denies women freedom and dignity, their ability to grow as individuals and become fully autonomous within family and society. In particular, she targets the Central African custom that denies a wife the right to inherit anything on her husband's death and argues her case with clarity and force.

Narrator Moya is in court awaiting a judge's verdict—which immediately charges the text with suspense. She has pleaded her case before a local tribunal, rather as Lawino in Okot p'Bitek's classic poem pleaded before a jury of her clan. The legal thrust is pivotal. Moya demands justice, and the title's "legacy" means the family inheritance Moya risks losing to her dead husband's brother and local tradition, which makes such an outrage possible.

Economy of event and scene and swift narrative tempo conspire to stress the case's urgency. The plain facts, simply stated, will speak for themselves: wordy advocacy would only blunt their sharpness. On Ba Mudenda's death, tradition demands that the bulk of the estate, including family home and ten acres, should go to his brother, leaving Moya and her children virtually penniless. But she has contributed substantially to the family's welfare, raised her children well, and built a business to generate school fees. The brother-in-law, like Ba Mudenda an alcoholic womanizer, has spent long absences drinking and whoring and has inflicted violence on Moya. The case, she knows, will be of landmark importance. As she puts it, "The outcome of my case would affect many other women's lives," and her lady advocate makes plain that "we were contesting our culture and its laws of inheritance and succession." While it is bad enough for Moya to be insulted by her in-laws, tradition's demand that she be "cleansed" of her husband's death by sleeping with his brother is the last straw.

A passionate believer in education, yet forced to abort her own for an arranged marriage, Moya wants something better for her daughters. They must understand education's liberating rewards, learn that a woman need not be wife and mother to feel fulfilled. Her efforts partially succeed. Choole becomes a schoolteacher, Mazuba a personal secretary, Mutinta a bank clerk, and Chipo (triumphantly) a civil engineer. But they all, says the text, had to learn the hard way. Choole, who hated school and was expelled for pregnancy, never saw the value of education until the eleventh hour. Mazuba, accepting the traditional view that her status was gender-determined, became mistress to two rich men and faced abandonment consequent on pregnancy.

Moya bluntly asks why men but not women can let modernity transform their lives. Women wanting this are told they are forgetting their culture. Anxious not to be seen as an iconoclast, Moya respects custom but insists that its rationale be scrutinized. She also notes how modernity has polluted traditional practice. Initiation ceremonies that once alerted society to a girl's new adult status are now merely a voyeur's chance to peer at women's bodies and stress subservience to husbands. Similarly, widows and children, traditionally protected by in-laws, could keep the land they had been farming. Selfish materialism has now taken over.

The judge, fortunately, descries double standards—one law for men, another for women. It will not do, and he finds in Moya's favor.

Further reading: *Dispossessing the Widow: Gender Based Violence in Malawi*, ed. Seodi White, Dorothy nyaKaunda, Tinyade Kachika, Asiyati Chiweza, and Flossie Gomile-Chidyaonga (Blantyre, 2002).

Hove, Chenjerai (b. 1956). Zimbabwean novelist, poet, and essayist. Born in Mazvihwa Zvishavane, he attended Catholic mission schools at Kutama and Dete, received teacher training at Gweru, and, while teaching secondary-school English, studied for a South African external degree in literature and education. He has lectured and read his poetry internationally and held writing residencies at the universities of Zimbabwe, Leeds, and Leiden and at Lewis and Clark College in the United States. He now lives in Norway. His work has been translated into French, German, Japanese, Norwegian, Swedish, Dutch, and Danish.

Using both Shona and English, Hove's published fiction includes *Masimba Avanhu?* (1986), *Bones* (1988), *Shadows* (1991), and *Ancestors*. His nonfiction (mainly essays) includes *Shebeen Tales* (1994), *Guardians of the Soil* (with Iliya Trojanow, 1997), and *Palaver Finish* (2002). Since 1980, when fourteen of his poems appeared in *And Now the Poets Speak*, he has published *Up in Arms* (1982), *Swimming in Floods of Tears* (with Lyamba wa Kabika, 1983), *Red Hills of Home* (1985), *Rainbows in the Dust* (1997), and *Blind Moon* (2003). A radio play, *Sister Sing Again Someday*, appeared in 1989. Honors garnered include the Zimbabwe Literary Prize (1988) and the Noma Award for Publishing in Africa (1989).

Like his late compatriot Yvonne Vera, Hove moves African fiction toward the norms of verse. Indeed, though working mainly in prose, he told the Dutch publisher Jan Kees van de Werk (who wrote the prologue to the 1997 edition of *Shebeen Tales*), "I am a poet in my bones." Placing him beside contemporaries like Mungoshi, Marechera, and Zimunya, Rino Zhuwarara says that Hove's is mainly a postindependence emergence. He skillfully indigenizes his prose, and through intense engagement with soil, seasons, landscape, climate, flora, and fauna, he can define the Shona worldview in language as gnomic as Achebe's. But this is always accessible writing, problems arising only from disturbed chronologies as Hove goes for historical amplitude. Especially when capturing the brutal Liberation War and its sequel (random murder by dissidents, children forced to bludgeon to death family members, innocent peasants having their throats cut slowly and sadistically), and showing how tradition's life-affirming values encounter their opposites, the writing achieves a searing poignancy.

Hove wants to "write books that remind us of what it is to be powerless or, indeed, to be powerful, and at the same time, strive to retrieve our historical conscience." Thus advocacy for the weak and for accurate history are pivotal. Writing as a countryman (rural beauty is pervasive, urban description rare), he portrays a peasantry stoic under drought and flood, on whom history has inflicted colonialism, land eviction, and rural warfare (urban areas are virtually unscathed) in which they suffer barbarism from either side. With this nightmare over, they face another when opponents of the new regime return to the bush and start slaughtering peasants again. Hove's are the countryside's "small" people (especially women, whose humanity and heroism he urgently trumpets), wanting only to live useful lives in harmony with nature and ancestors, powerless under colonialism and modern weaponry, yet always dreaming of better days.

Recurrent components of Hove's rural apologia are diverse and sometimes surprising. Along with soil and sand, forest, winds, water, birds (raptors significantly), sun and moon, buried umbilical cords, locusts, cattle, snakes (especially the python and black mamba), and, always, the ancestors, there is psychological loneliness, war-caused insanity, disempowerment, and pain ("pain is stored in the stories of land since the beginning of time").

Bones, which takes place on a large white-owned farm, that classic symbol of settler colonialism, foregrounds a feminist perspective on colonial injustice. Its heroes are heroines. The title recalls Zimbabwe's prototype anticolonial martyr Mbuya Nehanda, who predicted resurrection for her bones, while Marita, the protagonist, shares Nehanda's prophetic fire and integrity. She and her associate Janifa (the novel becomes a dialogue between them) represent African woman's defiance of oppression, arising externally from colonialism or internally from patriarchy. The menfolk—Marita's husband Murume, Chisaga the cook, Chiriseri the farm overseer, black soldiers—are complicit in the women's predicament. Stripped of patriarchal props by colonialism, they behave dysfunctionally: craven toward whites, brutal toward their own women. Chisaga's violent rape of Janifa triggers mental breakdown, marital rejection, and asylum chains. Marita, seeking her only son after the bush war, dies after torture and rape by government soldiers. Inspired by Marita's life, Janifa seeks the body for burial, but, tellingly, receives only abuse from the new regime.

Nehanda speaks in a flashback to the first uprisings of 1896 and 1897, denouncing the diseases whites have brought, and invoking all nature—cattle, clouds, sky, locusts, birds, rivers, hills—to show that this is "the land of rising bones." Melodrama is avoided partly because Hove depicts an integrated, albeit wounded, culture. But his text leaves us wondering whether this snapshot of tradition will erase the image of an incarcerated Janifa, who is Marita's, and thus Nehanda's, disciple. Nehanda's call is heeded. Peasants revolt and the whites are conquered. But Janifa, Nehanda's moral daughter, lies in free Zimbabwe's chains.

In *Shadows*, life disillusions villagers wanting independent agency beyond white areas—especially those who buy government land where, in theory, they can be as free as white farmers. Racial trickery, the Liberation War and its aftermath, repeat the *Bones* experience. Dedicated to warfare's innocent civilian victims, the book includes Romeo-and-Juliet deaths and the slaughter of almost an entire family. Johana's proud father, after years in arid Gutu, moves to the land of Gotami (a nineteenth-century male counterpart to Nehanda), where honest labor should guarantee prosperity. But there is dislocationary pain—abandoning ancestral graves and umbilical cord burial sites, the complex tapestry of new relationships with landscape, climate, and strangers. There is also white deception, for, unexpectedly, the land is malarial, an area of elephant and lion. Exile and aloneness become motifs.

Tragedy arises. When Johana the cattle girl falls for neighbor Marko, paternal disapproval triggers a double suicide—admired by contemporaries because at least symbolic of autonomy in an age of disempowerment. The guerrillas see Johana's father as a sellout and mark him for death. Escape to urban garbage scavenging and psychological devastation leads him, as with Janifa in *Bones*, to asylum chains. Cheated, guerillas now kill one of his sons—their leader, in Senecan detail, telling the boy's brothers to "slice a lip, slice an ear, slice another ear, slice an eye, slice the genitals, slice the thighs, until the man collapses dead." After the war, the opponents of the new regime ("the enemy had changed his color") return and again wreak slaughter. They take another son and give sticks to his siblings; then "they asked the sons to club their brother to death, to crush his head with big sticks, to pound his brains out of his skull." When Johana's father finally returns home in rags, guerillas come in the night, drag him from his wife's side, slit his throat slowly and sadistically, and finish him off in the forest. Slaughter by Rhodesian troops, guerrillas, and then dissidents inflicted on the peasant backbone of liberation struggle— this bloodshed produces some of Hove's most poignant writing.

In *Ancestors*, Hove wants to make sense of history by linking past to present. Disability marks heroine Miriro, as it did the great Nehanda. Born deaf and mute in 1850, and dead soon after a loveless marriage, she speaks posthumously and spiritually possesses a twentieth-century youth. Chronology is fluidly postmodern, dates ranging from 1850 to 1963, 1966, and 1989. Miriro recalls an early life of oddness and solitude: Christianity's arrival with a vengeful God, its missionaries bringing cattle disease, sexual disease, and a gun culture. Against white land theft and commercialization she counterpoints a traditional life of harmony with nature: "Imagine, forests and animals sitting alongside men and women, talking about the destiny of the land."

Under white hegemony this is unimaginable. Yet traditional narrative, Hove reminds us, has been overwhelmingly chauvinist—hence the importance of Miriro's story. That "the victors are the only story-tellers" means not only that historiography has come from colonial pens but also that local men, winners in the gender battle, have effectively silenced the women.

Impeccably equipped for verse, Hove evidently feels that Zimbabwe's modern predicament needs a public voice, which suggests prose, albeit poetic. Poetic lyricism might seem self-indulgent. His anthology *Red Hills of Home*, however, continues to echo his prose concerns: bloodshed, violence, exile, alienation, material and economic impotence, savaged innocence, injustice, irresponsible power. The prologue is Pablo Neruda's answer to any call for conventional aestheticism: "Come and see the blood in the streets." Hove himself calls his poems "sore songs." By 1985 the country has been five years independent, and yet is already in chaos. "Mother," an antiwar poem, asks, "Where does one see love / in a military grimace?"

"Inaugural Thoughts" conjures a president's future in images of a corpse in handcuffs, uncaring interment, curses, and the hollow ritual of military honors. In "Child's Parliament," a mother is dying of poverty while parliamentarians form committees, demand higher salaries, play with statistics, and complain about a lack of seating.

By 2003, when *Blind Moon* appeared, Hove had chosen to live overseas. The verse reflects non-African scene and event ("african farmer's son in europe," "in Rambouillet, France," "marson's bar. Doncaster, 1995," "st malo"), though home clings to the poet's consciousness. The poem "trail" catalogues a politician's sins committed on the road to power: broken hearts, tears, "footprints of blood," skulls, orphans, widows, nameless graves. Nature itself is victim—"you wounded even the trees, / the birds, / our butterflies of hope." The Matabeleland atrocities following independence struck writers dumb: "the birds went silent / afraid to sing of their freedom." A long poem titled "what are you doing?" portrays the leader, beautifully dressed, talking only of procedure as "the land overflows with despair," "streams of children's blood / creep on your desks," mothers have lost their husbands, and "every hill harbours a political corpse." The future, glimpsed in "ahead," looks equally bleak:

> from now on
> we tread the road,
> the footpath of illegitimacy
> to the tune
> of praise singers
> flatterers
> charlatans

Hove's social conscience also informs his journalistic essays. A set written for the Dutch newspaper *De Volkskrant* and included in *Shebeen Tales: Messages from Ha-rare* gives a foreign audience an insider's view of modern Zimbabwe. Villager Hove spotlights urban sex shops, AIDS, back alleys, unemployment. Two themes dominate: alcoholism ("A Zimbabwean is either drunk, just about to become drunk or is recovering from drunkenness"), and popular jesting about disaster ("AIDS means American Idea for Discouraging Sex"). Harare is "The City of Problems and Laughter." Hove wrote *Shebeen Tales* for *The Standard*, a newspaper Robert Mugabe constantly threatened with closure—a platform beyond verse and fiction on which to defend the powerless and remind government of broken promises. This recalls the anterior example of Kenya's Philip Ochieng, a provocative 1960s columnist in Nairobi's *Daily Nation*, and of Nigeria's Tai Solarin, whose *Daily Times* column long attacked multiform endemic corruption. Perhaps the Weaver Press had this in mind in 2002 when it published some of Hove's *Standard* essays in *Palaver Finish*, whose title piece has a peasant in West African pidgin vigorously attacking politicians as parasites: "He no produce nutting. He go eat everything dat you and I produce. . . . All he go do is palaver palaver palaver."

These essays offer such memorable statement as "a historian is one who thinks and analyses history, and a writer or artist is one who feels history." They sketch national oppression, rapidly resembling Malawian Banda's vicious censorship and silencing; a bullying youth movement; informer networks; exile, prison, or worse. The police in "Violence, Tear-gas, Handcuffs and Democracy" remind Hove of apartheid South Africa: "Their faces are stamped with the language of brutality and mercilessness. We have become a police-army state." In "Zimbabwe's Lost Visions" the excitement of independence counterpoints modern disillusion, golden chances wasted. Politicians have become a "demolition squad," believing that "African economies never collapse until there is no food in state house." Finally, "The Violence of Gokwe" records—in concise detail—horrors visited on this area during and after the Liberation War, when guerrilla and Rhodesian forces were, as he puts it, "hunting each other down," and, as it happens, including the Hove family as their quarry. As much antixenophobic as antiracist, he notes that the saddest victims of the government's recent land grab, supposedly aimed at white farmers, were scapegoated Malawian and Zambians—faithful workers on the land for up to forty years.

Further reading: Emmanuel Ngara, *Form and Ideology in African Poetry* (Nairobi, 1990); Flora Veit-Wild, *Patterns of Poetry in Zimbabwe* (Gweru, 1988); Veit-Wild, "'Dances with Bones': Hove's Romanticised Africa," *Research in African Literatures* 24, no. 3 (1993); Rino Zhuwarara, *Introduction to Zimbabwean Literature in English* (Harare, 2001); Rino Zhuwarara, "Gender and Liberation: Chenjerai Hove's *Bones*," in *New Writing from Southern Africa*, ed. Emmanuel Ngara (London, 1996); Annie Gagiano, "I do not know her, but someone ought to know her," *World Literature Written in English* 2 (1992); Caroline Rooney, "Re-possessions: Inheritance and Independence in Chenjerai Hove's *Bones* and Tsitsi Dangarembga's *Nervous Conditions*," in *Essays on African Writing: Contemporary Literature*, ed. Emmanuel Ngara (London, 1995); Landeg White, "The Language of Two Novels from Zimbabwe," *Southern Africa Review of Books*, February 1990.

I

Imenda, Sitwala (b. 1952). Zambian novelist, poet, and folklorist. He was born in the Western Region. After high school there, he studied chemistry and education at the University of Zambia, then took an M.Sc. at SUNY Albany and an Ed.D. at the University of British Columbia. He has since taught at the universities of Zambia and Swaziland and, within South Africa, at the University of Transkei, the University of the North, and Tshwane University of Technology, where he has held deanships in education, information science, and social development studies. In addition to research fellowships, he has held visiting appointments at Britain's universities of Bristol and York. A man of science and letters, Imenda strives, through rigorous analysis and synthesis, to blend the best of modernity and tradition within issues religious, educational, and customary. And though long resident in South Africa (setting his first novel there), Zambian concerns, especially decolonizing the school syllabus, remain close to his consciousness. His first novel, *Unmarried Wife* (1994), was followed by *My Grandfather's God* (2004), *Mind Over Matter* (2004), *Dancing Mice and Other African Folktales* (2004), and an epic poem, *The Blairing Kofi Bush War of Iraq* (2004).

Unmarried Wife appeared from Kenya's Spear Books, after initial publication in South Africa, and joined popular work by Spear authors David Maillu, Sam Kahiga, Charles Mangua, and Aubrey Kalitera. Thus racy fellow titles included *Sugar Daddy's Lover*, *The Girl Was Mine*, *Lover in the Sky*, *My Life in Crime*, *My Life with a Criminal*, *Son of Woman*, *Twilight Woman*, *Prison is Not a Holiday Camp*, and *Life and Times of a Bank Robber*. If Sitwala's dedication, "to all the victims of love," signals ephemera, what emerges (raunchy comment and Wodehousian humor aside) is serious analysis of modern sexual mores and ways of having them cohere with both African tradition and Christianity. Tsepo Molefe (TM for short), a leading Catholic businessman, is happily married to a nurse, Naledi. But he has recently had two children by girlfriend Bongiwe, an Anglican vicar's daughter. His problem (shared with his chum Wiseman, a sexualized Bertie Wooster) is how to square this with Catholic teaching; Bongiwe's is how to placate parental outrage and give her children their father's surname.

"We all need extramarital relationships to remain emotionally balanced," TM insists, and proceeds to a scholarly analysis of Catholic doctrine in order to graft it, transformed, onto traditional polygamy. While he gets into apologetics with Father Michael, the elderly pastor of Umtata, Bongiwe mobilizes an Unmarried Wives' Collective and marches successfully for legal change. A theologian conveniently arriving from Rome stresses "putting the word of God within a people's cultural context" and says that the Bible speaks of Christ (not the Church), being the same yesterday, today, and tomorrow. This backs TM's point that a major Catholic problem "may be attributable to the lack of proper integration between Christianity and the realities of social life as lived by the majority." Indeed, legalizing second marriages could even help to counter AIDS. And since TM's predicament is so general (the rural majority wonder what all the fuss is about), surely this is a compelling case of *vox populi vox Dei*. Traditional polygamy was honest and open; present practice is all hypocrisy and deceit. Fr. Michael is persuaded (though not Bongiwe's father), and TM celebrates a "triumph of love over idealism and Utopia." What his wife Naledi thinks is unknown.

Religious debate continues in the novella *My Grandfather's God*. Conflict between a traditional grandfather, Mr. Nyama, and an austere headmaster, the Right Reverend Nicodemus, sees Imenda eliding spiritual and academic aims. In the tradition of pioneers such as Ajayi Crowther, Aggrey, Solarin, and Samkange, Imenda wants an educational blueprint for African youth. The document that debates this is part Socratic dialogue, part scholastic disputation, and part updated *Emile*, with an occasional dash of Coleridge. It pursues with rigor an apologia for ancestral religion, exposure of Christian weakness, and a desire to blend both traditions for posterity.

Expulsion of the narrator Thomas from Mongu's St. Brian's School brings the two men of God into theological collision. In Imenda's splendid phrase, Grandfather is "unschooled but greatly educated." In any case, a transplant of the authorial brain lets Grandpa produce an intellectually distinguished account of African religion (its fairness, inclusiveness, family-centeredness, gentleness, pragmatic flexibility, openness to new thinking), while demonstrating that Christianity, Nicodemus-style, is all division, rigidity, unreason, and vindictiveness. On St. Brian's, the old man says, "No one in this institution appears to be concerned with trying to reconcile the Christian doctrine with the ways of life of an African person. . . . You are teaching us as if our lives started today." Then, addressing Nicodemus as "My child," a witheringly patronizing touch, the old man describes cultural vertigo in persuasive detail:

Our people are confused. They do not have any stable frame of reference. Sometimes they behave like white people and at other times the hard facts of life remind them that they are still Africans after all. In essence, they are people without a culture; people without a proven and tested social order; people without a history; people without a tradition; people without an identity. . . . They are a lost generation.

With the dice so loaded, Nicodemus loses the case and, like Fr. Ryan, accepts the African worldview. But Grandpa wants no rejection of Christianity, only a rich marriage of both traditions. When Nicodemus's second baptism produces the desired educational blueprint, a local zealot spots acute insanity and, in an echo of Zambia's historical Archbishop Milango affair, Nicodemus is strong-armed off to Europe for corrective treatment.

In *Mind Over Matter*, a long story, in which Imenda judiciously uses oral-style narrative, the focus is again academic and its stated target audience school grades 5–7. Jele Joyo (JJ) is an Emile figure being introduced to a traditional African education. Nyala is a traditional kingdom but Imenda's modern scientific picture of it is a beautiful lesson for modern youth. Its entire ecology receives detailed and systematic treatment and a world emerges where humans live in peace with nature. No disciple of Bentham or Mill, Imenda preaches holistic education. Beyond analysis and rational decision-making skills, JJ must develop creativity and imagination:

Many people suffer because they lack imagination. You have to look at the world from different vantage points in order to experience the fullness of life on earth and above. Other cultures elsewhere have conquered nature in different ways for their benefit and convenience. In our case, this is our way of conquering nature in order to derive maximum benefit and convenience from it, without destroying the natural environment. Look at how beautiful our land is. Unlike other cultures, we have conquered our world without destroying it.

JJ is thus steadily inducted into the traditions of his society, his final emergence as a solid Nyala citizen being described as "a triumph of mind over matter."

Dancing Mice and Other African Folktales is Imenda's most orthodox work. Eight Lozi tales are engagingly retold, each concluding with "*So it was, and so it will ever remain.*" Key problems arise to test traditional morality. They include matricide and patricide, euthanasia and greed, cannibalism, lethal polygamous rivalry, and witchcraft. Famine and drought are constants that trigger action and test character.

The Blairing Kofi Bush War of Iraq breaks new ground. In an epic poem of three thousand lines, Imenda addresses international issues, its provenance paralleling the nocturnal genesis of Soyinka's *Idanre*. The U.S.–led "Shock and Awe" attack on Iraq provoked outrage and insomnia; he rose in the deep watches feeling like a victim compelled to write both for healing and protest. The result, naturally, is more spontaneous overflow of powerful feeling than emotion recollected in tranquility.

Aim here dictates style: hence hammer-stroke repetition reflective of oral practice and modern reggae; short lines for immediacy; *vivace* speed for urgency; succinct statement for voltage; copious imagery for visual impact. Recalling 9/11's horrors, the poem sweeps on to Iraq with breathless backward glances at Japan, Korea, Vietnam, Afghanistan. Anger and empathy suffuse every line:

They must kill us
They must slaughter our wives
They must slaughter our husbands
They must slaughter our children
They say we did 911
About which we know nothing

Contradiction of rhetoric and deed is driven home:

Promises of love
Promises of hope

Promises of democracy
Promises of freedom
Promises of honour
Promises of dignity
Promises of prosperity
Promises of integrity
Promises of respect
Promises of tranquility
Promises of peace
But they are vicious
They are vengeful
They are aggressive
Their actions vitriolic
They're a killing machine
Marching and killing
Door to door
City to city
Town to town
River to river
Person to person
Killing with a passion

Rotting corpses stink in every town; waterborne disease becomes endemic; but "it is only Arabic life," the victims' sin only to be citizens of their own country. The speaker constantly demands explanation:

Was it justified
To blow up innocent children
And defenseless women
And old men on walking sticks
For the sake of revenge
Or regime change
Or oil?

The poem laments a world in which democratic governments can run amok like mad dogs, and shrewdly asks (Blair and Bush having been told by the pope that war was not justified):

Is it Christian
To dismember innocent children
Of another country
Is it Christian
To dehumanize the citizens
Of another country

Is it Christian
To rob another nation
Of its pride?

Decrying what it sees as a world dictatorship born in the ashes of Nagasaki and Hiroshima, the poem asks who are the terrorists? And who was insane?

K

Kachingwe, Aubrey (b. 1926). Malawian journalist and novelist. Born in colonial Nyasaland, he was educated there (when it had just four secondary schools) and also in Tanganyika. After five years with Kenya's *East African Standard*, he studied journalism in London, worked on the left-leaning *Daily Herald*'s foreign affairs desk, and moved home to Nyasaland's Department of Information. He thus witnessed the climax of his country's freedom campaign and used this in his novel *No Easy Task* (1966). Preferring radio to print journalism, in 1963, a year before Hastings Banda led Nyasaland to independence, he returned to London and the BBC's Africa Service, subsequently working with Ghana's national radio before finally returning home as Head of News with the Malawi Broadcasting Corporation.

Kachingwe is Malawi's first published novelist, *No Easy Task* appearing a year before Rubadiri's *No Bride Price* and two years before Kayira's *The Looming Shadow*. Set roughly in 1959, five years before independence (its title alludes to the freedom struggle), the novel captures colonial Nyasaland's political mood: impatience with glacial progress toward independence; anger at minimal educational opportunity; South African–style discrimination; admiration for newly free Ghana and Nigeria. Anger, too, at white colonial rhetoric about the need for the colony to stay in "civilized hands," expressed in the infamous *res nullius* argument: "Where our tea farm is now was nothing but bush, roamed by wild animals. There was not a single person living anywhere near. I transformed that wild land into what it is now." Organized opposition to colonial authority arose with the Malawi Congress Party, here called simply The Movement. A familiar pattern emerges of demonstration, riot police response, and imprisonment of liberation leaders. The struggle, as fictively realized, is authentically demotic, its main actors including a ragged ex-army sergeant night watchman (Britain's post–World War II broken promises to his ilk fueling demands for freedom), a lady of easy virtue, a journalist, and a taxi driver. Tension between Africans bent on freedom and those happy with colonialism (called here *akapilikoni*) is resolved with characteristic local forgiveness and reconciliation.

The novel is part autobiography. Like Kachingwe, Jo Jozeni, a would-be journalist, joins a national paper and then a leading London one. His humble pastor father seems partly Banda-inspired, employed in the Presbyterian interest and emerging inexplicably as the freedom movement's leader. Though a medical doctor, Banda was also an elder of the Church of Scotland, and an old man when invited home from overseas to lead Nyasaland's independence movement. Like Banda, too, Jo's father returns from London constitutional talks in a smart suit, enjoys traditional dancing in public, is jailed by the colonial authorities, and has a gift for oratory.

But Kachingwe could not anticipate all the irony that would arise from his fiction. For example, when Jo is briefly jailed, an old man says to him, "Do be careful next time. We don't want our educated people to waste their talents in jail for foolish reasons." He could not know then that among the most

heinous crimes of the real Banda was that for thirty years he would, for no good reason, waste the talents of large numbers of the country's intelligentsia by imprisoning them without trial. He was also ironically prophetic of another aspect of the detention saga. Commenting on the release of a certain Njoka Maki, Jo's friend says, "He came out this morning. . . . He gave us the latest information. Somehow, the people there are better informed than we who are out here. They know almost everything that's going on in the country. . . . We are a God-fearing people in this country, but our patience can run out if the Government continues to lock up our people indefinitely."

Such comment could have been taken directly from work by Mnthali, Mpasu, Mapanje, Mpina—later writers recalling years of actual incarceration and extramural and intramural networks that helped inmates to survive.

Further reading: J. Bardolph, "Aubrey Kachingwe," in *Encyclopaedia of Post-Colonial Literatures in English*, ed. Eugene Benson and L. W. Connolly (London, 1994), 753.

Kadhani, Mudereri (b. 1952). Zimbabwean poet. Born in Mhondoro, he was educated at the Jesuit St. Ignatius College, at the University of Zimbabwe, and at Britain's University of York. Passionate about a role for literature in national life, he published his *Quarantine Rhythms* in 1976, at the height of the Liberation War. A similar concern underpinned *And Now the Poets Speak* (1981), a collection edited with Musaemura Zimunya. Celebrating freedom, this volume covers the traditional world, the colonial scourge, the gathering storm, the guerilla war, and final independence. The introduction captures a national spirit eager to poetically hail victory in an historic struggle. Kadhani and Zimunya wanted a people's exercise in catharsis, an exorcising of historical nightmares, a "clearing of the ground" to lay foundations for a radiant future.

Individual talent, advanced scholarly training, and maturation under colonialism drove Khadani to make his verse serve political change. Anticolonial protest thus blends with postcolonial vision. Widely read, he can be eclectic in influence and experimental in form. He enjoys short-distance work and compressed statement that does not diffuse its energy. Seeing a poem as a logical argument produces an architecture recalling the verse of Malawi's Felix Mnthali. For example, his "Creation (For a Banket farm worker)" opens with "If the sweat of your brow / Flows..." and ends with "Therefore you lack / Control." The first stanza of "On the (Re)Detention of Advocate Edison Sithole (1974)" begins, "So, / If all the roads lead / To the same cell" and ends with a resulting clause of resignation to guerilla war in the bush. His command of imagery can be seen in "Chimoio," his response to arguably the war's worst atrocity, when Rhodesian forces in 1977 bombed a complex of military and civilian refugee camps in Mozambique, killing more than three thousand people. Years later, the mere buzz of flies is enough to recall the horror: "A severed leg sun-drying on a bush top. / A head, abandoned ruthlessly below a tree." Verbal adventure is evident in such coinages as "Kwashiorkored bellies," "Inhibits our ladenmarch to Freedom City," and in his poem "Direction (Lecture from My Student, March 1979)," where he wittily urges his new nation to reject free-market capitalism and "Economise on econo-mists"! Kadhani faces the common dilemma of academic poets in times of turbulent change: how to capture political vision and moral grandeur in memorable metaphor without drifting into abstraction.

Further reading: Mpalive-Hangson Msiska, "Mudereri Kadhani," in *Encyclopaedia of Post-Colonial Literatures in English*, ed. Eugene Benson and L. W. Connolly (London, 1994).

Kala, Violet (n.d.). Zimbabwean novelist. When her novel *Waste Not Your Tears* appeared in 1994 as an urgent response to the AIDS pandemic, it did so without biographical detail, suggesting perhaps a nom de plume. Its blunt opening seems to say that if writers hesitated to attack the Matabeleland massacres that followed independence, they will not be silent before a peril transcending division of every kind.

Though Zimbabwe's violent birth in guerilla warfare eroded proprieties in traditional African discourse (Mungoshi and Marechera are exemplary), Kala's opening scene still surprises. A man and woman in bed have just had sex. There is no discreet indirection or euphemism. No vagueness. The objective fact lies clear on the page. Further, the male, Roderick, is HIV-positive and has subjected (yet another) partner, Loveness, to unprotected intercourse. Psychological wrestling with his sickness swiftly follows, as do the terrifying social implications of his selfishness. Immorality's tentacular reach from this opening scene is made immediately and shockingly apparent.

Explanation of Roderick's selfishness (Don Juan fantasies and bad parenting) must wait upon urgent exposition of the disease's rhythm: initial well-being amid trivial symptoms, speedy reassuring remission, symptoms recurring, and so on. Loveness's background—orphaned early and institutionalized—counterpoints Roderick's. But we learn that, despite delinquency (rebellion at school, flight from an aunt's home), she craves the norms of motherhood, husband, and a secure marriage. This leads to Roderick, and to AIDS, about which, like so many contemporaries, she is ignorant. The tragedy of all Zimbabwe's Lovenesses rings out from the narrative.

The flight of impoverished girls into dysfunction and prostitution flows from social and economic injustice. Meanwhile, the gulf between Roderick's selfishness and Loveness's total love leaves us in no doubt where the text's sympathies lie.

AIDS professionals—doctors, nurses, counselors, women's refuge organizers—emerge positively, though scorned by Roderick as white liberals who can be manipulated. Is it significant that they are mainly church or private-sector personnel and not government employees?

This is a courageous novel, never hysterical, yet blunter than similar work from Zambia and Malawi. Its prose moves briskly, ensuring that figurative decoration will not blur a message to be understood fully and at once. The opening of chapter 7, which moves from worry to suicide plan in one paragraph, captures Kala's manner:

> The next day when she was alone in the house Loveness sat and thought back on her life and how miserable she was. Roderick was drinking a lot and when he came home drunk he insisted that they have sex. If she tried to resist he would beat her, and all the time she was afraid she would get pregnant again. Roderick seemed to dislike the pill as much as he disliked condoms, and when he had found a packet in her bag he had made her tell him where the rest were and flushed them all down the toilet. She couldn't bear the thought that she might give birth to another child to suffer as little Solomon had. She could only see one way out of her misery. She decided she would kill herself. She went to the kitchen and found a bottle of bleach. She took it to her room, and was staring at it, wondering about the best way to drink it.

Where AIDS strikes, not even fiction can fashion happy endings. But at least resurrection from the depths is hinted. Roderick dies wretchedly at home—only Loveness will arrange his funeral and mourn by his graveside. Though now HIV-positive herself, she gets an extended lease of enhanced life and, as an example to fellow sufferers, attends an international AIDS Conference in Brussels.

Kalitera, Aubrey (b. 1950). Malawian novelist and short-story writer. Irrepressible, self sufficient, jaunty, dynamic, resourceful—these words best describe a writer gloriously free of colonial angst or damaged self-esteem, a man who would no more genuflect to literature than to baking or carpentry. With a primary school education in Zomba and random reading in the British Council library, he epitomizes an enterprising spirit that makes Malawians admired throughout Central and Southern Africa. Defoe would have embraced him as a kindred spirit and Samuel Smiles could profitably have sat at his feet. A pioneer of self-publishing, he created both Power Pen Books and the short-story journal *Sweet Mag* (for which he wrote everything); he has written more than a dozen books and claims to be the nation's first full-time writer. His specialty being ephemeral literature (so ephemeral that he cannot recall what all his early work was about), he resembles the freewheeling writers of Nigeria's Onitsha Market and their Gikuyu vernacular contemporaries in Kenya's Karatina, for whom literature is simply another tradable product, like fishing traps or bananas.

Like Tutuola, Nigeria's unschooled author of *The Palm-Wine Drinkard*, Kalitera began to write through boredom. He told Bernth Lindfors, "I had nothing to do at home in the village. . . . If you've got a little education, you may want to express it." Hence, with one bound, he leapt from village lethargy to urban frenzy. Futile assaults on London publishers outraged a writer who would call no man master: "I had this feeling that if I published my own books and sold them myself, possibly I would get a living out of them. I had no money. In fact, I had nothing, so I picked up an old duplicating machine and then bought some stencils."

Life became frantic: writing books all morning ("It was ABC. Writing them was very easy") and selling them by hand in the afternoon. Soon twenty sales assistants were needed—some, alas, apt to flee with the takings. Kalitera told Lindfors that, while averaging four books a year, he was sometimes working simultaneously on three. He was equally revealing about his short stories (some accepted for discussion in Felix Mnthali's Writers' Corner radio program): "I started by producing a thousand copies, but when they didn't sell, I produced only five hundred the next week. Those I did manage to sell. By the following week, there was a greater demand, so I went back to a thousand, then fifteen hundred." Again, when asked about the future, he replied, "At the moment I'm working on three books." Thematic questions, however, triggered amnesia: "Books are like children—you leave them for possibly ten minutes and you can't remember what they look like, especially when you've got over ten! So when I'm here talking about them, I can't remember what all the books are about." He is clear, however, that among his titles (*A Taste of Business*, *A Prisoner's Letter*, *Why Father Why?*, *She Died in My Bed*, *Mother Why Mother?*, *Why Son Why?*, *Daughter Why Daughter?*, *He Died in Her Bed*, and *To Ndirande Mountain with Love*) some examine adultery and the problem of fathers who work in the mines of South Africa and forget their family responsibilities.

There is nothing ephemeral about themes such as these.

Further reading: Bernth Lindfors, *Kulankula: Interviews with Writers from Malawi and Lesotho* (Bayreuth, 1989).

Kalonde, Ken (b. 1969). Malawian poet and playwright. Born in Lilongwe, he attended secondary schools in Mitundu, Mvera, and Bilila before training as a teacher. At twenty-four he wrote a prizewinning radio play, *Welcome, Mr Mwaya*. In 1994, his poem "Okondeka Mzimundilinde" won the Wasi Writing competition and his screenplay *Maaya* a national prize for video scripts. Kalonde pursues the welfare of fellow writers by working as director of Malawi's Copyright Society.

His anthology *Progress After Referendum* (1996) covers the period of the historic referendum of 1993, forced on President Banda, precipitating both his downfall and the coming of multi-party democracy. Given the false dawn of Malawi's 1964 independence, however, the poet's speculation on the future is distinctly ambivalent.

There is ferocity of statement here, Kalonde being another writer wrongly pitched into Banda's jails who deplores the dictator's mauling of his homeland. Ferocity, however, ill serves the need for editorial revision and *labor limae*. Hence at times verse not rough-hewn, inchoate, or impenetrable through modernist whimsy, but simply verse unrevised. A poem called "Nothing" ends well with "Please, die and let die," but begins with "Retortion, shoeing and rerocking aparts" and continues with similar opacity. Plainer statement appears in "Of Being":

The art of being a good visitor is to
    know
When to leave
The art of being a good Politician is
    to know

When to lie
The art of being a humorous
    President is to know
When to die . . .

"Little Path to Chiwamba," though not fully realized, carries fine imagery, while in "Of Ngala wa Pakamwa" the startling coinage "these jiggerflead persons could be gods" signals strong potential, and "Sadaka mood," a funeral poem, begins well with "It's morning / worms skidding / they wake, they walk, they catch / hoes in hand, tears in eyes."

Kalonde is forgiving about his incarceration but cites chapter and verse anyway:

At Kachere prison
We survive by God's art
And Devil's performance
Just as we quiz our faces to odours
    and carry
Unidentified corpses from Bottom
    Hospital
To Sacred Heart cemetery

Youthful misbehavior might well have prepared the way for his detention:

I was fourteen then
And always in stolen school
    uniforms
A scandalmonger. A mobmaker
A nuisance, a rapist
A Jehova's [sic] witness and a
    becoming dissident

Admirable commitment emerges in Kalonde's poetry for children, whose situation across Central Africa hurts him deeply. His *Smiles Round Africa* targets hunger, crime, abuse, abandonment, and AIDS-caused orphanhood. This is plain poetry, uncluttered and compelling. "Phwetekere Township" censures child labor in the home:

Oh dear! We are too young to lift
    firewood

We are too young to work for pay,
    Mama
Please, try us tomorrow when we
    grow
Try us tomorrow when we are tall
Try us tomorrow when we are strong

In "Mother and Child," children sing:

Treat us good, mother
Teach us good, mother
And we will be good citizens
Sweet sweet Mama

Street children appear in "Kamuzu Procession Road":

Kamuzu Procession is a busy road
    here
We walk and steal more money, dear
Tobacco farmers are too loose to
    play here
It's not our wish, but Mummy died
And Daddy died of Malaria and
    Tuberculosis
And we know life is too bad here

Even children with living parents suffer. But in "We Walk in Teams" they show solidarity when visiting the town dump:

But we know that food is scarce
Mummy goes to town begging
Daddy goes to town robbing
Pretty sister goes to town picking
    men
Rude brother goes to town raping
    disabled
Every school holiday
We walk in teams sadly
To our poor homes and poor hearts
And sleep with singing stomachs

Kalonde's work has range, energy, and moral core. A scholarship to the Iowa Workshop (it worked wonders for compatriot Mpina in the 1980s) would be investment in a talent that, like the children in the poet's second volume, cries out for care and attention.

Kamkondo, Dede (d. 2006). Malawian novelist, short-story writer, and playwright. Born in the northern region, he graduated from the national university in the 1970s. His first novel, *The Innocent Boy*, won a British Council prize in 1976 and his play *The Vacant Seat* a university award in 1977. Subsequent work includes *A Tattoo for the Soul, Truth Will Out* (1986), *The Children of the Lake* (1987), *The Family Secret* (1988), and *For the Living* (1989). Kamkondo combined writing with a post in communication at the University of Malawi's College of Agriculture, where his research interests included the role of women in land issues and smallholder estates.

The Children of the Lake bears Kamkondo's distinctive style: tight prose delicately blending realism and fantasy, and lively dialogue. Behind it is an incisive mind and confident creativity. Not to choose a Malawian protagonist but a South African "colored" female bespeaks courage. To capture a woman's viewpoint, with appropriate linguistic register—and make her the socially alienated "mother" of a daughter neither white nor colored but black—suggests mature literary skill.

Florence portrays herself briskly:

> I was born some forty-four years ago in a shantytown outside Greater Durban. My father, I was told, was a Tonga from Nkhata Bay (I never saw him for he disappeared when I was seven months old inside my mother's body) and my mother was a Cape Coloured who never knew which Boer farmer was her father.

Kamkondo is confident with white portrayal too. Hence Rex Smuts, whose speech and racist posture Florence catches when recalling employment with him:

> Rex Smuts wasn't a bad man. . . . His instructions to me were simple: Look here, girl, no kids, no visitors for you, jah? You can go visit your Mum once in two months, jah? You go to bed at 10 p.m. and up at five. . . . You will be given your rations every Thursday, enough for breakfast, lunch, dinner, jah? There's a good girl.

As someone disturbing the racial mosaic of Central and Southern Africa, Florence's plight is pitiful:

> Can't you see that I've nowhere to go? I'm not black; I'm not white; I'm not Asian. I'm me . . . Coloured me. I don't know my father; I don't know my grandfather. Leave me alone, you people.

Vignettes of fast life in Blantyre's Ndirande slums counterpoint idyllic Lake Malawi, where, with the sinking of the *Viphya* in 1946, the plot's action begins, Florence's "daughter" Anita being a disaster survivor. Florence constantly addresses readers and a dead husband as if they are a jury whom she must convince that her behavior is always for Anita's welfare. Yet, slowly, through her own protestations, she emerges as a woman of poor judgment and suspect values. If, as she hopes, Anita is to be a lady, she must have wealth: "I am one of those people who are convinced that no poor woman is worth the title 'lady.'"

Like other contemporaries, Kamkondo accepts the importance of writing for children. His *Sivo and the Cruel Thief* shows no compromise on quality. Sivo and his sister Nyembezi win five hundred kwacha for helping police arrest a Blantyre thief called "The Hat." The children are interviewed on national radio, which then broadcasts their story of action, suspense, and responsible citizenship. Narrative pace is swift, characterization engaging, and, as in *Children of the Lake*, arcadian lakeside scenery (the family's home area) contrasts Blantyre's urban criminality. Young listeners can emulate Sivo's heroism because he is no fairy-tale star:

> Sivo Phiri was not tall. He was twelve years old. His face was round and smooth. His eyes were as small as the eyes of a rat. His ears were as large as the ears of a hyena. Fortunately, he was not ugly.

There is nothing inert in *Sivo and the Cruel Thief*. Invention constantly feeds the imagination in a story that gives didacticism a good name.

Truth Will Out (a book revealing Kamkondo's admiration for Kenyan popular writer David Maillu) exhibits symmetrical plotting at its best. The aesthetics of style are manifest—a prose effectively brisk that pushes along event and character development and reaches for the figurative just often enough not to suggest gilding the lily or narrative delay: "like a rat fleeing before a raging bush fire," "That dirty face that is like an old bicycle saddle," "like a little child left to face the dentist alone." A happily married couple with the author's own university background become haunted by revelations from the past—sexual behavior producing babies that could, if revealed, destroy current connubial joy. Tension builds via inner dialogue in each partner and, as it were, with each other. Confessional exposure is contemporaneous and the marriage is saved with room enough for both anterior offspring.

For the Living, which also has the episodic features of the picaresque, reconfirms Kamkondo's storytelling powers. If Rossini could make music from a laundry list, Kamkondo could probably create fic-

tion from one. Bennett Nthali, a clever, sensitive, guilt-prone Hamlet figure, is obsessed by memory of his dead mother and tiny deaf mute sister, Teresa; his every thought and action are for or related to them. Kamkondo's fertile invention, his instinctive understanding of how to create compelling narrative, his capacity for skilful plotting on levels realist and surrealist, his understanding of the popular love of school experience and humor, the importance of shifting scene across the nation, and the need for event, and more event— they are all here.

Kamlongera, Chris (b. 1949). Malawian poet and dramatist. He was born in the Central Region and educated at Zomba Catholic Secondary School. After undergraduate training at the University of Malawi, he took an M.A. and Ph.D. at Britain's University of Leeds. Initially appointed to his home university's Department of English, in 1981 he became a founding member of its Department of Fine and Performing Arts, where he is now a professor.

Kamlongera developed during the Banda era, a time of political terror and literary awakening. While detention centers were filling, the university's Writers' Workshop flourished. Manifest were the creative energies of such figures as James and Patience Gibbs, David Kerr, Felix Mnthali, Mupa Shumba, Steve Chimombo, Ken Lipenga, Paul Zeleza, and Jack Mapanje. A traveling theater was active, an open-air theater built. Dramatic experiment stimulated vigorous critical debate. When the anthropologist Matthew Schoffeleers urged the protodramatic traits of Malawi's cults and oral texts as a basis for local theater, Kamlongera, like his colleagues Steve Chimombo, James Ngombe, Joe Mosiwa, Bayani Ngulube, and Innocent Banda, was keen to respond. His own *Love Potion* and *Graveyards* were well received during 1976 in Malawi and Leeds.

Since then he has written plays for the BBC and contributed seminally to the growth of theater for development, a field with clear political risks during Banda's rule. His *Theatre for Development in Africa with Case Studies from Malawi and Zambia* (1989), informed by the thought of Brazilian reformer Paolo Freire and by collegial cooperation, shows how literary art can cause social change. As he writes: "The distinction between a work of art and the real world commonly made in the west is difficult to discern in the African experience." Conventional theater practice contrasts that in theater for development. Unlike the pattern of the former (Script—Auditions—Interpretation of script—Rehearsal—Technical input—Publicity—Audience—Reviews), that of the latter is markedly communal: Catalyst—Research with villagers—Further scenario creation/improvisation—Improvisation leading to sketches loose enough to accept comment from villagers during performance—Performance, which changes in response to audience comment—Evaluation—Follow-up. As Kamlongera observes, "Whereas the script and the actor dominate in the 'professional' theatre, it is the creative process which is dependent on research that is central" to Theatre for Development. Among his case studies is one from Mwima. In Freirian style, the villagers debate their problems (absence of a nurse or clinical officer, lack of clean water, diseases such as malaria, schistosomiasis, diarrhea, measles, scabies, lack of health leadership, up to two hundred deaths per thousand live births, distance from hospitals, and so forth). Loosely dramatizing them (villagers as actors, audience as active commentators) results in sinking better wells, keeping them clean, digging latrines, and setting up village health committees.

Kamlongera's early verse was introspective, less engaged with landscape or season than with the human predicament, Africa's postcolonial disenchantment, and

oppression under Banda. Circumstances demanded an ironically oblique poetic statement, heavily metaphoric. A newly decolonized undergraduate syllabus had also exposed him to writers such as Wole Soyinka and Chinua Achebe, who had already drunk deep in postcolonial gloom. The vision was existentially bleak. To colleagues urging the humor of a Mongo Beti or Ferdinand Oyono or the mythic world of an Amos Tutuola, Kamlongera would reply that the zeitgeist made such mirth and fantasy artistically irresponsible. Life overall seemed dark, certainly uninviting of celebration:

> Eggs hatch into chicks
> Sunrise gives way to sunset
> And babies grow to fit large coffins

Reflecting an existential gloom understandable under Banda, he suggested that growth simply meant you could see life's disasters more clearly:

> We are maggots
> Wriggling
> Within the glitter
> Of faeces
> That give us birth
> Only to slip back
> Where we began.

Poems abounded in images of weevils, disease and mucus, owls hooting doom from rooftops, snakes whispering death in the grass, stricken birds flapping helpless in the dust. Soyinka emerged as a favored figure for prophet and lofty satirist: "Soyinka has been / Up Idranre rocks / Seen it all . . . / Nigeria's witness / Teiresias."

Kamlongera liked the idea of the poet as prophet and seer, but the speaker in the following lines presents a pathology of deep disillusion:

> I'm a cancer patient
> Another Bone Chewer

Impotent in this ward
Hospitalizing my cancerous truth

Further reading: Martin Banham, ed., *A History of Theatre in Africa* (Cambridge, 2004); David Kerr, *Dance, Media Entertainment and Popular Theatre in South East Africa* (Bayreuth, 1998); Adrian Roscoe, *Uhuru's Fire: African Literature East to South* (London, 1977).

Kanengoni, Alexander (b. 1951). Zimbabwean novelist and short-story writer. Born at Chivhu, Zimbabwe, educated at Marymount Catholic Mission, Kutama College, and St. Paul's Teacher Training College, he taught in schools until 1974, when, like other contemporaries, he became a freedom fighter, serving in the border areas between Zimbabwe and Mozambique. After independence he studied English at the national university and became a government education officer working with ex-combatants and refugees. Since 1988 he has headed research services at the Zimbabwean Broadcasting Corporation. His work includes the novels *Vicious Circle* (1983), *When the Rainbird Cries* (1988), *Echoing Silences* (1997), and a short-story collection, *Effortless Tears* (1993), which won him the Zimbabwe Book Publisher's Literary Award.

Vicious Circle shows solidarity (family, worker, national) buckling under the onslaught of late colonialism. The rural Mavhu family has rebounded from earlier colonial damage—Baba Mavhu was lured to South African mines and returned to find a broken home. And it has achieved the limited progress the system allows: a son with GCE O levels working in a paper mill, a daughter married, and a son, Tendai, at university. Tendai's decision to join the bush war is the simple act that triggers family tragedy. The long arm of white security soon reaches into the family network.

Baba Mavhu, old, dignified, proud of the solidarity he has rebuilt, profoundly moral, and not at all complicit in his son's decision, is dragged before the District Commissioner and subjected to a degrading and fatal beating:

> "Come, fix the kaffir," the DC shouted. The DA unleashed his left leg and the big boot thudded into the old man's groin. The old man doubled up and sprawled on the floor. The DA raised his boot again and landed it with all his might on the head of the old man.

The incident typifies Kanengoni's ability to lay bare, without ideological comment, colonial reality. While Baba is dying in hospital (he tells his son Noel "You are taking over the ruin I have left"), his wife and their deaf mute child Lovemore receive a government visit in which their possessions are smashed and thrown onto a lorry for removal to the arid Limpopo Valley and their barns and huts burnt by laughing officials. Baba's dying words to his son reemphasize the urgency of family solidarity. But Noel decides to join his brother in the bush war and is killed while daydreaming on the road.

Echoing Silences explores paradox in a Liberation War conceptually simple yet complex enough in self-destruction and psychic trauma to produce initial literary silence. This, in turn, says Kanengoni, spawned postindependence injustice— veteran rejection, urban profiteering, nepotism, corruption, national lying—and a distorted history. He writes: "We deliberately kept silent about some truths . . . because some of us felt that we would compromise our power. This was how the lies began when we came to tell the history of the country and the history of the struggle." This is the echoing silence the book breaks as it joins a regional effort to get history right. Nightmare horror appears with diarylike immediacy (mirroring accounts in fellow writers like Nyamubaya and Samupindi). With thirty thousand dead, the nation emerged dazed and traumatized from the war, conscience-stricken by internal and external atrocities, initial idealism almost destroyed. Hostility erupts between allies ZAPU and ZIPRA. Guerillas die pointlessly in Tanzanian training camps. Munashe survives the conflict, only to see soldiers after independence on their way to inflict civil war massacres on Matabeleland. Female cadres are sexually abused (Kudzai's military career is a litany of rape, prison when she objects, and death by South African commandos—but not before being raped again). Half-mad commissars' sadistic execution of anyone suspected of betrayal includes the book's central atrocity. A starving woman with a baby on her back, suspected of being merely the wife of a sellout, has to dig her own grave before being beaten to death with a hoe by Munashe, the high-minded recruit who has abandoned study to fight for what he thought a noble cause. Memory of this murder (merely one of many) recurs ad nauseam, driving Munashe to the conviction that "war is the greatest scourge of mankind" and to a death in the eastern mountains that nothing, not even traditional exorcism, can prevent. Guerilla war devastation is key. But nation and protagonist had already suffered psychologically under colonial rule—being shifted so often from ancestral land to make way for white farmers that, in Munashe's case, he speaks of home as "a place where one stayed with one's bags packed."

His detailing the massacre at Nyadzonia is not untypical. The attack on this refugee camp was one of the vilest outrages of the Liberation War:

Whole bodies of little boys and girls, young men and women, old men and old women lay scattered amongst those with decapitated heads, crushed skulls, shattered faces, missing limbs and shredded stomachs. Flies, swarms of heavy, green flies hovered over the bodies moving from corpse to corpse. . . .

Flashbacks, narrative interruptions, and digressions here are less structural flaws than representations of Munashe's mind, which is countering psychic sickness.

Kangende, Kenneth (b. 1953). Zambian short-story writer. He was born in the Kangomo District. After education at Monze Secondary School, unusually among African writers, he graduated in chemistry and is currently petroleum manager for the Energy Regulation Board of Zambia. His writing harnesses his science but emerges, he says, from an acquaintance with written literature of only secondary school level. However, his *Zambian Myths and Legends of the Wild* (2001) displays a formidable knowledge of local tradition and lore. His first publication, *Night Whispers* (2000), a short-story collection, announced an important new Zambian voice. Though ill served by his editors, it speaks of a natural talent skillfully employed. Its characteristics include variety, engagement, and the sheer nosiness of journalism, though married here to fiction's way with verbal aesthetics, narrative, and characterization.

The writing exudes decisiveness. Kangende knows his strengths and aims. A short story means precisely that—it will occupy one sitting—and when he strays further, as he does exceptionally in a longer piece, "Ordeal Fire," he can lose his way. He wants crisp, economical openings: "Eagle's Nest is a pub notorious for flouting the law," "Squatting like a kangaroo in a five meter pit, Kani felt a sudden violent jerk," "The dark river of ants fascinated me," "I had never been conscious of my looks until

I graduated from college, joined a parastatal company and moved into a flat with Mulonga."

Dialogue echoes the tough Americanized argot of Alex La Guma's Cape Town: "Let's go, you thief. Tonight, we'll fix all of you aliens. This area is completely sealed by paras," "You," barked the first officer, "have you ever slept in the cooler?"

A further strength is Kangende's intimate knowledge of village life as well as fast-track city ways. He can register the smell and feel of a witch doctor's kit as acutely as the sex-and-booze rhythms of a township nightclub. He is equally compelling on both peasant and townie psychology—witness his accounts of witch doctor chicanery in "Ordeal Fire" and "The Witch Finder's Drum," the mental workings of a slum-dwelling winner of the national lottery in "The Street Vendor," and of a girl jealous of her prettier friend in "God, Why Was I Born Ugly?"

Kangende can dazzle with cameo portraits while minimally interrupting his narrative. Thus in "Ordeal Fire": "He was a frail old man with a permanent sourly grimace and a red neck that rivaled a rooster's wattle"; in "Cure for Jealousy": "He was a tall bloke with steel muscles bulging from his sleeveless shirt. He looked haggard and his chin was unshaven"; and, in "The Disciplinarian": "Marina was a beautiful woman. She had the gaze of the moon and the succulent bottom of a wasp."

If Kangende commands the clarity of scientific discourse, more important is his flair for the figurative. To reflect the richness of his African landscape he resorts to conventional devices that assault the senses and bring a work to echoing life: "Toads and frogs were having rowdy parties in the flooded plains," "He peered down like an owl trying to locate a rat," "He hurled himself out of the pit like a fish suddenly surprised to find itself stranded in hot sand,"

"My eyes popped out like a chameleon swallowing a fly," "He was a short old warthog with the curse of elephantiasis in the left leg," "The fresh air hit his face like honey on the tongue," "A visit from a bloke like Zyle was like being visited by a rabid dog," "His face was a cataract of wrinkles," "His teeth gleamed like ice cubes," "A piano brooded in the corner."

Kangende is a most sociable writer. A true child of the society he paints, he loves people, rumor, prattle, eccentricity. Unsentimental, never strait-laced, his writing celebrates life cheerfully, often mischievously, on the surface. Yet he can poignantly depict the misery of street children, as he does in "No Surname," and hint at postindependence greed in the same story: "Do you know why you're poor? . . . The answer is simple. You're poor because somebody else eats on your behalf." But there is no wallowing in postcolonial gloom or white settler sin.

Katiyo, Wilson (1947–2003). Zimbabwean novelist. He was born in Mutoko, but circumstances drove him to live with cruel relatives elsewhere. He gained admission to Fletcher High School, a leading institution, but, as with many contemporaries, government harassment (including a month's jail in 1965) forced him into exile: first to Zambia, where he was befriended by the Hodgkin family (his first novel's dedicatees), and then to England to complete his education. After independence, he became popular among Zimbabwean writers and journalists; his books were prescribed as school texts. But he fled again in the late 1980s, first to France, then to Britain, where he died. His main works were *A Son of the Soil* (1976) and *Going to Heaven* (1979).

Childhood trauma determined the autobiographical nature of Katiyo's first novel, whose narrative drowns in detail. Seeking writing's exorcism of morbid memory, his prose is rough-hewn and repetitive, minimally decorated and patterned.

Yet such weakness is also a strength. Stylistic rawness, torrential detail, and sober plainness persuade the reader that so much suffering cannot be imaginary. His account of colonial Rhodesian life, with its Byzantine network of apartheid-style laws, casual police brutality, and red-scare neurosis ("comrade" automatically signifying "communist") is all too quotidian to be untrue. This is so even in the book's rural sections. Alexio, fatherless, is farmed out to relatives, who physically and mentally abuse him, a foreshadowing of life in the capital, where the police, suspecting a Moscow-bound "terrorist," abuse him again. Absence of bias also enhances credibility. Mistreatment by black rural relatives balances mistreatment by white urban police; kindness from black rural relatives balances kindness from some urban whites.

Tonal innocence merely records the illogic of the colonial madhouse—all the better for hardly interrogating it—its racist laws especially: Africans must drink no spirits, carry town passes, use separate buses, avoid benches reserved for whites. After torture in a darkened prison cell, where an interior dialogue shows Katiyo's writing at its best, Alexio flees to the mountains, joining four hundred others ready for rebellion and escape across the border.

Further reading: Musaemura Zimunya, *Those Years of Drought and Hunger: The Birth of African Fiction in Zimbabwe* (Gweru, 1982); Rino Zhuwarara, *Introduction to Zimbabwean Literature in English* (Harare, 2001); Primorac Ranka and Pauline Rodgson-Katiyo, "Wilson Katiyo 1947–2003," *Journal of Commonwealth Literature* 39, no. 2 (summer 2004): 123–125.

Kaunda, Kenneth David (b. 1924). President of Zambia (1964–91). Born at Lubwa of Malawian parents, a circumstance his political opponents exploited, he grew up imbued with a love of education and Christianity. Like many politicians across the continent, he became a teacher, first in Northern Rhodesia, then in Tanganyika. In 1949 he became interpreter and African affairs adviser to Sir Stewart Gore-Browne, a liberal white member of the Northern Rhodesia Legislative Council. Political activity began in the 1950s, first at a local level, and then as secretary general of the African National Congress, the country's first national political party. He famously broke with the ANC leader Harry Nkumbula, finding him insufficiently committed to freedom. He favored Gandhian nonviolent action within a philosophy of humanism (David Kerr calls it an "unofficial state ideology"), created to unite Zambians around such core family and community values as respect for the aged, willingness to share, and a strong work ethic. Indeed, Kaunda saw this as a model for a world lurching toward capitalist individualism. Despite his humanism, he was detained by the colonial authorities, and on release in 1960 he joined UNIP, the United National Independence Party, founded in 1959 by Mainza Choma, which, with 300,000 members, demanded independence from Britain and an end to the hated Central African Federation. With the Federation's collapse (Malawi's President Banda claimed the credit), Zambia became independent in 1964, with Kaunda as president. He was reelected six times—after 1973 in one-party elections.

Admiration for Kaunda's integrity brought him chairmanship of the Organization for African Unity (1970–71, 1987–88), of the Non-Aligned Movement (1970–73), and of the Front Line States (1985). He is a radiantly warm man, but unfortunate policies and the global economy frustrated his plans for Zambia. Receiving rich copper revenues, he unwisely neglected agriculture (unlike Banda in Malawi). The fall in copper prices and massive rise in oil prices in the 1980s wrought havoc with development, collapsing living standards and provoking mass protests. Kaunda lost power in competitive elections in 1991, defeated by the Movement for Multiparty Democracy. He graciously handed the government over to his successor, Frederick Chiluba.

Zambian writing reflects the positive and negative in Kaunda's rule. History will perhaps view him kindly as a good man who could have achieved more in quieter times. His humanism was unobjectionable, his intentions benign, his attitude to power different from Banda's and Mugabe's. His principled decision to let Zambia become the leading Front Line State in the struggle against white Rhodesia and apartheid South Africa (he hosted Joshua Nkomo's ZAPU forces) cost repeated bombings and economic body blows that Malawian pragmatism avoided.

Among Central African leaders, Kaunda is the most published. Despite absorbing national and international affairs, he has found time to write numerous books. They examine violence, dominion status for Central Africa, economic reform, and include letters to his children; he has coauthored texts (with, for example, Kenya's Tom Mboya) and written introductions to books on themes that appealed to him. His autobiographical *Zambia Shall Be Free* (1980), wherein he describes his Christian background, growing political awareness, and anger at apartheid-style practices in his country, was well received. His thinking on freedom, humanism, and Africa's future as it moved beyond colonialism was outlined in *Black Government* (1966) and *A Humanist in Africa* (1966). Central arguments were based on the thinking of Teilhard de Chardin and on the view that colonialism devalued man. Independence, he said, was the triumph of a "Man-centered society over a Power-centered society."

Further reading: Richard Hall, *The High Price of Principles: Kaunda and the White South* (London, 1969); David Kerr, *Dance, Media and Popular Theatre in South East Africa* (Bayreuth, 1998).

Kayange, George (b. 1976). Malawian fiction writer. Born in Chintheche in Nkhata Bay District, he attended three primary schools and St John's Secondary School, Lilongwe. Holding a diploma in journalism, he currently works for the Malawi News Agency, joining a growing cohort of writers who have developed outside the walls of academe.

After essay prizes in 2001 from the Malawi Writers Union and the Ishmiri Religion of Peace Organization, in 2002 Kayange produced his first book, a novella called *Gone for a Walk*, whose fresh conception and thematic boldness give it a significance disproportionate to its modest dimensions and first attempt at prose beyond the essay.

Sharing a national anxiety, Kayange decided to tackle the AIDS scourge head-on, without, however, rejecting Old Africa's tactful indirection around sensitive topics (a group survival strategy) for Western explicitness. The book is thus a creation of gentle originality and even beauty, its didacticism, wrapped in human interest, offered with calm reflection rather than dogma. Freshness even marks its characterization. Kondwani ("be happy"), is thirteen. His father is a lecturer at Mzuzu University. Two of Kondwani's sisters have already died from AIDS. As he journeys to Lake Malawi, Kondwani's bus breaks down, providing a chance meeting with a Mrs. Mills and her eleven-year old daughter Sue, from New Zealand. The delay lets the children walk, chat, and touch on AIDS, while Kondwani also expands on African life— its village camaraderie and rich folklore. He censures female initiation ceremonies because in them "some men, known as *afisi* (hyenas), are invited to sleep with [the initiates]. . . . And what if these men have AIDS?" Sue cites her mother's view that poverty is the root problem because it forces girls into prostitution.

Here the book's explicitness ends, yielding to a forest walk of edenic overtones and even suspense. When, after finding and eating mangoes, Kondwani pulls Sue to the ground, it is for a happy chat and not for sex. But, perhaps as a symbol of what might have been or of the AIDS danger, a python destroys this idyllic interlude and chases the pair away.

The AIDS discussion gets balanced treatment. While Kondwani approves of government condom advertisements, he does not explicitly oppose the Christian message of Job-like patience and abstinence:

> Most churches in Malawi such as the Roman Catholic and the Church of Central Africa Presbyterian, including the Pentecostal churches themselves had been bitterly opposed to the government's promotional campaign for condoms. The government claimed that condoms were effective whereas the churches disapproved of them on moral grounds, instead emphasizing behavioural change like the practice of abstinence.

Kayange is strategically placed at the Malawi News Agency to monitor the unfolding ravages of AIDS and deserves credit for a text both bold and timely. *Gone for a Walk* shows Malawian literature confronting contemporary issues, thus continuing the moral role of Africa's oral literature, which, in its more oblique mode, traditionally tackled major problems, too—famine, for example, chiefly misrule, and drought.

Sporting a glossary and essay topics, *Gone for a Walk* addresses an audience of secondary school children. A cover blurb by Sambalikagwa Mvona also urges its suitability for primary schools. That, too, would mean breaking old patterns.

Kayira, B. M. C. (b. ca. 1953). Malawian novelist. Born in northern Malawi, he studied French at the national university and lectured there for five years before, like others, fleeing from Hastings Banda's oppression. He traveled to Zambia, Zimbabwe, Swaziland, and South Africa, where he still lives. His first and only novel, *Tremors of the Jungle* (1996), was published simultaneously in South Africa and Malawi.

Tremors is a campus novel without comic core. Events at Fearfong University in Manthaland critique national politics and explore ways in which the system might be changed. This is clearly a roman à clef. Here is Chancellor College's campus in Zomba, Malawi's old capital lying beneath Zomba Plateau, called Tumblefeet Mountains. The high street, Kham Kham Highway, is Kamuzu Highway; Scotland, the town to the south, is Blantyre, and nearby Lake McSilence is Lake Chilwa. Testing-time Hotel, where Mati, a young staff associate, comes to stay, is the former Government Hostel (Sir Harry Johnston's original gubernatorial residence) where new Malawian academics were housed to be discreetly vetted by Banda's Special Branch.

Postcolonial literary criticism will sometimes descry the shaping traits of the former colonizer. Nigeria might reflect British pragmatism and Senegal, say, French idealism. When Kayira, though educated in a former British colony, writes Central Africa's most cerebral novel (intense ratiocination and Socratic dialogue dominate), its allusion to Breton, surrealism, and Chateaubriand suggests the influence of his French literary specialization. The book's generous dedication to Jean-Louis Joulié, Kayira's instructor and colleague, suggests this, too. British pragmatism adds action and violence.

Young Mati, exiled, recalls his closing years at Fearfong. Staying on after graduation to prepare for an academic life, he feels proud to be seen now as a colleague by Professor Chiselwood, whom he idolized as a free spirit, famous for noteless lecturing (it brings imaginative free play and death to rigidity). Chiselwood counterstates the buttoned-up-and-suited culture of the regime, and extended exchanges among him, Mati, and law-lecturing Vivi address dilemmas facing academe: how, with its commitment to truth and new knowledge, should it respond to a dictatorship that despises all this ("Intellectuals, like the poor, we will always have with us," sneered Banda, and jailed them in numbers). Polarities are in tension. Chiselwood's world of intellectual solutions (he is writing a book on Being, and an extempore apologia for the life of the mind is one of the novel's highlights) opposes the crude world of physical violence, represented not only by Banda but also by law-lecturer Vivi. Mati swallows Chiselwood's view that life is all about language, in the way St. John of the gospels saw it (*In principio erat verbum*—in the beginning was the Word), but Vivi will have none of it. "The problem with most revolutionaries," he says, "is that they end up embracing words. And so find themselves in the very politics they set out to fight!" To his claim that in global crises writers are the last to stand up, Chiselwood replies that they "stand up in their writings," which address not just discrete incidents but all such incidents for time immemorial.

Amid endless partying ("another round of drinks" constantly refuels the narrative) and frequent recourse to Einstein, Yeats, Shelley, Shakespeare, Wilde, and French counterparts, students target the police, who then, in local phrase, "accidentalize" Mati and his friends in a road smash that also kills Vivi, Chiselwood, and the hapless Kettie, Mati's pregnant girlfriend. Recalling the horrors of a regime that snuffed out freedom dreams so swiftly, Mati reflects, "I cannot help but wonder how anyone can fight a system with full justification—and then, at the first opportunity, turn around and embrace the same system, with full justification, too!"

Kayira, Legson Didimu (b. 1939). Malawian novelist. His autobiography, *I Will Try*, though denying knowledge of a birth date (circumstantial evidence suggests 1939), says it was into a Tumbuka family in the hill village of Mpale in the Karonga district of Northern Nyasaland. It also records that, being a fat baby, Kayira was flung into the Didimu River but was rescued by a neighbor. A further burden was the name Chalangani, meaning stupid, given him by his grandfather. He was educated first at the Presbyterians' famous Livingstonia Secondary School, which he left in 1958. His subsequent life reflects sadly on Nyasaland, which, though founded partly on Livingstonian values, was a land from which many literally walked away.

Banda himself famously walked for schooling to South Africa, from where he sailed to America and qualified as a medical doctor before his career in Scotland, England, and Ghana. But Kayira out-trekked even Banda. With Lincoln his hero, his walk, begun on October 14, 1958, took him nearly two thousand miles to Khartoum in the Sudan, where he arrived on September 25, 1960; he carried a Bible in one hand and *Pilgrim's Progress* in the other. He also wore his Livingstonia School khaki shirt sporting the motto, "I will try." His plan was simple: "Leave home and walk to America!" His dreams led him to Skagit Valley Junior College and the University of Washington, where he took a B.A. in 1965, later moving for graduate study to Britain's Cambridge University.

Kayira's literary output was achieved within a single decade. *I Will Try* (1966) preceded his first novel, *The Looming Shadow* (1968). Three further novels were *Jingala* (1969), *The Civil Servant* (1971), and *The Detainee* (1974). Malawi itself has undervalued Kayira's achievements, perhaps because, as witness contemporary South Africa, tensions may develop between readers who remain at home and writers in exile wanting to evoke the home scene. Certainly Malawian students in the 1970s saw Kayira's work as detached from harsh local reality, offering a genial pastoralism that only slowly mutated into political engagement, while they craved frontal attack on Banda's terror. Having, like others, admired Banda as liberator, Kayira paid the price of moving too slowly to attack the metamorphosed leader, which he eventually did in *The Detainee* (1974), written after a rare visit home and immediately banned by the authorities.

Detachment and nostalgia, once rebuked, now seem to find post-Banda favor. Kayira's fine capturing of Malawi's old rural world, with its arcadian landscapes, steady life rhythms, ritualized social event, and distinctive cultural patterns can be enjoyed—even its gently Horatian satirizing of human foible.

Kayira's position in the first novels, despite a slow-dawning social emphasis (rural poverty, domestic damage by work in South Africa's mines) lies in the broad middle ground that attracted Fielding, Leacock, Smollett, and Chesterton, where the comic spirit thrives, and where life proceeds pragmatically, shunning extremes. People transcend ideology here, with minimal hint of negritudist angst, cultural vertigo, and colonial disruption. His characters smiling in the midst of adversity reflect a human spirit widely manifest yet, during the colonial and postcolonial struggle, not always given literary shape.

Kayira's first novel pits a village doctor against a headman over a suspected bewitching. As in Gogol's or Gulliver's world, its spice derives from the disjunction between the actors' exaggerated sense of their village stage and an outsider's wider perspective. Yet there is hinted sadness too as these men are reminded that a coming political order will bring them redundancy and mere decorative status. Their world reappears in *Jingala*, but within advanced plotting and characterization. Jingala, with a small man's dreams of grandeur, opposes for traditional reasons his son Gregory's desire to become a Catholic priest. A comic figure, he is a sad one too as modernity edges him and his like to the sidelines. They are becoming as cosmetic as the symbolic keys and stopped timepieces they ostentatiously carry. Mirth and autumnal sadness blend when the headman keeps looking at his watch during a visit to Gregory and Jingala and suggesting that he is very busy and must be off to his garden:

> The chief swung his left arm around and looked at his watch as though it was functioning, and even said something to the effect that it was getting late. As if it was some sort of ritual, Jingala also pulled his clock from the breast pocket of his waist-coat, took an examining look at it, then shook it once and looked again. It was getting late, he agreed with the chief's pronouncement, then put it back in the pocket.

Yet Jingala is shrewd, with debating skills that make his "educated" son seem slow-witted. His formation, described by the headman for Gregory, makes a point about modern schooling that Ivan Illich or Paolo Freire would applaud:

> Neither your father nor Devera nor myself can read. In your eyes we are

therefore not educated; but we know how to live with other people, how to raise our children, how to appease our ancestors, and how to bury our dead. Now, is that not education?

Kayira's vision darkens with *The Civil Servant*. While his eye for absurdity remains, he foregrounds problems within city and village, and his characters typically inhabit both milieus. When the adulterous George arrives in Isabella's village she tells him: "We are very poor here as you may have guessed already. We eat no bread and drink no tea. We eat nsima and beans and spinach." She herself, vulnerable to seduction, a victim of the poverty that drove her husband to his death in South Africa's mines, dies tragically in childbirth walking to the city and carrying George's child. Alongside her we find George's wife Vera, a stranger in Malawi and mother of many dead babies, and Enid, tradition's ideal woman, who, with a hare lip nobody wants to mention, waits vainly at home to be called to the city to marry Demero: "I am afraid that I am only living in a dream, that you will not marry me or, if you do, that you will always regret it. I know that I am not beautiful and not well-educated. I am only a simple girl."

In *The Detainee*, Malawi's timeless rural world has disappeared. Detention without trial affects families everywhere. Banda paranoia is running wild. His Young Pioneers are terrorizing villagers and flinging Jehovah's Witnesses into wells. This is the kind of text Kayira's countrymen had long wanted—a frontal assault on the injustice, deepening poverty, human waste, and suffocation of free speech that ordinary citizens witnessed daily and whose reality Kayira now acknowledged.

Further reading: Thomas H. Jackson, "Legson Kayira and the Uses of the Grotesque," *World Literature Written in English* 22, no. 2 (1983): 143–151: Adrian Roscoe, *Uhuru's Fire: African Literature East to South* (London, 1977).

Lessing, Doris (b. 1919). Zimbabwean novelist, poet, and short-story writer, born Doris Tayler in Kermanshah, Persia (now Iran). In 1924 her family emigrated to Rhodesia, her bank-manager father hoping to make money in the short-lived agricultural boom of the early 1920s. He never succeeded, and Lessing's childhood on their farm near Banket in the northern part of the country was characterized by real poverty. She left school at fourteen and moved to Salisbury, working as a nanny, telephone operator, and secretary in a law firm. She began to identify with various progressive groups whose Marxist agendas became more doctrinaire as refugees from Europe and members of Britain's Royal Air Force swelled their membership. Her earliest published short stories appeared in the local RAF magazine *Rafters* and her first published poems in *New Rhodesia*, which opened its pages to ideas seen at the time as dissident. This period of her life provided the background for the first four volumes of her novel sequence "Children of Violence": *Martha Quest* (1952), *A Proper Marriage* (1954), *A Ripple from the Storm* (1958), and *Landlocked* (1965). When she left Rhodesia for England in 1949, she had already completed *The Grass Is Singing*, which was published the following year to immediate acclaim. A volume of short stories, *This Was the Old Chief's Country* (1951), confirmed that here was an important new writer, and *Five Short Novels* (1953) was enthusiastically reviewed. Included in the former volume were "The Old Chief

Mhlanga" and "Winter in July," and in the latter "A Home for the Highland Cattle" and "The Antheap," which are perhaps the best known of her shorter African fictional pieces. In 1956, Lessing was commissioned to visit Rhodesia and report on the progress of the Central African Federation, to which she was bitterly opposed. South Africa declared her a prohibited immigrant. Back in England, she found herself also forbidden from visiting all three countries comprising the Federation. Only with Zimbabwean independence was this ban lifted, and she was allowed to return to the country that had been her home for twenty-five years. She called the account of her 1956 journey *Going Home* (1957), ironically rejecting the settler habit, which persisted until the late 1940s, of referring to England as "home," even by people who may never have left Africa.

While her later work in science fiction and in a novel like *Briefing For a Descent Into Hell* (1971) was set outside Rhodesia, all Lessing's early work was located within the country, although she generally referred to it as "Zambesia," claiming at the time that she was not writing about Southern Rhodesia and that the society in which Martha Quest grows up is representative of any British colony in Africa in the 1930s and 1940s. The first volume of her autobiography, *Under My Skin* (1994), acknowledges, however, how faithfully the narrative of the "Children of Violence" novels reproduces both the public and private events of her life in Rhodesia, and she claims a greater "truth" for the world of her fiction than can be recovered by the memory on which autobiography depends. None of the novels is an historical record and each uses different fictional modes to examine the various stages in Martha Quest's growth in consciousness. *A Ripple from the Storm*, for example, is often a gentle satire on a group so locked into Marxist orthodoxies that any engagement

with the material realities of Zambesia is impossible, although some critics read it as a contemporary example of social realism like its predecessors in the series. In 1962, Lessing published *The Golden Notebook*, which uses an elaborately fragmented narrative to examine the breakdown of public and private relationships in the contemporary world and calls into question the stability of society and self that the realist novelist has traditionally assumed. The autobiographical elements of "Children of Violence" are still discernible, however. The principal character of *The Golden Notebook* is Anna Wulf, the author of a successful novel set in Africa; and one of the notebooks that make up the novel, "The Black Notebook," is set in what is clearly Rhodesia during the Second World War. When Lessing resumed the "Children of Violence," her experimentation with different types of narrative in *The Golden Notebook* is evident. The Zambesia of *Landlocked* lacks the objective reality it had in the earlier volumes and is mediated for the reader through Martha's consciousness.

With Zimbabwean independence in 1980, it was possible for her to return and in 1984 she made the first of many visits to the country, the first four of which are described in *African Laughter* (1992), which uses and subverts the forms of travel writing both to rediscover Zimbabwe and to test the validity of expectations, memories, and associations. She has recently written two other novels partly set in Africa: *Mara and Dann* (1999), located in the distant future when the continent is transformed by global climate change, and *The Sweetest Dream* (2001), where the fictional Zimlia can be read as a Zimbabwe that has betrayed the promise of its first decade with massive corruption and misgovernment. The setting for the novella "The Grandmothers" in *The Grandmothers* (2003) is probably South Africa.

Critics of her early work identified Lessing as a writer about the "color bar," a label she rejects along with others like "Marxist" and "feminist." From *The Grass Is Singing*, her writing is aware of the pressures of collectives compromising individual integrity by demanding conformity, and she wrote that "Children of Violence" is "a study of the individual conscience in its relation to the collective." These collectives can be segregationist or Marxist, marked by utopian strivings or nostalgia for an invented past or indeed a combination of any of these. Throughout her career, Lessing has noted the particular pressures exerted on women to conform to roles not of their choosing, among which is the pressure to marry, which Mary Turner experiences in *The Grass Is Singing*, or, conversely, to voice contempt for marriage and married women by women who name themselves as feminists in *The Sweetest Dream*. Often Lessing shows the language of collectives withering individual imaginations and this may be the crude racist terms of her Rhodesian novels and short stories or the clichés of benign political programs that take over our minds and refuse us the possibility of alternative and dissenting vocabularies. We may as easily lose our own words in the language of imperialism as in the rhetoric of an opposing nationalism. Lessing has never rejected the necessity of political action and its dependence on collective decisions. Throughout her work she has insisted that our allegiances must be tentative and that the language we use must express what we have felt or seen or known. It is not difficult to see the origins of this lifelong preoccupation in her early experiences in Rhodesia, where briefly it seemed that only the certainties of Leninism could oppose the certainties of British imperialism as they had been transmuted into white Rhodesian nationalism. Lessing worked with those who opposed Rhodesia and anticipated the

birth of Zimbabwe, but that does not mean that Zimbabwe commands her unreserved loyalty. Her record of Zimbabwe's failure in *African Laughter* or as Zimlia in *The Sweetest Dream* or in an essay on Zimbabwe in *Time Bites* (2004) is as scathing as anything she wrote about Rhodesia. She is as rigorously unsentimental about black collectives as she ever was about Rhodesia or indeed Britain itself.

Further reading: Jenny Taylor, ed., *Notebooks/Memoirs/Archives: Reading and Rereading Doris Lessing* (London, 1982); Lorna Sage, *Doris Lessing* (London, 1983); Eve Bertelsen, ed., *Doris Lessing* (New York, 1985); Katherine Fishburn, *The Unexpected Universe of Doris Lessing* (Westport, 1985) and *Doris Lessing: Life, Work, and Criticism* (York, 1987); Ruth Whittaker, *Doris Lessing* (London, 1988); Judith Kegan Gardiner, *Rhys, Stead, Lessing, and the Politics of Empathy* (Bloomington, 1989).

Lipenga, Ken (b. 1954). Malawian short-story writer, poet, and playwright. Born in the Mulanje area, he attended Nazombe Primary and Mulanje Secondary School, and then the University of Malawi. He earned a B.A. with distinction in 1976, took an M.A. at Britain's University of Leeds, and received a Ph.D. at Canada's University of New Brunswick. Critical acuity, darting imagination, a flair for irony, and taut writing enabled Lipenga to shine among a vintage cohort of young Malawian authors and academics. He had written his first story when finishing primary school in 1966 and told Bernth Lindfors that, submitted for a national competition, it won first prize—"a bed and mattress which I gave to my father." At secondary school, encouraged by a Peace Corps volunteer, he succeeded again, with a story written in French. His University Writers' Workshop contributions (prose and verse in English and Chichewa struck off with apparent ease) raised the question whether his future lay in fiction, poetry, or criticism. Acknowledged influences include Wole Soyinka, Ayi Kwei Armah, and Nuruddin Farah, prerevolutionary Russians such as Anton Chekhov, Nikolai Gogol, and Leo Tolstoy, and, in verse, Pablo Neruda ("a giant in this century . . . a beautiful human being").

Light satirical eroticism was a favorite in Lipenga's early verse, as in these unpublished lines from "You Used to be Nagama," mocking a remembered village maiden turned sophisticated townie:

I've seen your face before I swear
Sweating beside an earthen pot,
With that long, long drawing gourd,
Waiting patiently
For water to gather
At the bottom of the deep village
    well;
And you used to be Nagama.
Since you grew into a Priscilla
We men have not eaten life,
We can no longer deal in
    grasshoppers
Nor brag about our mouse-traps
Nor even call you Nagama.

But he also reflects disappointment and resentment at postcolonial developments in poems about his relationship with Mulanje Mountain and its mythic associations. "I Salute the Wise, I Mourn the Future" is shrewdly shaped to sound like honor to Banda instead of the anti-Banda statement it really is:

I stand to praise the wise of the land
Before whom there was nothing,
After whom will be darkness and
    tears

His early poems and short stories regularly featured on Radio Malawi, his critical reviews in the journals Odi and The Muse (which he cofounded); and since then his verse has appeared in such anthologies as The Haunting Wind: New Poetry from Malawi (1990) and The Unsung Song (2001). His reviews in Odi and The Muse contributed seminally to critical debate on local drama emerging under the guidance of David Kerr, James Gibbs, Mupa Shumba, and Chris Kamlongera. In a morning-after review of a vernacular play and two English ones, Mr Death and She Is Too Polite, staged in Chancellor College's open-air theater, he famously backed the position held by Ngugi wa Thiong'o on linguistic nationalism:

And talking about language, it so happened that the Chichewa play . . . crushed the two English plays . . . into oblivion . . . so let us go, you and I, now the Dawn is here, let us sit ourselves beneath the mango tree, and, with our pencils, teach Messrs Sophocles, Shakespeare, and the rest, teach them the rudiments of Chichewa, and take them to the people.

An undergraduate collection of thirteen short stories, Waiting for a Turn (1981), confirmed Lipenga's precocity. With minimal marks of an apprentice using simplistic event or thematic cliché, each story creates situations afresh, to be explored, puzzled over. "A Cloud of Dust" shows ironic angles on the tradition-modernity theme. Town-educated Betty organizes a village birthday celebration but withdraws tearfully when a child's funeral begins nearby. Yet her traditional mother accommodates both funeral and party, seeing no conflict, and wonders why modern schooling has not taught her daughter to do the same. Kefa, a serial adulterer in "A Gentle Fall," suffers psychological stress: his wife is so "abnormal" she ignores even flaunted evidence of his affairs, thus causing him feelings of abnormality too! "The Drunkard of Kumbi Kumbi" (about which Lipenga has confessed mixed feelings) confounds the received wisdom that alcoholism and failure are synonymous: "Che Sunche Salumphan-jira is not only a successful sot, but also a successful farmer, basket-weaver, judge, and maker of mortars."

Waiting for a Turn thus suggests an early leap to maturity. A fertile mind records, exploits, and wonders at life's Chinese box complexities. Be it cultural vertigo or town-country antagonism, Lipenga weaves art without angst, his imagination constantly producing fresh perspective and little tidy closure. Narrative lengths vary, first and third-person viewpoints alternate, and, tellingly in a writer with dramatic instincts, personae are diverse: six are village grave-diggers, one a philosophical bus conductor, another a city tailor, and yet another a young husband with an inexplicably anorexic wife. "At the Graveyard," where six characters chat endlessly around a rich man's grave they are preparing, reflects Lipenga's feeling for theater. And in the manner of Cameroon's Mongo Beti and Ferdinand Oyono, Lipenga's hairspring sensitivity triggers laughter as readily as tears. Writing of his characters in his "Author's Note," he says:

> I have allowed them to surface partly because they have caused me some measure of mental and emotional torment, and partly to express a rather base obsession with tears, produced as they are by both pain and laughter. My grandmother used to insist that the two were inseparable, although she never got round to explaining just what the relationship was.

Yet Lipenga's work is rarely flippant. The issues are serious, the tone elegiac as well as ironic. Death, often tragically premature, stalks his landscapes; so, too, grinding poverty, guilt, and domestic dysfunction caused by men leaving for South Africa's mines.

The title story carries an especially bold satire on Banda's times. A depressed tailor contemplates suicide by leaping from Sapitwa, Malawi's highest peak. He "wanted an original kind of departure, not something ready-made which you had only to put on when the time arrived. No, a ready-made life was to be rewarded with an original death." About to jump, he is rudely seized by restraining hands, for there is a lemming-like queue behind him—the whole nation apparently—and he must wait his turn! Another anti-Banda satire, "The Tiger," censored out of *Waiting for a Turn*, was published after Banda's death in *The Unsung Song* (2001), edited by Reuben Chirambo, Max J. Iphani, and Zondiwe Mbano.

After doctoral studies and some lecturing at his alma mater, Lipenga turned to journalism (an early dream), becoming editor of *The Daily Times*, and then, with Banda's fall, moving into politics. In Bakili Muluzi's administration, which ended in 2004, he held ministerial portfolios for education and resources and an advisory post in the president's office. Though he is still a serving parliamentarian, rumors in publishing circles suggest that he is again turning his talents to writing.

Further reading: Bernth Lindfors, ed., *Kulankulu: Interviews with Writers from Malawi and Lesotho* (Bayreuth, 1989); Adrian Roscoe, *Uhuru's Fire: African Literature East to South* (London, 1977).

Lwanda, John Lloyd, Chipembere (b. 1949). Malawian poet, novelist, and biographer. Born in Northern Malawi and educated at schools in Zimbabwe and Malawi, he qualified as a medical doctor at Glasgow University. A man of wide interests, he then secured a doctorate in history from Edinburgh. He has spent many years outside Malawi—as he puts it, from 1970 to 1979 for educational reasons and from 1981 to 1993 for political reasons, after falling foul of the Banda regime. While exiled in Scotland, working as a general practitioner and as honorary senior lecturer in primary care at Glasgow University, he created a publishing house specializing in Malawiana. During Malawi's transition to multiparty democracy (1993–94), he went home to work for the new United Democratic Front, but returned disenchanted to Scotland when, as he saw it, businessmen swiftly marginalized thinkers and intellectuals. His books include *Promises, Power, Politics and Poverty: Democratic Transition in Malawi* (1996); a verse collection, *Black Thoughts from the Diaspora* (1994); a novel, *The Second Harvest* (1994); a political history, *Politics, Culture and Medicine in Malawi* (2005); and a biography, *Kamuzu Banda of Malawi: A Study in Promise, Power and Paralysis* (1993).

By any standards, Lwanda is highly productive. Praised by historian George Shepperson and the literary critics Angus Calder and Landeg White, his work exudes an exile's determination to do something for the home scene and a conviction that African voices, especially Malawian, must be heard. His energies climaxed during signs in the early 1990s that Banda's thirty-year tyranny was ending. Thus, within a three-year period, he wrote a substantial Banda biography (1993), the verse collection (1994), the novel (1994), and a major work of political history (1996).

His poem "The Writer" announces, "Today, I really must write," an exhortation repeated eight times. But obsession with political change did not exclude skepticism: false African dawns had taught caution. Not for Lwanda the premature British praise for France's revolution or its later Russian equivalent. Too many politicians known to him could still be dismissed as "Plump plutocratic posers." Hence his cautionary "The Second Harvest," addressed "To our new government":

Hope?
Should I dare?

This bitter sweet moment of
    freedom,
Snatched from tragedy by the barrel
    of a gun
Intoxicates me momentarily.
    Tantalising!
Hope?
Should I dare?

His verse elsewhere praises the Catholic pastoral letter that proved the tipping point for Banda's downfall. But bleak decades had taken their toll, home becoming "The fading memories of a romantic youth / Pampered innocence and boarding schools, / Among the poverty and misery of my peers." His poem "Despair" moves from optimism that Malawi's nightmare could end to gloom and resignation. The years have slipped by, with effort unrewarded, dreams unfulfilled. An uncle had reminded him, "Like mushrooms wisdom comes late in the season":

Today I am tired, old and weary;
I no longer care or dare.
Somalia, Bosnia, Burundi . . .
Even Malawi, don't excite my
    anger . . .
Such is the depth of my despair

He is after all, as he puts it in "Black Thoughts from the Diaspora 1986," "A free-thinking human imprisoned in the murky, dark / Mysteries of Malawi, the warm bleeding heart of Africa." Yet he can laugh ironically at the hypocrisy of liberals ("ever so clean, nice and caring") because "I am one myself" and portray with harrowing nostalgia his old mother saintly amid her poverty:

Shrivelled, stooped and old, for her
    time had lost its march.
Yet with scrawny, shaking hands she
    tends her small patch
Of mother earth's dwindling
    resource.

Bending but not seeing the toes she
    cannot touch,
She gathers the grass for her hut's
    thatch.

No new dispensation could be simple. Apart from human nature, venal politicians, a national psyche "deep as Lake Malawi," there was "the stalking lion" of AIDS. His piece "Viral Spirits" blends pity with medical precision to picture an AIDS victim of twenty-nine, close to death, sitting motionless as flies massage his "dry, scaly, itchy ulcerated skin," his wife, probably infected too, looking on, and two children already dead before the age of four:

He sits cross-legged on the earthen
    verandah, eyes
Staring straight to God and cheeks
    sunken like
The dambo in the driest drought.
    Thinking those
Thoughts only known to prophets.
    As he coughs
The echo from the cavities of his
    sails, those
Caves excavated by the tubercle,
    threatens to
Capsize his frail frame before the
    journey's end.

The Second Harvest, a novel ("as told to John Lwanda"), fictionalizes Banda's fall, though with its factual landscape only thinly veiled. Reflecting perhaps the notorious practice of "accidentalization," and the mysterious death of Mozambique's Samora Machel, Lwanda has Banda (here called Mwari) and most of his cabinet die in a plane crash over (with undisguised symbolism) Switzerland. But filling the political vacuum generates the same instincts for power and self-aggrandizement that marked the thirty years of Life President Mwari's rule. While airing skepticism about the new dispensation, the book summarizes Banda's record:

collaboration with apartheid South Africa; covert help for Renamo rebels in Mozambique; hatred of local intellectuals; summary arrests and detention without trial; waste of expensively trained talent; the notorious Viphya Pulpwood scheme that threatened to pollute Lake Malawi; and the hideous educational experiment at Kamuzu Academy.

Madanhire, Nevanji (b. 1961). Zimbabwean novelist. Born in Masvingo, after receiving a B.A. at the University of Zimbabwe, he was first a teacher, then a journalist, becoming editor-in-chief of *The Financial Gazette*. He is the author of two novels, *Goatsmell* (1992) and *If the Wind Blew* (1996). His journalist background explains the boldness of *Goatsmell*, a text frontally tackling sensitive national issues—in particular ruling elite corruption and Shona-Ndebele tension, which dogged the freedom struggle and arguably caused some thirty thousand deaths.

The plight of Musiiwa, the narrator-protagonist, reflects this pathology. Though an orphan, alcoholic, and crippled, he fights ethnic prejudice to pursue a dream of national unity. A Shona, he is in love with Ndebele Katazile, a relationship opposed by his adoptive parents and her family (the calculus of prejudice is neatly balanced). Attacks on the political elite begin early. His adoptive father, Chief Mbire, is a corrupt parliamentarian straight from the pages of Achebe and Ngugi—a people's representative who rarely visits them, a rich man with a castle among the poor; the owner of several farms and murderer of albino twins; an ex-headmaster who seduces a colleague's wife and absconds with the building fund; the man who smashed the student demonstration that crippled his son. Protest anyway is evenhanded: beaten by Ndebeles in Bulawayo, Musiiwa wonders why the nation's heroes died. Was it "so that we could kill each other because one spoke a language with clicks while the other spoke one without"? This, and memories of liberation comrades forcing him to watch an innocent headman being murdered, provoke the finding that "man is inherently cruel." The new political elite craves deification, and the retained colonial emergency powers that killed Musiiwa's parents almost kill him. Intertribal mudslinging continues; a hated white farmer confidently fences his land again; a road is driven through an ancestral cemetery, as in colonial days; a well once communal now belongs to one man; and a family forcibly removed by the Smith regime is being moved again, this time by an African government.

Escape into alcohol and art is tested, and, as in the fiction of Yvonne Vera, finding ancient rock paintings provides some inspiration. But in answer to a question from the loving Katazile, Musiiwa ends the novel with the words "No. There is no HOPE."

Mahoso, Tafataona (b. 1949). Zimbabwean poet and historian. Born in the Chimanimani District, he holds an American doctorate in history and is current director of the National Arts Council.

His main publication, *Footprints About the Bantustan* (1989), divides into five sections: "Zimbabwe," "South Africa," "Facing the North," "Gleanings," and "Nibs and Blades." Mahoso says the book arose "out of the necessity for a poetry of solidarity which is accessible to our international comrades, and representative of the international and internationalist role which Zimbabwe has so clearly assumed. This necessity has been my daily experience in the last ten years of studying and fighting

apartheid." A foreword by Vimbai Gukwe Chivaura pinpoints the book's characteristics: its visionary breadth and gravitas, its location of Zimbabwean experience, colonial and postcolonial, within world history. While contemporaries such as Zimunya and Nyamubaya aesthetically reflect Zimbabwean life, says Chivaura, Mahoso contemplates a global order that needs radical explanation. Contemporaries may blame a wider world and pillory adoption of the very system the Liberation War sought to reject, but none does so more systematically than Mahoso.

Readers may find the book "dated" (historian Mahoso is in any case keen on dates, often announcing the chronology of a poem's creation and revision), not because of timeless themes like poverty and exploitation, but because its favored Marxist idiom has now slipped quietly into silence. In the Mahoso world, the Cold War rages, the Soviet Empire looks permanent, the Berlin Wall impenetrable, and Mandela still breaks stones on Robben Island. New nations like Zimbabwe are mere pawns in a global game. Hence Mahoso's Marxist discourse and insights as, more anti-West than pro-East, he scourges capitalism and colonialism. His anger, despite Britain's central role in Zimbabwe's colonization, is fiercest against America.

As Mahoso says, this is a poetry of international solidarity, embracing unemployed workers in Appalachia or naked children in Kentucky and Harlem as much as their African counterparts. It also honors a free Zimbabwe, which, in 1989, still commanded moral respect—convening Unaligned Nations conferences, World Council of Churches gatherings, and playing a vigorous role in the Southern Africa Development Council. Seeing this now against a background of power abuse, economic delinquency, election-rigging, ruinous military escapades, and manipulation of justifiable land claims, is to be reminded of the disillusion other Zimbabwean writers are expressing.

But the collection also pictures a private life of affection for friends and family and a poignant maternal invocation reminiscent of Laye's overture to *African Child*:

> Mother of dream and memory,
> you whose teaching is gradual
> like a stair, you who lilt to wake me
> to the silent strides of daybreak,
> remind me of the years when
>   streams meandered over
> fallow fields in tropical
>   moonlight . . .

But the anticapitalist polemic dominates. The West in general is an "iron bitch," with "breasts that drop her milk of napalm / on naked refugee children." Walt Rostow's trickle-down theory is spurious, and, as for capitalism's vaunted free enterprise, it gave Africa only "commercial slave trade / and Apartheid." On the carrot of mass consumption, the poet asks:

> Will you teach us how to survive
> Mass consumption with nothing to
>   consume?

Meanwhile, if Washington wants the world to sleep to the "Voice of Amnesia," the poet will use literature's waking power to remind us of Chile, My Lai, Sharpeville, Wounded Knee, Blood River, the Bay of Pigs, Franco, El Salvador, Kasinga, and Matola. And while the "Wall to Wall Journal" pumps out lying messages to a hungry world and its laid-off workers, and Mandela rots unnoticed on Robben Island, the

> Connivy League universities sleep,
> Quite safe from the ferment of the
>   age,
> Quite secure behind their piles
> Of clean monographs and
>   dissertations.

The modern world is "frantic," a quality the poet abhors, commits structural sin in its trade (wherein consumer grinds the face of producer), and generates a searing postcolonial gloom. For all this, the United States is to blame, stemming from a neurotic distrust that Mahoso enjoys deriding:

> In God we trust
> so never trust the Russians.
> In God we trust
> but the Cubans are dangerous.
> In God we trust
> but never trust the Vietnamese.
> In God we trust
> but never trust the Angolans.
> . . .
> In God we trust
> but the bomb is what will save us.

And so on, to include the Ethiopians, the Nicaraguans, Allende, children who must pray in public but not at home, and Gideon's Bibles that only visitors read because, between TV and *Reader's Digest*, Americans are too busy to bother.

The final broadside in "To a Western Poet / Critic" targets not the United States but a supposed non-African critical establishment. It reads as if Mahoso, anticipating Western reviewers' censure of his ideology, is getting a blow in first. This high-voltage irreverence attacks what Mahoso sees as an all too anodyne, aseptic, uncommitted (and thus immoral) view of culture and poetry:

> From your position
> Culture is a medium by which to
>   escape
> The tedium of forced leisure,
>   something
> To take or leave personally, your
>   poetic licence,
> A hobby, sabbatical or dessert.
> From my position, it is a condition,
> collective as the famine, abounding

in cravings darker than absorption
   nebulae.

The Western critic, as he puts it

Has antennae of logs solid to the
   core,
Well-seasoned and clogged with
   shit.
If he sneezes you have to spit.

Mapanje, Jack (b. 1945). Malawian poet. Born of Yao and Nyanja parents in Kadango Village, Mangochi District, he was educated at Kadango Anglican School, Chikwawa Catholic Mission School, and Zomba Catholic Secondary School. A B.A. and Diploma in Education from the University of Malawi preceded an M.Phil. and Ph.D. from the University of London. One of Central Africa's leading poets, he was an Amnesty International Prisoner of Conscience during a three-year period from 1987 when President Banda detained him without trial or charge. Now in Britain, and recently poet in residence at Wordsworth's Lake District cottage, he has held university fellowships at York and Oxford and writer residencies at Leiden and the Open University. International prizes include the Rotterdam International Poetry Award (1988). His main publications include *Of Chameleons and Gods* (1981), *The Chattering Wagtails of Mikuyu Prison* (1993), *Skipping Without Ropes* (1998), and *The Last of the Sweet Bananas* (2004). He has also edited *Gathering Seaweed: African Prison Writing* (2002), coedited *Oral Poetry from Africa: An Anthology* (1983), *Summer Fires: New Poetry of Africa* (1983), and *The African Writers' Handbook* (1999).

Student enthusiasm for Mapanje's *Of Chameleons and Gods* alerted Banda's censors, who, though finding its ironic surface impenetrable, ordered its withdrawal from sale. Banda, for his part, said he detained the poet not because of the book but on the (groundless) claim that he was preaching politics in the lecture hall. The volume revealed Mapanje as a poet of marked independence, who, though widely read, had a personal style owing little to others, African or European. An introduction captures the psychic stress experienced under Banda's rule: "The verse in this volume spans some ten turbulent years in which I have been attempting to find a voice or voices as a way of preserving some sanity. Obviously, where personal voices are too easily muffled, this is a difficult task; one is tempted, like the chameleon, who failed to deliver Chiuta's message of life, to bask in one's brilliant camouflage. But the exercise has been, if nothing else, therapeutic; and that's no mean word in our circumstances." Within a compass covering UK-Malawian contrasts, Portuguese massacres in Mozambique, the Year of the Child, and rural eccentrics, the text cryptically satirizes the regime's contempt for human rights, its shameless cheapening of tradition, and its waste of human talent precisely when nascent Malawi required urgent development. Even the legacy of the nation's martyrs is exploited, their achievements invoked for political advantage but their mothers ignored:

Do we now troop past the skeletal
   mothers
Before their sons' burial mounds
   weeping
With broken bowls of rotten weevils
And shards of sour brew for the
   libation?

The Chattering Wagtails of Mikuyu Prison, jail-conceived and published when, helped by his friends Pádraig Ó Máille, David Kerr, Landeg White, and the British High Commissioner, he had become an exile in England, joined others' verse and prose as a record of horrors encountered in this dreaded detention center.

The dedication to family of *Skipping Without Ropes* touches the difficulties faced after leaving home for a life of exile:

> I thought I would offer you more
>   muscular
> Lines to help you reach the summits
>   of this
> Wandering seclusion without the
>   tether; I
> Remember pledging to myself I
>   would plot
> My own hope for you to surf these
>   swells
> Forever lashing our shores, a pledge
>   I feared
> I would never deliver but *pole sana*
>   and may
> These narrative symbols ease the
>   torrents of
> Your haven instead, may you skip
>   your globe
> More defiantly without my leash,
>   with your
> Hope recovered, may the bedrock of
>   chuckle
> Treasured heal our blisters with tons
>   of love!

The text journeys geographically and thematically. Pieces on Botswana, Blantyre, Bergen, Rwanda, and Holland accompany such topics as acacias in Gaborone, the hanging of Nigerian writer Ken Saro-Wiwa, and the newly canonized St. Margaret Clitherow of York. Mapanje has not found it hard to settle on poetic subjects in the aftermath of Banda's thirty-year oppression, but the traumatizing memories of imprisonment constantly recur. The title poem itself recalls Mikuyu, where, with no physical exercise allowed, a metaphorical skipping without ropes was the only exercise possible. Mapanje says, "This verse skips on its own terms wherever the human spirit takes it; it celebrates the potential hope for hu-

man fortitude in times of hopeless reconstruction." A warmly happy poem, "The Fish Eagles of Cape Maclear," shows Mapanje during a home visit in nostalgic mood addressing the writer David Rubadiri, his "Uncle," by the waters of Lake Malawi. The horrors of Banda and Mikuyu seem behind him at last:

> Today, we've deserted
> The salty waters of Europe for the
>   lap-lapping
> Breakers of this lake, we've come
>   back home
> For the curative waters to cleanse the
>   hurt of
> These three decades of despotic
>   desires; we've
> Come back home to watch fish
>   eagles swoop
> Down and nestle on baobab tree
>   branches as
> Cape Maclear fishermen haul ashore
>   twine
> Laden with prime *kampango* and
>   *chambo*.

Mapanje was preeminently equipped to edit *Gathering Seaweed: African Prison Writing*. Choosing material from across the continent, he wanted his anthology to be "waved as a warning banner to present and future African political leadership." His introduction laments how African independence, perversely, seemed simply to domesticate the excesses of colonial rule:

> Watch the irony. It was the African nationalists exiled by colonial administration to the barren African bush or tortured in infamous colonial prisons who became despots after independence, intolerant of multiparty politics, preferring to imprison, exile, even kill their political opponents, writers, journalists, lawyers, musicians, radi-

cal thinkers and other rebels, instead of accommodating them within the fabric of their liberated societies.

Mapanje's verse has received international acclaim. On *Skipping Without Ropes*, Angus Calder writes, "His latest work is mellower in tone. But the conscience, the wit and the craftsmanship which it displays have characterized his work from the beginning. His wholly original, unsubdued voice is still unlike that of any other poet writing in English, from Africa or anywhere."

Further reading: Alastair Niven, "Jack Mapanje: A Chameleon in Prison," *Poetry Review* 80, no. 4 (1990–91): 49–51; Angela Smith, *East African Writing in English* (London, 1989); Steve Chimombo, "The Chameleon in Love, Life and Literature: The Poetry of Jack Mapanje," *Journal of Commonwealth Literature* 23, no. 1 (1988): 102–115; James Gibbs, "Of Chameleons," *The Literary Half Yearly* 23, no. 2 (1982): 8–10; Innocent Banda, "On the Poetry of Jack Mapanje," *Stand* 24, no. 2: 14–26; Angus Calder, "Under Zomba Plateau: The New Malawian Poetry," *Kunapipi* 1, no. 2: 59–67; David M. Jefferes, "Saying Change in Malawi: Resistance and the Voices of Jack Mapanje and Lucius Banda," in *Ariel* 31, no. 3: 105–123; Lupenga Mphande, "Dr Hastings Banda and the Malawi Writers Group: The (un)Making of Cultural Tradition," *Research in African Literatures* 27, no. 1 (1996): 80–101.

Maraire, Nozipo (b. 1966). Zimbabwean novelist. She was born into a Shona family at Mangula near Mutare. The dislocation of the Liberation War meant that, before the age of eighteen, she had lived and been schooled not just in Zimbabwe but also in Canada, the United States, and Jamaica. Back home before the war ended, attending a formerly all-white high school (where

"the air seethed with anger and hate"), she won a scholarship to study biology at Harvard, took a medical degree at Columbia, and pursued a postgraduate specialization in neurosurgery at Yale. The medical profession has been productive of literature, but this has typically meant early career abandonment or late career relaxation. Few can claim, while bent beneath medical training's burdens, to have written a novel that won the *New York Times* Notable Book of the Year Award and reviews in the *New York Review of Books* —and this while also studying for a master's degree in public health at Yale and publishing research on intercranial cavernous malformations in a specialist journal of neurosurgery! If, as Maraire says, she wants to inspire African women with her achievements, already, by the age of thirty-eight, she has done so with élan. *Zenzele: A Letter for My Daughter* was written only for therapy and relaxation, not publication; still, London's Weidenfeld and Nicholson issued it in 1996.

This is an intelligent and emotionally strong autobiographical novel. It uses the epistolary form seen in writers like Mariama Bâ and Buchi Emecheta that allows the first-person narrator to range widely. It also provides room for the arrival center stage of other characters with their own narratives. A Zimbabwean mother who has lived with her husband and family throughout the freedom struggle, and who, it emerges, is dying of cancer, reflects on those times in a long epistle to her daughter Zenzele, who has won a scholarship to Harvard. Readers might conclude that Zenzele is the author herself, who, by way of imaginative leap, is narrating the story from within her mother's consciousness. Maraire comments, "I have been through the depths of Zenzele's soul. In a way I am each of the characters in the book as all authors are really." These other figures who inhabit the book include Zenzele's father, a successful human rights lawyer with enviable oratorical skills; her sister Linda, a woman destined for liberation; and Cousin Tinawo, who joined the struggle because of a pretty dress that a white shopkeeper refused to sell her, and who becomes a spy-servant in the home of the Rhodesian Army's senior general.

The text rarely loses its piquancy, even around issues standard in colonial Rhodesia—absurd white prejudice, arrogance and ignorance, verbal abuse, the passion for education, missionary roles in passivity, dogs being privileged over black domestics (a complaint most famously raised by South Africa's Es'kia Mphahlele in *Down Second Avenue*). Maraire reminds us of press mendacity during the Liberation War and how city whites lived safe while rural peasants were slaughtered. Zenzele's mother wants a God of the downtrodden and not the one "who lied to Adam and Eve about the fruit of knowledge and then banished them from the Garden of Eden."

The narrative, begun in sober discursive prose, steadily absorbs emotional warmth before a climax of great maturity, replete with human intimacy, spiritual poetry, and a sense of universal interrelatedness: "We are all bridges." Though the central narrative comes from a mother living a middle-class life in Harare's former white suburbs, it ends, appropriately, in the home village of Chakowa in the Chimanimani Mountains, scene of so much maternal reminiscence. She is back there now writing this letter and each dawn visiting the family graves literally to talk to the ancestors—those who have gone before, whose help she has sought and seeks, who suffered down the years, who never gave up, who taught and practiced love, and who are key links in the chain from past to present and future. She tells them in that silent graveyard that "even though the armed struggle of in-

dependence is long over, there is never a want of underprivileged and forgotten people" who need their help.

Marechera, Dambudzo (1952–87). Zimbabwean novelist, poet, dramatist, and short-story writer. Dead at an early age, like so many contemporary Central African writers, Marechera was the quintessential *enfant terrible* of Zimbabwean writing—and a shooting star doomed to early burnout. Born in bleak Vengere, a township near Rusape, he attended mission schools before beginning English studies at the national university in 1972. Briefly jailed and expelled for antiracist protest, he secured a scholarship to Oxford. But, like Soyinka earlier and Dangarembga later, he found Oxbridge uncongenial and was rusticated after an arson attack on a college building. A Sheffield writing residency proved equally disastrous.

His life (the natural fruit, he would say, of Rhodesian experience) was all alienation and disconnection, confusion, psychic hurt, existential angst, and emotional outrage. With his consuming dedication to literature, pursued with the desperation of a trapped miner gasping for air, he seized a trusted humanities tool to explain a world clearly insane, oxymoronic, pitiless, and empty of moral meaning. If religion, African or other, could not help ("In Africa, of course, it seems we have inherited the shit kind of religiosity"), perhaps the running streams of world literature might. Others have described themselves as so situated, but none with Marechera's obsessive insistence. His brutal township provenance, Zhuwarara suggests, denied him rural nourishment and triggered this frantic reaching for a literary identity. Marechera might well be saying, "I'm not the despicable, self-hating, dope-smoking, lost and volatile creation of township filth and white barbarity you think I am. No, my people include Sophocles, Virgil, Petronius, Skelton, Boccaccio, Chaucer, Shakespeare, Donne, Swift, Sterne, Carlyle, Worsdworth, Shelley, Lawrence, Cervantes, Forster, Pushkin, Turgenev, Gogol, Chekhov, Lermontov, Salinger, Hughes, Achebe, Beti, Mphahlele, Okara, Okigbo, La Guma, Soyinka, Ngugi, Senghor, Armah et multi alii." This is no bluffer's guide to world literature but a living part of the Marechera universe. The literary life, then, was pivotal, yet he could satirize his own vocation to it, as he does in *House of Hunger*. The character Harry says, "You literary chaps are our only hope," and the narrator says, "I choked politely on my drink. Then we are sunk, I thought."

Comparison with Dylan Thomas or Brendan Behan would not have upset Marechera. But Taban Lo Liyong's early career provides an African parallel anyway—a similar iconoclasm, energy, breadth of reading, and determination to penetrate conventional walls into gardens of creativity—though without Marechera's coruscating bitterness and lack of tradition's safety net.

The complete cultural rebel, Marechera believed with South African township poets that the truth could best be found with personal variations of chaos theory, contempt for formal boundaries and conventional taxonomy. The resulting fragmentary corpus did not fit publishers' pigeonholes, and we owe it to Flora Veit-Wild that, in death, she imposed on Marechera's work a tidiness impossible in life. After the acclaim of *The House of Hunger* (1978), which won *The Guardian* fiction prize, *Black Sunlight* (1980), and *Mindblast* (1984), Marechera's star began to wane. It was left to Veit-Wild to publish posthumously, in Liz Gunner's phrase, the writer's "brilliant, fractured shards"—in *The Black Insider* (1990), *Cemetery of Mind* (1992), *Dambudzo Marechera: A Source Book on his Life and Work* (1992), and *Scrapiron Blues* (1994).

Marechera's distinction is now clear. His cocktail of modernism and existential absurdism loosened the reins on received literary discourse. *The House of Hunger* repeatedly cocks a snook at traditional taboos. The title-piece narrator describes his brother masturbating in public before boys from across the township ("he came and came and came like new wine that cannot be contained within old cloth"). He sees his mother committing adultery ("there were tremendous groans and grunts erupting from that bed and the energy of it was like god's fist shaking Satan's shirtfront"). He watches a whore returning from the bush dripping with semen ("we could see on the gravel road splotches and stains of semen that were dripping down her as she walked. Years later I was to write a story using her as a symbol of Rhodesia"). Such coarseness is heard even from usually sacrosanct quarters. Impatient with the narrator's sexual tardiness, his mother angrily cries: "You stick it in the hole between the water and the earth, it's easy. . . . You strike like a fire and she'll take you and your balls all in. Right? Up to your neck . . . You were late in getting off my breast; you were late in getting out of bedwetting. Now you're late jerking off into some bitch. You make me sick up to here, do you understand?" Whatever reader response this elicits, it seems worlds away from the delicate indirection traditionally characterizing African discourse on such intimacies.

Marechera rates "the tyranny of straightforward things" as more oppressive than such "idle monstrosities as life and death, apartheid and beerdrinking." Hence the advice in his story "The Writer's Grain": "Insist upon your right to insist on the importance, the great importance, of whim. There is no greater pleasure than that derived from throwing or not throwing the spanner into works simply on the basis of one's whim."

Powerful statement and message invariably chime well: "Literacy is the surgeon's needle with which I bind my wounds," "I tell you, insider, the hills of Africa are red with wounds from long ago," "The desire to awaken in all things a community with what we experience within ourselves is not a phantasy but a reality. We call it love," "I have a sort of bellows which puffs up the forge of my mind now and then about issues like obscenity or squatting or the next meal's imponderable absence," "I detest teaching. I'd hate to have the next generation's night-mares on my conscience," "While we, im-mersed in the minutes of our last rehearsals (what we call tradition, civilization) think only of our own lines and footnotes, perhaps the grand drama of all the things we do not take into account is itself approaching a cli-max whose debris and shrapnel will devas-tate us," "Hammering nails into a coffin in which the image of a whole historical notion lay with its arms crossed over its breast," "I began to recount to myself trivial incidents which had left me feeling like a cat thrown without extreme unction into a deep well."

Veit-Wild salvaged enough of Mare-chera's verse (often binned) to produce *Cemetery of Mind*, a volume of some one hundred and fifty pieces. Verse, more than prose, demanded pattern and delineation, improving completion rates and making Marechera look the disciplined artist. However, as with the Nigerian Christopher Okigbo, who also died young, there is little sense of audience. Though Okigbo became a little more public in his later verse, Mare-chera's lyricism seems entirely self-directed. External landscape is sacrificed for internal landscape, humor is rare and a darkness at noon pervasive.

Admiring Shelley, Marechera avoids his penchant for abstraction. His preference for concrete imagery with a dusting of the abstract can be effective. In "The History Class" we find "Dress the question in jeans / And sweater," while "Mind in Residence" begins:

On grey twilit balconies
In T-shirts and shirt sleeves
Each shrouded in preoccupied misty
    thoughts
The several pasts of my life
Wait for this and all other days to
    end.

In "Drunk After the Misunderstanding,"

Emotion creeps under the carpet
Rational butts overflow the ashtrays
Memory's empty wine bottles clink
    in every room.

"My Arms Vanished Mountains" cap-tures the poet

Writing angry poems to the rats in
    the attic
To the girls tightening belts against
    unwanted pregnancies
To the mothers, whores out of grim
    necessity

His existential plight as a man desperate to harmonize a turbulent inner and outer life appears in "To Langston Hughes":

Let me in, Spirit
Nothing out here but darkness
And frantic images
Let me out, body
Nothing in here but darkness
And frantic images

The verse covers the poet's career from 1982, when he returned from Britain, until his death in 1987. Closing pieces privilege reflection over voltage and volume—apt in a poet now mortally sick. "Ice to Reprieve," an experimental sonnet, breathes only gloom:

Death wears, from within all faces,
a secretive smile;
from within all gestures
an incomprehensible movement;
from within all voices
a sound beyond hearing.

My eyes glow at sight of sights
Never again to be seen;
And if the restful grave slumber in
    dream
Then is heaven a recapitulation of
    known delights!

"I Used to Like Tomatoes" mentions the lung disease that is killing him:

I get tired of the blood
And the coughing
And more blood

In "Darkness a Bird of Prey" the young poet is sinking fast, his fires no longer burning hot:

What are the things, bright-winged
That within me no longer move
No longer 'bruptly leap clear to soar
Towards the stars above this dead-
    weight night?
Where is that ecstatic turmoil
Which once fired my youth into
    desperate acts
Visions beyond any known to the
    hideous devil?
Where! That demented force that
    hurls Death
"Get thee behind me"?
The hundred knocks on the door
To my thirties-old life
And th'impatient question "Is
    anyone in there?" I have
No strength to shudder, to utter, to
Scream YES or painfully mutter "Go
    away."

And the collection's final line asks poignantly:

Is life the Nightmare death has when
    death is asleep?

Further reading: Musaemura Zimunya, *Those Years of Drought and Hunger: The Birth of African Fiction in Zimbabwe* (Gweru, 1982) and "Dambudzo Marechera: Portrait of an Extraordinary Artist," *African Literature Association Bulletin* 14, no. 1 (1988): 15–18; Flora Veit-Wild, *Dambudzo Marechera, 1952–1987* (Harare, 1988), *Dambudzo Marechera: A Sourcebook on His Life and Work* (Harare, 1993), and *Patterns of Poetry in Zimbabwe* (Gweru, 1988); Rino Zhuwarara, *Introduction to Zimbabwean Literature in English* (Harare, 2001); Liz Gunner, "Dambudzo Marechera," in *Encyclopaedia of Post-Colonial Literatures in English*, ed. Eugene Benson and L. W. Connolly (London, 1994): 983.

Masiye, Andreya S. (b. ca. 1930) Zambian novelist and dramatist. Born in Eastern Zambia and educated at Munali Secondary School, he trained as a teacher, taught in Katete, and was recruited from there into radio work with the Central African Broadcasting Services. David Kerr's definitive study, *Dance, Media Entertainment and Popular Theatre in South East Africa* (1998), employing personal communication from Masiye and material from his autobiography, *Singing for Freedom* (1977), narrates how, to undermine the hated Central African Federation, Masiye and compatriots Moses Kwali, Samuel Kasankha, Francis Magiya, and Fundula Chisha used especially vernacular radio programs (adapting Nyanja and Bemba songs, for example). After studying BBC tapes and scripts, Masiye wrote radio plays, whose scripts the colonial authorities eventually seized and burned. On the advice of Kenneth Kaunda, he left CABS to become Tanganyika's first African head of broadcasting. Michael Etherton, says Kerr, successfully adapted Masiye's one surviving play, *Kazembe and the Portuguese* (1973), for performance at the University of Zambia's open-air Chikwakwa Theatre, eventually changing its name to *The Lands of Kazembe*. Based on the diary of Francisco de Lacerda, an eighteenth-century Portuguese explorer,

Masiye, Kerr says, wanted to make anticolonial points with dexterity and balance. Europeans and Africans thus share praise and blame, though Lacerda's getting bogged down in the African wilderness hints clearly at Masiye's basic viewpoint. Masiye told Kerr that he wanted to offer an alternative version of history "from an African viewpoint." That his play initially prompted the newspaper headline "African Writes a Play!" reflects the racist ignorance of the ruling whites. Chris Kamlongera is quoted as praising Masiye's courage in writing in English at all when the Northern Rhodesian authorities, like their racist brethren in Salisbury and Pretoria, were advocating local languages to undermine tribal solidarity.

Though best remembered for his radio work, Masiye's novel *Before Dawn* (1971), which charts a young man's journey from village life and back, is no idle adventure among commonplace themes. Few novels treat so well the village-town dilemma as a matter of rational active choice rather than passive inevitability, and even fewer resolve the dilemma in favor of the village. Nor is the two-worlds phenomenon so wryly rendered as when protagonist Kavumba, home from heroism against the Japanese in Burma, locks his door at night against hooting owls and laughing hyenas. Again, few novels emphasize so vividly the imperative of group and individual survival at the heart of African culture. Banda Village faces extinction as a working entity without the leadership that Kavumba will provide. And while African writing often cites World War II as a catalyst for freedom, no text offers so detailed an account of an African soldier's experience of it. Kavumba is press-ganged into fighting the Italians in Abyssinia and the Japanese in Burma—and is even, in that hallowed British phrase, "mentioned in dispatches."

The novel also chronicles an important phase in Zambia's socioeconomic history. The late 1930s and early '40s mark the growing magnetism for village youth of the colony's Copper Belt—as opposed to the older lure of South African and Rhodesian mines. This accelerated rural denudation, agricultural neglect, and the tragedy of desperate village girls, without youths to marry, throwing themselves at passing truck drivers—creating a seedbed for the AIDS pandemic of the 1980s.

That Nyanja songs and prayers adorn the text suggests Masiye's allegiance to both local tradition and Christianity. Kavumba, narrator and new Banda Village headman, ends by saying, "I reminded Ganizo Phiri of the troubles which our village, and all its people, had to experience as a result of the irresistible external foreign influences whose first victim was my father." He also shows a lofty humanity when his white South African company commander dies at the hands of the Japanese:

> Captain Marais was dead. . . . The troops were very sad at losing such a gallant officer. . . . I shovelled in the last lumps of earth and remembered the sweet memories of my brother-in-arms and former employer—Captain Marais, the Lusaka Kabwata Location Superintendent and my erstwhile brilliant Company Commander. . . . "Let your life be evergreen," I said, wiping drops of bitter tears from my face. . . . "Sleep well, Captain Marais," I muttered and departed."

What could better capture the humanism Kaunda was promoting for the new Zambia?

Further reading: Martin Banham, ed., *A History of Theatre in Africa* (Cambridge, 2004); David Kerr, *African Popular Theatre* (London, 1995), and *Dance, Media Enter-*

tainment and Popular Theatre in South East Africa (Bayreuth, 1998).

Mbano, Zondiwe (b. 1952). Malawian poet. Born into Malawi's Ngoni people, who trekked north from Natal in the nineteenth-century *mfecane* caused by Shaka's oppression, he was educated at the University of Malawi, where he was exposed to the Writers' Workshop. He currently lectures at the university in language and communication skills. His poetry has appeared in such collections as *The Fate of Vultures* (1998), *The Haunting Wind* (1996), *The Unsung Song* (2001), and, most recently, *Operations and Tears* (2004).

Mbano likes a short line and clutter-free statement. Banda-era verse, lamenting ravaged tradition, ruling elite greed, and a people with "backs trained in stooping," foregrounds imagery of sunset and darkness, shadowed lonely paths, and irrational behavior. Ngoni leaders in "Princes" feast while the edifice over them crumbles; ordinary folk squabble while danger threatens; elders narrate folktales unaware that their time is up. The poet blames all this for the despotism the nation has allowed to take root. In "Why, Oh Why?" the target is Banda himself. How could daughters, mothers, sons, men and elders, so foolishly welcome this tyrant? The daughters dressed colorfully for him, but he didn't notice. The sons whistled and chanted praise; the men danced the favorite Ngoni dance. Yet "When a he-goat is mad, / Don't you knock off its horns?" The late Anthony Nazombe, editor of *Operations and Tears*, said that Mbano's "Beware, Millipede" is "one of the few good poems inspired by the political transition of 1992–1994," when Banda was losing power. Imagery is of new growth, green trees, singing birds. Pro-Banda forces, seen as millipedes, must not subvert the new order:

Beware millipede, do not burrow
For bulldozers lift the earth
And grit it between their teeth.

Mbikusita-Lewanika, Akashambatwa (b. 1948). Zambian poet. A prince born at Nkana-Kitwe into the Lozi royal family of the Western Province, where his father was the Litungu of Barotseland, he was educated in schools at Wusakile Tunduya-Munali, Kalela, and Chalimbana, as well as in England. He also holds master's degrees from Cornell, Jackson State, and Carleton universities. National positions include the posts of minister of Science, Technology and Vocational Training, secretary general of the National Party for the Western Province, and chair of the National Economic Advisory Council. A Fellow of the Economic Development Institute of the World Bank, he has published on marketing boards, agricultural development, and the move from one-party government to multi-party democracy. As a poet, he is best known for his volume *For the Seeds in Our Blood* (1981).

The book appeared when Central and Southern Africa were in turmoil. Zimbabwe was emerging from a bush war that had economically ravaged Zambia as a frontline state. In South Africa, the ANC's anti-apartheid struggle still raged. Namibia's SWAPO was fighting to free itself from South Africa. Pretoria was complicit in civil wars ongoing in Angola and Mozambique, while Malawi groaned beneath Banda's heel. Fittingly, Mbikusita-Lewanika's poetic vision embraces continental rather than private circumstance. He dreams of a Mother Africa reborn, free, no longer bleeding. It is hard to render creatively an entire continent, but "Even the Vaccinated Are Infected" symbolizes Africa's condition in the speaker's personal experience of "civilized" thieves / ("from the cold / green deserts / beyond the burning sands / of the Sahara"). However, Mbikusita-Lewanika is more comfortable when he chooses a local topic, as in "A People of the Plain: Ku-umboka." Here he admires the survival struggle of the Lozi people against seasonal flooding by the Zambezi, a river both "blood stream" and life threat, both "the ruler of death" and "the lord of life." The floods create a communal survival ethic. The people learn "to sway / with / and / in / the wind." And, as his neat antithesis puts it, "we know of life / by rubbing shoulders with death."

Miti, Lazarus Musazitame (b. 1948). Zambian novelist. Born in Chipata, he was initially educated there and then at universities in Zambia, York, and London. With a doctorate in linguistics, he has taught at universities in Zambia, Swaziland, and South Africa, where until recently he was professor of linguistics at the University of Venda. He is currently Language Rights Research Fellow in Pretoria. Alongside much academic output, there are two novels, *The Father* (1989) and *The Prodigal Husband* (1999), while two more await publication in Nigeria.

The Father, a bildungsroman, features a village youth, Manzuno, dreaming of medical studies and an educated wife—a vision underpinned by Christian values of restraint around premarital sex. Miti exploits the twists and turns of a journey from idealism through human imperfection to disenchantment. Manzuno's father, patriarchy incarnate, respects schooling, but not if it takes a child from home and village. Following his star, the boy successfully pleads for fee-free education, but is psychologically haunted by father and duty. Contemporary mores are also against him, leaving his Christian purity besieged among schoolmates enjoying a sexual free-for-all. A Chipata relationship with Jane seems ideal, until she inexplicably allows herself to fall

pregnant to a sleazy, Mercedes-driving, married inspector of police. A good man in a bad system, Manzuno moves for money to the Copper Belt, turns to drink and even sex, and concludes that reality after all demands a village life and marriage. Education's light has been more *ignis fatuus* than heavenly guide:

> I must now change. I must help my younger brothers and sisters. I must become a father to my father. To do this well, I should follow my father's advice. I am going to marry the girl he found for me. I know she is illiterate. I know she is dirty but it doesn't matter. I will change her. . . . I will never beat her. I will never tell her to go back to her parents. . . . I will try to keep her happy at all times. . . . And I will do my very best to completely forget all the girls who have disappointed me. All of them. . . . Me, I will marry this innocent village girl and make her very beautiful. Oh yes, I will do that. . . .

Amidst much else, Miti dramatizes starkly how the modern academic calendar of training for work and married life conflicts with the biological calendar, in all societies, but especially in those where life expectancy is short. Coincidentally, sexual license here (the plot is set in the late 1970s), sanctioned or otherwise, prepares the scene for the AIDS pandemic that erupted in the 1980s.

The Prodigal Husband recalls the 1950s. Zambia was still Northern Rhodesia, Zimbabwe was Southern Rhodesia, and Malawi was Nyasaland. It also encompasses Zambia's 1964 independence and ends in 1972, when its hero, Isaki, unlike his predecessor in *The Father*, joins the national university's first medical graduates. Core concerns again include education and a puritan Christian ethic urging hard work and monogamy.

Musa, from Northern Rhodesia, is foreman on a white farm in Southern Rhodesia. With a good wage, employer respect, and seven children, he feels it befits his status and Ngoni tradition to take the Shona girl Rhoda as a second spouse. Tisa, his devoutly Christian wife, objects, citing Corinthians 7:10–11. Ensuing debate around polygamy, wherein Musa cites the Old Testament and Father Abraham himself, is well handled; so too exposition of Ngoni marital lore covering husbands, wives, and brothers.

Marrying Rhoda, Musa packs Tisa and children off home, and, in Prodigal style, gradually abandons his responsibilities, thus hurting not just Tisa but also young Isaki, Christian like his mother and aglow with academic ambition. In a reprise of *The Father*, the narrative pits incandescent faith against multiform obstacles to education. If an earthly father will not help, the Heavenly Father will. For every tense encounter with academic authority (he is apt to arrive at new schools in bare feet carrying only a paper bag) Isaki prepares with silent prayer. Total faith plus brains bring successive bursaries until independence under Kenneth Kaunda introduces free education.

As the idealistic doctor that Manzuno failed to become, Isaki helps his father with a blend of traditional and Christian morality. In 1976, laid off in Southern Rhodesia (his white employer has no respect for age), Musa returns home to embarrassing drudgery on the Copper Belt. Isaki rescues him and reunites him with his mother—Rhoda failing to come north for fear of the area's witchcraft.

The novel captures a key period of transition in Central African history, debates around tradition and religion, and insight into a people's passion for modern learning. Miti also makes judicious use of epistolary communication. The tone is cool. Emotion remains controlled even when

conflict peaks, while traditional procedures allowing patient debate on complex problems show village democracy in rude health. It seems no part of Miti's purpose either to highlight postcolonial disenchantment (Kaunda's appearance is applauded) or to weigh heavily on colonial injustice, though Northern Rhodesia's neglect under the Central African Federation emerges implicitly via the widespread unemployment Musa finds on returning home and Musa's whole career has symbolized his country's status as a mere labor pool for the south designed by Rhodes—a fate shared by neighboring Nyasaland.

Mkamanga, Emily Lilly (b. 1949). Malawian novelist and social historian. Born at Chilumba, she was educated at Livingstonia, Uliwa, Lilongwe Girls' Secondary School, and the University of Malawi, graduating in 1971. After seven years with the Chitedze Agricultural Research Station, she joined the National Bank in 1978 as an Agricultural Information Officer. On retirement in 1993, coinciding with Dr. Banda's exit and democracy's arrival, she began a media campaign to persuade women to break their long political silence. Her novel *The Night Stop* appeared in 1990 and her account of the Banda years, *Suffering in Silence: Malawi Women's 30 Year Dance with Dr Banda*, in 2000.

Unthinkable as a Banda-era venture, *Suffering* is a study in appearance and reality: an analysis of the obsessive psyche of a modern tyrant and of what is called here "governance by intimidation"; a study, too, in how the extremes of right and left embrace with brands of brutality indistinguishable from each other. The world believed (was made to believe) that Banda loved his nation's women, rural poor women especially. He even styled himself their *Nkhoswe* (protector) Number One. But Mkamanga heaves up this rock and exposes the crawling things below. Banda exploited rather than protected "his women," used them indeed to protect and sustain himself in power. Even his trademark image as the centerpoint of a circle of dancing women suggests more protection than protector.

Mkamanga, just fifteen when Banda's reign began, has total recall of it and its democratic aftermath. She systematically deconstructs the cultivated image, but without personal agenda or coat trailing. There is only relief at setting straight the historical record before, as in colonialism, false image becomes false history.

Paradox abounds. The avuncular Nkhoswe exploits his *mbumba* ruthlessly—extorts the widow's mite for gift or party card (of the latter pregnant women must buy two); tolerates female abuse in jails where even old women can be paraded naked, raped, sexually tortured, and left to rot. The kindly medical man, preferring palaces to hospitals, deviously bullies his women not just into dancing, but into being ready—always, everywhere, no matter what the weather or their health—to literally dance attendance on him; leave the domestic hearth for weeks to attend practice camps and be sexually exploited by party officials. And far from enjoying lofty status locally and internationally, as propaganda claimed, Mpamanga says the typical Malawian woman was forever "powerless, poor, and pregnant." Nor would Banda disturb patriarchy (except to urge wives to inform on husbands) or move to reform its notorious system of widowhood dispossession. On key indices, women were substantially worse off than their sisters in Tanzania, Zambia, Zimbabwe, or even impoverished Mozambique. When Banda lost power, 85 percent of Malawians were still illiterate.

Mkamanga does not completely exculpate women: she blames them for their lack of solidarity, for futile rivalry, for being duped into destructive messianism, and even for polygamy. As for Bakili Muluzi's new democratic order, though the author rejoices that "anybody can be somebody in a democracy," she regrets that, just as Banda opportunistically exploited the change from colonialism, because people were diffident and inexperienced, something similar seemed to be recurring. The men *know* about democracy and how to use it; the women do not. With few exceptions (she singles out the late Mary Kerr-Ndovi for special praise) women are not speaking out or debating issues in the media.

Suffering in Silence exposes for us a core feature of Banda's governance. The extraordinary pathology of Banda's psyche itself still awaits clinical analysis.

Mnthali, Felix (b. 1933). Malawian poet, novelist, and dramatist. Proudly Malawian, his work, while constantly hymning landscape and people, also embraces a wider world—Southern Africa, West Africa, North America, Europe, Australasia. His background itself reflects a Central African interrelatedness. For though his parents were Tumbuka from northern Nyasaland, they were in Selukwe, Southern Rhodesia, when he was born. And, while his maternal grandfather had worked there for Rhodes himself, at home his great-grandfather had been a co-opted elder among the Ngoni, who had fought their way up from their Zulu homeland to settle near Lake Nyasa and become troublesome neighbors.

Mnthali's formation reveals a similar pattern. Southern Rhodesian and Nyasaland schools (including a Catholic seminary) preceded undergraduate study at the then University of Botswana, Lesotho and Swaziland and a doctorate from Canada's University of Alberta. A career fundamentally academic has also included exposure to diplomacy, radio broadcasting, university administration, and commerce. He is currently Professor of English at the University of Botswana.

Botswanan sanity followed Malawian madness during Banda's thirty-year rule, when Mnthali, with numerous colleagues, suffered constant harassment and then detention without trial. Marking much Malawian literature, this inhumanity spawned its own school of prison writing, from Mnthali, Sam Mpasu, Frank Chipasula, Jack Mapanje, and others. David Kerr, a leading figure in Central African literary scholarship, and in Banda's downfall, poetically captures this period's absurdity:

This is the man who was taken.
This is the brother-in-law
Of the man who was taken.
This is the neighbor who saw
The brother-in-law
Of the man who was taken.
This is the playboy who moved with
   the wife
Of the neighbor who saw
The brother-in-law
Of the man who was taken.
This is the newsboy who said hello
   every day of his life
To the playboy who moved with the
   wife
Of the neighbor who saw
The brother-in-law
Of the man who was taken . . .

Mnthali's verse registers it resignedly:

and so,
whether we like it or not
whether we spit or not
we are bound to be
the next to go
for all those that have spat
or have refused to spit
have sooner or later
sooner rather than later
gone

Mnthali's poetry began appearing in the 1970s, in the *East African Journal, Busara, Odi,* and the Irish missionary magazine *Africa.* His first collection, *When Sunset Comes to Sapitwa* (1980), was followed by essays, short stories, and a novel, *Yoranivyoto* (1998). An elder statesman of Malawian letters, familiar with colonial and postcolonial times, his core values might be called Afro-Catholic humanist. While his verse registers private pain (though always "communally"), seminary and university had taught a patient contemplation of large moral and political issues.

After colonialism, he suffered the trauma of independence when Banda overnight changed dream to nightmare. It was not enough that Mnthali was an intellectual ("Intellectuals, like the poor, we will always have with us," sneered Banda, who saw educated compatriots as rivals); he was also from the north, an area whose educational leadership stemming from Livingstonian pioneering triggered jealousy and spite.

Banda-era waste emerges as, soon after independence, the intelligentsia rot in jails: "these howling walls," "this walled wilderness," "walls / as inspiring as the shaft of a grave," "We have been entombed / by all that is ugly in this land / and in lands like this." Instead of a new dawn, life is "a sit-in of whispering skeletons" during which one can only contemplate "the emaciated ghost / of our diminished selves." We see the poet perched on his cell's feces bucket amid a scene of human wreckage:

wrinkled
wizened
pained
beyond their years and hanging on
   bodies
that once looked human clutching
   with iron hands
filthy plates of lukewarm porridge
without sugar and without salt

Yet Mnthali redeems his world by filling it with splendidly resilient souls—close family, relatives, friends, colleagues, other writers past and present—and inscribes human community at its heart. There is no pomposity, despite a distinctly oracular tone. And, whether painting a Corpus Christi procession or prison release, the verse moves at a steady pace: considered statements are carved, as it were, after careful thought (ambulatory composition being a favorite practice) and pieced together with care for logic and good draftsmanship. Melodic strength is apparent, too, and his *andante* rhythms provide a ground for elegiac tonality.

Rather than a spontaneous overflow of powerful feeling, we find powerful feeling modulated into artistic statement. And like many contemporaries, Mnthali also wants to get history right:

Write then erase all this
in the waters of the lake
before historians disturb what was
while inventing what was not

The poetry provides emotional release and its morality a challenge to surrounding chaos. George Steiner's words in *Real Presences* fit Mnthali's work precisely: "Be it realistic, fantastic, utopian or satiric, the construct of the artist is a counter-statement to the world."

Oral literature and debate were a survival strategy in Banda's prisons, where reading and writing materials were forbidden. A bookless university emerged, with inmates becoming widely informed and with Shakespeare's political assassination play *Julius Caesar*, unsurprisingly, a hot favorite. Such was the resilience of the human spirit:

And yet within these walls
as inspiring as the shafts of a grave
eloquence blooms like mushrooms
    in the rainy season

and irony and satire
cut deeper than blades of steel.
we are buoyed by each other's wit
and the stubborn faith
of men adrift
on uncharted waters
for between this tomb
and the sun and bloom
of the world beyond these walls
yawns infinity

The poetry's characteristics flow into the novel *Yoranivyoto*. Its title, meaning sweeping away the ashes, begins Mnthali's prose attempt to explain thirty lost years of Malawian history. The world of the poems becomes the world of the prose—a framework within which Banda's sociopolitical wasteland can be contained and inspected. Beyond a first-person commentator, the controlling narrative device is epistolary, correspondence between key figures providing contrasting comment on mutually important issues.

The book's blurb is helpful:

What keeps an attractive academic tied to the memory of a man she marries when he is about to die [in detention]? What do people who have been jailed without trial have to say to one another and to posterity? What do they really long for as they languish in detention? What is love? How does it survive persecution? Has the last word been written on Dr. Banda? What really brought him to power and how did he manage to wield it for so long?

The attractive academic is Dr. Anniversary Yoranivyoto Mganthira, a Malawian geologist at the University of Botswana (home to many Malawian exiles), her husband Woodson Wavasinga Mganthira, a civil engineer detained, like many others, only weeks after returning from graduate studies abroad.

The book's letters comprise conflicting statements to Yoranivyoto on Banda's behavior from figures still in Malawi—victims' cries and villains' special pleading. The villains damn themselves out of their own mouths. Chiswaswa Mataanjoka, Minister of National Integration and Mass Mobilisation, a suitor of Yoranivyoto constantly urging her return, explains that her husband and his friend Pachipembo deserved detention for a madcap scheme called Project Isanusi.

Like the verse, the prose is steady-paced and reflective, befitting a narrative on the nation's intelligentsia. It systematically lays bare the pretensions of Banda's lockup regime, yet more in sorrow than anger. Chinangwa Chamawa Mchosamantha, the hero's friend and cellmate, laments his approaching death to Yoranivyoto but suggests,

It is no longer good enough for the living to merely mourn the dead. We have been whispering in the dark and dying in silent despair for far too long.

From prison he later issues a plea to those still at liberty:

All you who seek change in this country, listen to the voice of a wasted soul. This is no time to whisper in the dark and die in silence and despair. Organize yourselves. Unite! You have nothing to lose but the lies of this regime and the suffering and despair of these times. Enough is enough. There comes a time in the life of a people when the fear of force must give way to a common anger and a common hope. I say that that time is now. . . . As the poet Agostinho Neto once wrote, "I wait no more. It is I who am awaited." God bless you all!

The Neto reference belongs to a thread of poetic allusion woven into the prose—just as adulatory citation of other poets informs Mnthali's verse. Indeed, civil engineer Wavasinga is a poet himself and a keen reader of African verse:

Wavasinga had almost recovered from the beating he received on the day of his second arrest. He had once more become his usual humorous and witty self. He would once in a while recite with passion verses from both his own poetry and from well-known writers such as Senghor, Okara, Okot p'Bitek, Awoonor, Kgositsile, Serote and a host of others whom we were hearing for the first time.

Elsewhere Eliotian interpolation registers shock at detainee numbers ("so many, / I had not thought death had undone so many"), while the main narrator, near the close, sees himself in Yeatsian terms: "An aged man is but a paltry thing, / A tattered coat upon a stick, unless / Soul clap its hands and sing"). Dr. Shuwa Mkwapatira Wakumkachi, ex-detainee and, after Banda's downfall, interim prime minister, writes to Yoranivyoto, citing her dead husband's favorite lines: "And what rough beast, its hour come round at last / Slouches towards [Blantyre] to be born?" But in life Wavasinga himself had secreted from prison prose that caught the heart of these years of madness: "Why am I here? I, Woodson Wavasinga Mganthira to whom crime is alien and malice an absurdity, why am I now here?"

Further reading: Adrian Roscoe and Mpalive-Hangson Msiska, *The Quiet Chameleon: Modern Poetry from Central Africa* (London, 1992); Adrian Roscoe, *Uhuru's Fire: African Literature East to South* (London, 1977), "Proceed with Joy: The Poetry of Felix Mnthali," *The Month* 253, no. 1492 (1992): 29–33, and "Dizzying Vortex: A

Portrait of Felix Mnthali," in *The Listener*, May 1986.

Modern Stories from Malawi. This anthology, edited by Sambalikagwa Mvona, was published by the Malawi Writers' Union in 2003. Economic constraints (Zimbabwe's Chenjerai Hove complains that books never appear in African budget plans, yet the continent is awash with luxury cars) meant that, as with such sister anthologies as *The Heart of a Woman* (1997), publication required donor help, in this case from the Norwegian Agency for Development. Forty stories by forty authors encourage Mvona's claim that Malawian writers have found their "identity and roots." Borrowing and imitation, he says, is now a "game of the past." An author himself, Mvona is pleased that the book captures history from ancient to post-Banda times: "We are talking about our beliefs . . . dating back to the Maravi era, the coming of the white skin, the AIDS pandemic, what democracy has brought." He welcomes new publishing channels, especially the *Malawi News* and *Weekend Nation*, which weekly feature emerging writers; and, with commercial eye, he notes that the stories "suit the Malawian readership and market." Editorial finesse is not Mvuma's forte, but his potted biographies are unrivalled models of encouragement.

Home from exile, author David Rubadiri graces the text with an appreciation. Work filtered to him between 1965 and 1994 had borne "the heavy hand of censorship," which is no longer the case. The collection, he says, reflects exactly the energy he finds at Writers' Union workshops, where he has been "awakened by . . . freshness, enthusiasm and sheer burning interest." It is reassuring that "there is still life even after poverty."

Writers here include Shepherd Adam, Gracious Changaya, Shadreck Chikoti, Victoria Chilowa, Joe Chinguo, Richard Duwa, Lawrence Kadzitche, Everson Kalinda, Peter Kalitera, Adonis Bongololo Kamphilikamo, Janet Karim, William Selemani Kayanga, George Kayange, Stanley Onjezani Kenani, Ken Lipenga, Mike Andrea Maele, Mufananji Magalasi, Kelvin Maigwa, Benedicto Wokomaatani Malunga, Levi Zeleza Manda, Linje Manyozo, Mariam Nthambile M'bwana, Temwani Mguda, Joe Alec Mlenga, Maureen Mercy Mlenga, William Mpina, Costly Ronalds Mtogolo, Charles Muthothe, Adamson Muula, Mike Sambalikagwa Mvona, Ndongolera Mwangupili, Phillip Pasula Nkhoma, Emmanuel Mzomera Ngwira, Godfrey Dinga Nyasulu, Nelson Nyirenda, Edwin Nyirongo, Sosten Yairo Abraham Phiri, Roy Sagonja, Nyakwawa Usiwausiwa, and Rhoda Zulu.

That texts rarely exceed two thousand words might reflect oral tradition, Writers' Workshop practice, media requirements, readership considerations, or all these. There is historical reach, but most authors are young with modern interests and, after Banda's 1994 departure, capture the new democratic climate. Because overwhelmingly male, feminist concerns are left largely to them. Free to break old taboos, heady candor marks their discourse as Banda puritanism yields to a looser ethic in writing and behavior. Liquor-store culture, sexual license, and scatological anecdote take a higher profile. Characters can now announce their tribal origins—whether Sena, Tumbuka, Chewa, Yao, or Lomwe—and there is, crucially, passionate concern about AIDS and prostitution.

Though primarily mirroring an urban meritocracy of cell phones, college, and the professions, the texts reveal, more substantially perhaps than Zambian and Zimbabwean writing, living links with rurality and tradition. If narratives do not exactly privilege rural life, protagonists have a village provenance from which they have not yet completely escaped. College graduates and busy professionals, they recall rural schools and village love affairs that still impinge on urban life. Nor is their world so modern as to exclude witchcraft (albeit treated skeptically), demands arising from famine back home, and "stylish cyclists" who pedal and wave to flaunt new wealth. Orality's fantasy yields to realism, but bequeaths its symmetrical plots, defeated expectation, and didacticism. Yet change is pervasive. As Temwani Mgunda puts it in "That Friday at Katoto," "these are the days when girls drink like their fathers and gone are those days when they cooked like their mothers."

Irony abounds. While sexual license and inebriation escalate and the mini skirt screams posthumous contempt for Banda, a religious voice grows louder. Oral text morality becomes born-again Christian discourse. Emblematic is a T-shirt in Temwani Mgunda's story crying, "It's not a secret I love Jesus." In Janet Karim's "Vain Vengeance," a schoolboy, losing his parents to AIDS, becomes a bullying, womanizing, drinking and smoking "monster," cursing AIDS and the whores who gave it to his dad and thus his mother. But he recovers by becoming so keen a Christian that he converts all his school friends. Joe Mlenga's "The Ignorant Matchmaker," an engaging venture into tragicomedy, features a Malawian Bertie Wooster driven into marriage by a bossy Aunt Agatha and then to an early death from AIDS caught from his village bride (there's talk of past involvement with truck drivers). Moral symmetry informs Charles Muthethe's "Devil at the Other End." Bernard, a businessman married to childhood sweetheart Chikondi, has a phone-triggered affair with Eileen—"only" a company receptionist, but smarter than he is. It transpires later that she has another lover, too, who gives her AIDS, which she passes to Bernard, who is now dying in hospital and anxious about the fu-

ture of his innocent wife and children. In Roy Sagonja's "Walking Corpses," Jimmy, a top executive married to schoolteacher Nabetha, on falling for bargirl Ethel, swiftly dismisses wife and children. But Ethel is blamed for Jimmy's AIDS eight months later—she has slept with 120 men, including Jimmy's own father. As the text says, Jimmy can divorce her but not his AIDS. They are now both "walking corpses." Nabetha survives. She is, after all, "a dedicated Christian." Soyinkan shades hover over Costly Ronalds Mtogolo's "This Road!" New highways spur economic activity, this one bringing Chinese shoes and radios, private buses, and a pub; it also brings traffic deaths, truck drivers, and the AIDS they pass on to village girls. Religion, AIDS, and widows' rights all emerge in Levi Zeleza Manda's "Kuhara." Charles and Catherine Phiri are married, having met at school in the Student Christian Organization. Charles begins drinking and whoring, and dies of AIDS. Following the *kuhara* tradition, his brother inherits Catherine, who infects him with the disease picked up from Charles. The diagnosis itself kills him, while Catherine's once lovely face is already showing ominous symptoms. The warning to those who abandon SCO morality is clear enough.

Rhoda Zulu's "Power of Prayer" omits AIDS but answers the chauvinist problems pervading Zambia's anthology *The Heart of Woman*. Robert and Juliet are born-again Christians in an initially good marriage. Not drink but twin girls drive Robert to wife beating and adultery. After prayerful Juliet saves him from public disgrace, when caught by a rival husband *in flagrante*, his gratitude restores domestic peace. Christian wisdom also operates in Godfrey Nyasulu's "The Rotten Mango" when two boys sweeping their schoolyard argue over a mango fallen between them. Ulemu, whom Sunday school has taught that those who entertain fighting are slaves to hate, steps in, picks up the fruit, and prevents violence.

A recurrent theme, exemplified in Gracious Changaya's "The Broken Promise," suits oral tradition's circular plotting. Noel makes pregnant Nyasongi, an orphaned fellow villager. College, city life, and a mendacious promise of marriage, make him vow "never to set foot again at home." How can he, a graduate accountant, marry a girl with only two years of high school education? Deceit climaxes in a letter saying that because he's going on a ten-year course overseas, Nyasongi should feel free of any commitment! But justice is at work. Even a Form Two training is a match for degrees in accountancy. Nyasongi tracks him down, with a new man and in a nice car, and leaves her baby on Noel's desk. A smart marriage to a graduate colleague is now off. She tells him "Waste not your time here."

No Malawian anthology could fail to reflect a national spiritedness and mirth, even amidst adversity. In Sosten Abraham Phiri's "Tit for Tat," there is nimble thinking and humor around a noise problem in a hotel. Peter Kalitera in "Asailunda" applies comic irony to the endemic problem of debt. The eponymous hero at month's end, exploiting social sensitivity around funerals, passes the hat around at work to collect for a deceased relative. Money flows. But so, awkwardly, does practical sympathy. Colleagues insist on accompanying the coffin to the home village for burial. They arrive just as a celebration begins for the arrival of the "deceased" relative from South Africa! But such inconvenience does not defeat wily village folk.

Moetsabi, Titus Bonie (b. 1963). Zimbabwean poet. Born near Bulawayo, and a law graduate of the University of Zimbabwe, he has no formal literary training but an internationalist vision as likely to lead him to Neruda as to Ngugi. He exemplifies how modern African writers often engage a wider world than do their Western counterparts, who seem often, in George Steiner's phrase, to be mired in trivia and domesticity.

Moetsabi has been described as "a lawyer by training, a development practitioner by practice, and a writer, actor, and theatre director by inclination." His area of special interest, communication, is apt. Currently SADC Communications Training Adviser and an expert in "participatory approaches," his values embrace community, justice, education, democracy, and language—human development broadly conceived. But seeing a fertile role here for the arts, and as a keen theater-for-development man, he is currently researching methods of communicating legal issues via drama. He is also associated with the Zimbabwean Association of Theatre for Children and Young People.

His verse, in *Fruits and Other Poems* (1992) and *Fated Changes* (1999), is attractively pragmatic. Moetsabi celebrates life in both its general and private dimensions (unusual in African verse, he even reflects his own young married love); and while Zimbabwe is highlighted, he also portrays community life in Sudan and Botswana. Due concern for postcolonial ills and development issues does not prevent gentle satire of donor agency aid; and whether writing on AIDS in humans or rinderpest in cattle, he exudes optimism, commitment, and even humor. Life is good. It can get better. Problems will be overcome.

Themes and positions are diverse. There are poems—the speaker can be male or female—on rural and urban life, Kalahari topography, Sudan, Zimbabwe, gender and patriarchy, black government violence on squatters, birth and parenting, ordinary people and their work. An overarching political sense enables him to talk learnedly about the North-South Dialogue, but always without the posturing of a pundit.

Postmodern oxymoron becomes a stylistic device of choice. Hence such titles as "Day Night," "Hell of Hope," "Wealth's Poverty," "Seeing Noises," "Sweet Torture," "Sour Milk is Sweet," "Cold Comfort," "Soft Like the Maiden's Hard Breasts." Despite a chance echo of Nigeria's Okigbo or Malawi's Mpina, Moetsabi seems free to experiment—untrammeled by models and rules, though on occasion he must fight the strangling register of his legal profession. A temptation to rhyme can also spoil effective poetic statement, as in:

Since you left, up to this day,
I am like a horse without hay
Pray I will not bray
From this distant bay
Like a horse without hay
Without you everyday.

Fortunately, better imagery appears, as in "Centre Ballad":

Oh, come with your long lady fingers
To pour cool water over my burning
    blood

And in "Smiling Lara":

In the village
They know me as the smiling
    drummer
One who silences the passing wind
With music to his love.

Some of the volume's early verse is perhaps too elliptical—Moetsabi seemingly flinging down unconnected thoughts—though sunshine clears the clouds in later poems:

Tolerance the vine of peace
Endurance the way to peace
Patience the line of peace
Forbearance the bridge to peace
Compromise the manifesto of peace

Moto, Francis (b. 1948). Malawian poet. After undergraduate training at the University of Malawi and doctoral studies overseas, he became professor of Chichewa at Chancellor College, where he is now principal. The country's leading authority on vernacular writing (a tradition dating back over a century), he has authored the standard work on the subject, *Trends in Malawian Literature* (1999). His concerns include women's rights and female portrayal in literature. A verse collection, *Gazing at the Setting Sun* (2000), was issued by Fegs Publications. He is also the author of *Language, Power and Politics in Malawi* (1999). Most recently his verse has appeared in *Operations and Tears: A New Anthology of Malawian Poetry* (2004), whose editor, the late Anthony Nazombe, comments that his contributions are a rare case of work reflecting the dawn of the new post-Banda democratic order. This is appropriate, for in *Trends in Malawian Literature*, quoting fellow poet Lupenga Mphande, Moto stresses that the university's famous Writers' Workshop, founded in 1970 by six students, was set up "to find spaces for political criticism and literature of dissent." His long association with the university has given him extended exposure to the workshop and its aims. Hence a keenness to mark poetically the changing weather as Banda's regime tottered to its end.

"The Child Chilungamo Will Be Born" rehearses the pain of a "people's reasoning" being taken prisoner, after an order which "had arrested creativity / in its useful tracks." It offers an apologia for the intelligentsia's weakness under oppression ("Silence, our friends, was an art learned / for the sake of simply wanting to be there"), but also announces that the new child, Justice, will soon be born. While "Where Will You Be?" admits that the new age is still unclear because a "white mist hanging over the hills / still veils my vision of a new tomorrow," it contains images of new dances in "the circles of a changed time" and a final slaying of the *chidangwaleza* or bogeyman. In "Escorting the Mother of Years," the poet is standing by the Thames in London as the new millennium dawns, dreaming of a rebirth that will reclothe and rebaptize homeland hills. "Songs from the Anthill," recalling past horrors, sweeps to climactic euphoria in seventeenth-century acrostic fashion with a crescendo of clarion calls to send out a message that the new order is here and old horrors over.

Moyana, Tafirenyika (b. ca. 1920). Zimbabwean teacher and poet. Moyana, who died in the 1980s, epitomized the charismatic teacher who pushes pupils toward fame in professions more honored than his own. He was also an astute analyst of the system he worked in and designed blueprints for its transformation. An educational pioneer in the mould of Nigeria's Tai Solarin, and urging syllabus reform of the kind pioneered in the late 1960s by Kenya's Ngugi wa Thiong'o, Taban Lo Liyong, Henry Awuor Anyumba, Philip Ochieng, and Okot p'Bitek, Moyana wrote *Education, Liberation and the Creative Act* (1988), which pinpointed and attacked major flaws in colonial education. The system, he argued, merely underpinned white domination—its Christianity, discipline, and manual labor emphasis creating a loyal black underclass. Models for every segment of life were British not African.

History rarely honors schoolteaching (hence its abandonment by generations of aspiring African politicians), but Moyana's achievements within modern Zimbabwean literature have been acknowledged. He taught the poets Samuel Chimsoro and Musaemura Zimunya at Chisore Secondary School, and an interview with Flora Veit-Wild shows Zimunya paying him golden tribute for inspiring him to love literature and seek a career in it. The instruments

were infectious teaching, an electrifying love of poetry, a school magazine, and bold excursions into African writing (especially Achebe and the negritude poets Senghor and Diop) when it was either banned or generally unknown:

> The primary inspiration was a man called Toby Moyana who taught us English in Form I and Form II and also in Form III. . . . When I was in Form I, a friend of mine got an article published in the [school] magazine and I got very envious that he had published and so I started to scribble something and I sent it in to the magazine and it was published. Thenceforth I became more excited about writing but I did not know what I was really doing until Toby started to teach us African literature. We read *No Longer at Ease* in class for many, many weeks and then he also introduced us to the poetry of negritude, the poetry of Senghor and the poetry of Diop.

Negritude was never a model for Central African writers, but its inspirational power and beauty, its affirmation of African worth, struck exactly the right nerve in aspiring writers still under colonialism and wanting their seeds of poetic ambition watered. "Moyana," Zimunya adds, "was very full of conviction and the way he taught made us aware of literature at a very early stage." Keen to see published the verse of pupils like Zimunya, Pote, Mazani, and Chimsoro, Moyana dispatched a collection to Heinemann, but without success.

Zimunya had earlier honored Moyana by including him in *And Now the Poets Speak* (1981), the collection he edited with Muderei Kadhani. The verse here reveals a gift for wit, striking imagery, and pungent statement. In "The Cashier," Moyana exploits the irony in a workaday racial confrontation with a white woman abusing him for the capital crime of wanting to pay a bill the day before it was due. She is seen sitting "Taut / in a chair . . . Eyes blazing through / Gold rimmed spectacles / Pointing at my heart," her lips described as "two thin slices of flesh." His poem "Apathy" captures the gloomy disbelief caused by Ian Smith's fatuous declaration that there would be no black rule for a thousand years. The stupidity of this and the regime's "ideological drycleaning" he captures in the lines, "Bones without all marrow / Make hollow oboe sounds / Of common sense." His poem "At the Meeting," where the persona seems to be awaiting sentence by a white colonial official, carries the tight lines:

> Pronounced my own benedictions
> On my own crucifixion
> Chanted my own requiem
> Purchased my own coffin
> Planned my own funeral procession.

Further reading: Flora Veit-Wild, *Patterns of Poetry in Zimbabwe* (Gweru, 1988); Rino Zhuwarara, *Introduction to Zimbabwean Literature in English* (Harare, 2001).

Mpasu, Sam (b. 1945). Malawian novelist and biographer. Born in Khuzi Village in Ntcheu District, he was educated at mission primary schools, Dedza Secondary School, and the University of Malawi. Among the university's first graduates in English and economics (1969), and finding infectious the vibrancy of its Writers' Workshop, he developed his literary and political interests during a decade in which the full details of Banda's dictatorship were still unclear. His early career, therefore, breathed the fresh air optimism of a new dawn. Nor had his vision for a decolonized Africa been dimmed by postcolonial failure elsewhere. He was proud on graduation to become a diplomat and secure a posting to West Germany, where, heady with youthful success and a desire to combine literary and political interests, he wrote his novel, *Nobody's Friend*.

A fast-track appointee, Mpasu then returned to major promotion at home: first to Trade, Industry and Tourism, then to the Office of President and Cabinet. Unfortunately, his novel's publication coincided with a spike in Banda's paranoia and a vicious tightening of security; and when, during 1975, the Censorship Board examined the book's contents (a body notoriously edgy and unlikely to smile at "fictive" disclaimers), it was immediately banned and Mpasu thrown into Mikuyu Detention Centre. He joined large cohorts of compatriots there, from villagers to cabinet ministers and academics.

The experience, maritally but not spiritually destructive, provided fertile material for a second book, the autobiographical *Political Prisoner 3/75*, published in 1995 after Mpasu had helped to remove Banda and introduce multiparty democracy. Within this new dispensation, Mpasu has been a respected Member of Parliament, Chief Whip, Speaker of the House, and Minister of Education, Science and Technology.

Nobody's Friend was a handy receptacle for youthful idealism. Its issues—colonialism, gender, town-country conflict, marriage, polygamy, philosophy, religion—suggest excited undergraduate debate, with at times minimal plot impact. Urban picaresque in nature, the novel recalls Nigeria's Ekwensi or Kenya's Maillu—city bars and drunk students here eclipsing rural Malawi, which is rarely captured. Yet the work is an early contribution to a genre still uncommon in Malawi and a valuable chronicle of issues engaging local youth in the late 1960s and early '70s.

Without *Nobody's Friend*, Mpasu's second book could not have happened. The Special Branch, he says, detained him because his novel's title clearly referred to the president. While the solipsism this signals is perfectly plausible, given Banda's paranoia and a Censorship Board that banned *The Green Revolution*, Mpasu had perhaps been too preoccupied to see the emerging reality of Banda's character—Victorian puritan morality, towering hubris and egocentricity. How else to explain a novel portraying sexual license, adultery, scenes of drunkenness (there is much delight in vomit), opposition to gerontocracy and one-party states, leaders for whom women must dance, political detention, and even African presidents who refuse to leave office or acknowledge a successor? If this was not enough, the narrative attacks government corruption and nepotism, incompetent lackeys being fast-tracked to the top, ministers getting "accidentalized," opponents being fed to crocodiles, predawn arrests, water and electro-genital torture, and thugs of a youth movement. As a document prophetic of life under Banda, this would be hard to equal. More banally, the hero even claims credit for introducing television into the country—an innovation, everyone knew, that was only possible under the Wise Leadership of the President.

Written with the benefit of personal trauma, journalistic skill, and freedom from fictive strictures, *Political Prisoner 3/75* makes absorbing reading. It delivers narrative pace and sustained focus on key features of Banda's rule—a climate of fear, wanton talent waste, widespread psychological destruction, and the rise and fall of henchmen like Focus Gwede and Albert Mwalo. Explaining how a long-awaited dawn became sudden nightmare, Mpasu makes a major contribution to the historical record.

Readers familiar with prison conditions in, say, Scandinavia or the USA, will find Mpasu's Mikuyu account scarcely credible: "Cell . . . the size of a small bedroom but . . . twenty-two of us in it . . . no beds, mattresses or mats . . . our old blankets were literally crawling with thick black lice." It was also "infested with large black rats. They ran all over us in the darkness. . . . Fleas from the rats were even more troublesome than the lice." Among the cell's twenty-two inmates there were at least a dozen madmen and a poor schizophrenic whose "wild, unintelligible singing," like the rats, made sleep impossible. Mpasu gives us a thumbnail portrait of him:

> He was tall and filthy. During the day he used to go to the garbage bin and eat from there. . . . Once I saw him chase a huge black rat in broad daylight. He caught it just before it could squeeze itself into a hole. Squealing and squeaking, the rat was put into his mouth, head first, and it was chewed off. With its blood dripping from his lips, he finished off the raw rat, bit by bit, and squeezed its long tail into his mouth.

Next door were the condemned cells where men "were chained to steel hooks on the floor, all day, every day, waiting for execution . . . they were never let out of the cell until they were executed." There were "fifty-eight people executed in one night . . . hanged three at a time . . . finished off with blows to the back of the skull, with a hammer or with powerful pliers which crushed the testicles." Relatives "went away sobbing as the condemned men gave instructions regarding who was going to inherit which chicken, which goat or which pair of trousers." In Mpasu's cell at least one man died every month, and suicide attempts were numerous. When one man, already in a punishment cell called Ku Mdina, or place of darkness, made a second attempt to hang himself, further punishment was swift and brutal:

> They opened the punishment cell hurriedly to cut him down. . . . He was

swiftly sentenced to seven days. . . . This time he was completely stripped of his clothing. Then they chained his legs together. Lastly they chained his hands between his chained legs. That way he could not sit up or stand or even roll over. To crown it all they poured three pails full of cold water over him. The water never flowed out and he lay in it . . . they nearly succeeded in killing him and thereby granting him his death wish. The first two days, they gave him no food or water to drink.

Amid such barbarism, where Christian brutalized Christian, friend brutalized friend, all to feed the vanity of a presidential elder of the Church of Scotland, prison authority preached reassurance. Inmates were told, says Mpasu, "how fortunate we all were to be detained by a civilized and humane leader, like Dr. Banda, when our fellow political prisoners in Eastern Europe got their heads smoked while dangling from the ceiling where their legs were tied."

Other Mikuyu prisoners during Banda's rule, all innocent of any crime, included Peter Mwanza, principal of the university's Chancellor College, writers such as Felix Mnthali and Jack Mapanje, Kirby Mwambetania, and many others. Picked up for the most ludicrous reasons, it was enough, say, that they were northerners, showed too much ambition or, in the case of Alafeo Chilivumbo, that they had perhaps dressed untidily for a graduation ceremony where Banda officiated. Mpasu's text takes its place among a growing body of Malawian prison writing.

Further reading: Richard Carver, *Where Silence Rules: The Suppression of Dissent in Malawi* (*Africa Watch* report, October 1990); Jack Mapanje, ed., *Gathering Seaweed: African Prison Literature* (Oxford, 2002).

Mphande, Lupenga (b. 1949). Malawian poet. Born at Thoza, near the Vipya Plateau in Northern Malawi, an area his verse celebrates, he studied with the Presbyterians at Embangweni, one of Malawi's leading secondary schools, and took a B.A. at the University of Malawi, an M.A. at Lancaster, England, and a Ph.D. at the University of Texas. In 1984 he chose exile in the United States and is currently associate professor of African languages and literatures at Ohio State University. His verse, which won prizes in 1985 and 1988, has appeared in such anthologies as *When My Brothers Come Home: Poems from Central and Southern Africa*, *The Heinemann Book of African Poetry in English*, and *The Fate of Vultures: New Poetry of Africa*; his work has also appeared in the journals *Poetry Review*, *West Africa*, and *Index on Censorship*. A long overdue verse collection, *Crackle at Midnight* was published in 1998, not, curiously, in Malawi but in Nigeria.

During the 1970s, Mphande enjoyed a Byronic reputation as an anti-Banda activist, a courageous risk-taker who left Malawi only to avoid arrest by the Special Branch. Apart from his passion for freedom and detestation of state bullying, it was enough that he was a Northern intellectual, a group Banda—whom Mphande in a poem for Jack Mapanje calls "a palsied tyrant / that scorns his subjects"—especially hated.

The romantic allusion is also apt because Mphande is in love with the natural world. His fellow exile Frank Chipasula observes in *Crackle at Midnight*'s introduction that "Of all the Malawi poets, he is perhaps the only one who has faithfully, and lovingly rendered the beauty of rural Malawi, exemplifying the intimacy many of us feel with the land." One could claim this for others (Edison Mpina, for example, who emerged in Chipasula's absence), but no one quite so sensitively captures the scattered graces of Malawi's hills and waters (Lake Malawi he calls "that ultimate beauty"); and like a true romantic, his best effects blend landscape with moral reflection. These early lines are typical:

> Herds of cattle and goats move
>   slowly across the hillside
> And pause to look like red and white
>   blossoms on a village tree
> A cloud of shadows brings life to the
>   far off hills. . . .

And

> In youth the future is like a hazy hill
>   in the dawn light of winter
> When fog in riverside deciduous
>   trees propitiates glory in a winter
>   day.

Crackle shows other romantic markers, too: a love of dream, melancholy, lyricism, nostalgia, tradition, country people, and solitary reflection amid rural beauty. The opening of "On the Vipya" is positively Keatsian:

> I sit in a sea of pink grass high up the
>   Vipya plateau,
> All around wild flowers sparkle like
>   stars against
> A lake breeze that blows the grass to
>   endless waves

But if this prompts European comparison, it also recalls the work of Nigeria's Gabriel Okara, a poet of similar sensibility. His love of rurality grows combative, however, when Mphande attacks forest rape by tobacco farmers and the polluting effects of pesticides—just as the poet Ogaga Ifowodo (author of *The Oil Lamp*) laments Shell's despoliation of the Niger Delta.

Crackle embraces a span of life from rural childhood, through student days, to a middle-age casting up, though chronological precision is sometimes absent. The volume reflects strengthening power, verbal overload yielding to compressed statement and short tighter lines. Rhyme ceases and *in propria persona* lyricism steps back for the distancing effect of created personas. A man, for instance, is called home from South Africa's mines:

> I was sent for,
> As happened in our country. That
>   morning,
> I lighted the mine shaft for the last
>   time:
> Miles by air, miles by land, Welkom
>   to Mzimba.

And in "Getting Past the Darkside," Orton Chirwa, feared rival of Banda, ambushed on the Zambian border, jailed in leg-irons and doomed to a prison death, speaks for himself:

> I walk, falter, listen to aches in my
>   joints,
> alone or with inmates,
> I creak step by step, wade under
>   floodlights,
> edge fence heights trimmed with
>   glass.
> I trip, sometimes, peeping at the
>   moon,
> and hasten along grey walls
> trying to get past the dark side.

In "Freeing the Barbarians," a spokesman for Banda's vicious Young Pioneers (an organization Robert Mugabe was to imitate) describes their response when peasants throw stones at Banda's passing motorcade:

> We descended and set fire to their
>   village.
> The women howled curses
> at our badges shining in the bonfire.
> Yelling of women is worse than
>   men's
> so we shut them up forever
> and went our way.
> . . .

Let the smouldering ruins
we left behind
be a warning to all who curse us.

But neither landscape nor solitude stifles Mphande's love of people. As with all good romantics, the lonely voice celebrates social life. Hence moving poems on the death of friends; a memorable dialogue with his grandfather; tributes and dedications to fellow poets and scholars like Jack Mapanje, Frank Chipasula, and Anthony Nazombe, and to victims of Banda's terror such as the hapless Chirwas, Vera and Orton; a portrait of an innocent old village woman in "Charged with Treason (for the mother of Amnon Phiri)," sentenced to be hanged, and then doomed to die in prison,

Where she sat all day cross-legged,
Waking each morning to stare at the
    sunrise
And a world she no longer recog-
    nized from dreams.

One poetic grouping is a portrait gallery of loved women: Tasiyana (so smitten by her that he attacks sacred tradition because it frustrates their relationship); peasant beauty Maria; a certain Perdita; the student Anjana; Ndindase (chided for fleeing to the bright lights of the city); and lastly Natasha, presumably a girl in Ohio, whose viola playing transports him to village days when he was expert in traditional dances such as ingoma, vimbuza, mutoyi-toyi, and gumba-gumba.

Further reading: Adrian Roscoe, *Uhuru's Fire: African Literature East to South* (London, 1977).

Mpina, Edison (1942–2001). Malawian poet and novelist. Born in Mulanje District, he was educated at Zomba Catholic Secondary School and became a banker, turning to writing in middle age. Taught little poetry at school, he later said, "I've fallen in love with Octavio Paz and Pablo Neruda and after my Iowa visit of 1982 American poets— Allen Ginsberg, Louis Simpson, and Marvin Bell, among many others—keep coming my way. Then also Soyinka and Brutus on the African and Brathwaite and Naipaul on the Caribbean scene. Biographies of writers— Auden, Frost, Lawrence—still inspire me. I keep reaching out for them." Mpina's life was a litany of hardships—among them serious personal and family sickness and imprisonment (including solitary confinement) without charge in the 1970s. He came to public notice in 1981, winning a major BBC award with his poem "Summer Fires of Mulanje Mountain," a success leading to his formative visit to the University of Iowa's International Workshop. After Dr. Banda's fall, he set up a Malawian branch of PEN to support new authors, founded a writers' workshop in the nation's capital, and was first president of the Malawi Writers' Union.

More than most contemporaries, Mpina celebrates physical Malawi and the agrarian round of village life:

We live in our fields most of the day
Hoeing Reaping Weeding Grafting
    Pruning
Because we believe that to mould
    Malawi verse, poets
Must first learn to master the craft of
    rearing animals, birds, plants

This earth-toil-poetry equation, with its spaced and capitalized honoring of agriculture, links to an argument aired in his *Malawi Poetry Today* that the nation's verse in English had been wrongly launched—in the groves of academe rather than in the fields of the countryside. Malawi's is not a poetry "that's given birth in a workshop / Like a coffin. Complete with formic . . ."

It enters into our eyes as arrows.
Into our ears as bees' buzzing,

It affects our skin as itch-beans.
A mosquito bite.
A bluegum falling on a hut where an
    old woman is sleeping.
As a ten pound hammer on a loaf of
    bread.

In 1991 Mpina turned to fiction with two short novels, *The Low Road to Death* and *Freedom Avenue*. The first, unblushingly didactic, structurally symmetrical, and spare in event, contrasts the moral codes of Nathupo and Napolo, ex-banker and lawyer, who leave prison committed to a new life. Nathupo, refusing to escape domesticity by fleeing the country, becomes a born-again Christian; Napolo, a religious skeptic, embarks on a life of business, sexual profligacy, bribery, corruption, and drug trafficking.

Narrative tempo is brisk, dialogue a Socratic exchange about God and Mammon. Nathupo knows his bible; but so does Napolo, in addition to books by Dickens, Naipaul, Nkosi, Okigbo, Eliot, Solzhenitsyn—and Can Themba especially, whose *The Will to Die* is a major influence. When Napolo hangs himself, Nathupo reflects, "I had read Can Themba's suicidal manner of drinking and my mind quickly related Can's death to Napolo's. One craved . . . drink while the other's search for money was phenomenal. Drink and money had proved bad priorities in the life of man."

Freedom Avenue is a better book, its didacticism more subtly woven into a plot of increased scene and event. Like Banda himself, protagonist Samsoni walks away from colonial Nyasaland's poverty, treks to Southern Rhodesia, and stays eleven years before returning for Malawi's independence.

Repeating poetic practice, Mpina highlights Nyasas' workaday concerns (sugar and salt supplies, the price of paraffin or fertilizer) and how, despite white pride in a colony founded partly on Livingstonian values, they must escape adversity born of hut tax and a forced-labor system dating to Sir Harry Johnston's policies in the 1890s.

Samsoni's dangerous safari through Portuguese Mozambique brings plentiful farm and mine work in Southern Rhodesia, where Nyasas are highly favored. Surviving racism, he supports compatriot burial societies, negotiates rivalry from local Shonas and Ndebeles, and returns home with dignity.

Irony arises from Mpina's twinning impoverished Nyasaland with racist Rhodesia with its food, work, basic health care, and even rudimentary education. Overwhelmingly, survival outpoints ideology. Arriving illiterate in Rhodesia, Samsoni leaves trained in first aid, butchery, and dairy management, is well married with three children, and, again with irony, is schooled in the liberation politics of East, West, and Central Africa.

Beyond noticing the abandonment of "good" Nyasaland for "bad" Rhodesia as a freedom avenue, readers in 1991 would also have noticed, rather glumly, the reprise of euphoria around dawning independence. Vignettes show patriots singing hymns to Banda, who, released from Rhodesia's Gweru Prison, is returning to seize freedom and smash both the hated *thangata* forced-labor system and the Central African Federation:

We are united behind our Kamuzu
Tili pambuyo pa Kamuzu!

That Banda should so swiftly betray the affection of his people and then, after thirty years, leave them still among the world's poorest, ranks high among the scandals of modern history. Why, then, should this novel honor Banda, especially when Mpina was himself one of his victims? Perhaps fidelity to history is one reason. Banda was certainly idolized during

Nyasaland's colonial struggle—the only man, it was believed, qualified to bring freedom, forced labor's demise, and an end to the common sight of people without "fat between skin and flesh." Authorial caution is another reason. As a late 1980s creation, the novel predated Banda's downfall by a number of years. Further, the book's intended audience (the pervasive use of the Chinyanja, Yao, and Shona languages suggests that it was local) would already know the horrors to which its hagiographic close was prelude. Thus seen, Mpina's text emerges as subtly satiric.

As a final irony, Nyasas, literally the Central African Federation's poor relations, emerge as its most politically astute citizens—leaders in a freedom campaign that black Rhodesians could only follow at a distance. Samsoni, in Rhodesia, says, "Rhodes came to this country, I don't know from where. But what I do know is that he came as a hungry wolf. David Livingstone came to Nyasaland . . . not . . . as a hungry wolf . . . but to teach and preach. . . . Livingstone was not hungry for land."

Mpina's poem "Monkey Bay," published in the 2001 anthology *The Unsung Song*, epitomizes him at his nature-and-land-loving best, longing for the next life, when he will live in the title's idyllic location and "recline on my past blurred with jail." His untimely death after so few years of recognition ended a career that promised much more than we have before us.

Further reading: Alfred Msadala, *Destined for Great Things: Papers* (Blantyre, 1999); Adrian Roscoe and Mpalive-Hangson Msiska, *The Quiet Chameleon: Modern Poetry from Central Africa* (London, 1992); Angus Calder, Jack Mapanje, and Cosmo Pieterse, eds., *Summer Fires* (London, 1983); Ken Kalonde, *A Special Guide to the Anthology of Malawian Literature for Junior Secondary* (Lilongwe, 2000).

Mpofu, Stephen Obert (b. 1955). Zimbabwean short-story writer and journalist. Born in Mberengwa, he left Zimbabwe as a youth to study journalism and creative writing at Zambia's Africana Literary Center. After twenty years with the *Zambia Times*, he returned home in 1980 to become *The Herald's* first African news editor, and then, in 1984, editor of *The Chronicle*. He is now governor of Matabeleland North.

The short-story collection *Shadows on the Horizon* (1984) announced a new writer mining journalism's rich deposits of human, political, and historical material. The prose was pungent, the openings were crisp, and incident was conveyed with authority. Narratives, often ironic, tracked social and political event without heavy ideology, though pithy comment always seemed ready, as when the reserves whites forced Africans into were dubbed "a place of slow genocide."

In "The Village Priest," a widow's mite story, an old woman brings to the church offertory a bucketful of monkeynuts and draws the priestly reply: "Amai, Christ needs money, not monkeynuts." In "The Black Poet," a villager, after city success, returns home with individualist values, and gets comeuppance when his broken-down Chevrolet needs muscle power from the community whose values he so despises. "Midnight Operation" recounts an innocent villager's arrival in Bulawayo, awed by its possibilities until, suffering racism and unemployment, he ineluctably falls into crime. Rural-urban contrasts, illusion and disillusion, suspense, the complex psychology of the unemployed, the breakdown of black solidarity via corruption—all feature in this brisk-moving plot.

"Nyamandu" depicts the complexities of the Liberation War. Africans privileged by colonialism's fringe benefits, and now keen materialists, deny help to the local poor and pay a deadly price when freedom fighters exact justice. This recalls Kenyan Mau Mau–era narratives, where a simple freedom issue, complicated by the twisting tentacles of history, led to fratricide and virtual civil war. In "The Criminals," the white regime's black bullies terrorize and torture even defenseless nurses. "The question remained unanswered," says Mpofu, "whether these men were entrenched in the "wrong" political camp because of their lack of political foresight or whether it was a fanatical loyalty which made them cling to a system whose life-chances they knew little about, or a combination of both." But Nurse Moyo's symbolically one-eyed tormentor finds himself years later as her patient—when she, too, now faces a serious moral and ethical dilemma. "Hunters of Fortune" shows that tribal relations need not, after all, generate corruption. A young man hands over to the police a tribal brother precisely for such behavior. "Behind the Mask" exposes white hypocrisy when those pretending to work closely with black colleagues privately articulate vicious racism.

The title story best shows Mpofu's strengths. Dramatizing key historical moments through events in a single village, Central African literature here once more seeks to get history right and draw conclusions. In 1949, a year of major new white immigration, the people of Mpopoti West are driven off their land by a farmer called Franschoek, who has "bought it." Most are dumped in a reserve, but one young couple, their dream of a land-based future shattered, join the guerilla war. In 1981, victorious, they proudly show their children the home area and the land that independence will now restore. Euphoria is short-lived. Their land has been bought again—now by a black buyer, Gambura, dismissed by the husband as "a spy, a sell-out." Postcolonial gloom descends:

'When we became independent we thought we had won the war. . . ."
"But we have."
"No, *sekuru*, we still have to fight on . . . but a different enemy this time. A black enemy trying to live like the old enemy."

Msadala, Alfred (b. 1956). Malawian poet, short-story writer, essayist, and journalist. Born at Nkhotakota, he was inspired as a University of Malawi undergraduate by the Writers' Workshop to write and pursue a role for literature in national development. Publications include a verse anthology, *Reminiscence* (1996), an essay collection, *One, Steve Chimombo* (1996), collected critical journalism, *Destined for Great Things* (1999), a long poem on AIDS, *We Lost Track of Ausi* (2000), and an edited short-story collection, *Neighbour's Wife* (2002).

Reminiscence's introduction says that, in addition to university influence, credit for Msadala's literary growth must go to the Malawi Broadcasting Corporation's Writers' Corner—a program, along with press reviews, far more significant for Malawi than, say, the *London Review of Books* for Britain or the *New York Review of Books* for the United States. University study exposed him to African and Western writers, ranging from Kenya's Jared Angira and Nigeria's Okigbo to T. S. Eliot and Samuel Johnson (who taught him patience).

Mainly short, some of his poems, like "Illusory," "Chisomo Spoke from a Window in Chilobwe," "Mon Ami," "The Past," and "A Letter to Lilongwe" could be apprentice work for *Haiku*. But "Blantyre" stimulates by its bluntness:

The city is stinking
Of crime, it is stinking
Of immorality, it is stinking
Of sewage, it is stinking

Of economy, it is stinking
Of corruption, it is stinking

"The Visit" reflects a delicate situation when a lady visits her jailed lover:

On that Saturday afternoon
Jokingly to her lover,
She was becoming used then,
'c'mon, surely
no need to sit like that!'
He looked up somberly
His eyes meeting the warder's
And courageously and calmly
Replied 'we do not'
And changed tone 'put on
Underwear, here'
Silence fell on them.

In the nine sections of *We Lost Track of Ausi*, Msadala addresses child abuse and neglect. With Blakeian sincerity, he narrates Ausi's childhood abandonment (at three months by his father, at seven by his dying mother), leaving him "an outcast, / a refugee, a boy in bond, / a leper." But there is a clear message for all Ausis: God will reward their hard work and faith because, after twenty years, lost Ausi grandly resurfaces as a modern success:

Yesterday a local tabloid
carried his profile:
Ausi Mafinga is high court judge,
    widower
his nephew, Chagoma, whom
he has brought up
is a teaching associate at Moni
    University
and his two sons, twins Mmwemo
    and Momo
are at St. James High School.

One, Steve Chimombo comprises five essays on Msadala's admired compatriot. Both writers are passionate about Malawian literary growth, and Chimombo's *Wasi Writer*, founded for this purpose, gets repeated citation. Chimombo's productivity—twenty books in a variety of genres since 1978—is lauded; so, too, his calm acceptance of criticism. Important literary milestones include the 1975 premiere of Chimombo's play *The Rainmaker*, an overnight classic; the 1990 publication of *Python, Python*, Malawi's first modern epic; and a pioneering entry into the feminist debate with the play *Sister! Sister!*

Msadala's *Destined for Great Things* (thirty critical pieces previously published in newspapers) parades not only good cross-continent literary models (Ngugi, Okigbo, Taban Lo Liyong, Okot p'Bitek, Musaemura Zimunya, Es'kia Mphahlele) but also aspiring locals: Patrick Jere, still at school; Patience Chimongeni and Tholakele Likupha, diffident and unsure about publishing procedures; some "dead poets," killed by poverty, who need a wakeup call. He praises John Lloyd Chipembere Lwanda, the exiled physician with his own publishing house, whose verse collection, *Black Thoughts from the Diaspora* (1994) saw the post-Banda leadership already "strangling the new constitution with its own umbilical cord." And he honors Sambalikagwa Mvona, because literary fame is elusive if you have not trodden "renowned academic corridors" and are thus seen as coming from "a small ant-hill."

Msadala also praises Du Chisiza Jr.'s *One Bright Night* for expanding the possible in post-Banda days. The play's high-flying female protagonist, chief accountant with a pharmaceutical conglomerate, is not only sexually demanding but seduces her own daughter's suitor. This, says Msadala, reverses reported local practice wherein older men seduce young girls to avoid AIDS. Nothing like this would have escaped the puritan eye of Banda and his Censorship Board.

Msora, Bertha Sithembiso (b. 1947). Zimbabwean playwright. With an unusual background in a musical and acting family (her father was a film actor and magician), she was on stage at the age of five. Since the early 1970s, she has appeared in such plays as Ama Ata Aidoo's *Dilemma of a Ghost* and *Finian's Rainbow*, and worked with the Zimbabwean Christian Council, the Urban Female Development Council, the Ministry of Local Government, and the Archdiocese of Harare.

I Will Wait, her first published play, won the 1984 Zimbabwe Publishing House Playwriting Prize and was included in their *Plays for Schools* series, its intended audience upper secondary pupils and adults. The year 1984 brought Zimbabwean independence, but the play is silent on politics and omits mention of the freedom struggle. Instead, Msora dramatizes older problems around tradition and modernity, town and country, a central focus being conflict between traditional custom and individual freedom, patriarchy and emerging feminism.

Tambudzai's will instructs husband Togara to marry her sister Rudo (still in seventh grade) to ensure care for her two children. Togara pays Rudo's school fees and expects her to join him. Her parents approve, but Rudo, like aunt Atete Rutendo, does not, because she has fallen for the stylish Leo-James Chizema. Plotting this conflict to completion proceeds with Jonsonian intrigue and the intertwinings of a Restoration *Romeo and Juliet*. A "tragic" ending with Togara's death brings the lovers together anyway, but not before Msora displays her flair for creative coincidence, go-between maneuvers, and identity confusion (the lawyer whom Togara and his sister unwittingly consult is Leo-James himself). Msora clearly knows her audience intimately and what will succeed on the Zimbabwean stage.

Muchemwa, Kizito Zhiradzago (b. 1951). Zimbabwean poet. Born in Chirimuhanzu, after education at Holy Cross School, St Ignatius' College, and the University of Zimbabwe, he became a teacher. Like contemporaries Kadhani and Zimunya, he has supported modern black writing as a poet in his own right and as an editor and commentator. In 1976, he became the first black editor of *Two Tone*, a journal open to all races founded in the mid-1960s; and in 1978, he edited the landmark anthology *Zimbabwean Poetry in English*, his introduction to which, scholars agree, remains the most authoritative introduction to modern Zimbabwean poetry. His own poetry appeared in this volume, in *Two Tone*, and in Tim McLoughlin's *New Writing in Rhodesia* (1976).

Oracular qualities made him a natural choice for Kadhani and Zimunya's freedom-celebrating *And Now the Poets Speak* (1981). His poem "Tourists" opens a section called "The Colonial Scourge." Colonizers, their baggage stiff with arrogant cliché, can never become flesh and bone of the land. Their British link may attenuate, yet their relationship with the soil never fructifies. They flaunt fetishistic geegaws as marks of superiority, import exotic plants, and live as though in a fortress. Their attempts to intimidate the ancient spirits of a land they think they have conquered will never succeed.

"Circular Roads (Wankie 28:1:76)" advances censure. White claims to enlightenment and superiority ring hollow in the coal-mining town of Wankie. Its blighted landscape, polluted streams, and choking air create a face soulless, unsmiling, and smelly. There was once beauty here. No longer. Though statistics are a state secret, "Thousands die for this coal town," and the surrounding roads, where "toxic pus flows on the landscape of this bandaged laager society," like white society itself, are "going nowhere."

In the section on the Liberation War, "My Friends, This Storm (1977)" pits radical black innocence, on which this struggle has been forced, against white pitilessness. Peace has been exiled to what Muchemwa calls "the vast prison of the wild." Meanwhile, readers are disappointed that he is not more productive.

Mufuka, Ken (b. ca. 1940). Zimbabwean short-story writer and journalist, born at Chiweshe near Masvingo. His family was thrice displaced to make way for white farmers—a blow the more painful because his grandfather was a World War II veteran. Mission school–educated, Mufuka holds an American doctorate and currently teaches African history at Landers University, South Carolina. Inspired by St Jerome's view that "If the truth cause an offence / It is better that an offence be caused, / than that the truth be denied," his nonacademic writing addresses human, political, and religious issues on both sides of the Atlantic. In the United States, he frets over young African Americans (unlike Colin Powell and Condoleezza Rice) rejecting opportunities and growing up fatherless. He also cites John Paul II's statement that it "is easier for men to father children than for children to have fathers." Best seen perhaps as a modern Alistair Cooke who can explain America to outsiders, Mufuka is correspondent for various African newspapers, including Harare's *Sunday Mirror* and *Standard*.

Like other African commentators, such as Kenya's Albert Ojuka and Nigeria's Tai Solarin, he exudes moral passion about global issues. While reproaching Robert Mugabe for shattering independence dreams within twenty short years (Malawi's Banda did it in as many weeks), he can ridicule the claims of Alabama's governor to Christian-

ity and a Washington that "hates evil dictators only if these evil dictators are not on its side." Brave in the face of political correctness, he can support feminist aspiration yet assert that American achievements have driven multitudes of "sissified men" into homosexuality. His short-story collection *Matters of Dignity* appeared in 1993, and in 1999 he published *Matters of Conscience: The Killers of a Dream*, nominated as one of Zimbabwe's seventy-five best books of the twentieth century.

Matters of Conscience (blurbed as "a damning satire on Zimbabwe's politics of greed") challenges taxonomy as neither an orthodox novel nor loose-linked short stories. Instead, it blends reportage, autobiography, short narrative, case study, and journalistic essay. A recurring feature involves a journalist or reporter whose newspaper piece, honest or fabricated, gets quoted; another is dancing peasant women who provide a choral background to postcolonial Zimbabwe's unfolding tragedy. Mufuka says, "The stories in this book and the personalities are fictional." But this is more faction than fiction, so diaphanous is the satiric veil. The jailed Rev. Indaba Kithole here is clearly the seventy-four-year-old Rev. Ndabaningi Sithole and the *mukuru mukuru* is Mugabe himself. Lord Thomson of Fleet is Lord Thomson of Fleet and feisty Sister Aquina is the real Catholic nun of liberation fame.

Despite uneven narrative quality (sometimes weak on focus and finish), Mufuka sharply details crime by a black "kleptomaniac aristocracy." "Khan Loses His Farm" highlights fraudulent land seizure from an Asian with impeccable liberation and postcolonial credentials. Demonstrating how right and left oppression embrace each other, other narratives uncover a housing ministry gifting flats for sex, the leg-breaking and general terrorizing of any kind of dissident, jobs only for party card holders, and a warning to the likes of Mufuka that virtue and learning will be of no avail: "It is our time to *eat. Eat* we are going to. And who is going to stop us? You, with your books, your little articles here and there?" But there are lighter moments. A flashback to Mugabe's schooldays shows Jesuits punishing him by making him read St. Thomas Aquinas's *Summa Theologica* in its entirety!

Mugabe, Robert (b. 1924). President of Zimbabwe. Mugabe is a Mshona born at Kutama Catholic Mission, Zvimba, Southern Rhodesia, where Jesuit schooling preceded correspondence courses that qualified him for secondary teaching in 1941. He later enrolled at South Africa's Fort Hare University, graduating with a B.A. in English and history in 1951. In 1952 he taught at government schools in Highfield and Gweru, but in 1955, after a B.Ed. from the University of South Africa, he secured a post in Northern Rhodesia (now Zambia) at Chalimbana Teacher Training College. In 1957 he was in Ghana teaching at St. Mary's College. Nkrumah, the country's president, fired his liberation instincts (Ghana was Britain's first sub-Saharan colony to achieve independence) as perhaps did Hastings Banda, who was also there before returning to Nyasaland. Back home with a Ghanaian wife, he began his political career at a time of growing tension.

When his Zimbabwe African People's Union, founded in 1961, split along ethnic lines in 1963, he stayed with the new Shona-dominated Zimbabwe African National Union. Charged with "subversive speech" by the colonial authorities, he went into exile in Tanzania in 1963, returned in 1964, and was jailed for a decade. This period marked the rise of Prime Minister Ian Smith, whose Rhodesian Front Party resisted all notions of black independence, despite a decolonizing tide engulfing most of the continent. Smith's 1965 Unilateral Declaration of Independence triggered the guerilla war in which Mugabe's and Nkomo's armies ended white colonial rule in 1980. When the ZANU-PF party won the 1980 elections, Mugabe became president, the only effective opposition being his old party ZAPU, now Joshua Nkomo's minority Ndebele grouping. Mugabe-Nkomo rivalry deteriorated into a brief but bloody civil war with massacres monstrous enough to inflict on literary Zimbabwe a stunned silence.

It is said that Mugabe, a skilled politician, is adept at bringing opponents into government: hence he invited defeated Nkomo to become Zimbabwe's vice president. Less skilful at economic management, however, he has overseen a collapse of living standards (inflation topping 1000 percent in 2006; life expectancy, at forty, the world's lowest) and a mischievous handling of legitimate land concerns that has only added to economic decline. Like Kaunda (but unlike the psychologically flawed Banda), Mugabe created great optimism on his nation's independence—a hero even of white farmers and *Time* magazine. But age seems to have sharpened an autocratic tendency almost to Banda levels. Indeed it is reported that in Banda's last years the two often met; and the Youth Brigade that Mugabe has used so cruelly against his opponents closely resembles the Young Pioneers who terrorized Malawians during the Banda years.

Mujajati, George (b. 1958). Zimbabwean novelist and dramatist. Born near Chivhumudhara and educated at Gweru Teachers' College and the University of Zimbabwe, he is a principal lecturer at Harare's Morgan Zintec College. His plays *Children of God* (1988), *The Wretched Ones* (1989), and *The Rain of My Blood* (1991) have won national awards. In 1993 he published a novel, *Victory*.

Though *Victory* is short—it opens with the Prophet Amos's warning to "those who trample on the needy" and closes with a gloomy afterword on the interlocking meanings of "victim" and "victory"—its focus is poverty, colonial oppression, and powerlessness, and how, combined with land loss, these lead to guerilla warfare and hollow victory. Deeply spiritual ("sin" becomes a motif companion for Amos), Mujajati defends with Old Testament zeal the oppressed who labor at white farmers' whim. He depicts barbarous punishments in eyewitness detail, and, through protagonist Zuze's life, enwraps all in historical context that reaches back to Rhodes and Nehanda and forward to independence. His identity with the poor is so passionate that he is apt to slip from the third person into the collective "we." And just as he flays white farmers, like English Jones and Afrikaner Boschgrave, who grind the faces of the poor, he lambastes the new black elite who do the same. Harare authorities use batons and bulldogs to hound Zuze and his ilk from station waiting rooms and plastic shelters. Food rioters sing in the streets while the President receives an international prize for his "relentless fight against hunger"—"the rhythms of hunger," as the text puts it, "clashing with the rhythms of power."

Zuze was born on Jones's Little England Farm into an unhappy marriage (his father, Jairos, industrious, demoralized by alcohol, impotence, and his wife's adultery; his mother, a feisty woman who teaches him survival). Destined for farm laboring, he witnesses atrocities committed by Rhodesian soldiers in the Liberation War, his mother's sordid adultery with a soldier, and the resulting death of both parents. Yet in 1984, by chance the year of Zimbabwe's formal independence, an award for work with pigs (one notes the Orwellian echo) precedes his fall from fame and dismissal on contracting tuberculosis. Thereafter he must scavenge among Salisbury's dustbins ("the earliest tramp catches the fattest leftovers") and face a cave's cold comfort. A seriously ill son of the soil reduced to troglodyte life in independence year needs no comment. Imbued with his mother's resilience, however, Zuze defies a white prospector wanting his cave and leads a hunger riot that smashes Harare shop windows to get at fried chicken.

Though sometimes with rhetorical overload, Mujajati can write with power. Poetic prose can literally become verse. A despairing Zuze wishes God had created him a tree or animal, since dignity and pride had been stripped from him by "the pricking crown of thorns which humanity had planted firmly on his head." The story proceeds:

> Suddenly a rat raced past him in full flight. Hot on the rat's heels was a viper. The beauty, the peace, the innocence of the blossoming flowers that had hung all round him turned into a jungle. A jungle where only the poisonous would survive. The viper sank its fangs through the tender skin of the hapless little rat. Within seconds the little rat quivered in violent spasms as it expelled the last tremors of life from its harmless body. Thus, the weak, the harmless, the non-poisonous, those that cannot defend themselves, shall all perish. They shall become food for the powerful and the poisonous. Their remains shall, however, be laid to rest in the tomb of their innocence.

The rat-and-viper irruption into Eden is arresting, so too Zuze's identification with the snake's victim. But Mujajati cannot resist switching into prophetic register and pointing a moral that announces itself.

Less rich stylistically, *The Rain of My Blood* foreshadowed the novel's objective, recording settler devastation of African lives, the bush war, ensuing atrocities, liberation in 1980, and subsequent disenchantment. With land settlement colonialism's central issue, the play, like the novel, also begins on a white-owned farm. But, with writers at this time still perhaps hesitant to express postcolonial gloom, Mujajati constructed his work defensively. Tawanda, a neglected freedom fighter, meets an anonymous dramatist keen to feature the struggle, and merely narrates his story, including his treatment as a disabled veteran. Thus, in a sense, this is not Mujajati's work, and not even his protagonist's.

Negomo and Munjai, a couple working on Mr. Sanderson's farm, have a clever son, Chamunorwa, enrolled at Chegato Mission School, who is beaten unconscious for daring to protect his father against the blows of Sanderson's son, who merely tripped while jogging past the family hut. Evicted, the family moves to Chegato Mission, from where Chamunorwa and a friend are expelled for contesting the white version of the first Mashona rebellion of the 1890s. Like Zuze in *Victory*, they descend to the dustbins of Salisbury ("this Devil's Paradise") before leaving for Tanzania and Zambia to join the struggle, returning later to kill Farmer Sanderson, suffer comradely betrayal, and death by hanging after a show trial. Munjai dies under torture and Negomo is driven insane. The play's denouement shows Tawanda leaving the home of his educated brother (a noncombatant but successful new order accountant), who finds the freedom songs of Tawanda and his veteran friends an intolerable intrusion on his bourgeois lifestyle.

Recalling *Victory* are the play's swift action and scene shifts. The demands of spectacle and debate are met with energy; dialogue rarely submerges action. Chamunorwa's public beating, his degrading treatment in racist Salisbury, the Senecan torture of Munjai, and Negomo's wild insanity—

these are captured with signal power. Tawanda's summary is poignant: "Then came 1980 . . . the combatants marched victoriously into a liberated Zimbabwe. . . . A new sun rose in the sky, shining brightly, full of promise. And we gazed up full of expectation, our souls full of song, our hearts full of pride. We marched into Zimbabwe, and waited . . . and waited."

Mujajati's work has incurred such government hostility that Chenjerai Hove in *Palaver Finish* (2002) has written: "He is the most tortured writer in this country at the moment. He cannot sleep in peace in his own house. And the violence against him means he is supposed to fall silent, to disappear as it were."

Mulenga, Luke (1935–2003). Zambian poet. Born in colonial Northern Rhodesia, he attended the Jesuit St. Francis' Secondary School, Malole, and then Munali High School. After British A-levels, taken by correspondence, he studied theology and philosophy at the Jesuit seminary in Salisbury, Southern Rhodesia, sociology and anthropology at Britain's Sussex University, and social studies and literature at Canada's University of Regina. Wide travel preceded work in independent Zambia, first with Malachite Films, Chingola, and then in the copper industry with NCCM Ltd of Kitwe. A passion for peace and justice led to membership of Amnesty International and of a Belgian group called Hearts Open to the World. He also joined the New Writers' Group of Zambia because, as he put it, he was "interested in being associated with those who strive to serve the world through poetry." Nostalgic for Old Africa's values and cultural richness, he lamented modern damage not just to tradition's accidentals but also to its very essence. Verse reflecting these concerns has appeared in journals in Zambia, the United States, the United Kingdom, and

Scandinavia. His collection *Zambia I Love* was published in Sweden in 1982, but its poems have been often recited at cultural gatherings within Zambia itself.

If Mulenga shows nostalgia for old Africa, "One Zambia One Nation" celebrates also the new country's birth, its title an early Kaunda slogan. Lusaka, the burgeoning capital, he calls a city "that thunders with vitality, / A new center of attraction, / in the heart of Africa." Proudly African, though no jingoist, Mulenga in his poem "Determination" hymns his people's stoicism under colonial rule and attacks the theft of their copper to make foreign racists wealthy. Imperialists' motive was simple, "Exploitation of man by man," but the country, "so young but rich and big," rose up and drove them away.

Zambia I Love is beautifully illustrated by Margareta Oscarsson. Her mother-and-child drawings amid leafy bowers, migrating swallows, hummingbirds feeding their young, hands in barbed wire, women abandoned, hungry, or infirm, concretize values informing the verse. She symbolizes "Torture in South Africa," for instance, with a powerful sketch of a white raptor tearing apart a black dove, its victim meanwhile looking bewildered. "What can remain of love," asks the poet, "In such a life teeming with evil"? Yet Mulenga's love of African natural life is everywhere manifest. His "Singing Birds of Africa" begins:

> With eyes like beads
> So satisfied and happy
> Sing the sweet birds of Africa.

Migratory swallows and their round trips to Europe capture his imagination:

> Lovely seasonal birds
> Sweet swallows,
> Hover in and out of Zambia
> And in twinkling clouds,
> With golden voices sing.

> From different foreign lands
> They come in choirs across vast
>   waters,
> And over mountain tops they fly.

His nostalgic poem "Back to the Land" aches for lost rural simplicities and indirectly recalls young Zambia's mistake in privileging mining over agriculture. It was in the countryside, says Mulenga, that he left not only his ancestors' songs and dances, the fields of millet and cassava, but also, crucially, "my God." Meanwhile, he mourns over our modern world: its lack of social justice or cures for poverty and sickness, its ravaged family life wherein husbands abandon wives and children to penury. Old customs "disappear like chaff" and the effect is painful:

> It makes me sick and sad,
> Our beautiful culture of love, peace
>   and joy is gone.

But the female persona in "Little Mother" broaches a different problem. Her father "shakes his head and weeps" because she has become a nun. Her vocation seriously disturbs a value system based around group survival's imperative of new births and the concept of a family comprising those dead, those living, and those yet to be born. Hence the paternal response:

> My father will now say,
> "You have delivered life to all
>   disasters,
> Because you will bear no children.
> You have cut me
> At the bottom of my roots" . . .

This states baldly the inherited position. And though the persona reaches for arguments that at least do not deny her basic womanliness, it is unlikely that the poet agrees with her:

> God called me one day,
> Because He is Almighty.

And somewhere deep inside me,
Femininity and maternity
Are blossoming fully,
In a life dedicated to God.

Meanwhile, the poem "Creation" constructs the larger picture Mulenga urges us to see and love:

Look at the stars,
And see the beauty of creation,
The inner soul of order,
And source of harmony,
Look at the planets and beyond
And see gleaming galaxies afloat
Like wind-driven balls of fire
In the fullness and fruitfulness of
      creation.
Look at the face of the Earth,
And see the innermost nature of
      creation,
Blossoming bright
Like mother's love.
Look at the gift of life far and wide,
And see the whole system of
      creation,
In full bloom
Like miraculous flowers of Babylon.
Look at yourself
And see the eye of God
With penetrating light of creation
The sweet source of life.

It is unclear if Luke Mulenga was active politically. But his work reveals a man whose overflowing love of family and nation, continent and nature, justice and peace, seems a splendid flowering of the spiritually conceived humanism that Kaunda, Zambia's first president, was so keen to preach to his new country.

Mulaisho, Dominic Chola (b. 1933). Zambian novelist. Born in Feira, Zambia, and educated at the Jesuit Canesius College (which revealed Catholicism's role in the liberation struggle), he grew up under colo-

nialism but lived to see independence. Teacher training taught him about Zambia's educational needs, while study at the University College of Rhodesia and Nyasaland exposed him both to Western literature and Rhodesian racism. Important for his writing, public service showed him the inner workings of colonial governance and its relationships with London, Salisbury, and Pretoria. Periods as permanent secretary in the ministries of Education, Lands and Natural Resources, and Mines preceded a move into international business. In 1971 he was chairman of Roan Consolidated Mines and Nchanga Consolidated Copper Mines; in 1971 he was executive chairman (and in 1972 Managing Director) of the Mining and Development Corporation—experience that exposed capitalist mendacity when Zambian copper fortunes were riding high. After years in yet another field of national industry, as general manager of the National Agricultural Marketing Board, in 1976 Mulaisho was appointed special assistant to the president for economic affairs and thus worked for a decade in close cooperation with his admired leader, Kaunda. This led to governorship of the Bank of Zambia (1991–95), during which period Kaunda's successor, Frederick Chiluba, arrived. Few public careers anywhere can match such diversity.

Mulaisho used all this to good effect in his novels *The Tongue of the Dumb* (1971) and *The Smoke That Thunders* (1979), with Kaunda personally helping to launch the former as the first Zambian novel. Though initially tentative, as it dramatizes a struggle between good and evil during the late 1940s, it analyzes incisively the strengths and weaknesses of two competing entities: the traditional village world and the world of the missionary. Both emerge flawed and fissile. Village fickleness, power hunger and cruelty, and a ready resort to the *mwavi* test for witch-sniffing balance an unrivalled warts-and-all portrayal of missionaries. Jesuit-trained himself, Mulaisho shows the order's human face—sublime humility and identification with the people on one hand, intellectual arrogance and racism on the other; ordained priests as a mandarin caste and lay brothers as disdained inferiors. But the strengths of both worlds unite to resolve the book's conflicts. An incidental finding is the chiefly use of youthful bullies to sustain village power—a fictive feature soon to appear with terrifying reality in Hastings Kamuzu Banda's Young Pioneers and Robert Mugabe's Youth League.

In *The Smoke That Thunders*, Mulaisho uses his experience with more assuredness as he attempts an all-encompassing account of Central Africa's freedom struggle. While the three territories played out their colonial history differently, the book weaves together their commonalities of struggle. And among writers seeking to rectify the historical record, none comes better equipped than Mulaisho: insider and outsider to the colonial process, active player and concerned spectator. The eye and ear of memory are keen, too, and his Kaundan humanism gives the novel its moral core.

Mulaisho's fictive colony Kandaha is an island in the Zambezi and thus symbolically midway between the three territories of the Central African Federation. Here he can invest enough material from the neighboring states to make his novel representative. Thus Ian Smith's racism and rhetoric around his Unilateral Declaration of Independence (1965) blend with life under Baker, the diminutive Kandaha governor (probably a recreation of Nyasaland's first governor, Sir Harry Johnston), and a freedom movement led by one Kawala, who is clearly Kaunda in disguise. The settler-capitalist alliance is drawn from Mulaisho's experience in the copper industry, while the white leader Sir Roy Norris (an ultimate convert from crude racism), boxer,

ex–engine driver, and Polish immigrant uneasy among British colleagues, clearly recalls the extraordinary Sir Roy Welensky of Rhodesia.

Mulaisho captures to a nicety the varied discourse of black freedom fighters, white capitalist businessmen, working-class British miners, Afrikaner expatriates, Bloomsbury and Whitehall officials, Asian pragmatists, African traditionalists, and the Holy Ones lashing biblical millennialism to the wheels of revolution. Given Mulaisho's linguistic relish, and particular love of African rhetoric, he fashions passages of memorable oratory, for or against independence, from speakers in the whites-only parliament no less than from speakers in rural villages and guerilla camps.

Mulaisho paints the brutality inflicted by both sides in a struggle white intransigence makes inevitable. And while gracing his narrative with cameo portraits, minutely and memorably sketched, he also probes mind and motive among his key players—Kawala, Norris, Malherbe, Kangone, Fr. Lafayette, Governor Baker, and Norris's rebellious son George. If Achebe's *Things Fall Apart* is the classic account of colonialism's arrival in West Africa, Mulaisho's novel memorably depicts Central Africa's farewell to it.

Further reading: John Reed, "Dominic Mulaisho," in *Encyclopaedia of Post-Colonial Literatures in English*, ed. Eugene Benson and L. W. Connolly (London, 1994), 1052; Fanuel Sumaili, "Literature and the Process of Liberation," in *Literature, Language and the Nation*, ed. Emmanuel Ngara and Andrew Morrison (Harare, 1989), 7–14.

Mulikita, Fwanyanga Matale (1928–98). Zambian short-story writer and playwright. He was born in Sefula in western Zambia, and his early schooling was in Mongu and Lusaka. He later studied English and psychology at South Africa's Fort

Hare University College, graduating in 1954, and in 1961 completed an M.A. in psychology at Stanford University. He was awarded a doctorate in laws by South Africa's Rhodes University. Mulikita shares the diverse career profile of many contemporaries. Before Fort Hare he was a clerk interpreter in Northern Rhodesia's High Court. From 1954 to 1956 he taught at Mongu Secondary School, and after a brief spell as welfare officer with Kitwe Municipality, he moved in 1957 to Kitwe Teacher Training College. Fired with an educational idealism reminiscent of Nigeria's Tai Solarin and Zambian compatriot Sitwala Imenda, in 1961 he opened Chalimbana Secondary School and served as headmaster. In 1964 he was at Columbia University taking a course in diplomacy and international relations. On independence, he was appointed Zambia's first ambassador to the United Nations. In 1996 he assumed such ministerial portfolios as Labour and Social Services, Transport, Power and Works, and Education. In 1988 he was appointed speaker of the National Assembly and guided government through its sensitive transition from single-party to multiparty democracy in 1991. A respected figure in Kaunda's United Independence Party, he served terms as chancellor of the University of Zambia and of Copperbelt University (1992–97). His career parallels that of Dominic Mulaisho, a compatriot whose literary energies were also curtailed by the demands of high office during Zambia's fraught early years of independence. Mulikita is best known for his short-story collection *A Point of No Return* (1968) and the play *Shaka Zulu* (1971).

The eleven stories in *Point of No Return* (expansive tales rather than conventional short stories) show Mulikita coolly surveying contemporary Zambia but within a traditional context. Setting, plot, and event are local, but frequent cultural explanation suggests an alien target audience. Part of a tiny intellectual elite at this time, Mulikita feels a natural moral concern for the nation as a whole. Imbued with education's transforming potential, he also espouses key tenets of Kaunda's humanist philosophy. He wants to move beyond colonial pain and his "The Tender Crop" points one way. Thus the sacking of Mateyo Chilufy by white farmer Paul van Zyl after thirty years' service becomes a moment of promise, not protest. Mateyo returns to his abandoned village and, like colonial settler van Zyl, starts a prosperous, but communal, farm, a magnetic model for others. Mulikita here is warning his new postcolonial nation besotted with mining profits and perilously spurning agriculture. His message, alas, went unheard.

Mulikita is interested in rationality and its impact on issues traditional and modern. Exposing the psychological trickery of venal medicine men (in "Chikoli's Ghost"), he also tilts at an American academic (in "A Doctor of Philosophy Changed His Mind") whose rational skepticism is sufficiently disturbed by village superstition to cause flight. A narrative on rural crime ("A Baby Reforms a Notorious Thief") stirs modern reflection on kleptomania, and the closing story, "The Borders of Reality," reads like a puff for the practice of psychological regression. Its success with a disturbed schoolgirl, despite professional medical skepticism, precedes a suggestion that maybe all humanity could thus be treated—with edenic results.

Mulikita's prose is attractively unhurried and eschews flamboyancy, proceeding at oral storytelling pace. Indeed, "What Old Hankwamuna Said" is cast as an actual oral performance, its narrator pausing, teasingly withholding information, lighting his pipe, and interacting with his audience.

The Shaka story, a natural for drama, and of course a subject of much writing in prose and verse, stirred the African imagination far beyond Zululand. If colonialism exploited division, Shaka created a great nation from "the oddments of more than two hundred unruly clans"—an object lesson in suprasectional vision and solidarity. While his military genius (innovated weaponry, Amazon and bachelor regiments, iron-clad discipline) intimidated whites, it also inspired others keen to avoid conquest. Even the nineteenth-century *mfecane*, which his faults triggered, dispersing Zulu groups north to what are now Zimbabwe, Malawi and Zambia, inevitably spread the glow of his reputation. Then, too, Shaka's personal life—obscurity, illegitimacy, supreme power, psychic flaws, bachelorhood, maternal worship ("I have conquered the world but lost my mother"), and assassination—was a study in tragedy of classic Aristotelian dimensions. Mulikita has his play (successful enough for a reprint in 1974) blend staples of western and African practice: a chorus-like chronicler, prophecies, reported-speech battles, onstage executions, and highly dramatic witch-sniffing. Using E. A. Ritter's biography, he captures well the essence of his large subject.

Muluzi, Bakili (b. 1943). Former president of Malawi. Born into a poor family at Kapoloma in Machinga District, he was educated locally, in Denmark, and in Britain. Qualified in technical education, he became principal of Nasawa Technical College, Magomero (by chance the location of the Chilembwe uprising of 1915, the first against British colonial rule in Nyasaland), and helped the Malawi Congress Party to win independence. Though a minister during Banda's thirty-year rule, from 1983, when several cabinet members were murdered, he began work to oust Banda via a new democratic party, The United Democratic Front. After the country's first free multiparty elections, he became president in 1994. His term of office, if not without blemish, was sufficiently regarded to bring honorary doctorates from Lincoln University, Missouri, Glasgow, Strathclyde, and Taipei, and the International Peace Maker Medal in 2002. His main publications are *Democracy with a Price* (1999), coauthored with D. Y. Juwayeyi, Mrs. M. Makhambera, and D. D. Phiri, and his autobiography, *Mau Anga: The Voice of a Democrat, Past, Present, and Future* (2002).

The Muluzi story has rarity value. Unlike West or East Africa, Central Africa has produced little autobiography. Muluzi was not just the first genuinely democratic president of a country hitherto subjected to one-party rule, but also the first Muslim to hold such high office in a country inaccurately represented as overwhelmingly Christian: not wholly for their historic links with slaving, Malawi's Islamic communities were virtually ignored in political discourse during the Banda years. Though an elder of the Presbyterian Church, Banda's prejudice contrasted sharply with Muslim Muluzi's religious tolerance; his book, for example, repeatedly citing the key agency of a Catholic pastoral letter in triggering Banda's downfall. The poet-priest and academic Pádraig Ó Máille, a tireless supporter of the oppressed during Banda's reign, in his autobiography *Living Dangerously*, recalls waking during serious illness (poison was suspected) to find a concerned Muluzi at his bedside.

Creative writers have captured the profound misery of the Banda years. But *Mau Anga* comes from a political insider, someone who saw Banda close-up and had access to documents and events outsiders could only guess at. It narrates succinctly how Banda came to be involved at all in

Nyasaland's decolonization and the Orwellian speed (July 6 to September 30, 1964) with which he turned freedom's dawn into despotic night. Muluzi covers John Chilembwe's failed uprising of 1915 (an early decree of his portrayed Chilembwe on all Malawi's banknotes, an honor unthinkable under Banda); the catalytic effect of the imposed Central African Federation of Rhodesia and Nyasaland; the recall of Banda from medical practice in Ghana by young leaders seeking an older man with international experience; Banda's accession and leap to autocracy, which triggered the Cabinet Crisis of 1964; and so on to the decade of Banda's slide from power. There are cameo portraits of those, skilled and eager, who fled into exile, their names constantly reviled in Banda's interminably repetitive speeches. Attorney General Orton Chirwa was one. He lived for decades abroad, was seized with his wife near the Zambian border, and died miserably, leg-ironed in Zomba Prison. Others included Henry Chipembere, Kanyama Chiume, Augustine Bwanausi, Willie Chokani, Yatuta Chisiza, and Rose Chibambo—an enthusiastic intelligentsia lost to a nation scarcely three months old.

The book breathes fresh air after the Banda nightmare. It shows Muluzi's democratic spirit striving, with difficulty, to build a new political and civil culture and dismantle Banda's oppressive machinery—not only the legislation designed to entrench autocracy, but the instruments too—the hated Young Pioneers, for example, the Special Branch, press censorship, and the appalling detention centers at Mikuyu, Dzaleka, and Nsanje. Party manifesto and parliamentary policy speeches exude openness and honesty, and an inclusiveness previously unknown. Under Banda only good things happened—always attributable to the president. The world must see only peace

and calm, law and order, growing prosperity. Muluzi tears back the conjuror's curtain to tell the truth. Malawi ranks among the earth's poorest nations, despite Banda's boasting. There is an "infant mortality rate of 135 per 1000 live births; a maternal mortality rate of 620 per 10,000 deliveries; over half under-fives are stunted from chronic undernutrition; an average life expectancy of 48 years is among the world's lowest. There is a high prevalence of HIV/AIDS with 33,000 laboratory confirmed cases recorded by March 1994 and an estimated number of 950,000 Malawians carrying the AIDS virus. Malawi is number 15 from the bottom on the scale of UNDP human development indicators out of a total in 1993 of 173 countries." Drought means the country has urgent need of 450,000 tons of imported maize. Illiteracy is far too high. Too few children are in primary school. Deforestation ranks second only to the Ivory Coast's. Lakes Malawi, Chiuta, Malombe, and Chilwa, and the River Shire are being grossly overfished. The road infrastructure needs urgent repair and extension.

Such candor released the nation's energies. While the Muluzi years were not free of backsliding from high ideals, new hospitals really were built, new water supplies installed, and roads improved or extended. The Mikuyu detention center became a museum and a photo shows Muluzi handling leg-irons there. Primary education became free with enrolments up by 1.3 million in a year. Press freedom engendered an explosion in publications. Externally, Malawi began contributing to peacekeeping in Rwanda and Burundi. Strikingly, in neat reversal, Muluzi's narrative, with its rise to democratic openness and optimism, implicitly crosses the descending graph lines of Zimbabwe, where Robert Mugabe's impressive democratic beginning has descended relentlessly toward the oppression and political manipulation of a Banda. Muluzi was succeeded in May 2004 by Bingu Wa Mutharika.

Further reading: Eunice Nihero Chipangula, *Political Reporting Trends in Malawi: 1980s and 1990s* (Makwasa, 2003); Pádraig Ó Máille, *Living Dangerously* (Glasgow, 1998); Steve and Moira Chimombo, *The Culture of Democracy* (Zomba, 1996).

Mumba, Norah M. (b. ca. 1956). Zambian short-story writer, poet, and autobiographer. Born in Petauke, she began her education in Lusaka and Mufulira, and then attended Roma and Kabulonga Girls' Secondary Schools. At Zambia's national university she graduated in English and librarianship (1978). She currently works as a librarian and is a moving spirit within the Zambian Women Writers' Association. Her play *The Birthday Party* won first prize in a Radio Deutsche Welle competition in 1989, and her short stories have featured on radio and in *The Heart of a Woman* (1997), a collection she edited with Monde Sifuniso. She is perhaps best known for her autobiographical *A Song in the Night: A Personal Account of Widowhood in Zambia* (1992).

As a woman's autobiography, *A Song* is rare in itself, the human saga it narrates compelling, and its unique assault on a cornerstone of traditional custom courageous. The central event of Mumba's young husband dying from leukemia is harrowing enough; her widow's home being stripped by relatives following custom is almost as bad. This secondary focus, on widows' property rights, appears also in Tsitsi Himuyanga-Phiri's Zambian novel *The Legacy* (1992), Senegalese Mariama Bâ's *So Long a Letter* (1980), and the multiauthored *Dispossessing the Widow: Gender-Based Violence in Malawi* (2002). Mumba's prose is lean, carries its sad burden efficiently, and on occasion even moves into verse:

Look at me twice, old friends
Yes, I am the one who once walked
    with my head held high
Now I stoop all day long
To hide the haggard face lined with
    ridges
Like a bare hillside whose soil
Has been eroded away by a heavy
    storm.

As proof of literature's transforming power, Mumba's book was seen as instrumental in winning new protection for Zambian widows when, with President Kaunda's full support, the 1989 Interstate Succession Act became law in May that year.

The house stripping prompts theoretical reflection. In a traditional communal society practice around widow-and-orphan inheritance presumably arose to provide protection for the bereaved: their survival would lie in cleaving to the deceased's extended family, with food and shelter guaranteed. Estate contents (traditionally not the car and fridge Mumba loses) would be needed for the new situation. For Mumba to see the custom only as heartless must mean that social change has indeed been radical, so that from her modern perspective (professional, middle-class, educated, Christian) the custom indeed seems pitiless and predatory. The key factors in this change (presumably Christianity, capitalist individualism, education, urbanization) are not explored.

In *The Heart of a Woman* (1997), a feminist anthology edited with Monde Sifuniso, Mumba's contributions echo *A Song*. But whatever is causal in woman's predicament, her view of men is not totally bleak. Her title story, showing that prostitution usually means the girl next door facing penury, features the affluent and caring Michael whose humanity creates loving happiness for young prostitute Leya. While "Waiting"

attacks Don Juans and bosses who make fe-
male promotion conditional on sexual fa-
vors, "Come Back Nancy" sensitively
analyzes male psychological fragility. Shy
Ben and Nancy fall in love, plan marriage,
and buy wedding clothes. But Nancy is
found dying of an overdose and an at-
tempted abortion. When relatives have re-
vealed her tragic background (raped at
seventeen by her father's friend and psychi-
atrically committed after killing her baby in
a fit of depression), Ben will don his new
suit on their planned nuptial date, visit the
cemetery, and "deliver a beautiful bouquet
of flowers to my bride." Doubtless with her
own happy but tragically short marriage in
mind, Mumba can offer positive male por-
trayal and optimism about life's potential
for happy gender relations.

Further reading: Martin Banham, ed., *A
History of Theatre in Africa* (Cambridge,
2004).

Mungazi, Dickson A. (b. 1939). Zimba-
bwean novelist. Born near Mutare in east-
ern Zimbabwe, he attended local schools
before receiving a Methodist scholarship to
study in America. With a B.A. from Morn-
ingside College, Sioux City, Iowa, he re-
turned home in 1964 to teach at Old Mutare
Methodist Center. From 1966 to 1968 he
studied for a London University Certificate
of Education and then returned for gradu-
ate study to America. The University of Ne-
braska awarded him an M.A. in 1975 and a
Ph.D. in 1977. A prolific academic author,
he is currently regents professor of educa-
tional foundations and history at Northern
Arizona University, Flagstaff.

Mungazi's novel *Humba Kumba Goes to
School* (2002), a curious work, is part educa-
tional history, part sociopolitical tract, and
very much autobiography. Its publishing
provenance is also curious for it comes from
the Southern African Political Economy

Trust, a nonprofit organization aiming "to
promote and nurture social science research,
debate, teaching and publication in South-
ern Africa." The trustees evidently decided
that Mungazi's work supported enough of
their objectives to merit acceptance.

Education, implicit in objectives and title,
is the book's focus and a given of Central
African writing. It is recommended for anti-
colonial struggle, for personal growth and
identity, for economic advancement, and for
understanding historical process. Mungazi
describes a colonial government afraid of a
rising educated class (Africans, largely, must
remain hewers of wood and drawers of wa-
ter) and keen rivalry among individuals
lucky enough to get into the system. Argu-
ably *Humba Kumba Goes to School* fore-
grounds education as comprehensively as
any other Central African novel. Its 220
pages narrate efforts by the Kumba family,
devout Methodists for whom teacher is sec-
ond only to preacher, to get an education for
young Humba. Mungazi says his book will
inform readers of conditions under South-
ern Rhodesia's white government just as
"one learns about the social conditions in
Britain during the Elizabethan period by
reading the works of William Shakespeare,
or those of the Victorian period by reading
the works of Charles Dickens."

In colonial times, white farmers, using
the Native Affairs Department and the no-
torious Land Apportionment Act, could
close down or refuse to open any school
deemed to be on their land or too close to
it. This seriously disadvantages Humba,
who stumbles from pillar to post striving
to get first a primary and then a secondary
education. A disciple of his Methodist
preacher grandfather, whose mantra-motif,
"success is failure to accept adversity as a fi-
nal act of circumstances," echoes unend-
ingly, Humba narrates a career that leads
him from village-school rudiments to a

distinguished professorship at Northern Anozira University and global travel on research funds as an American citizen with a white partner. Shaped by Grandpa's Methodism, with its passion for education ("Methodists were rare human beings and a vintage creation"), Humba's mind and vision blossom before us. There is also help from Socrates, Tom Paine, Hemingway, Shakespeare, Rousseau, Donne, Browning, Biko, Kenyatta, Keats, Pope, Booker T. Washington, R. L. Stevenson, Russell, Aristotle, Swift, and Frost.

Politics and educational sociology aside, romance provides insight into cross-cultural tensions and traditional imperatives. Solemnly sworn to return after graduation and marry a Methodist girl at home, Humba falls for Jane Philips, a white girl born in the Congo to Methodist missionaries. When Grandpa dies, Humba's family fear that breaking this solemn promise to a relative now deceased will bring a curse. With Jane's consent, the relationship ends and Humba marries Rosalyn, who, though Methodist and a local girl, has only a primary education, is insecure and depressive. Back in America, and despite three children, the couple divorce, and the novel ends with Humba and a new lady, colleague Dr. Harriet Traber, traveling to Africa for research but with return tickets clutched firmly in their hands.

Though defending his African upbringing (yet censuring its proscription of debate between the young and their elders), Humba chooses life in America—its dearth of African-origin professors apparently more urgent than the need for intellectual leadership at home. And while he contrasts a materialist and polluting America with frugal, earth-friendly Africa, he unsportingly exalts white women's characteristics over those of ladies at home with only a primary-school education ("The thought of getting married to any of them was repugnant to me"). He says:

> Using Jane and Harriet as two white women I have come to know closely, I could not resist the conclusion that African women were conditioned by their culture and colonial system to reduce themselves to the level of inability to have meaningful social interaction with men. This sad reality robbed them of their self concept. . . . At the same time African women were extremely jealous of white women who dated African men forgetting that African men liked women who were intelligent and assertive, not because they were white, but because they were who they were.

The Kumbas' fight for colonial educational justice produces Humba's closing advice to unnamed African leaders who abandon attempts to solve problems and who, to retain power, allow corruption and crime to proliferate. It is, laments Humba, "a continental tragedy that has no end."

The novel, then, intertwines issues broad and specific, individual and racial, colonial and postcolonial. The competing claims of individual and group, central to African sociopolitical debate, is one such issue—Grandpa stresses that African society needs both individual growth and communal solidarity. Mungazi also wants to slay colonial dragons while suggesting that liberal but anti-smoking-and-drinking Methodism, a colonial companion, is a special gift to African society. Meanwhile, the Methodist Kumbas oppose Catholicism and withdraw Humba from a school where Jesuits are trying to convert him.

Other threads in this novel's tapestry include differences between French, Portuguese, and British colonialism, the hated forced-labor system instituted soon after Rhodes conquered Lobengula, the invidious role of chiefs under indirect colonial rule, a defense of traditional premarital sexual morality, wife abuse in traditional society, and how colonialism creates psychological self-hate and dependency.

Mungoshi, Charles (b. 1947). Zimbabwean novelist, short-story writer, poet, and dramatist. A leading Central African writer, he was born at Chivhu in colonial Rhodesia's Manyene Communal Land. Primary education at All Saints and Daramombe School preceded secondary training at St Augustine's, Penhalonga. Two years as a research assistant for the Rhodesia Forestry Commission brought experience later used in his short fiction. Following work with Salisbury booksellers (1969–74), he became a Literature Bureau editor in 1975 and in 1981 literary director and editor with the Zimbabwe Publishing House. Speaking and academic engagements overseas include New Zealand's Wellington International Festival and a writing residency at the University of Florida.

Three Shona novels, *Makunun'unu Maodzamoyo* (1970), *Ndiko Kupindana Kwamazuva* (1975), and *Kunyarara Hakusi Kutaura* (1983), and a Shona play, *Inongova Njakenjake* (1981), were among early publications. His involvement in theater has made its mark on his fiction. His first short-story collection in English, *Coming of the Dry Season* (1972), preceded his only novel, *Waiting for the Rain* (1975), and further collections: *Some Kinds of Wounds* (1980), *The Setting Sun and the Rolling World* (1987), and *Walking Still* (1997). A volume of poetry, *The Milkman Doesn't Only Deliver Milk* (verse, he says, sharpens his prose), appeared in 1981 and *Stories from a Shona Childhood* in 1989. His work has brought international acclaim, translation into several languages, and award recognition from

PEN, Noma, and Zimbabwe's national Literature Bureau.

The Mungoshi world glimpsed in *Coming of the Dry Season*, especially in the title story, "The Lift," "The Ten Shillings," "The Setting Sun and the Rolling World," and "Shadows on the Wall," has features that become constants. For example, against a classical community background, there is minimal evidence of large interactive families, nuclear or extended, or of vibrantly healthy human relationships. Domestic violence seems routine, affection rare (love apparently a taboo word), and suspicion, drunkenness, jealousy, and hate abundant. Within the encircling gloom, humor and optimism die, "shadows" are ubiquitous, and the phrase "imprisoned by life" echoes from the title story. Orientation is toward death, and domestic guerilla warfare eclipses the Liberation War that is being fought in the bush. Narrators are mostly male, while existential loneliness, alienation, angst, and sterile introspection embrace solitary personae also overwhelmingly male. The few women present—wives, mothers, sisters—are low-status victims of a brutal patriarchy.

The pathology is complex, but lack of wholesome communication is a root cause. Few rival Mungoshi's sensitivity to the labyrinthine nuances—verbal, unspoken, physical, psychological, emotional—of human discourse: its tempos, pauses, crescendos and diminuendos, its alternating stress and relaxation. Patriarchy denigrates talk as female and exalts silence as male. Miscommunication afflicts not only spouses, children, and friends, but exchange between the races, between town and country, tradition and modernity. Talk, good communication, Mungoshi suggests, would ease the depressing futility of unceasing joblessness, rejection, racial contempt, and disillusion with a vaunted schooling whose price is personal dysfunction. "Deserts of the heart," to use

Auden's phrase, are at one with the arid landscapes of the home area and "city awe," that natural force luring rural folk to escape.

When *Some Kind of Wounds* appeared in 1980, Mungoshi seemed to privilege short fiction, despite the resounding success of his novel. Though these narratives are now longer, more reflective of landscape moods, the human and physical scene remains unchanged and the Liberation War unemphasized. Whatever the theme—sexism, violence, alcoholism, miscommunication—hatred, suspicion, despair and loneliness predominate. Happy families showing carefree children, humor, love, tenderness do not appear. The Abrahamic theme of "The Mount of Moriah" features a father wanting to murder an only son, not for God, but for *muti* to restore his luck in gambling. Gratuitous violence against women is again pervasive; but now, in "The Flood," "Who Will Stop the Dark?" and "The Day the Bread Van Didn't Come," strong wives may beat weak husbands. "The Flood" contains a virtual misogynist's manifesto: "A woman is what destroys a man," "We live because of them and die because of them." Miscommunication is again cardinal. The opening story describes the father as "trying to trap Hama into talking"; a father who thanks the ancestors for "our physical language" and wishes "he could say something in words." But while miscommunication is radically complicit in social and spiritual malaise, so too is drink. Though Mungoshi is not given to "statements," "The Brother" is a comprehensive depiction of alcohol's evils, causing here brutal violence against women and the destruction of key features of decent human life: truth, respect, discipline, fidelity, industry, patience, endurance, and family solidarity.

Change and development, as well as continuities, characterize *Walking Still*. In "The Slave Trade," independence has supposedly brought Zimbabwe new immigrants with new thinking. But white dinner hosts exploit Marara's weakness for drink, and when his loosened tongue brackets them with the original Rhodes/Jameson gang, he is made to feel inferior in the old way and is even physically threatened. "The Empty House" catches up with the world of Michael Jackson and O. J. Simpson. It explores an interracial marriage and shows Mungoshi teasing out modernity's ironies with its borrowed and shifting values amidst the standard fare of hopeless father-son relationships, suicidal despair, xenophobia, suspicion, destructive alcoholism, and inadequate communication. Gwizo's painting blossoms commercially with American Agatha's arrival, but his marrying the West kills its inner life. Confusingly, the westernized father despises art but admires Agatha's American entrepreneurism, which, ultimately, she herself wants to jettison for African village values. Yet the volume rescues some optimism from its moral and social squalor. In "The Homecoming" an old widow (her biggest problem, typically, "the loneliness—the impossibility of communication") finds her orphaned grandchild becoming a caring youth able to handle even her malodorous incontinence. "The Little Wooden Hut in the Forest," which finally gives the war some space, encompasses violence, drunkenness, and bad communication, but ends with war-damaged Gavi and his expectant wife rescued by a peasant couple who choreograph the expected child's nativity in a Bethlehem scene complete with animals. Birth screams resonate in Gavi's memory with screams of death. Out of the war new life emerges into a context of domestic beauty—and the new child is a girl.

The international success of *Waiting for the Rain* makes it puzzling that Mungoshi should appear suddenly to abandon novels for more short stories. Stylistically curious in that it reads like a play, even using stage directions, the book is also remarkable for the intensity of its claustrophobic gloom, pent-up hatred and violence, scenes of external and internal aridity, and the uncompromising rejection by Lucifer, the ironically dubbed bringer of light, of his home, family, village, landscape, and traditional world. Home is the hot, dusty Tribal Trust Lands into which the whites have pushed the blacks. Every village needs its rainmaker. This is home in "naked white earth criss-crossed by the eternal shadows of the restless vulture." This is home but also "the failure's junk heap," a place of hopelessness and capricious rains that breeds "paralytic inertia," terrifying entrapment, and "the smell of loneliness," where "the worms set to work on you the very day you are conceived." Nature's sterility parallels the people's spiritual and psychological sterility. Internecine strife and hatred spare no one, with drink and violence routine solutions. For Lucifer, childhood's golden kingdom here meant nightmare fear of witches and memories of "the crack of the oxhide whip on bare flesh and the distorted face of a mother in pain." Having been educated at boarding school, he passionately resents having been born to these people, in this place. Once overseas on scholarship, he swears, he will never return, no matter what family problems and duties arise.

The book censures the village world, but does not eulogize Lucifer. It offers two dimensions: the boy's internal life as a schooled, cosseted, westernized youth, and an external view from a rustic world that cannot understand or reach him. To his brother Garabha, he is a "lofty mountain. And I am only a fly in his milk." Rural society thinks school has made him a selfish, unpredictable stranger, lacking even a child's social skills. Paradoxically, his smart new language has crippled his communica-

tive powers. He can converse easily with nobody, routinely meets questions with silence, ignores letters from home, and constantly feels there is nothing to say when everyone else feels there is everything to say. Mungoshi avoids didacticism, but Lucifer's behavior, crass, yet not guilt-free, emerges as unacceptable by any standards. Having avoided his mother's farewell lunch, smashed bottles of protective medicine, and spurned his father's porterage, he leaves home, village, and rural world without a backward glance. As he does so, he hears the white priest driving him reflect, wistfully, "Beautiful country," "Beautiful people," "Such beautiful manners. I envy you, I really do."

Mungoshi seems hesitant to sheet such horror totally to colonial politics and white greed, not because he doubts their catastrophic agency—which anyway informs his own texture of event and reflection—but because it would mean omitting, or inadequately acknowledging, the universals of fallen humanity and life's intractable complexities, whatever the physical or historical context. Hence, despite reference to the First Chimurenga and land loss, he does not mention UDI, the Liberation War, or the Ian Smith regime. When room is made for a trenchant statement on colonialism it comes, obliquely, from the lips of Lucifer's drunken uncle. The centrality of land to a people's psycho-spiritual and physical health is of course a given, and an implicit riposte to the crime of land theft is pervasive. But one wonders if Mungoshi is entertaining a loftier ethic when we find the text saying, "What grows in the land first grows in the heart."

Why Mungoshi left the novel with this book remains unclear. Perhaps short stories provided wider literary exploration. Perhaps, like South Africa's Es'kia Mphahlele, he needed the swift therapy short stories could provide for daily vexation. Perhaps, too, publishers' advice suggested the short story's advantage in terms of audience size, flexibility, and even income—the form most easily transmitted to journals and newspapers, radio and television.

Further reading: George Kahari, *The Search for a Zimbabwean Identity* (Gweru, 1980); Musaemura Zimunya, *Those Years of Drought and Hunger: The Birth of African Fiction in Zimbabwe* (Gweru, 1982); Rino Zhuwarara, *Introduction to Zimbabwean Literature in English* (Harare, 2001); Emmanuel Ngara, *New Writing from Southern Africa* (Harare, 1984); R. Zinyemba, *Coming of the Dry Season: Charles Mungoshi* (Harare, 1989).

Mungoshi, David (b. ca. 1960). Zimbabwean novelist and short-story writer. Born in Bulawayo, he is brother of the writer Charles Mungoshi. Teenage ambition produced poetry and short stories that appeared in the journals *Two Tone*, *Parade*, and *Mahogany*. His collection *Broken Dream and Other Stories* appeared in 1987 and *Stains on the Wall*, his best-known work, in 1992.

Stains is distinctly postcolonial, its anger targeting the human wreckage independence has produced. Recalling the revolutionary ideology that produced liberation, it tests current health against original purity, with results profoundly disturbing. Broadly Marxist (though never the mainstream species the white government pretended it to be), this ideology abjured racial inequality and class formation, stressed care for the poor and marginalized, the equality of women, and access to the instruments of self-improvement. The narrator finds all this unrecognizable in the new dispensation.

Ex-freedom fighters Tahara and his wife Nonhlanhla, now comfortably middle-class, realize that for the impoverished masses—the real victims of colonialism and liberation warfare—nothing has changed, except

that township slums are now called "high density suburbs." They conclude that "armed conflict alone does not make a revolution." There has been merely "stagnation in progress," while a black bourgeoisie has become "glossy with the fat of the land." Society's rejects, its beggars and transients, become the couple's focus of care. Founding a Society for the Downtrodden (their mantra is "Be among the destitute as the fish in water"), they organize for its launch an Olympic-style parade of the unwashed to embarrass the ruling party. These are the title's stains that government wants scrubbed off the nation's wall. The movement frightens government and there are warnings of a new war: "The real war was coming," "There would come a time when the people would no longer settle for promises."

The middle-class couple counterpoint a wretched-of-the-earth duo: Old James, ex-Malawi but now among Zimbabwe's dustbins, and Rachel, with apparent Lesotho connections, who collects scrap bones for a living. A moral strategy here is to show that, while the downcast might be externally repulsive, they might well have inner transforming skills. Old James has a philosophic mind, a considerable command of oratory, and political acumen; Rachel, in her sixties, can discourse persuasively on cooperatives. Ill-smelling James, dining in Tafara's lovely home, rekindles the host's dormant revolutionary zest and the hostess's social conscience. More, in an extraordinary imaginative leap, Rachel creates a sexual incident that breathes new life into her hosts' flagging marriage, which in turn energizes Tafara for struggle against the regime. The message seems to be that if the privileged look after the downtrodden, they will garner all manner of surprising benefits. This even covers Zimbabwe's white males, for in a wry twist to the idea that liberation is salvific for oppressed *and* oppressor, they can now publicly urinate by the roadside, free of having to maintain a bur-densome image.

With nice symbolism, and echoing Armah, La Guma, and the Psalms, the novel begins with Old James, as far from his Malawi home as from new-order pros-perity, sitting, not quite by the waters of Babylon, but on the banks of a cesspool in Shirugwi. The new regime's political com-missar, who wants to exterminate such compatriots, tells Tafara not to "promise your destitutes and vagabonds a heaven on earth. We shall allow a few benefits to trickle down. . . . Classes are the bonds that hold society together. . . . We remain stead-fastly Marxist-Leninist. There is no doubt about that, but we cannot ignore the up-heavals all around us. People are happier when they struggle. . . . I have just re-packaged your ideology."

Muronda, Elfigio (b. 1951). Zimbabwean poet. Born in Harare, he was educated in Zimbabwe and the United States, where, in 1982, he received the Kurnitz Writers' Award. Media-skilled, he has written and directed work for television and has illustrated his own texts. When his collection *Echoes of My African Mind* appeared in 1982, it bore his own photographs, prompting the Malawian scholar Mpaliwe-Hangson Msiska to ob-serve that they "enrich the reader's reception of individual poems, as they draw attention to the limitations of language as a descrip-tion of reality and focus on the intertextual-ity of African poetry."

While hymning the centrality of moth-erhood in his celebration of life—an ingre-dient of African literature and culture never to be underestimated—Muronda identifies himself decisively within the his-tory of his home country:

I was born in a now defunct racist
    country called Rhodesia.

All Africans born in that country
    were without
political rights
human rights
or any kind of rights
but in spite of it all
my spirit was always free.

The pan-Africanism of Ghana's Nk-rumah long predated Zimbabwean inde-pendence, but it inspired Muronda to embrace its large vision and ideology. Thus, as Msiska puts it, "He views Zimbabwe in the context of Africa rather than the other way round." Hence, too, the torment of his own people is pictured within a larger con-text of suffering across the continent. A poem fusing, say, the stridency of Malawi's Frank Chipasula and the detail of South Africa's Dennis Brutus, includes "red blood tears," a "police bloodhound," "sweat drenched sag-ging blankets," "screaming and pleading" and "black and white / colonial monsters / that seek to drag you away." But heart and imagination fly elsewhere before closure:

The dead disfigured faces
Of your brothers and sisters
From Sharpeville to Soweto of 76
Flash in your mind
Like the rocky horror picture show.

Indeed the vision embraces the colo-nized beyond Africa. "Visions of My Land" has its persona standing amidst the sadness of America's Malibu Canyon, reflecting, sympathizing, and identifying with the "collective presence" of "the long departed Indians."

Further reading: Adrian Roscoe and Mpalive-Hangson Msiska, *The Quiet Cha-meleon: Modern Poetry from Central Africa* (London, 1992).

Musengezi, H. G. (b. ca. 1960). Zimbabwean playwright. He grew up during the long years of Zimbabwe's freedom struggle and earned a B.A. from the national university in 1983. His play *The Honourable MP*, conceived while he was an undergraduate, was performed on campus before finding publication in 1984. Echoes of Achebe and Ngugi wa Thiong'o are audible (the text actually mentions Ngugi, and the satirized MP Shakespeare Pfende calls himself, in Achebe's phrase, "a man of the people"), while the play's epigraph, a sideswipe at the postindependence carnage current in Matabeleland at this time), comes from Okot p'Bitek's *Song of Lawino*:

> And while the pythons of sickness
> Swallow the children
> And the buffalos of poverty
> Knock the people down
> And ignorance stands there
> Like an elephant,
> The war leaders
> Are tightly locked in bloody feuds,
> Eating each other's liver . . .

The play's attack on the new government and its stark rendering of peasant protest against betrayal are remarkable for following so swiftly on the heels of independence. Conceived within a contemporary socialist paradigm, the play highlights class division. On the one hand are peasants who fought for freedom, suffer still under poverty and drought, and have an absentee parliamentary representative in Pfende ("We sent a fly into a pot of milk. It got drowned in the feast."). On the other hand are the new bourgeoisie, represented by Pfende and wife, who shop expensively abroad, have three cars, two houses, a farm, and money stolen from the public purse. In between, supporting the masses but in touch with both groups, is a teacher, who, symbolically in Zimbabwean writing, plays a role as hated by the new ruling class as by their white predecessors. Women, the MP's wife excepted, become the sexual toys of the new elite. Tellingly, when the peasant masses denounce Pfende, he draws a pistol and threatens violence. The play is visually strong, contrasting the fat, poorly educated MP (who despises university people like the author as much as the constituents he represents) and thin starving peasants; it is strong, too, in its flights of moral rhetoric. Its adornment with vernacular interpolation suggests that Musengezi was writing for a local and national audience.

Musonda, Kapelwa (n.d.). Pen name of a Zambian who, like Nigeria's Tai Solarin, Kenya's Albert Ojuka, and South Africa's Can Themba, exemplifies journalism's importance in modern Africa. Where prose fiction delivers selected and framed experience, journalism enjoys freer flight, captures breaking news on the wing, stoops suddenly on descried targets. It must communicate with an audience whose identity it shares—or die. It must interpret contemporaneity when creative prose is only just beginning its reflections. It can swiftly change both mind and tone, entertain, censure, play the prophet. And yet (witness Addison or Macaulay) it faces no veto on using the figurative and rhetorical strategies of creative writing, not even excluding invented character and event. Across much of Africa, journalism dominates the literary menu of the poor.

Thus, between 1967 and 1977, a turbulent decade, Musonda's weekly *Times of Zambia* column alerted and illuminated while conventional literature lay dormant. To his credit, he produced a most engaging chronicle of Zambian life during these years. Independent in 1964, but soon a casualty of Rhodesia's 1965 Unilateral Declaration of Independence, Zambia took a costly moral stand within the liberation struggles raging across Mozambique, Angola, South Africa,

Namibia, and Rhodesia. All around it, white colonialism's death throes were becoming violent and intrusive. While neighboring Malawi slipped quietly into isolationist despotism, Kaunda's Zambia faced crippling adversity: bombing and incursion by the Rhodesian Front; expensive hosting of freedom fighters from across the region; a disastrous collapse of world copper prices; export route restrictions to the Indian Ocean; drought; and a fatal policy that privileged mines and minerals over agriculture. Creative writers later captured the misery of all this, and the IMF's Structural Adjustment Program that exacerbated it. But Musonda's journalism, collected in *The Best of Kapelwa Musonda* (1979), provides an unrivalled view of times resembling those neighboring Zimbabwe was to face thirty years later.

Musonda is your Horatian satirist, not vicious like Swift or Solarin, but genial like Fielding or Wodehouse (he even features an aged relative called Aunt Agatha). If he attacks snobbery, arrogance, self-righteousness, complacency, immorality, greed, and hypocrisy, as a foreword by J. M. Mwanakatwe observes, he does so without malice. His column is a multicolored umbrella under which he sits transmuting sin into anecdote and humor. He likes masks. Unidentified himself, he creates a fictional character, Bonzo, barfly and gossip, through whom information and comment get filtered. There is also a gift for paradox, an ear for register, and a nuanced way with irony.

Matters parochial and global arise as Musonda records this age of Henry Kissinger and John Vorster, President Ford and Harold Wilson, James Callaghan and Idi Amin, Ian Smith and Samora Machel, Joshua Nkomo and Bishop Muzorewa, Ndabaningi Sithole and Gordon Chavunduka, Josiah Chinamano and Robert Mugabe. There is rumor and intrigue,

sanctions-busting and suspicion, conspiracy theory, endless shuttle diplomacy. From an opening sally entitled "When in Doubt, Deny Everything!" Musonda gaily cleaves his way through problem and crisis. Dominant are economic collapse, ensuing poverty, dire shortage of essentials like cooking oil, detergents, sugar, coffee, fish, salt, toothpaste, beans, butter, margarine, and even the staple mealie meal. Rumor holds the CIA responsible. Zambians will soon be queuing for fresh air, says Musonda. Because Chibuku beer is always available, Musonda suggests the brewer, Tiny Rowland's Lonrho multinational, as prime choice for making and distributing everything else. Gentle satire on Kaunda's cherished humanism and foreign policy ("How KK Discovered Malawi") sits by wonder at Chinese humility as they build the Tanzam Railway. Public transport and the parastatals so popular in independent Africa are ridiculed for their wasteful inefficiency. Railway officials pray that coaches will be swiftly wrecked and so relieve them of further concern about them. Employment corruption means that all jobs become merely avenues for second-income rackets. Back-to-the-land campaigns are laughed out of court. Inept economic modeling sends Musonda to garbage men for more accurate data. For the price of a drink, Comrade Bonzo (an impoverished borrower like everyone else), who plans to found a League of Disgruntled Customers, supplies vital information on everything.

Beneath the mirth, serious comment runs on the role of the extended family. And a splendid piece on the hackneyed topic of town and country shows a nice calculus of woes: while a village mother complains to her absent daughter about urban bandits, prostitution, and road accidents, she mentions, with insouciance, a cousin impregnated by the old village headman, a knife fight caused by the village drunk, an uncle who has divorced his youngest wife after finding her *in flagrante delicto*, a village headman's son killed by a lion, and a fracas at the village school between parents and the headmaster's wife, who is now in hospital.

Musonda, unmasked, assures us that on column content there was never editorial or political pressure—a sign of Zambian freedom and tolerance at this turbulent time unimaginable in neighboring Rhodesia or Malawi. His excellent pieces predated the rise of AIDS—a scourge that would have tested his powers of irony and humor to the limit.

Mutasa, Garikai N. (b. ca. 1952). Zimbabwean novelist. Born in Chivi, he schooled at Dadaya, Mzingwane, and Goromonzi before qualifying as a teacher at Gweru Teachers' College. He then taught at Chivi Secondary School, where he worked concurrently as a *mujibha* or guerilla helper during Zimbabwe's bush war—experience substantially informing his novel *The Contact* (1985). Before assuming his current post as a lecturer in education, he completed a bachelor of education degree in Britain.

The Contact covers the closing stages of the country's armed struggle. With a prologue revisiting, like other narratives, the hanging of the spirit medium Nehanda in the first Chimurenga or anticolonial uprising of the 1890s, *The Contact* embraces an action-driven plot, memorable portraits of black and white fighters, rigorous analysis of motive and morality, scenic description that affirms the centrality of land, and contextualizing to clarify the stage reached in this confusing struggle. It is the interregnum of Bishop Muzorewa, strongly backed by South Africa, but rejected by the rest of the world. Ironically, Britain's rightist Thatcher government is having to impose a settlement that hands power to leaders seen as dangerously left-wing. The narrative is candid about gaps already appearing between the idealistic blueprint for war and subsequent developments.

Claiming moral purity for neither cause nor fighters, Mutasa constantly stresses the struggle's just-war and nonracial status. The protagonist Gadzirai, holding a white officer at the point of death, lets him live but startles him with questions that define the moral strength of one side and the moral vacuity of the other. Frequently in Zimbabwean writing, such analysis invariably reveals white attitudes as childish parochialism. Thus all Africans are "Commies" and terrorists. Mugabe himself and all such leaders are, by definition, "Commies"—and this after the evidence of Kenya's Kenyatta, Malawi's Banda, Ghana's Nkrumah, Nigeria's Abubakar Tafawa Balewa, and a string of military dictators. The book also shows whites underestimating black skills and intelligence in a frozen paradigm of racial prejudice. Hence allusion to numerous "contacts" (concealed by government propaganda) in which small guerilla bands (helped by the *mujibha*, of whom the author was one) outwit and outgun Rhodesian Army professionals and inflict heavy casualties.

The war's moral squalor (Mutasa estimates fifty thousand deaths, others thirty thousand) is best seen in the mercenaries Mutasa draws: men like Mike Hoare, familiar from the global tabloid media, who fought in the Congo, Vietnam, Angola, and are here only to kill and be highly paid. Yet their wider experience lets them swiftly see how their white Rhodesian colleagues are seriously underestimating the fighting skills of the ZANLA guerillas. The novel's postscript shows some fleeing to South Africa. One, ominously, has bought a farm in Marondera. Another, now one-legged, is in an Angolan jail. Of the freedom fighters, group leader Gadzirai, the pure ideologue, is working for a multinational. His colleague Bazooka is a brigadier, overweight and driving a Mercedes. Hondoinopisa, a thief before the war, is a poverty-stricken thief after it. An African farmer who dreamed of land reform still cultivates his small patch next to a large white farm. How such eventualities match the vernal freshness of the struggle's manifesto Mutasa leaves to the reader. As he says in his closing words: "Not everyone was lucky."

Mutswairo, Solomon M. (b. 1924). Zimbabwean novelist. Born in Mazowe, from 1946 to 1947 he did teacher training at South Africa's Adams College, while busy handwriting his first novel, *Feso*. Admiring his parents' Christianity, he accompanied them during missionary work in Northern Rhodesia. Career details are sparse, but he gained a doctorate at Howard University and was recently an associate professor in the University of Zimbabwe's Department of African Languages and Literature. The first black Zimbabwean novelist to be published in Shona, his best-known works in English are *Feso* (1957), *Chaminuka: Prophet of Zimbabwe* (1983), and *Mapondera: Soldier of Zimbabwe* (1988). A collection of his work, *Solomon Mutswairo: Poetry and Prose,* also appeared in 1988.

Feso carries a checkered history. Its modern editor, Donald E. Herdeck, says it was the first Shona text sponsored by the state's Rhodesian Literature Bureau for publication by Oxford University Press, Cape Town, in 1957. America's Three Continents Press then published the first English edition in 1974, though Mutswairo's acknowledgments for the 1995 edition (HarperCollins) suggest that it was 1979. The Literature Bureau excised the first chapter (restored in the 1995 edition), which discusses the infamous Land Apportionment Act of 1930, using a literary fig leaf: the act, it said, was surely an anachronism in a nineteenth-century plot. The book sold briskly with its winning formula of adventure, espionage, suspense, violence, and morality. Without its opening chapter, the Bureau thought it harmless (merely precolonial event rendered in a vernacular) and thus prescribable for Rhodesian schools. In apartheid Pretoria, the University of South Africa agreed.

But readers found it an illuminating allegory of Rhodesia's colonial predicament. Soon a cult text for impatient nationalists, it was read with fascination, quoted at rallies, rather as revolutionaries elsewhere were quoting Che Guevara and Mao. Inevitably, there arose state embarrassment pursued by a banning order.

The book in fact appears to ignore colonialism to focus on two related African tribes: the VaHota and the VaNyai. Nyang'ombe, the VaHota chief, wants a bride. Pfumojena, chief of the VaNyai, has the ideal candidate, Chipo, but denies her marriage because she is more spirit than flesh. Through espionage among the VaNyai, brave Feso abducts this African Helen (though echoes are more African *Shaka* and *Mhudi* than Greek) and warfare erupts. The VaHota are trounced, rebound, stiffen regiments with Amazons, and sweep to their own victory. Friendship with the VaNyai ensues plus quiet retirement for despotic Pfumojena. The tribes become known collectively as the VaMbire and face a golden future together.

Allegory whispers insistently in the central theme. One group high on hubris is terrorizing another. The swaggering VaNyai are clearly colonial whites oppressing despised VaHota blacks. Like whites, Pfumojena is cruelly insensitive. Like them, he inflicts unbearable taxes, forcing folk to flee to the forest and start a guerilla war. He is dubbed a "vulture king," a favorite epithet for white rulers. The cry of justice denied becomes a motif. Chipo comments echoingly, "Freedom is a word I haven't known from birth," and she has ideas too about racial equality: "We still share human attributes of touch, taste, smell, sight and hearing, and all other things that make human life complete and enjoyable. . . . It is wrong that we are all so separated."

Once allegory is signaled, liberation sentiment flows. A VaNyai whose relatives Pfumojena executes beseeches guiding spirit Nehanda in words inviting immediate allegorical interpretation:

In every house and every village
Our people are being pulled out and
    punished;
In every place and every court
Where they are accused, they are
    treated like flies,
Killed without reason—without an
    honest trial.
Today all the wealth of the land has
    been taken.
The top dogs, the kindred of
    Pfumojena, share the spoils.
Today they are eating the fat of the
    land,
And we are reduced to eating the pus
    of our wounds.
    . . .
Where is our freedom, Nehanda?
Won't you come down to help us?
Our old men are treated like
    children
In the land you gave them, Merciful
    Creator!

Though in context Pfumojena is the target, readers know he stands for the whites. Likewise the VaHota regrouping to fight the VaNyai instantly become Africans after their failed uprisings, girding to strike another blow for freedom. A scarcely disguised textual comment says that no enemies are invincible and that "the liberation of a nation" requires "the efforts of ev-

eryone." Even female troop deployment prefigures the unisex armies of Mugabe and Nkomo. The postvictory VaMbire solution suggests the reconciliation crucial for an independent Zimbabwe, while the quietly retired Pfumojena looks like the defeated Ian Smith now growing roses in Harare.

In *Chaminuka: Prophet of Zimbabwe* Mutswairo explores his passion for Zimbabwean tradition (he is another Central African writer contesting white historiography's grand narrative) and humane Christian values. The life of Chaminuka, a guiding spirit like his sister Nehanda, is an ideal choice. Chaminuka is a nineteenth-century figure whom the author's Shona people revere for his pivotal role in their struggles against Lobengula's Ndebele. His spiritual and pacifist values are both profoundly African and resonant of the author's Christianity. There is a Christlike pattern in his life of betrayal and death, and his appearances before the people recall Christ on the Mount and in the Temple. Significantly, he expresses approval of reports that he has heard of Jesus, at which point the prose assumes a scriptural tone and cadence. Mutswairo's acknowledgments say that the book is "not only a defence of traditionalism, but an attack on excessive greed for power."

While Central African history and literature often portray Lobengula as victim, cynically cheated by Rhodes and Helm, Mutswairo paints him as a despot, cruel to his own people and crueler to the Shona whose land he occupied. Jealous of Chaminuka's charisma, he lures him to his death and sacks the Holy City of Chitungwiza. But not before Chaminuka has prophesied defeat: "Look now to the south! See, there comes a race of men, shrewd and daring—a kneeless people—who shall subdue the land." Lobengula will be "like the dove that the falcon pursues to its death, and his people like the lambs scattered by wild dogs."

The Shona prophet also predicts that, because the Ndebele have offended the spirits of the land, "when Chaminuka is gone, his seed shall prosper and overwhelm your seed. Your land shall be accursed and famine-stricken as punishment from the ancestors. For this land belongs to Mambo and his chosen people, their Mbire, and their descendants."

Verbal abuse of the Ndebele ("southern grasshoppers . . . bloodthirsty imbeciles . . . a sadistic group of murderers . . . morally depraved and lawless aggressors . . . self-imposed political refugees") rather dims the book's closing statement: "Today there is peace and mutual respect between the Mbire and the Ndebele, and all that remains now are memories of their past history, and the desire to build a unified nation."

Further reading: George Kahari, *The Search for a Zimbabwean Identity* (Gweru, 1980); Rino Zhuwarara, *Introduction to Zimbabwean Literature* (Harare, 2001).

Muzorewa, Abel Tendekai (b. 1925). Zimbabwean Methodist bishop and nationalist leader. He was prime minister of what was briefly called Zimbabwe-Rhodesia in a coalition that failed to create a biracial government and end the Liberation War. He began his clerical life in 1947 as a lay preacher for five small congregations while he studied theology. Ordained in 1953, he spent several years as a circuit preacher before beginning work for a master's degree in the United States. Like his Methodist colleague Canaan Banana, he channeled religious energy into the freedom struggle. He led protests, for example, against the white government's deportation of American bishop Ralph Dodge, who had opposed increased oppression following UDI in 1965. Succeeding Dodge in 1968, Muzorewa became the first black cleric to lead a major church in Rhodesia, though his activism

got him banned from the tribal trust lands where most of his flock lived. His autobiography *Rise Up and Walk* was published in London in 1978.

Seen internationally as a guileless moderate, who rejected factionalism and violence, including the eventual bush war, Muzorewa came to prominence in 1971. Britain had agreed with prime minister Smith on a slow transition to majority rule in exchange for removal of international sanctions. Muzorewa ensured the agreement was stillborn by uniting with his clerical colleague Canaan Banana to form the African National Congress and oppose it. This briefly increased ANC stature as the other liberation movements, Ndabaningi Sithole's ZANU and Joshua Nkomo's ZAPU, came under its aegis. But in 1975, emerging from eleven years of village restriction, Ndabaningi Sithole and Joshua Nkomo seized control of the ANC, formed their own groups, and isolated Muzorewa politically as the guerilla war intensified and neighboring African states endorsed it.

In 1978, however, Muzorewa was still strong enough to join with Sithole and agree with Smith on installing a majority government within a year. Indeed his ANC won an election, and he became prime minister of an entity called Zimbabwe-Rhodesia. Denied recognition internationally, and by the major groups determined to pursue the guerilla war, it was short-lived. Muzorewa was snubbed at the UN, and when Zimbabwe emerged in its present form, he became an ordinary member of parliament, his party winning only three seats. He served for four years until, in a repeat of colonial practice, he was detained by Mugabe from 1983 to 1984. Deciding to abandon politics, in 1985 he moved to Scarritt Theological Seminary in Memphis, Tennessee, though retaining an interest in his farm back home.

Further reading: John A. Wiseman, *Political Leaders in Black Africa* (Brookfield, 1991); Alan Rake, *Who's Who in Africa: Leaders for the 1990s* (Metuchen, 1992).

Mvona, Mike Sambalikagwa (b. 1958). Malawian poet, fiction writer, and journalist. Born in Undi Village, Mvona, sometimes described as "a writer without school and an academic without university accolade," typifies a trend in modern Malawian literature. Hitherto associated mainly with academe, and especially with the university's Writers' Workshop, it now grows at a popular level. This is relevant for Mvona. Lacking canonic literary exposure has left him free to ignore orthodoxy and to experiment, pursuing writing commercially. His links might be seen as less to scholarly contemporaries than to, historically, the eighteenth-century world of Defoe and chapbooks and, currently, to Nigeria's Onitsha Market Literature, Maillu's Comb Books of Kenya, and Malawi's own Aubrey Kalitera.

Mvona's career has been all shifting scene and adventure, the latest happening to be literature. By the age of forty-three, he had attended no fewer than four primary schools and tried a vocation as a Catholic priest. But geography and economics overcame theology and led him into meteorology. Still dissatisfied, he took up journalism, then public relations. Such restless energy and worldly savoir faire underpin eighty short stories in journals; Malawi's first thriller, *The Special Document* (2002); and a verse recollection, *The Sun at Njuli* (2001). Serious about the nation's literary health, he also chairs the Malawi Writers Union.

The Sun at Njuli reveals an upbeat and entrepreneurial Mvona. It opens with a "Sonnet to Mountainous Malawi," hymning local landscapes ("from the crafty Misulu Hills" to "the majestic white-puffed Sapitwa"), and closes with "Notes Intended for Contemporary Secondary or College Students," which, as a species of literary term glossary, variously covers music in poetry, eternity, portrait painting, patriotism, alliteration, and onomatopoeia—all illustrated from the text. School adoption is earnestly desired—amid Malawian poverty, one must spot every chance of turning a penny.

The poems show Mvona out in the world. Now he describes Cairo, where men "with drooping faces / Sluiced and slobbered the light shisha / with long orchestral pipes / siphoned by wet moistened noses"; now he pities refugees from Mozambique's civil war ("Creatures that are threatened with bullets / weary eyes wandering to and fro / seeking peace, seeking comfort"). Elsewhere he writes to his beloved ("I have envied those hide and seek luminous eyes"), visits Palestine ("The old road to Calvary is now / decorated with arcs and holy candles / but life in Jerusalem is as mean / as the Biblical hard road from Egypt"), or captures his father's work as a market tinsmith. He can strike an attractively casual tone:

A poet, taking an evening stroll
behind his gardens
stood at one of the ridges
and started appreciating
the wonder and beauty of nature.

Concern about poverty producing prostitution emerges in "Plight of Bargirls," which begins "Their only dream is to defeat marriage / Always hitting the street / To cruise for other women's men," and ends with "no hope to regain their old beauty / For time wasted can never be recovered / By hard Aids-infected bones." But he shows no sympathy for suicides ("You have broken the law of heaven / God will announce to you: 'Your space is with Lucifer!'"). Nor does he much admire a "Poet Who Excelled in an Anti-AIDS Poetry Contest," winning first prize then stupidly, through pride and drink, falling victim to the disease himself. The poor man lies unmourned:

> You left the earth still sweet
> Sophisticated dames still flower the
> streets
> Wise men still dance and live
> But you went young.

The section "Of Idols and Heroes" comprises cameos of John Chilembwe (Malawi's pioneering rebel), the Nigerian poet Okigbo, Kwame Nkrumah, Nelson Mandela, and, curiously, the Boertrekker Louis Trichardt. His portrait of President Banda is also unusual. It censures the despot's pride, wonders how such a scholar could "Prattle with a Bible in one hand and a sword in another," but completes most of the picture talking about Nkrumah, Kenyatta, and Qaddafi.

"Trek of the Lomwes" reminds us that many Malawians are immigrants of recent vintage, in this case from neighboring Mozambique. The migration motif is strong here, as it is with fellow Lomwe, Edison Mpina. It is unclear who the Lomwe woman Silvesta Mwikhoni is, but her death produces effective lines:

> Her soul gone now
> And her body left with cold wood
> All the graveyard trees shake
> All to welcome Silvesta Mwikhoni.

The Special Document is Malawi's first thriller. Set in a mythical landlocked country, it blends the genre's formulaic components—violence, hot pursuit, suspense, sex (subdued), power, and money—with the modern African theme of coups, and ends with old-fashioned morality:

> And what message has this brought to us all? Greed and lust for power are all evil! Men of the wilderness, how you have despised and rejected wisdom and justice and perpetrated

murder, bribery and corruption! . . . I have lost my personal wealth in this document chase and so has our motherland lost all donor support let alone its good image.

Narrative speed prevents in-depth characterization and, as the murderous villain Oliver Mamba pursues hero Morrison Mutunya, who is carrying the earth-shaking document (the blueprint for the colony and its future), we get lost in the subtropical vegetation. The form's clichés include its register ("dough," "dope," "smart cop," "buddy," "chum") heard among characters whose first language appears to be either Lomwe or Chinyanja.

Mvona's writing can be roughshod, with editing often a casualty. But, as with Kalatira and Chimombo, his enterprise has found a market and opened a path for others.

His latest work is a substantial volume, *Modern Stories from Malawi* (2003), which features some forty young authors. Its introduction, by the writer David Rubadiri, sees it as evidence that "we are building a rich writing tradition in Malawi. . . . There is still life after poverty."

Nazombe, Anthony Joseph Mukomele (1955–2004). Malawian poet and critic. Born at Nguludi in Chiradzulu district, he schooled first in Blantyre and Chiradzulu and then at Pius XII Minor Seminary. In 1973 he moved to the University of Malawi to study English and French, his first-class mind winning widespread respect, an academic post, and an M.A. and Ph.D. at Sheffield University. His time there, however, left him disturbed at how British universities, desperate for foreign student fees, are, in a "reverse of the Robin Hood saga," stealing "from the poor / To give to the rich." He died in 2004 after a long illness, during which his former colleague, the priest-poet Pádraig Ó Máille, unwell himself, gave him constant help and support, including academic visits to Ireland.

Care and rigor stamped Nazombe's work. Typically, an interview with Bernth Lindfors produced the most succinct chronicle of Malawian literature's growth, the University Writers' Workshop influence on it, its Banda-period strategies, its likely future, publication outlets, place in the university curriculum, and links with other African regions. On his own writing, he felt he had yet to find his own voice but was grateful to those who had encouraged him. As a child, he found his father's copy of *The Poet's Progress* and soon began to "scribble my own lines." At Pius XII Seminary he wrote for teachers and friends, and at sixteen he won a national prize. After Mupa Shumba urged its submission to the university's Writers' Workshop, his verse began to appear in the local journals *Odi, Umodzi,* and *Denga,* and later in Scandinavia's *Kunapipi* and South Africa's *Staff Rider.* Felix Mnthali and Jack Mapanje were key teachers. Influential poets, besides Mnthali, Mapanje, and Steve Chimombo, were Nigeria's Christopher Okigbo and Wole Soyinka, and Britain's Keats and Wordsworth.

Nazombe edited *The Haunting Wind: New Poetry from Malawi* (1990), a model of critical tact and patient diplomacy, given draconian censorship and the need to include poets already banned, exiled, or jailed. Only the nation's second collection, it followed the much slimmer *Mau* published twenty years earlier. Critical acumen also radiates from Nazombe's "Poetry and Liberation in Central and Southern Africa," a contribution to Arthur Ngara and

Andrew Morrison's *Literature, Language and the Nation* (1989). Basically reviewing Frank Chipasula's edited collection *When My Brothers Come Home,* it proceeds in the Macaulay style, becoming a luminous survey of all Central and Southern Africa and even reaching the Cape Verdes and Guinea-Bissau. Encompassing literary histories, current performance, and future problems, it is as informed about Angola's Agostinho Neto and Mozambique's Jose Craveirinha as it is about South Africa's Sipho Sepamla, Botswana's Albert Malikongwa, or Zimbabwe's Alec Pongweni.

Nazombe died in February 2004, but not before completing (though not seeing in print) *Operations and Tears: A New Anthology of Malawian Poetry.* Among its forty-six poets and one hundred and thirty-nine poems, nine of his own pieces appear, including the admired "Battle for Chingwe's Hole." This gently chaffs fellow poets such as Chimombo and Mapanje, for whom this deep cavity on Zomba Plateau by the Namitembo River (literally "a bearer of the dead") had become an obsessive icon and symbol of injustice, its role in history, especially its use as an execution instrument, a matter of ongoing debate; but it also inserts stretches of Malawian history and some anti-Banda satire. "Misty Presences," on Malawi's poor, echoes Soyinka's "Death in the Dawn":

I have heard them trudging along
   the gravel path
In the small hours of the morning
Misty presences murmuring in the
   wind
Across streams, through labyrinths
Of matchbox huts and waking
   markets
Travellers from the rim of the city
Earmarked long ago for swift
   demolition
. . .

They have trodden through my
   dreams
Marching as to war in discarded
   boots
To feed the conveyor belts at the
   heart of the web.

"This Temple" conjures years of mina-tory Catholic teaching on the Eucharist en-capsulated in the words *Domine non sum dignus*. A guilty speaker tells Christ he is unworthy to receive him under his roof, but a northern John the Baptist will come to "cleanse our pig-sties / In readiness for your second coming." "Emigrant Pole" captures misery in a Polish mother and children coming into Africa "with a fluttering heart" to find a new life and censures John Paul II for defeating the Communists while failing to see how this might scatter his sheep from home, often as victims of fellow sheep turned human traffickers. "Blind Terror" personifies death as a blind man blundering into a home to carry off residents one by one. For the speaker there is no escape:

But in a mirror I saw death
Spring from the hand of this blind
   man
Weaving through the living
To fall on those he had already
   marked;
In vain had mother hidden them.
I feared death
From the groping hand
And the rattling staff
I feared the unseeing eyes
And the unfeeling face.

Gloom and marginalization continue in "Tuberculosis," which bears the poignant marks of a poet speaking *in propria persona*:

The spittle, sapping blood and
   weight,
Flows into spittoon under a lid
And I await another quake.

. . .
And we live quarantined in this
   ward
Bored with counting our ribs
Awaiting another quake.
. . .
Sometimes when the whooping stops
We read texts from the Bible
Sent to us by pastors we have never
   seen,
To fight against the malady.
Plans are underway for a church of
   our own,
With a shepherd from this flock,
So we can go, after the last quake,
To spread the Word among those
   outside.
We hope they won't persecute us
Fearing the Word is infected.

Crucially, Nazombe ensured that his vol-ume embraced new post-Banda verse. He himself symbolized the profound damage, emotional and physical, that thirty years of Banda's cruelty inflicted on young talent. His creative and scholarly flair deserved a freer dispensation. But postdoctoral exile he would not, or could not, choose.

Further reading: Bernth Lindfors, ed., *Kulankulu: Interviews with Writers from Malawi and Lesotho* (Bayreuth, 1989); B. Phiri, "A Call for Female Participation: An Answer to Dr. Nazombe," *The Muse* 90 (1988): 9–10.

Ndhlala, Geoffrey (b. 1949). Zimbabwean novelist. Born at St. Mary's Mission, near Harare, he was educated at St. Augustine's Mission in Mutare and then at Britain's Keele University, where, in 1973, he achieved joint honors in English and history. He has since worked as a Zimbabwean civil servant. His first novel, *Jikinya* (1979), pictured an ar-cadian rurality that white colonialism rav-aged, a view (which Rino Zhuwarara calls romanticized) that Stanlake Samkange,

Wilson Katiyo, and Charles Mungoshi shared but city-bred Dambudzo Marechera rejected.

Historian and literary scholar meet in *The Southern Circle* (1984). Set in the early 1970s, the Liberation War a distant forest echo, the narrative covers three generations, with the narrator Rugare himself a writer. Recounting the tragic life of his father, Masutu, he also recalls the times of his grandfather, Zengeza. White prejudice and chicanery test Masutu's traditional pride virtually to destruction. Despite long loyal service, he loses his city job and returns to village life and little sympathy in Ruva. Rugare, perfectly schooled for the new order (he has ten British O-level and four A-level certificates), must surely manage escape from a life of village idleness and drunkenness. Five humiliating interviews with a city firm that finally rejects him (his interviewers are far less qualified) crushes his spirit and leads to menial estate work in the Eastern Highlands. However, as his father drifts into insanity, self-exile, and death in the bush, Rugare rises from despair and cultivated anonymity to rebuild a life solid enough to write his story.

The book impresses structurally and stylistically. Masutu and Rugare's employment disasters are rendered well, their psychological impact compellingly recorded. The minutiae of Rugare's embarrassment are painful enough for the novel to have been called simply *The Interview*. Occasional scenes of beauty and happiness relieve a harrowing *via dolorosa*. These include lyrical evocations of rural Africa at dawn and sunset and dramatic hunting vignettes from his grandfather's time; but they are clouded by memories of forced removals to land so bad that Masutu's "fat cattle all raised their heads to the heavens in disbelief" and crops tried to shrink back into the earth.

Like many contemporary texts, the book invokes the memory of Sekuru Chaminuka and Ambuya Nehanda, the nineteenth-century spirit-mediums hailed as Zimbabwe's first freedom fighters. They receive allusion at the opening and close of a book about whose sad events the narrator observes, "Time wears sorrow to a noble memory."

Further reading: Rino Zhuwarara, *Introduction to Zimbabwean Literature in English* (Harare, 2001).

NDP. The National Democratic Party. A nationalist party founded in 1960 in Southern Rhodesia, with political independence as its objective. Led by Michael Wawema, it included such future leaders as Robert Mugabe, Herbert Chitepo, Leopold Takawira, Ndabaningi Sithole, George Silundika, Eddsin Zvogbo, Simon Muzenda, and Enos Nkala. Banned by the white government in 1961, the NDP reformed as ZAPU, the Zimbabwe African People's Union.

Ngara, Emmanuel (b. 1947). Zimbabwean poet and critic. Born at Mhondoro in Southern Rhodesia, he was educated by the Jesuits at St Ignatius' College, Chishawasha (where, among other writers, Lawrence Vambe had earlier schooled), at University College Rhodesia, and finally at London, where he was awarded a doctorate. A senior lectureship in English at the National University of Lesotho (until 1980) preceded appointment as deputy ambassador to Ethiopia and ambassador to the Organization of African Union. Thereafter he held the chair of English and was deputy vice chancellor at the University of Zimbabwe. He currently holds similar positions at South Africa's University of Natal.

His books of careful scholarship have made him a leading commentator on African literature and its pedagogy, and his contribution to literary growth in Central Africa continues to be substantial. A book of verse, *Songs of the Temple*, appeared in 1992, but his work had already been anthologized in *And Now the Poets Speak* (1981), edited by Muderi Kadhani and Musaemura Zimunya.

Unlike most compatriot poets, Ngara chooses a verse statement that sometimes needs what he calls two or three "movements." Profound immersion in world literature and a radical commitment to African history and the best continental scholarship producing it (West Africa's Cheikh Anta Diop's work on ancient Egypt stimulated his own curiosity about Great Zimbabwe) equip him with wide cultural and artistic reference. He can readily summon Eliotian or Yeatsian modernism and yet blend it with the formulaic devices of oral tradition. Among African poets he resembles in formation and cultural range Nigeria's Echeruo or Okigbo, Uganda's Ntiru, and Malawi's Mnthali. A first-class mind sits beside an emotional center that can, however, produce stylistic overload, as in his poem "Heroes of Zimbabwe." His "Song of a Child Who Survived Nyadzonia" revisits perhaps the bush war's worst atrocity, when white Rhodesian forces, disguised as blacks, invaded a Mozambique refugee camp and slaughtered hundreds of innocent civilians. A child persona narrates the brutality in horrific detail ("a leg flying from a falling person," "a human head bouncing like a bouncing ball," "a man walking on two legs without a head"), and with repetition and parallelism capturing oral practice. The child himself has lost both parents in the onslaught and a leg, too. He, his parents, grandmother, and brother had "All fled from Rhodesia / To find this life, this death, this horror at Nyadzonia."

Further reading: Douglas Killam and Ruth Rowe, eds., *The Companion to African Literatures* (Oxford, 2000).

Ng'ombe, James Lapani (b. 1949). Malawian playwright and novelist. An important figure in the growth of modern Malawian literature, he holds degrees from Malawi, Canada, and Britain, where he secured a doctorate. Nine years lecturing in communication at the University of Malawi preceded the managing directorship of Dzuka Publishing, Blantyre, and he is currently director of the Malawi Institute of Journalism, whose facilities (including a radio station) he uses for promoting journalist skills and debate on human rights issues around democracy, gender equity, and domestic violence. In 2004, his democratic concerns winning him a Reagan-Fascell Democracy Fellowship, he used his time to write about the decade of democracy following Banda's one-party rule. His publications include the plays *The Banana Tree* (1976) and *The Beauty of Dawn* (1976), the novels *Sugarcane with Salt* (1989), *Madala's Children* (1996), and *Madala's Grandchildren* (2005), and a children's book, *How the Pig Got His Snout* (1998).

Ng'ombe is associated with key moments in Malawi's literary history. He was among a small student group who, with the help of instructors like Jack Mapanje, Landeg White, and Mupa Shumba, founded the University's Writers' Workshop—at once the nursery for most Malawian authors and, under Banda's rule, a rare island of free speech and debate. Witnessing the appearance in 1971 of *Mau*, a pioneering anthology of new poetry, he also played a part, as both playwright and critic, in a drama renaissance at the university inspired by scholars like John Linstrum, David Kerr, James Gibbs, and Mupa Shumba. Responding to a call to root a new scripted drama in Malawian oral tradition and practice, he wrote *The Banana Tree* and *The Beauty of Dawn*, which appeared in James Gibbs's pioneering anthology *Nine Malawian Plays* (1976) along with work by his contemporaries

Innocent Banda, Chris Kamlongera, Joe Mosiwa, and Enoch Timpunza-Mvula. With deceptive simplicity (a sorrowing widower, seeing flora resurrect after rain, waters his wife's grave, whereupon a banana tree grows and bleeds on being cut down by the second wife), *The Banana Tree* explores timeless issues around mortality, its perceived oddness within the natural order, and wifely jealousy.

While *Madala's Grandchildren* explores the mixed fortunes of post-Banda democracy, with its problems of corruption and bad governance, *Madala's Children* looks at the harsh realities of life under Banda (it is now compulsory reading in Malawi's secondary schools). Pangani, known as Madala, survives the struggle for independence and sees a postcolonial era that brings nothing but pain for the nation and for his own family. Unsurprisingly we hear echoes of Shakespeare's *Julius Caesar*, that classic of political assassination so beloved by victims of Banda's tyranny, especially those he jailed. While *Madala's Children* covers a thirty-year period, *Sugarcane with Salt* works within a much smaller time frame. An earlier book, it is necessarily more circumspect. These were Banda's autumn years, but he was still feared. Hence a need for nuanced satirical indirection. Dr. Khumbo Dala returns from medical studies in London, keen to leave that hateful city and return to the warmth of home and service to his society. His euphoria scarcely survives arrival at the capital's airport. As the bittersweet title suggests, the text will walk a tightrope. Banda's hated Malawi Congress Party is praised for its social activism (as impressive as that of the churches); under Banda Muslims can now get an education without committing apostasy; it was Banda's government that sent Khumbo overseas on scholarship. On the other hand, rural poverty is widespread; hitherto discreet political class corruption

(Banda himself is never implicated) now burgeons as ministers make fortunes smuggling barbiturates and marijuana to South Africa; teaching has become a despised profession; gender problems multiply.

Further reading: Alfred Msadala, *Destined for Great Things* (Blantyre, 1999); David Kerr, *Dance, Media Entertainment and Popular Theatre in South East Africa* (Bayreuth, 1998).

Nine Malawian Plays (1976). Collected and edited by James Gibbs and issued by Popular Publications of Limbe, this landmark volume is essential reading on the rise of modern Malawian drama. Indeed, Gibbs's introduction suggests that as the continent's first national play collection, the text scored for Malawi "a modest first in African publishing." He explains the shaping influences of cultural tradition, annual school drama festivals, radio (especially the Malawi Broadcasting Corporation and the BBC), the university's Writers' Workshop, and creative writing courses. Though short, the plays capture a luminous burst of creativity amidst the growing darkness of Hastings Banda's despotism. James Ng'ombe is represented by *The Banana Tree* and *The Beauty of Dawn*; Chris Kamlongera by *Graveyards* and *The Love Potion*; Innocent Banda by *Lord Have Mercy* and *Cracks*; Spencer Chunga and Hodges Kalikwembe by *That Man Is Evil*; Enoch Timpunza-Mvula by *The Lizard's Tail*; and Joe Mosiwa by *Who Will Marry Our Daughter?* Gibbs praises the "awareness of the fragility of relationships" in Ng'ombe and Banda, the "subtle shifts of attitude which ripple through the dialogue" of Kamlongera, "a boldness of construction" in Banda, and the "many delightful touches" of Mosiwa. All are praised for their "awareness of form, a recognition of the range of traditional material available" and for not indulging in "superficial cultural nationalism and national romanticism."

Further reading: David Kerr, *African Popular Theatre* (Oxford, 1995); David Kerr, *Dance, Media Entertainment and Popular Theatre in South East Africa* (Bayreuth, 1998).

Nkomo, Joshua Mqabuko (1917–99). Former Zimbabwean vice president. Born in Matabeleland, he attended high school and college in South Africa, returning home in 1947 to work for Rhodesian Railways. Experience as a union leader—by 1951 his African Employees' Association was the region's strongest—rapidly made him the country's foremost African political figure. When Sir Godfrey Huggins visited London in 1952 for talks on a Central African Federation, Nkomo accompanied him, though vehemently opposing the plan. He became leader of Rhodesia's local African National Council in 1957 but chose exile in Britain when Edgar Whitehead banned it in 1959. There, collaborating with Kenneth Kaunda and Hastings Banda, he campaigned vigorously against the Federation and persuaded the United Nations to adopt the entire Rhodesian question as an international issue in 1962. In the same year, he became president of the Zimbabwean African People's Union (ZAPU), which replaced the banned ANC. This period was marked by serial banning orders, restrictions, and detentions and his consolidation as the country's most popular African leader. When Ian Smith's white Rhodesia Front declared its Unilateral Declaration of Independence in 1965, he correctly dubbed it "the suicide squad" and pleaded vainly for Britain and France to intervene. British cabinet officials subsequently trying to solve the Rhodesian problem consulted him in prison.

Robert Mugabe's departure from ZAPU to form the more radical Zimbabwean African National Union (ZANU) accelerated growing rivalry between the two men. The ensuing guerilla war found Nkomo's ZAPU forces based in Zambia receiving Soviet support and Mugabe's ZANU forces, based in Mozambique, Chinese aid. Zambia's 1973 border closure seriously disadvantaged Nkomo's forces, leaving the ZANU army in a leading position and as the natural destination for young recruits. Later, continental pressure, alarmed at such division in the freedom movement, united the two factions as the Patriotic Front in opposition to the transitional government of Bishop Abel Muzorewa. But in the postwar elections of 1980, ZANU and ZAPU competed separately, with ZAPU winning only twelve seats to ZANU's fifty-seven. Offered the presidency, Nkomo chose the home-affairs portfolio instead. When discovery of a ZAPU arms cache in 1982 drove him again into exile, ZAPU soldiers left the national army and began a rebellion against the ruling ZANU. A massacre occurred in Matabeleland when the government sent its Fifth Brigade to put down the rebellion. Returning to fight the 1985 elections, Nkomo again did badly, but in 1999 accepted the nation's vice presidency. He died in 1999.

Further reading: Joshua Nkomo, *Nkomo: The Story of My Life* (London, 1984).

Nyamfukudza, Stanley (1951). Zimbabwean novelist and short-story writer. Born in Wedza, Zimbabwe, he was dismissed from the University of Rhodesia and jailed by the white regime in 1973, a traumatic experience that reappears in his short stories. Like his contemporary Marechera, he then won a scholarship to Oxford, where, unlike Marechera, in 1977 he completed a degree in English. In 1980 he returned to a political independence about which he had already expressed foreboding. And he brought with him his novel *The Non-Believer's Journey*, London-published and explorative of reservations about the Liberation War. The novel was well received, but his subsequent work suggested a preference for a smaller canvas. Two short-story collections appeared, *Aftermaths* (1983) and *If God Was a Woman* (1991).

Nyamfukudza likes individual dilemma and response to unfolding situations. He rarely highlights the sociopolitical background against which (often from which) action arises, weaving it instead into the overall tapestry. This is manifest strategy, but it may also find roots in personal experience: growth to maturity and scholarly ambition during a colonial war in which contemporaries were being slaughtered. Thus, amid war's waste, lethal internal rivalries, or a trek to the front where the hero is killed by a guerilla leader, the novel remains focused on human relationships in all their intractable complexity. That he feels women's pain under patriarchy is clear; that he sees their moral and physical heroism shamefully ignored is also clear. His writing constantly celebrates courageous women towering morally over feckless, faithless, and alcoholic men. Violence against women is common, sexual encounters sometimes smack of misogyny, and the word "bitch" liberally peppers the texts.

Set in 1974, with the bush war raging, *The Non-Believer's Journey* explores enough skepticism and tension around individual and group freedom to make this a multilayered text. Protagonist Sam's predicament is cruelly representative. With an education long fought for, and essential for postcolonial reconstruction, his generation is asked to risk this legitimate prize by joining the liberation armies. This group understands the historic issues in play better than most and is well equipped to interrogate their implications. Among undergraduates, however, "fuck the war" individualism prevails—precisely the capitalist-imperialist sin ideologues see themselves opposing. But what if national freedom excludes an individual's freedom

not to fight or to offer, say, political, noncombatant support? To borrow Malawian Mnthali's coinage, these youths are semidetached intellectuals. They are of the struggle but not in it. They see its moral health and its moral disease, want a liberated future, but fear its shape. They are suspicious of the political elite, dub black professionals self-seeking, ridicule Shona-Ndebele rivalry, and highlight the cruel imbalance between city comfort and village slaughter. They would ask why poor rural youths (like Sam's brother) must abandon school to fight while the offspring of some leaders (known scoundrels among them) are safely overseas getting training for the best jobs back home. "And there you sit," Sam tells his father, "like every other peasant, your children getting killed, and you will probably end up with nothing."

Sam convinces psychologically. A township product himself, a drinker and early 1960s activist, his political acumen derives from a white man he detests. Physically and intellectually courageous, he hates colonialism and knows that land is the core issue around which, if around little else, there is national solidarity. He despises sentimentality but can wax sentimental. Bus passengers singing liberation songs draw him in, but only with an outsider's "amusement." Marching in the mountains with singing recruits, he joins in, but he hates himself for doing so:

It was the most desolate experience of his life . . . watching and despising himself for the lack of courage which prevented him from shutting his mouth and declaring how much he hated this sort of rousing, emotional politics. At the same time, he felt wretched at being cut off by his inability to share in the fervour of his fellow men, to open up and sing out his problems, his hates and his hopes, dispelling, at least for the duration of the song, all the doubts and the mistrust which gnawed at his being.

Nothing captures Sam's schizoid condition more vividly. After his chest-clearing novel, Nyamfukudza relishes a chance with short stories to range more widely. Yet the experiment in setting and viewpoint does not exclude consistencies. As if setting a mental exercise, he likes anonymous pronominal openings ("someone," "he," "she," "it," "we") within which he inserts a question that the text might answer. This creates the magnetism of curiosity and a hint of individual-yet-everyman experience. Its effect is to engage us closely with people and circumstance. "Opting Out" continues a theme of the novel (which ends, "He just wasn't political, he decided"), and looks like a dry run for it. It also once more privileges gender. Strong decisive women again loom loftily over perfidious and alcoholic men. This can involve pointed ironic twist. In "Crossing the River," with hair-raising suspense, a mother heroically gets her children over a flooded river, thus awing her small son, the narrator. He then wryly inverts the balance of courage by saying, "I let her talk, mothers like to talk." Having symbolically crossed a Rubicon of his own growth (his mother had commanded him to be brave), he sounds already like a new recruit to patriarchy.

"Lucia" narrates the tragic life and early death of an only child—brave, lovely, spirited, compassionate, but victimized at school and home. Her poignant innocence suffuses the narrative, and the diffident narrator pays heartfelt tribute by saying he has grown in confidence and courage from knowing her. In "Settlers," a husband lost in a forest cries out like a child to his wife for help. In "Guilt and Sorrow," the man of the house is seen "sunk in a sofa" and described bluntly as having "no balls." "Having Been Someone" begins differently. The male is

tough, ruthless, a man of action, but nightmares about his past sexual mistreatment of a girl expose him after all as frightened and guilt-stricken, weeping like a child beside his psychologically stronger wife.

Further reading: Rino Zhuwarara, *Introduction to Zimbabwean Literature in English* (Harare, 2001); Flora Veit-Wild, *Teachers, Preachers and Non-Believers: A Social History of Zimbabwean Literature* (Harare, 1992); Musaemura Zimunya, review of *If God Was a Woman, The Parade*, December 1999.

Nyamubaya, Freedom (b. 1950). Zimbabwean poet. Born in Uzumbe in Mashonaland East (her peasant roots, she says, sustain her happiness), she was in schools at Musanhi and Nhoma Mission until 1975, when she interrupted her education to join the Zimbabwe Liberation Army in Mozambique, becoming a frontline field operations commander and education secretary for ZANU. Despite this truncated education (she later spent two years at Oxford's Ruskin College, but in any case says bush warfare was an "open university"), wide interests led her seamlessly into peacetime life as an inspirational writer, rural activist (founder of a successful nongovernmental organization), and public traditional dancer.

Africa's wars are many, their poets few. Liberation song collections appear (Pongweni on Zimbabwe, Mapanje and White on Mozambique), but counterparts to Nigeria's Okigbo or Britain's Sassoon are rare. In Africa the front line has produced less than the prison cell. But Nyamubaya is both war poet and female.

Her collections *On the Road Again: Poems During and After the National Liberation of Zimbabwe* (1986) and the ironically titled *Dusk of Dawn* (1995) won enough acclaim among an impoverished reading public to need, respectively, four and two reprints.

If the blurb for *On the Road Again* mentions Nyamubaya's "prose-like style" as a compliment, she herself approaches poeticity with dismissive bluntness:

One person said,
You are not a poet,
But forget that . . .

And then, after listing ghetto deaths and suffocated miners ("Poetic stuff this"), she simply asserts, "Art serves." She will apply her military courage to writing verse. The imagination will fly free, guided only by truth and concern for radical decolonization. Her writing in part deconstructs warfare as private experience and does so in a manner uncommon in African discourse. No subject is taboo, whether abuse in the guerilla camps ("They beat me the first day I arrived at Tembwe / I was raped by the security commander") or postcolonial disillusion ("The survivors do not seem to love / the country at all").

The volume's title suggests another journey after liberation. It will be one of continuing struggle and with unchanged targets. With her AK-47 now abandoned, she writes,

Let my hands work—
My mouth sing—
My pencil write—
About the same things my bullets
Aimed at.

She will target pointless anger, disappointment at "a defeated victory," Lancaster House's ludicrous land deal, and intellectuals whom war has taught nothing ("The colonized intellectual buds again, / A society of individuals starts afresh"). There will be a plug for existentialism ("Miraculous Jesus, a mere tale, / It's us and us alone"), achingly sad tributes to military casualties, especially women, and, in "A Mysterious Marriage," pointed critique of the struggle seen as a planned marriage between Independence and Freedom in which Freedom failed to show up. Now, still unwed, "Fruitless and barren Independence staggers to old age, / Since her shadow, Freedom, hasn't come."

At her best with clipped lines, shooting comment like bullets, Nyamubaya commands varied poetic statement. The bluntly demotic ("We should accept / We have been fucked up / A training ground / For their armies") accompanies the warmly elegiac, seen in poignant lines for the dead ("In the hot air, her sound burnt away / Above the angry mountains / her voice echoed away"), or for abused women in the camps who went mad

Unknown by the world at large,
Forgotten by their male comrades
Who made them pregnant . . .

Dusk of Dawn appeared in 1995. Preceded by two war anecdotes, its verse maintains the first volume's jaunty resilience. Though analyzing contemporary issues, she revisits the war—partly for personal balm, partly for a readership growing distant from it. She recalls a camp baby born in the muddy discomfort of the bush, who "did not cry like all babies do at birth / But wriggled bravely in the whispering wind," and an old woman who lies dying "flat on rocks": her stomach had "disappeared into her back"—"somewhat skeletal but cheerful."

The volume closes with "My Beloved Country" (1992–93), an intriguing poem that shrieks "This country stinks," describes in nauseous detail the stench and sight of broken sewers and hungry children, and asserts that care here is "long frozen" and peace "a stranger." She hurls abuse at the country's moral corruption:

I spit at the windscreens of the stolen
Pajeros and Mercedes Benzes
That have eaten the brains of those
    who know it all . . .

Then, with a dash of defeated expectation, she reveals her target as Mozambique! Can this be the same land she hymned earlier in the collection with the words "I kiss you for sheltering my soul at that difficult time / Mozambique the land of life"? Or does she simply want some fertile ambiguity?

Further reading: Adrian Roscoe and Mpalive-Hangson Msiska, *The Quiet Chameleon: Modern Poetry from Central Africa* (London, 1992).

Operations and Tears: A New Anthology of Malawian Poetry. Edited by Anthony Nazombe, this title appeared in 2004 from the University of Malawi's Department of Theology and Religious Studies. The nation's largest anthology yet, its provenance reflects the continuing intimacy between Central African writing and religious agency. The pioneering Malawi Writers Series, which became an important outlet for prose writers, emerged from the Catholic Montfort Press. Nazombe himself had a mission education at Pius XII Seminary. Shadowed with a sense of mortality, his dedication is to

> the memory of numerous relatives, friends and colleagues who have died in the past thirty years. Some were carried away by the deadly HIV/AIDS pandemic just when an effective treatment was in sight. May their souls rest in peace.

Soon after this inscription, and before his work saw publication, Nazombe himself died, in February 2004. Among Malawi's most painstaking scholars, he was even unable to check the final stages of proofing. He mentions a seven-year gestation period

and the inevitable attack of editorial neurosis. The text had to be representative, yet there was a dearth of women poets. Verse reflecting Banda's political retreat between 1992 and 1994 must appear, yet the new dispensation also demanded that, as Writers' Workshop archivist, he dust off "censored" verse dating from the 1970s. Finally, poems appearing in a score of new independent newspapers also called for capture, inspection, and sifting.

The collection eventually comprised forty-six poets (including some expatriates) and one hundred and thirty-nine poems. Known poets included Innocent Banda, Steve Chimombo, Frank Chipasula, Zangaphee Chiseze, David Kerr, Ken Lipenga, Jack Mapanje, Zondiwe Mbano, Felix Mnthali, Francis Moto, Lupenga Mphande, Edison Mpina, Geoff Mwanja, Pádraig Ó Máille, Landeg White, and Nazombe himself. Where possible, their fresh work was included. Lesser known or entirely new poets were Hoffman Aipira, Kisa Amateche, S. E. Chiziwa, Dunstan Gausi, Cecilia Hasha, Maxford Iphani, Gustave Kaliwo, Kapwepwe Khonje, Joji Kumwenda, Monica Kumwenda, John Lwanda, Zeleza Manda, Alfred Matiki, Zondiwe Mbano, Rowland Mbvundula, M. Mkandawire, Bright Molande, J. J. Msosa, Khumbula Munthali, Ian Musowa, Sam Raiti Mtamba, Alfred Tyson Nkhoma, Immanuel Bofomo Nyirenda, D. B. V. Phiri, Kadwa Phungwako, Ambokile Salimu, Francis Sefe (Ghana), and Edwin Segal. An extensive glossary reflects the sharply increased use of vernacular terms and cultural allusion over earlier anthologies.

Hoffmann Aipira, a new voice, is represented by seven poems. His taut lines picture lake and rural life: the sanctity of taking seed to soil at dawn, drought that produces "an Eden / Denied," the sadness of village funerals when "the deceased exits / to a callous void / without best wishes," tradition's great symbolic dances like *Gulu Wamkulu* from which modern education cuts you off, and environmental degradation as "The globe fast forwards / to a massive construction site." The ultimate "concrete jungle" and the disappointments of a deracinating education produce nostalgia amid urban sterility and find Aipira's speaker now "wearing worried looks / staring at the world / with negative confidence / and in difficulty coordinating / speech and thought."

Kisa Amateshe's "For the Grand Old Man" honors the pioneering poet and novelist David Rubadiri, in whose eyes the speaker sees the "Pains of a derailed history" and in whose career is written Malawi's literary growth:

> We feel your stately presence
> At the creative milestones—
> Your works graciously walking
> With silent strides to eternity

Sai Bwanali's "This Family" reproves a national leader who preaches unity but only for his own glorification. S. E. Chiziwa's "The New Covenant" assembles sharp imagery around notions of dawn and shadow, risings and fallings, dry valleys of bones, biblical Egypt and Palestine. This is "The anniversary of our impotence" and the vehicle of state is racing out of control with "The Pilot snoring." Cecilia Hasha's "A Woman's Cry" joins a swelling chorus against the abuse of women. Her skillfully built piece rises on incrementally urgent pleas to a sister, if she sees "the man I married," to teach him what normal marriage is about. Hands are for caressing and fondling, not a sjambok for beating; lips are for kissing, not for calabashes of beer; eyes are for admiring wifely beauty, not for lusting "after teenage girls." Money should be spent on maintaining his wife and young ones,

> Not to purchase risky pleasures
> Which he can have free and safe
> From me, his wife, Abiti Daniel

Maxford Iphani writes with force, and sometimes too cryptically, but "Jaundice" paints a total demoralization that works at literal and sociopolitical levels. Because of the sickness, "My shadow does not go where I go, / It has chosen its own path / . . . My smile has come to be / A distortion of my face / My voice, a muted grunt." His hopes, merely a convenient word, "Have long degenerated into nothingness / In the massive holocaust of / What I dare to call the 'real' me." Gustave Kaliwo, whose postgraduate studies, disappointingly, led him to law and not literature, laments in a poem dated 1984 how the people prayed for a man to take them out of the land of Egypt. A Moses came, "silenced Pharaoh and his councillors," but "led us out into the wilderness / he alone and God knew where." Kapwepwe Khonje's "Choices" more frontally attacks the Banda years, scorning the president's Kamuzu Academy, an Etonian clone where Latin and Greek would be taught but where, for the first ten years, no Malawian teacher would be hired:

> Haven't we been taught classics
> At this transplant of Eton
> Where our skins don't qualify us
> And local graduates are snubbed?

Monica Brenda Kumwenda's response to Banda's legacy is to cherish sanctuaries of inner security symbolized by the shade of a favorite tree. The future seems locked into a disturbing globalization, and her "Unforgettable" recalls the hideous deception of someone (no prize for guessing the culprit) who came with the innocence of a butterfly, dove, angel, and child, offering love, peace and harmony, and instead brought their opposites. John Lwanda is a medical doctor who, in Scottish exile, has created his own publishing house and provides a valuable outlet for Malawian writers. His verse here features chronic bouts of nostalgia and guilty memory of privilege among penniless peers that leads him to say, "Sweet peace of mind would be my prize." A repeated daring to hope (the word begins each stanza) informs "The Second Harvest," in which he questions the democratic government succeeding Banda. It ends,

> Hope?
> Should I dare?
> Like the mother of five skeletal,
> Drought starved, sunken eyed
>   children;
> Let me live to see the second harvest!

Zeleza Manda's "Dried Bones, Steel, and Sirens" is another piece from Nazombe's "censored" file. Typical is its obliquely angled protest at yet another Special Branch arrest of a leading academic. Given its allusion to Chingwe's Hole, central metaphor and symbol of the Banda years, this is almost certainly the poet-scholar Jack Mapanje being dragged off to Mikuyu, called here "Golgotha—the valley of / dried bones / cold steel / and sirens." The poet wonders what to choose—patience or suicide at Chingwe's Hole. Should security eyes and ears grow suspicious, the poem has an appended footnote:

> Theme: strictly religious
> Personae: certainly Jews
> Time: probably all seasons
> Place: Doubtfully heaven.

Sadly, as in Alfred Matiki's "Whispers," indirection and opaqueness sometimes indicate intramural dissent rather than extramural protest, requiring glosses that Nazombe died before providing. Mikuyu as Golgotha reappears in Rowland Mbvundula's "Jacked Up (To Golgotha)," whose subject again is Jack Mapanje being hauled to a "bony calvary." But venom is reserved for academic colleagues suspected of complicity in the arrest, here called "The Iscariot soul mongers / Who trade in his (priceless) flesh and bone."

Bright Molande's "An African Tragedy" has a persona narrate a joyous homecoming from overseas study ("The long flight of the soul from Heathrow came to an end") only to face the misery from which he had temporarily escaped. He is told that "the grave is an insatiable stomach, it only swallows" and that his people have been "falling gently one by one like lonesome leaves in the wind." In the village cemetery, sensing a fate wider than Malawi's, he "sees" John Chilembwe, Malawi's first martyr, praying, Banda washing his hands in "steaming blood," Mandela, looking worried about distant thunder, and Mugabe "mauling raw flesh." A baby's scream suddenly rings out from a labor ward, and as suddenly falls silent. The poem ends:

> I am sick inside me, my inside is sick
> As Africa keeps delivering astride
>   hungry yawning graves.

J. J. Msosa's "Son of Tinkenawo" (literally, "let us go away with them") is one of many reminders of ambivalence around a modern education usually seized with enthusiasm. The persona, like some haunted Byronic hero, wanders in solitude over not a physical but an intellectual landscape. His long and torturous journey has taken him far from home, though the memory of that "season of sweet smelling" remains fresh. He has climbed peaks and descended into valleys, but always without those who gave him life. Whenever he sits to reflect, he can still hear kith and kin calling him to "return from the winding path." But the journey "maimed has left me / In need of crutches of wisdom." Meanwhile Khumbula Munthali, a female poet Nazombe was happy to recruit, writes of witnessing the seizure of a Banda victim called Benja. "I Saw It" describes him being seized at his house, dragged out, tied hands and feet, and blindfolded. Then, "bundled into the boot of a car," he is taken to a nearby river, beaten into silence, "tied in a sack."

Ellipses hide what all local readers would know—that the victim was to be thrown to the crocodiles, an end Banda often threatened for his opponents. Ian Musowa's "For Ayewo Who Was" reflects on the tense silence, "guarded by I-will-report-you-eyes," that Banda imposed on a noisy people, while Sam Raiti Mtamba, a brilliant undergraduate of the 1970s, laments in "Too Much Energy in Us Destroys" how modern man has denuded nature of its old frightening power: now "Mountains are mere mountains" and "We can do anything / Without fearing a landslide." D. B. V. Phiri is represented by poems written in Wales, where he raised his eyes to the mountains to search for life's meaning and hoped that the truth would finally out, just as "The whales trapped in ice once / broke barriers to unity." Kadwa Phungwako's "No Tears of Sorrow" uses a 1611 biblical register for messages from Mumbi, the Gikuyu Eve figure, and Mphambe and Namalenga, Malawian deity appellations, to assure "the children of Maravi" in apocalyptic terms that "thy grief shall be no more"—no darkness, no weariness, and no death by viper bite. Finally, the lawyer Ambokile Salimu, in "Then the Monster Rose and Failed," talks about man as "swallowing empty dogmas / While bathing in his own urine and blood," and worries about prophets and their sacred texts having somehow "preserved the camps" and spawned all the other horrors of the modern world.

P

Phiri, Desmond D. (b. ca. 1930). Malawian playwright, historian, and biographer. A model of how modern Africans can squeeze several lives into one, Phiri has had a remarkable career. Born at Mzimba in northern Malawi, he was educated at Blantyre Secondary School, Livingstonia, and Embangweni. Because two self-educated South African doctors inspired him to reach beyond his 1949 Junior Certificate, in 1950, while a government clerk, he took a Cape Town correspondence course, moved to Dar es Salaam, secured British A level passes for entry to the London School of Economics, and took a B.S. there. Commercial attaché and first secretary at the Malawian embassy in Bonn from 1966–69, he retired from the civil service in 1976, whereupon he founded the Aggrey Memorial School (named after the West African educational pioneer), which specializes in distance teaching.

Phiri's energies and courage are legendary. In the 1970s, a perilous time for praising anyone but Banda, he wrote biographies of five prominent Malawians for the Longman *Malawians to Remember* series. Their subjects were John Chilembwe, a national martyr figure; Inkosi (Chief) Gomani, a respected Ngoni leader during colonial times, who died in exile; James F. Sangala, founder of the Nyasaland African Congress; Charles C. Chinula, distinguished teacher, vice president of the Nyasaland African Congress, and advisor to Paramount Chief M'mbelwa II; and Dunduzu K. Chisiza, secretary general of the Malawi Congress Party, tragically killed in a car accident. Next, after learning SiZulu by correspondence to tackle sources effectively, he wrote *Nguni to Ngoni* (1982), an absorbing history of the Zulu-Ngoni exodus from South Africa north to Lake Nyasa. As his foreword suggests, so important was this exodus that "very few tribes between Natal and Lake Victoria were unaffected by the Ngoni. . . . In their march northwards most people in Zimbabwe, Zambia, Malawi and Tanzania felt their presence in a big way."

His most recent biography, *I See You: Life of Clements Kadalie, the Man South Africa, Malawi, Zimbabwe and Namibia Should*

Not Forget (2000), continues the Phiri style. Breezily concise and generous, a weaving of documentary evidence and interviews, it delivers sympathy without hagiography, patriotism without chauvinism. His subject is well chosen. Few Malawians know of Clements Kadalie, born in 1893. Yet in sixty-four pages Phiri resurrects a figure seen to be pivotal in Southern and Central African history, perhaps second in significance only to Mandela himself and a key agent in the long struggle toward South African freedom in 1994. Indeed, Mandela's *Long Walk to Freedom* cites him as founder, in 1919, of the Industrial and Commercial Union, South Africa's first black trade union—its motto "Awaken O Africa, for the morning is at hand"—and an ANC partner, but often outshining it in its appeal to workers rather than intellectuals. George Padmore, says Phiri, when listing Africa's decolonization heroes, bracketed Kadalie with Ghana's Nkrumah, Nigeria's Azikiwe, and Kenya's Kenyatta. A brilliant orator and natural leader, "he became the uncrowned king of the black masses. No other Negro in recent South African history has enjoyed the popularity that was Kadalie's at the height of his power. The whites feared him as they feared Dingane the last of the Zulu warrior kings." Kadalie organized strikes, urged pass burning, got better black wages, held his own at the ILO in Geneva, represented his people with Britain's Labour movement, knew Lord Fenner Brockway, and was on speaking terms with South African prime minister Hertzog. He knew communists like Sidney Bunting and James La Guma, father of writer Alex La Guma. A dominant figure in Southern African politics and unionism until his death in 1951, here was a small boy from a remote Nyasaland village with only a Scottish missionary secondary education. Phiri had wanted to include Kadalie in his 1970s Malawians to Remember series, but Longman was advised against publication,

Banda being too intimately associated with white South Africa just then. With the end of Banda's rule, Phiri found time and energy to help the new democratic president, Bakili Muluzi, to write his book *Democracy with a Price.*

Phiri had much earlier won prizes from the Nyasaland and Northern Rhodesia Publications Bureau, and four short stories were published as novelettes in his home language, Tumbuka. In 1972 his play *The Chief's Bride*, first published by Britain's Evans Brothers in 1968, was included by America's Delacorte Press in *All the World's a Stage*, an anthology of twenty-one of the "world's great modern plays" for the young—Phiri the sole African alongside such authors as America's Langston Hughes, Sweden's August Strindberg, India's Rabindranath Tagore, and Britain's Robert Bolt.

In 1999 he published an expanded edition of his *Let Us Die For Africa: An African Perspective on the Life and Death of John Chilembwe of Nyasaland/Malawi*. With a foreword by historian George Shepperson and an appendix by David Stuart-Mogg, this text finally defines Chilembwe's status as a pioneer in the freedom struggle, in the promotion of modern education for Africans, and in opposition to cruelty on British settler estates, which, in 1915, provoked his heroic uprising, hanging, and burial in an unmarked grave. Phiri's relentless promotion is partly responsible for Chilembwe's appearance now on all Malawi's banknotes.

Phiri, Virginia (b. 1954). Zimbabwean novelist and short-story writer. She was born in Bulawayo and trained as an accountant. The areas to which she has applied her skills reflect her values and vision. Like her contemporary woman writer Nyamubaya, she fought in the Liberation War. She is a leading figure in the Zimbabwe Women Writers organization, and her publications (in

Shona, Ndebele, and English) seek to enhance women's social status; hence her coauthoring *Women of Resilience*, which honors the lives of women freedom fighters. Echoing J. S. Mill's advice in "On the Subjection of Women," she has tirelessly urged women to tell their stories and write them down. She has worked as secretary to the Zimbabwe Academic and Non-fiction Authors Association and, as a leading horticulturalist, enjoys the rare distinction of having an orchid bear her name: *Polystachya phirii.*

Phiri's strongest writing appears in *Desperate* (2002), a collection of six short stories dedicated entirely to the plight of Zimbabwean women forced into prostitution. The topic is sensitive but the book is luminous, a work of gratitude and sympathy, a symphony of poignancy and moral heroism. Phiri explains its genesis:

> More than twenty years ago, in the mid-seventies, I, like everyone else, did not spare much thought for prostitutes. Because of my activism during the Second Chimurenga, I was constantly in danger. At one stage, prostitutes saved my life. For two weeks, they fed me, housed me, protected me and then let me go on my way when it was safe to do so. I had nothing with which to pay them for their kindness. I just thanked them and left.
>
> When I became a writer, I started to search for reasons why women became prostitutes. The answers are to be found in all our communities if we care to look for them. Women take to prostitution as the last resort when, as the title of this book proclaims, they become desperate. No woman enjoys being kicked about, tossed about, bullied and abused by different men. This book seeks to highlight what drives some of them into this profession.

> Perhaps this book will cause our communities to realize that sometimes this decision on their part would not have been made if we took a more caring attitude towards women in difficulties. . . .
>
> Writing this book is, for me, an act of gratitude and reparation to these women. It is difficult for me to find those women who had saved my life by helping me so long ago. Most of them would now be in their fifties.

Though *Desperate* carries a disclaimer as fiction, the distinctive styles of these first-person narratives—detail abundance, tonal and tempo variation—suggest that Phiri is working from personal histories. Their very titles suggest case studies.

Openings are terse and urgent. "Chido: Teenage Bread Winner" begins: "I started selling sex in the early seventies when both my parents died within a year of each other, leaving me, then fifteen years old, with my two young sisters, Kate and Chipo, and a young brother, Roger, who were twelve, ten and six years old, respectively." "Dorothy: Accused" begins: "I was stripped of my title as a wife, a mother, labeled a witch, and thrown out of my village. My five children were barred from seeing me. I could not even take the youngest daughter, Tandi, with me. She was only three years old. She cried and kicked but was dragged away by my mother-in-law. That broke my heart." "Sihle: Child Bride" opens: "When I was six years old, I was given away as a bride to a polygamist the age of my grandfather. My parents were poor. They could not afford anything more than a meal once per day. I was child number six out of eight children and the only girl, the hope for my mother." "Rachel: Why Me?" begins with exploded ambition: "I was to be the first woman in our family to get as far as the "O" level stage. I wanted to go beyond that. I wanted to be a doctor. I had admired female doctors when I went to visit hospitals." Brutal rape by two men pushes her to inexorable ruin. "Nhamo: The Black and White Girl" begins: "Nhamo Nkosi is my name. My mother was sixteen years old, still a virgin, when she was brutally raped by a member of the Rhodesian forces, a white man, as she was gathering firewood during the Second Chimurenga war, in the early seventies. For better or for worse, I was conceived."

Phiri resists simplistic explanation. Modern society, the war, poverty, history, colonialism, urbanization, culture collapse—they can all be blamed. But she rejects political posturing. There is no ideological manifesto. Answers instead are implicit in cameos of care and deep respect. A blurb, however, suggests that commonly these women "are victims of a society that shackles women to a dependence on men"—though these might not be Ms Phiri's own words.

Recurring fragments comprise this ugly mosaic of decline and fall: alcohol (to blur or blunt fear of commercial sex); apartheid-style family disruption—rural parents and city-working children; home visits in the dark to avoid gossip. Pivotally, there is heroic survival struggle—material, emotional, psychological—and constant temptation to suicide. Nhamo, a city prostitute, offers the heart-stopping words: "Once in a while I got a letter from my mother, which contained the usual greetings, happenings in the village and the last sentence always read 'Without you, we would starve to death, God bless you.'"

That colonialism has wrought grievous harm is a fact Phiri will not rake over. Unlike some contemporaries, she is not rewriting history, important though that is. Current distress must be faced and a way forward found. Nor will she canvas a negritudist return to the past. The village has its flaws and the city, symbol of selfishness, has its support groups and salvific encounters.

Village solidarity is not completely dead ("We work and eat together and entertain ourselves at least once a month with songs and dance"), and small urban churches offer new communal growth points ("At the mission every member worked. We produced our own food, made our own furniture and sold some. We also made our own clothes. Older children attended school, the very small ones played while older men and women were taught practical skills"). Phiri's values are humanly inclusive. In the final story, featuring a mixed-race girl, Nhamo, the product of rape by a white soldier, an admirable figure is Mr. Jackson, a white man welcomed into village society on marrying her.

Ambition flickers and flares amid career and prospects wreckage. Despite her squalid life, Rachel can still say: "While Sheila went out in the evenings, I read Form Three to Form Four textbooks in English that I borrowed from my workmates." But Chido, a childhood bride, reports in her moving story the arrival of survival's mightiest threat:

> I rented out all four rooms of the house and collected the rent myself at the beginning of every month. The house was for my retirement. I would still collect rent to live on when the world of sex-selling ended. My work is now risky. AIDS is now wiping out a lot of people: the innocent, the promiscuous, the young and even the naughty oldies have not been spared.

Rubadiri, David (b. 1930). Malawian poet, novelist, and playwright. Born at Liule, on the shores of Lake Malawi, his life has embraced the worlds of higher education, exile, and diplomacy as well as literature. In 1941, because Nyasaland's secondary education was exiguous, he was sent by his father to Uganda's King's College, a school academically progressive and, happily, a hotbed of literary activity. He told Bernth Lindfors, "I keep on coming back to that school because I think it's very, very central to having excited my sensibilities." That the Ugandan poet Okot p'Bitek was a contemporary recalls Rubadiri's status as a seminal link between East and Central African writing. A post at Ife, Nigeria, extended this link to West Africa, and another, at the University of Botswana, to Southern Africa. Though in each of these areas he strove to promote local writing, he complained to Lindfors that West Africans "gorged themselves with their own stuff and read almost nothing from East, Central and Southern Africa." About Southern Africa he was kinder, calling Botswana "this small island of highly cultured people."

Encouraged by the college's charismatic headmaster, Rubadiri began writing plays and poetry, and frequently acted in three productions a term—Caesar, Falstaff, and Othello among his roles. At Makerere University, Uganda, he continued to act and write, as he did later at King's College, Cambridge, where he read for the English Tripos. Arrested during the 1959 Nyasaland crisis (and jailed for a year in Bulawayo), on independence he became Malawi's first ambassador to the United States and the United Nations. An early Banda government crisis, however, drove him into long-term exile.

He entered exciting times when returning to Makerere in 1968. The literary journal *Transition*, under Rajat Neogy, was emulating the influence of West Africa's *Black Orpheus*; emerging writers included Robert Serumaga, Erisa Kironde, John Ruganda, Ali Mazrui, Okot p'Bitek, Okello Oculi, Richard Ntiru, and Paul Theroux. Rubadiri

and David Cook were editing *Poems from East Africa*, and in neighboring Kenya revolutionary syllabus change was being driven by Ngugi wa Thiong'o, Taban Lo Liyong, Henry Awuor Anyumba, and Philip Ochieng. President Idi Amin, however, brought sudden havoc to Makerere and the death of writers Pio Zirimu, Robert Serumaga, and Byron Kawadwa. Back in Malawi after Banda's downfall, Rubadiri is now vice chancellor of the national university.

No Bride Price (1967) was very much a pathbreaking novel, its main focus disenchantment with early independence leaders. But Rubadiri also wrote *Come to Tea*, a play that appeared in *New African*. Malawi's sole representative in Moore and Beier's pioneering *Modern Poetry from Africa* (1963), where "An African Thunderstorm" appeared, his "A Negro Labourer in Liverpool" and "Stanley Meets Mutesa" graced a later edition of the same collection. These poems were all significant as examples of internal African poetic influence beginning to supplant that of the West. Rubadiri's verse also appeared in *Black Orpheus*, *Transition*, and *Présence Africaine*. His collection *An African Thunderstorm and Other Poems* appeared in 2004.

Having returned to roots, Rubadiri is now an academic leader lionized by the young. In an Appreciation written for *Modern Stories from Malawi* (2003), edited by Sambalikagwa Mvona, he describes himself as a vice chancellor too poor to buy a newspaper every day but nevertheless feeling enriched by the new writing around him: "Each time I have attended writing workshops of the Malawi Writers Union at Lunzu I have been awakened by the freshness, enthusiasm and sheer burning interest that you could cut with a knife in that classroom. Having been isolated from my country for a good 30 years, I was isolated from the sources and energies that provoke the inspiration of Malawi artists."

Jack Mapanje, who calls him "the first and finest Malawian poet," dedicated to him "The Fish Eagles of Cape Maclear" in his anthology *Skipping Without Ropes* (1998). It celebrates the final homecoming:

> . . . the island's fish eagles sing
> Those familiar melodies of long ago.
>   My dear
> Uncle, welcome to the beach you
>   spent half
> Your life pining for

Further reading: Martin Banham, ed., *A History of Theatre in Africa* (Cambridge, 2004); Bernth Lindfors, *Kulankula: Interviews with Writers from Malawi and Lesotho* (Bayreuth, 1989); Alfred Msadala, "The Malawi Ambassador," *Destined for Great Things: Papers* (Blantyre, 1999); Adrian Roscoe, *Uhuru's Fire: African Literature East to South* (London, 1977).

Rungano, Kristina (b. 1963). Zimbabwean poet. Born in Zimbabwe, educated at Marindale Primary School and St John's High School, she studied for a British computer science degree before accepting a post with Harare's Scientific Computing Centre. She is the author of two verse collections, *Aloisa* and *A Storm Is Brewing* (1984).

Rungano's work has received warm critical comment. The work of her teens (its typical statement confidently concise) persuaded South Africa's Lewis Nkosi to write an introduction to *A Storm Is Brewing*. What Matthew Arnold would call a high seriousness characterizes the verse. It abjures trivia and its lyricism never descends into solipsism. The Malawian critic Mpalive-Hangson Msiska praises "the quiet majesty" of the writing: "Even when it treads in areas where direct experience might be called for there is a self-assurance, and an emotive as well as intellectual commitment which announce the arrival on the Zimbabwean literary scene of an exceptional talent." Imaginative

power is evident in Rungano's vivid scenes of a Liberation War in which she played no part and toward which she shows a nuanced blend of support for its cause, embarrassment at society's trite welcome for its heroes, and a pacifism she cultivates as central to the identity she is building:

> I'll never be subjected to a soldier's
>   ways;
> His ruthless servitude
> Nor kill another soldier who too has
>   his rights
> Inspired by some ambitious leader
> I'll never be conned into a military
>   force
> Nor accept that peace is maintained
>   by violence

Rungano typifies the artist who, while constantly wrestling with identity as it unfolds within time's shifting sociopolitical contexts and builds its moral core, avoids emotional self-indulgence, anchors herself in realism, and gazes out on the larger scene of humanity. Hence:

> My feeling for justice is unmovable
>   and true
> Every man deserves to be given a
>   chance
> I know God is colour-blind
> And money unimportant

For inner-life intensity she pays the price of loneliness and disconnection from family and society, though caring for these passionately. "My Best Friend," the typical statement of a section called "Exiled Self," begins "Never have I known such loneliness." Like many before her, she seeks solace, but never ultimate contentment, in the beauty of outdoors nature, in clouds and sky. Her existential solitude, though a mark of modern verse globally, stands out in poignant relief against a backcloth of African society traditionally communal and humanly embracing.

Further reading: Flora Veit-Wild, *Patterns of Poetry in Zimbabwe* (Gweru, 1988); Adrian Roscoe and Mpalive-Hangson Msiska, *The Quiet Chameleon: Modern Poetry from Central Africa* (London, 1992).

S

Sagonja, Roy (b. 1953). Malawian short-story writer and playwright. Born at Misesa Village, near Blantyre, he was educated in Malawi and at Britain's Wakefield District College. As of 2007 he was employed by the Ministry of Transport and Public Works. Keen to create a national reading culture, he is a prolific writer of Chichewa stories and plays for radio and the press and from 1995 to 1999 was General Secretary of the Malawi Writers Union. His publications in English include a short-story collection, *Night of Terror* (2001), and a long children's story, *Heroes Under Fire* (2002).

Sagonja's highly readable narratives portray not rural Malawi but an urban world of international business, top executives, luxury cars, posh hotels, and such attendant evils as AIDS, alcoholism, drug abuse, violence, and rape. A keen Seventh Day Adventist, he warns Malawi's rising middle class that sin and crime can never bring happiness. He comments interestingly on the post-Banda democratic order, calling it "this great romantic emancipation of the spirit," but notes how multiple parties have surfaced "like frogs from stinking swamps." Exploring the breakdown of traditional values and "new forces released from a Pandora's box" poses dilemmas. In his introduction to *Night of Terror* he writes, "I am caught between Elijah and the Prophets of Baal for interpreting society honestly. Should I support the organized lies of the group . . . earn a living as a peddler of literary opiates, or should I reveal the facts, stripped of their illusion?" The texts show that the second option is firmly chosen.

Saidi, William (b. 1937). Zimbabwean novelist and journalist. Born in Marondera, he grew up in the Salisbury township of Mbare and was schooled there and in Plumtree. University education was unavailable to him, so his literary interests in 1957 took him to journalism and reporting for the *African Daily News*. In 1963, in equal measure excited by Northern Rhodesia's dawning independence and depressed by Southern Rhodesia's slide toward UDI and guerilla war, he joined the *Central African Mail* in Zambia, where he published his first novel, *The Hanging* (1975), which examines squalid aspects of African politics. Other novels include *Day of the Baboons* (1980), *The Old Bricks Lives* (1988), *Gwebede's Wars* (1989), and *The Brothers of Chatima Road* (1990). His short stories have appeared internationally, most recently in *Writing Still: New Stories from Zimbabwe* (2003), edited by Irene Staunton. Zimbabwe's independence in 1980 drew him home as foreign editor for the Zimbabwe Newspapers group. He is currently editing *The Daily News on Sunday* and resisting a government assault on press freedom.

The Old Bricks Lives (its grammatically challenged title itself suggesting fracture) reads like a fictionalized autobiography based on life under the Central African Federation. This is no weakness. Saidi is preeminently qualified to write the classic account of life under the selfishly conceived Central African Federation, which, with London's approval, white settlers imposed on Southern and Northern Rhodesia and Nyasaland—and whose destruction Malawi's Hastings Banda always personally claimed. The book is another piece of the historiographic jigsaw writers are assembling to cure decades of enforced silence and deceit. Indeed, this task can be described in words Saidi himself uses of a journalist who embarks on a "mission of unmasking the mendacious." Federation targeting is pervasive. It is seen, for example, in a popular joke that "those who allowed federation to be rammed down their throats without fighting it were like the girl whose father forces her to marry a well-known village rapist because his father has the most cattle and the most land in the district"; and also in the novel's denouement, where Marudzanya tells the jailed Maskito that once he is free, "we make a baby" to celebrate the Federation's death.

Though white settlers would deny it, life in the Old Bricks settlement precisely mirrors South African reality in townships like Soweto, Alexandra, and Marabastad. Thus Saidi's narrative, with its legal monstrosities (hangings and death by police are almost ritualistic), babies in dustbins, prostitution, echoes the sad harmonies of South African Oswald Mtshali's verse or Es'kia Mphahlele's classic of slum life, *Down Second Avenue.* Nor should this surprise. British South African Police here are an umbilical link to South Africa, Rhodes, and his colonizing company. Southern Rhodesia brought its racism from the south. Its black citizens, in Saidi's memorable phrase, have all "tasted the vomit of rejection."

Hence, dignity in life and death becomes a motif. Its denial drives protagonist Maskito to attempt the castration of a "liberal" white missionary, who employs him, marries his sister Keriyana, but insults her honor by insisting she pose as a domestic for fear of scandalizing white neighbors. By contrast, one of the slum's oldest dwellers, Kazembe, is praised because "in the midst of squalor and despair, he had dared to live like minor royalty."

Like most modern African writing, the text celebrates a will to struggle and reach for light. Maskito loves his bookshop job,

seeing himself as a modern Raskolnikov (to this literary allusion add Swift, Wordsworth, Burns, Donne, Socrates, Melville, and Plato). Taking him toward the white world, this produces the relationship between his employer and a sister who, like other slum-dwellers, yearns to climb the ladder from native reserve and location squalor to the comfort of Salisbury's white suburbs. The violent results of moving toward a society felt to be collectively schizoid, however, suggest that this is not the way forward.

From downtrodden Old Bricks heroic lives emerge; also, however, an African politics based on class, with a certain Mr. Tigere's emphasis on "responsible" Africans providing a parallel temptation to selling out to the whites.

Samkange, Stanlake (1922–88). Zimbabwean novelist and historian. Born in Chipata to devout Methodist parents, he grew up in Bulawayo, where his father was a clergyman and keen nationalist. After attending Waddilove Institution, South Africa's Adams College, and Fort Hare University College (reading Honors English and history), he returned home in 1948 to teach and produce a blueprint for black education that was implemented at Nyatsime College in 1962. Samkange's Methodist background is important. The denomination privileges education (teacher is second only to preacher) and has strong credentials within the development of modern Western democracy. Methodism taught Samkange to use Christianity against colonial oppression and fired his love of fairness, justice, and truth. Its special contribution to Zimbabwean freedom was acknowledged when Ken Mew, principal of Harare's pioneering multiracial Ranche House College, received the Methodist World Peace Prize. Since Samkange's own views on racial partnership stirred little white interest, he left for the University of Indiana, receiving an M.S. in education (1958) and a Ph.D. in history (1968). He later taught at Fisk, Harvard, and Northeastern universities. His publications include *On Trial for My Country* (1966), *Origins of Rhodesia* (1968), *African Saga* (1971), *The Mourned One* (1975), *Year of the Uprising* (1978), *Hunhuism or Ubuntuism* (1980), *What Rhodes Really Said About Africans* (1982), *Among Them Yanks* (1985), and *On Trial for That UDI* (1986).

Intellectual rigor and imagination combine in Samkange's work. There is also polemical balance, and a descriptive clarity that arises from wide reading (early favorites were Shakespeare, Wordsworth, Tennyson, Dickens, Haggard, Buchan, and Shaw) and strong pedagogic impulse. His rather lonely status as a black historian made him a *vox populi* obliged to counter a white historiography that, at its worst, denied any African history anterior to colonialism. An infectious teacher, and early convert to the belief that most subjects are best taught by narrative, his blending of literature and history has become a widespread Central African practice.

On Trial for My Country (foreshadowing perhaps Mazrui's *The Trial of Christopher Okigbo* and Ngugi's and Mugo's *The Trial of Dedan Kimathi*) dramatically revisits Rhodesia's birth. An ideal text for black readers wondering how they were colonized, it was banned by settlers angry at seeing their vaunted rationality and judicial procedures turned against them. Before the bar of humanity, their forebears, and colonialism itself, were brought to account.

Selectively using oral tradition, Samkange employs mainly archive material for a cocktail of momentous event, characterization, psychological excavation, and emotion. The drama of relentless interrogation, forensic rhetoric, suspense, ideological conflict, international intrigue, gratuitous slaughter, even humor—they are

all here. An ancestor returns from the dead among the Matopos Hills (near Rhodes's grave) to narrate from the Hereafter the trial of two historical figures—Rhodes and Lobengula. The former appears before his clerical father in Bishop's Stortford parish church, England, the latter at the Great Indaba Tree Council of the Amandabele Nation. Lobengula must explain how he lost his kingdom; Rhodes how and why he seized it. Also cross-examined are colonizers like Frank Johnson, the Rev. C. D. Helm, the Rev. John S. Moffat, Charles Dunnell Rudd, Rochfort Maguire, Frederick Courteney Selous, and Dr. Leander Starr Jameson. The text asks if future generations will see themselves "indebted to Rhodes for a thousand years to come, as he once said, or will they curse him for that long?" As for Lobengula, "what will men think of him in a thousand years?" White treachery and deceit are admitted, so too Lobengula's cruelty to his own people (though not to whites), but the verdict is left tantalizingly open. Or, as Samkange's ancestral narrator says, it lies "in the bosom of the Spirits."

The Mourned One employs autobiographical detail and an actual 1930s trial and execution. Ndatshana, allegedly the author's kinsman and raised by whites, after suffering judicial mockery that shames Britain's colonial record, awaits execution for allegedly raping a white woman. His recollections document life since Rhodes: land seizure and population displacement, urban growth and rural decline, pass laws, job discrimination, tribal rivalry, missionaries, education hunger and ambivalence, and acquaintance with colonized neighbors in Northern Rhodesia and Nyasaland. Prominent are settler society's mind-numbing pettiness and obsessive materialism ("Yes, the white man has a God he has not told you about. That God is MONEY"), and wage scales that for the same driving job pay fifteen shillings to blacks, thirty pounds to coloreds, and eighty pounds to whites. Ancestral lore, though pervasive, never chokes the narrative; indeed, echoing *On Trial*, there are aesthetic gains from a judicious infusion of traditional rhetoric. The pedagogic drive also remains. Hence Samkange's closing words: "I trust that the mourned one's hope and wish that others may benefit from his experience and thoughts and be better able to understand 'this society, this culture, this civilisation' has been fulfilled."

The Year of the Uprising, on the 1896 anticolonial rebellion, though sometimes criticized for recycling *On Trial* material, allows a more dispassionate focus on this early response to whites—the opening chapter of a liberation process he felt professionally obliged to chronicle. *Among Them Yanks*, however, might be seen as part of a genre begun by Nigeria's John Pepper Clark with his *America, Their America*; while *On Trial for That UDI*, repeating his first novel's formula, indicts British Prime Minister Harold Wilson for his maladroit handling of Rhodesia's Unilateral Declaration of Independence and of Rhodesian leader Ian Smith, whom he would not use force to remove.

Samkange returned to Rhodes with his slender *What Rhodes Really Said About Africans*. He teaches compatriots a basic truth by tracing Rhodesian practice to whatever Rhodes legislated for in the Cape Colony. There, clearly, lay the basis for "native policy across the Limpopo." Pedagogy and historiography again combine in *African Saga: A Brief Introduction to African History*—popular enough to become a prescribed text in over eighty American colleges and universities. His *Origins of Rhodesia* won the Herskovits Award of the African Studies Association in 1970. *Hunhuism or Ubuntuism* (written with his wife Tommie-Marie) sought to identify, in a season of multiplying African ideologies, a political philoso-

phy for the new Zimbabwe. Zambia had its Humanism, Tanzania its African Socialism, and Kenya its *Harambee* self-help. With unintended irony, Samkange suggested Hunhuism, a radical counter to capitalist individualism but identical to the *Ubuntu* free South Africa espoused in 1994.

Further reading: Rino Zhuwarara, *Introduction to Zimbabwean Literature in English* (Harare, 2001); Eugene Benson and L. W. Connolly, eds., *Encyclopaedia of Post-Colonial Literatures* (London, 1994).

Samupindi, Charles (b. 1961). Zimbabwean novelist. Born in Mutare, he attended Sakubva Secondary School and Hartzell High School before studies at the University of Zimbabwe. After a civil service spell in the Ministry of Justice, he left in 1990 to become a subeditor on the *Herald* newspaper. His Mutare upbringing near the Mozambique border gave him both a ringside view of the guerilla war waged there against the settler regime and the core for his best-known work, *Pawns* (1992).

This is a novel of imaginative power. Complex terrain is tackled with energy and technical assurance and without recourse to moral naiveté. The publication date suggests there has been time to assess the Liberation War with detachment. Samupindi revisits its brutality (more than thirty thousand slain, countless numbers disabled for life), but also its causes, political complexity, and devastating damage to black and white lives, to race relations, and to psychological health—all viewed largely from one character's perspective. The book operates on diverse levels: the international level of Britain's Foreign Office and independence talks at Lancaster House; the level of relationships with Zambia's Kaunda, Tanzania's Nyerere, and Mozambique's Machel; the more local level of servant and employer relationships in white and black houses; and the level of peasant relationships with leaders such as Mugabe, Nkomo, and Tongagara. It further examines relationships between the educated and uneducated drawn together to fight in the bush, and between Marxist-Leninist ideologues and those simply cherishing a burning sense of injustice. Thus the scenario—large-scale tragedy played out against a backdrop of dying colonialism—is national and international, yet also local, personal, and private. While London talks loftily to Lusaka and Dar es Salaam, Robert Mugabe is starving in the Mozambican bush wearing a pair of blue tennis shoes. Multilateral complexity rules out the simplistic. And there are no trumpets and banners.

Central African writing moves once more into history. The novel, aimed essentially at the war's damage to individual Zimbabweans, documents with scholarly precision the years of struggle, major events, and actors: Mugabe and Nkomo, for example, Muzorewa, Sithole, Chitepo, Machel, Nyerere, Tongagara, Clutton-Brock, Walls, Sister Mary Aquina—and of course Prime Minister Smith himself, whose inability to foresee the logical result of his 1965 UDI (a task comfortably within the mental capacity of most primary school pupils) directly caused more than thirty thousand needless deaths. The blizzard of acronyms—ZANU, ZAPU, ZIPRA, ZANLA—only emphasized the war's early confusion (Mugabe ignored by Frelimo allies; a thousand of his people arrested by friendly Kaunda; "guerilla war within guerilla war"; tribalism; rape). It was a miracle there was any success at all.

Avoidance of the simplistic extends to textual structure. Linear chronology is reversed. For suspense and narrative pace, prose diary entries, inner dialogue, and media reports suddenly shift into verse. Characters (Fangs for example) can appear within the intimacy of first-person narration or in a more objective mode. Such fragmentation suggests both authorial skill

and the brokenness of war. Nor does Samupindi fight shy of irony and paradox. Hence the tension between the war as a grand communal enterprise and the haunted individualism it generates; hence, too, a white common foe employing black professional soldiers, or preaching equality in the face of the gulf between soldiers and political leaders. The supreme irony is the hero's reward a grateful nation gives to Fangs: life in the alleys and garbage bins of Harare, pursued like a common criminal and hauled into court as a vagabond. Such ironies are not lost on a Samupindi who undoubtedly recalls the fate of Kenya's Mau Mau freedom fighters from the pages of Ngugi, Kibera, and Kahiga. As Mugabe himself puts it in the text, "Waste, after all, is an inevitable adjunct of life."

Further reading: Rino Zhuwarara, *Introduction to Zimbabwean Literature in English* (Harare, 2001).

Seyaseya, Hopewell (b. 1952). Zimbabwean poet. Born in Kadoma, after schooling in different parts of the country, he went to the University of Zimbabwe. In 1973 he was expelled after a student demonstration and left the country along with fellow writers Stanley Nyamfukudza and Dambudzo Marechera, among others. Following a period in Botswana, he studied town planning at the University of Auckland, New Zealand, after which, in 1977, he worked for two years in the country's capital, Wellington. He returned home in 1979 to become a town planner in Harare.

A deeply sensitive man, passionate about improving the plight of women and children, he told Flora Veit-Wild in 1988 that loneliness in New Zealand started him writing ("I didn't find the people there very friendly. They keep to themselves. So I felt I was living in a land of no love." Nowadays, he said, poetry is merely "something I do on a part-time basis." He feels only tenuously

connected to traditional Zimbabwean life—
his paternal roots lying anyway in
Mozambique—but his brother Daniel died
for Zimbabwean freedom, a loss deeply
marking his inner life and verse. He says
frankly, "I am a very, very reserved person.
I think I am living in a sort of cocoon."
Wide reading has brought influence from,
among others, Pablo Neruda and Congo-
Brazzaville's Tchicaya U'Tamsi. His verse
has been published in the journals *Two
Tone* and *Moto Magazine* and in the an-
thology *And Now the Poets Speak: Poems
Inspired by the Struggle for Zimbabwe*
(1981), edited by Muderei Kadhani and
Musaemura Zimunya. He and Albert
Chimedza published the important collec-
tion *Counterpoints* (1984), an exercise in
distinct yet complementary styles—Seyas-
eya's deeply meditative, soft-spoken, hesi-
tant, at times abstract; Chimedza's demotic,
loud, and swashbuckling.

Seyaseya's contributions are called
"Hereafter" and arise from thoughts on his
deceased brother. The verse is entirely ele-
giac, the poet pondering on an afterlife in
which, he hopes, "there is a better world."
The title poem's transcendent strain, as he
seeks his brother's unmarked grave, can
reduce image concreteness—meditation,
world-weariness, and mystery being unpro-
ductive of earthbound solidity:

My brother's unmarked grave
Only takes me to a dream and I get
    no closer to him
This is my first death, and home-
    wards I turn
To the whims of life and the certain
    death of man.

Solitude and moroseness ("I long to re-
tire for the burden / Is heavy even for Atlas,
/ And no Simons of Africa will take the
load off me") are integral. More visual, but
equally melancholy, is "The Fourth of
June," which begins:

Today I will sit by the window
As children recite their poetry
To a hushed world. I will measure
The passage of time by the shadow
Cast by the mango tree in the
    garden.

The speaker goes on to say:

My eyes will remain closed as
The Ethiopian and Vietnamese
    children
Strum their ribs singing the final
    melody
Before curtains fall, ending their
    brief stay.

Though on occasion core material seems
incompletely realized, "Exile" succeeds
well. But again loneliness and bereavement
dominate the speaker's feeling of existen-
tial detachment:

It is history of mankind
That I am an exile, befriended to my
    shadow.
I will dance if I am asked to, but no
    one does
I will laugh if I am asked to, but no
    one does
My stories, my jokes fall to the ears
    of my shadow.

Further reading: Flora Veit-Wild, *Pat-
terns of Poetry in Zimbabwe* (Gweru, 1988).

Sibenke, Ben (b. 1945). Zimbabwean drama-
tist. Born in the Gweru area, and educated at
Cyrene Mission and Mutare Teachers' Col-
lege, he has contributed seminally to mod-
ern Zimbabwean theater. As independence
dawned he strove to promote landmark cul-
tural initiatives—the Mashonaland Art,
Drama and Cultural Association (1978) and
the People's Theatre Company (1982) are key
examples. A theater all-rounder, he contin-
ues to make his writing, directing and act-
ing skills (each of them award winners)

available to the National Theatre Organization. Like other African dramatists, he is also alert to modern media's rich communicative potential: hence work for radio, and for television, where, for example, his *Dr. Manzuma and the Vipers* appeared. That his first published play, *My Uncle Grey Bhonzo* (1982), was translated from a 1974 Shona version suggests that, as with Kenya's Ngugi wa Thiong'o, he feels acutely the vernacular's strengths over English for direct and immediate communication with his people. Sibenke's is a valuable comic voice within Zimbabwean drama as postcolonial malaise deepens. As with Ngugi, it will be interesting to see what linguistic choices he makes in the years ahead.

Further reading: Martin Banham, ed., *A History of Theatre in Africa* (Cambridge, 2004); Douglas Killam and Ruth Rowe, eds., *The Companion to African Literatures* (Oxford, 2000).

Simoko, Patu (b. ca. 1951). Zambian poet and journalist. He was born in Zambia's Petauke district. Secondary schooling in Sinda and Kabwe preceded journalism studies at Lusaka's Evelyn Hone College. Work followed with the *Zambia Daily Mail*, the *Times of Zambia*, Kenya's *East African Standard*, and Tanzania's *Daily News*. He later returned to Evelyn Hone to teach. He is best known for his verse collection *Africa Is Made of Clay* (1974).

Some poems collected here had already appeared in *New Writing from Zambia*; in Andrew Horn's Radio Zambia program *New Writing*; in Edward Blishen's BBC program *The Writers Club*; in *The Beacon*, an Evelyn Hone College newspaper; and in the house bulletin of the Swedish Development Authority, Zambia. The chronology of composition, however, is unclear.

Simoko has an intuitive feel for metaphor and wordplay: "Africa is the storm breaking her own pots," "how many faces did I see in the mirror of your dawn?" "proud blacks and the beautifools," "what i'm told by heavenseavesdroppers," "the books they read at school / were just extra legs / to flee from the village." A satiric cast of mind delights in irony, especially around freedom's disenchantment. The opening poem ("did we laugh or did we cry?") mocks those who had promised "schools in their minds," "hospitals on their tongues," and "tarred roads on their feet," and ends with three bleak words: "nothing has changed." Reflecting Simoko's international experience, the collection's geography reaches to Kenya, Tanzania and beyond. Hence such satiric targets as Kenyatta's corrupt post-Uhuru government and, more lightly, Nyerere's Tanzania.

A curious feature is the text's obsession with prostitutes and brothels—whether in Lusaka, Kinshasa, Nairobi, Dar es Salaam, India or Europe—and a resulting moral ambivalence. Carnal delight in this pre-AIDS publication allows scarcely a passing glance at the sex trade's degradation, material desperation, and disease implications. The poem "still i wondered" airily speculates on whether some or all of the speaker's encounters have produced babies and includes the throwaway remark, "oh / other people will watch my bastards grow." It is rare to find African verse quite so glamorizing of the harlot's world, so fixated on "thighs," or so ready to devote a whole poem to copulation, the word itself recurring thirteen times. The speaker certainly loves his ladies; but harlots outnumbering village wife-and-mother reference by about twenty to one is, to say the least, unusual African poetic practice. *Africa Is Made of Clay*, however, speaks volumes for freedom of expression in Kenneth Kaunda's Zambia; publication next door in Banda's Malawi would have been unthinkable.

There is ambivalence elsewhere. When the verse (rarely) excludes sexual adventure, it can switch, unconvincingly, into a faintly negritudist mood, yearning for abandoned rural simplicities. The speaker in "whisper of the eating son" assures his mother "that soon I must return / to the black thighs that made me white." Such nostalgia stirs faint echoes of Uganda's Okot p'Bitek, while occasional anticolonialism recalls Senegal's David Diop and the prodigal confessional mode of Nigeria's Christopher Okigbo.

Narrative viewpoint does not vary. If Simoko is not speaking *in propria persona*, then the speaker he creates has undergone the bulk of the volume's recorded experiences. No female voice is heard.

Sinyangwe, Binwell (b. 1956). Zambian novelist. Born into Zambia's Lungu people, Sinyangwe received an M.S. from Romania's Academy of Economic Studies in 1983. After government work promoting small businesses, he now manages a private company. By 1992 he had completed five novels, two of which have seen publication: *Quills of Desire* (1993) and *A Cowrie of Hope* (2000).

Quills of Desire ranks beside the first novels of Achebe, Laye, Oyono, and Ngugi. In particular, it resembles in some ways Achebe's *Things Fall Apart* (among its protagonist's favorite reading), but bears a distinctive Sinyangwe stamp. Occasionally school-life minutiae drown the narrative, but this simply highlights the passion for education lying at the novel's core. Far from the arrested adolescence around school that has characterized much British life and literature since *Tom Brown's Schooldays,* here it is firmly identified with paths from grinding poverty:

Wiza's dream was stark and clear. It was about education—a good education. . . . In today's world, education was everything. A good education meant integrity, employment,

dignity, and it meant material wealth. Without it one was nothing; one was as good as dead.

Such individualist thinking, inimical to old Africa, draws us into Wiza's tragic struggle. Rivalry cuts short his school career and threatens the chance of further studies; but his vision of academic status, solid income, and marriage to a fellow graduate (with at least a B.S.) will not dissolve—not even during unavoidable hand-to-mouth work in the slums of Lusaka. Few contemporary texts match the psychological angst of Wiza trapped between his academic ambition and parental plans for his marrying a village girl, Gelina. Loath equally to disappoint his family and make a marriage destructive of his dream ("He saw himself as he would be the following morning, standing next to an awkwardly spruced-up Gelina—all crude castor oil and beads before a crowd of jubilant villagers"), he performs the required nuptial rites, and then hangs himself.

Apart from thematic voltage and diverse characterization, stylistic strengths abound. Tonal and rhythmic sensitivity, gnomic flair, and a gift for telling detail, underpin a prose whose typical statement rises with expectation and falls to closure. Hence Wiza's reflection on the hell of Lusaka:

He had become enmeshed in the octopus limbs of the town, nursing a Herculean load of guilt in his soul. Walking the streets; scratching a living single-handed in the squalor of the world of the deprived . . . two years had seemed a decade, a tortuous and devastating decade, an eternity of Satan's furnace that had charred him from gold to charcoal, from the shimmering ore of intellectual potency to a deathly dross of intellectual inertia. He was deeply pained and shamed by it.

The cameo portrayal of Wiza's school enemy—"He was small, dark, and arrogantly erect; an uncomely little peasant with a confident display of self-importance and authority" counterpoints an arcadian rendering of village life: "The rain gone, the Chilumbeni homestead would slumber quietly beneath a coverlet of mist, wet and gloom. Then a bright resolute sun would return to the sky. The clouds would pass away, and the world would be bright again." There is memorable simile: "She is as quiet as water in a well." "He looked as serious as a man digging a grave." On Wiza finally cornered we read: "His eyes were red and fiery, the eyes of a trapped rat dying in a hole choked with smoke and guarded by a cat."

Wiza's father's assessment of modern schooling is a model of traditional African discourse. His overture reminds us that "when an elder does a dance there are aspects of it that the eyes of the young ones cannot see." He continues:

> Experience and the winds of caution from ancestral spirits have told us that you must marry now when your blood has started boiling with the whims and errors of early adulthood: that you must marry a girl like Gelina—someone with whom you can build a home rich in traditional wisdom, a home with roots. Not a marriage like the jokes of marriages you see in the towns and their spineless weddings, expensive and colorful for nothing. . . . Marry, my son, and avoid calamity. The world has teeth.

The finale gets skilful orchestration. While family members wallow in the blameless joy of a village wedding, Wiza silently drowns in end-of-the-world misery: "His mind was far away, staring into a dark void in mute desperation for a way to save himself from the fangs between which he was about to find himself resting."

A Cowrie of Hope appeared in 2000. Zambia's nine preceding years had been traumatic. Copper wealth disappeared with collapsing commodity prices. The IMF imposed a crippling Structural Adjustment Program. Kaunda's government fell. HIV-AIDS arrived, like some mediaeval plague, to compound economic disaster. More personally, Sinyangwe's young wife Grace died, the causes unstated.

Education dominates once more (impoverished widow Nasula must find money for her daughter's secondary schooling) but is now contextualized by Zambia's decade of devastation. Poverty, disease, and drought have savaged the family-based humanism Kaunda had preached in his *Zambia Shall Be Free* and *A Humanist in Africa*. Kinship bonds rot. In a patriarchal society where women now feel less valued than ever, destitute Nasula is abandoned by her in-laws, her child Sula now her only cowrie of hope. Secondary schooling, she is sure, will bring a life of dignity and security independent of men. Her own bad marriage to a convicted thief, shot dead by the police, had "awakened her to the indignities and injustices of a woman who could only put her life in the hands of a man." Those years "had turned her into a stream in which to wash and kill the stink of . . . humanity. . . . They had made her look like a non-human, a doll without thoughts or feelings of her own."

Pain metaphor is relentless: "Nasula was poverty, she was loneliness and aloneness. Suffering was her life. She wore it like a skin. . . . She was the gods' plant growing on poor soils without tendrils." As the narrative repeatedly stresses, "These were the nineties. . . . They were lean years. They were the years of each person for himself. . . . No, they were not years. They were the evil breath of a world turned upon itself." They were also the years when "the new disease of the world decided to sit down on a stool by the riverside and fish people like *cisense*." Even political change only delivered gloom: "You bring new people in government and hope the sky will open and spill honey on the earth; instead a dryness and a stubborn disease clothe it in harshness and blood."

Such is Sinyangwe's compelling imagery of modern poverty and sickness, despair, and the spiritual exhaustion of individuals determined, against impossible odds, to survive. Nasula's in-laws' once-profitable farm is destroyed by AIDS, "the new, unmentionable disease of the world that came of the taste of flesh, the one that made you thin before taking you, the disease of today." In chapters of churning anxiety, Nasula's hope diminishes to a single sack of beans, carried hundreds of miles to Lusaka, and then stolen by a city crook. A rare honest policeman saves the day. A sale is secured. Sula enters St. Theresa's School after all and won't end up on Lusaka's rubbish heaps, a prey to AIDS-infected men.

In 1992 the economist Allast Mwanza published a critique of the financial strictures that the IMF and World Bank imposed on Zambia. It is called *The Structural Adjustment Programme in Zambia: Lessons from Experience*. Taken together with *Cowrie of Hope*, no better picture of this decade of Zambian misery exists.

Sinyiza, Friday (b. 1972). Zambian novelist. He was born in Milango. His primary schooling at Nangongwe in Kafue preceded secondary education at Naboye and studies in English as a foreign language. After working in sales for Multimedia Zambia he founded Lome Publishers, which provided the ideal commercial background for a writer aiming at a popular audience. A humble man, with no pretension to producing laurelled literature, Sinyiza is delighted simply to be writing, and in his novel *True Love Is Scarce* (2001)

he acknowledges an important list of supporters. They include Susan Hope, Chapoloko Chitabanta, and Basil Mbewe, directors of Zambia's National Arts Council; Loveness Mbisi, head of languages at Naboye High School; Ray Munamwimbu, publishing manager of Zambia's Educational Publishing House; Mrs. Chibalange, inspector of schools; John Nsama, who lent the author his computer; and Mirriam Namukonda, his wife, for kindly, as he puts it, "sacrificing her image to be used on the cover."

This is not the rural Zambia of Sinyangwe or Miti. It is urban and suburban Lusaka and the Copper Belt—a world of cell phones, fridges, computers, counseling services, and television. But it repeats the focus of writers on education and the struggle to fund it ("Marriage can end at any time, but education is a life time investment"). At secondary school, devoutly Christian Ivy reforms Max, a beer-and-dagga youth, but spurns sex with him. When he is killed in a road accident, temptation comes from Kelvin, a rich Oxbridge engineer. But not even his dizzying cocktail of education, sex, and wealth (just when she urgently needs more funds for her nurse training) will tempt Ivy into a premarital relationship. A candidate much admired by Ivy's mother, Kelvin "lacked the patience to wait until they were married." Worse, he totally forfeits his chances by making Ivy's friend pregnant and has to marry her. But Ivy's heroic chastity is rewarded by a happy marriage to Peter, whom she nurses through a malaria crisis, and who secures employment as an accountant and "a big name house in the high cost area." Virtue is indeed rewarded.

True Love Is Scarce is popular literature in the style of Kenya's David Maillu, Malawi's Aubrey Kalitera, Nigeria's Cyprian Ekwensi, and the Onitsha Market writers.

Its significance should not be underrated, however, any more than the dimensions of the AIDS pandemic it seeks to address. Literature's social and moral role is writ large here within an African context. If characterization surrenders some depth, and the prose some luster, Sinyiza gives the central message gimlet-eyed focus: Zambians wanting a long life in a happy marriage must shape their sexual behavior accordingly. Bluntly, this means premarital abstinence and marital fidelity. Nothing else will do. The happy example of Ivy Bwalya, bright light within the encircling gloom, who resists temptation and lives to tell the tale, shows young readers what is possible.

The novel's focus on AIDS denies space to a sociopolitical context, beyond cursory allusion to Zambia's dire economy and unemployment rate. Colonial and postcolonial history and their possible role in the AIDS problem do not arise for investigation.

Sinyiza builds suspense (will Ivy, as with Richardson's Pamela, yield to temptation?) and his moral message is relentless. That its jacket says that it is "Approved by the Ministry of Education for use as a novel for Literature in English for Grades 10 to 12" shows that the author's commercial concern and moral commitment, like his Ivy and Peter, are very happily married.

Sithole, Ndabaningi (1920–2000). Zimbabwean novelist and political writer. He was born in Nyamanandhlovu. Schooling begun in 1932 was abandoned within a year for domestic work. But in 1935 he entered the Methodists' Dadya School, run by the New Zealander Garfield Todd, who later became a progressive Rhodesian prime minister. Extramural B.A. studies with the University of South Africa preceded theological training at America's Andover-Newton Theological College, Massachusetts (1953–56). Back home as a school principal,

he published *African Nationalism* (1959) and joined the new National Democratic Party. In 1961 he helped to form the Zimbabwe African People's Union, but when it was banned he moved to Tanzania to begin radio broadcasts. In 1963, he was home again, founding the Zimbabwe African National Union. Before Prime Minister Smith declared his Unilateral Declaration of Independence on November 11, 1965, he effectively jailed Sithole for a decade, though continuing to use him for sensitive negotiations with liberation leaders. In 1969, Sithole was accused of plotting to assassinate Smith, a charge, given Sithole's Gandhian credentials, both absurd and cruel.

Though he helped with the transfer of power to the interim state of Zimbabwe-Rhodesia (1978–79), the new entity's presidency went to coreligionist Bishop Abel Muzorewa. As a ZANU member of parliament, he was then defeated in the election of 1982 and went into exile in America. After returning home in 1992, he won another parliamentary seat in 1995. But 1997 brought yet another assassination charge—this time in respect of Robert Mugabe. He died in 2000 undergoing medical treatment in Philadelphia. His denial of burial in Zimbabwe's Heroes Acre prompted criticism that Mugabe's government was kinder to former white foes than to black comrades.

Integrity, moral courage, and single-mindedness marked Sithole's career and writing. Incarceration produced *Obed Mutezo of Zimbabwe* (1970), *The Polygamist* (1972), and a flood of morale-boosting correspondence smuggled to family and friends, published as *Letters from Salisbury Prison* (1976). His writing career had begun earlier with *Busi*, serialized in *African Parade* (1959–61), *African Nationalism* (1959), and *Roots of a Revolution: Scenes from Zimbabwe's Struggle* (1977). *Frelimo Militant* also appeared in 1977 and *In Defence of the*

Rhodesian Constitutional Agreement in 1978. Eminently readable prose draws on a gift for the figurative, wide reading in English literature, narrative verve learnt from his grandmother, pungent biblical utterance, and the echoing power of traditional oratory.

African Nationalism, appearing during early continental decolonization (only Tunisia, Morocco, and Ghana were then free), examines colonialism per se. It even risks a chapter on its positive role (along with Christianity it created African nationalism) and offers a consumer's guide to its diverse brands. The Portuguese thought God mistaken in making Africans African so their *civilizado* policy sought to correct that error. The "glass house" of French assimilation and the Belgian *évolué* system ("We dominate to serve") amounted to the same thing, while Afrikaner *baaskap* sought merely to create underdogs. North American revolts, he argues, taught the British to tolerate self-government, as in New Zealand, Australia, Canada, and South Africa, though, principally for business reasons, they wanted to hold on to these territories as long as possible. Sithole has fun pinpointing colonialism's screaming paradoxes, as in "When the British start arresting, full independence is around the corner." To replace white supremacy in Rhodesia, Sithole urges Christians to offer a philosophy that celebrates the universal over the particular, unites rather than divides, and emphasizes a common humanity.

Obed Mutezo of Zimbabwe (called *Obed Mutezo: The Mudzimu Christian Nationalist* in Sithole's *Letters from Salisbury Prison*) was smuggled to publishers in Nairobi. Kaunda wrote a foreword and historian Terence Ranger an introduction. As biography and anticolonial statement for a world audience, it joins the tradition of Kaunda's *Zambia Shall Be Free*, Kenyatta's *Facing Mount Kenya*, Awolowo's *Path to Nigerian Freedom*, Luthuli's *Let My People Go*, and Alhaji Sir Ahmadu Bello's *My Life*. Coolly distilling core elements in the Rhodesian Front's so-called civilization, it shows the colonized cherishing those values more than the colonizer. Settler case fault lines are deftly exposed—its lack of Christian love of neighbor, for example, of fair play, or concern for the underdog. Mutezo's case in particular demonstrates how the local version of British justice, overseen by Mr. Lardner-Burke, is a sham in which police act as judges immediately on arrest, beat and torture suspects before court appearance, and even after acquittal.

The brutal treatment of Mutezo, a devout Methodist of Blakeian innocence, provides the perfect model of bullying colonial giant terrorizing harmless underdog. But interrogation shows him morally dwarfing his police and settler tormentors in the Melsetter area, where he was ZANU's local organizer. For Sithole he is an African nationalist with a rock-solid faith in change based on Christianity, dreams, and contact with the ancestral spirits, *midzimu*.

Ranger remarks that Afrikaner settlers, in Mutezo's area in particular, seeking only cheap labor, saw missionaries as subversive. Indeed, it was missionary teaching that gave Mutezo his formidable inner strength, a fact that draws from Sithole one of his strongest comments on missionary achievements:

It is to the credit of the Christian Church in Southern Rhodesia that it pioneered, initiated and piloted African education which has resulted in the revolution of the African mental outlook without which the African in Rhodesia would have found it difficult to cope with the fast-changing conditions of the Africa of the latter half of the twentieth century. It was the Christian church that first introduced literacy which was to give birth to the

African nationalists, medical doctors, advocates, businessmen, journalists and graduates.

He adds,

uplifting Christian ideas fell upon the souls of those who were denied citizenship in the land of their birth as cool water upon their parched and burning souls.... The political set-up treated the African as if he counted for nothing, but the church, in spite of its many shortcomings, treated the African as counting for something.... In short the church helped that inner person of the African which puts up protracted resistance in the face of almost insurmountable difficulties.

Dismissing the childish settler mantra that all nationalists were communists, Ranger remarks that Mutezo knew and cared nothing for American capitalism or Chinese communism. He had learned of the triumphs of African nationalism elsewhere, but in him it sprang from his own grievances, his own hopes, his own past, his own present.

The Polygamist, another prison text, prompts audience questions. Is it personal therapy? A chance for mental spring-cleaning? Is it for an overseas audience—non-Rhodesian, non-Ndebele, non-Shona? A serious document, it can sometimes read like an extended Ndebele apologia, yet Sithole is Ndau and not Ndebele. Its best passages, however, are again counterstatements to the inhumanity of white settlers. They mainly take the form of affectionate accounts of tribal experience—the psychology of polygamous households, the minutiae of traditional court procedure, the wholesome beer-drinking tradition (degraded now by urban life), strategies to avoid confrontation (one must "walk like a chameleon"), the

hymning of cattle, and the radiant Ndebele dictum that "to be able to live well with other people is the greatest thing in life." Polygamy, however, is censured, because women are against it. So here is Christianity. The book urges unity in face of white oppression. Healed internal Ndebele splits, and between families over marriage, become a symbolic call for reconciliation at the national level between Ndebeles and Shonas.

Clyde Sanger, the veteran Canadian journalist, edited *Letters from Salisbury Prison* and the author himself provided an introduction. The text conjures the image of a coolly determined Sithole, president of ZANU, living like some brilliant spider along his lines, nocturnally penning uplift to family or freedom fighters in Lusaka and finger-wagging epistles to Harold Wilson, Edward Heath, and Lord Douglas-Home in London. For the directors of Nairobi's Transafrica Publishers, Ngumbu Njururi and John Nottingham (the latter coauthor of the seminal *Myth of Mau Mau*, an early promoter of East African literature, and of the journal *Busara*), Sithole's letters were a coup.

Roots of a Revolution: Scenes from Zimbabwe's Struggle was also smuggled from prison. Though appearing in 1977, the dedication is dated 1973. Contemporary with the bush war, for security reasons, however, the struggle is scarcely mentioned. Hence, too, its fictionalized contents. Key African and white characters reflect their concerns and the book also captures embarrassment about the country's continuing colonial status—Zimbabweans having failed to win what Zambian and Malawian neighbors won a decade earlier. Dr. John Moyo, addressing a forest gathering, roars: "We've become Africa's laughing-stock. We've become the world's laughing-stock. And we deserve it." Like their black South African contemporaries, the youth are itching to take over the struggle from their parents. Dispossession—of pretty much everything—rings through endlessly, together with conditions for peaceful co-existence long fulfilled by blacks but ignored by whites. It reminds us of Achebe's exasperation about being for too long clapped in the dock to plead before ruffians and "frauds masquerading as disinterested judges." "We are our own liberators" is Sithole's ultimate message.

Smith, Ian Douglas (1919). Prime minister of Rhodesia (1964–79). Born in Selukwe, he was a World War II fighter pilot (a fact used sentimentally in kith-and-kin propaganda during the confrontation with Britain over the Unilateral Declaration of Independence after 1965). Elected to the Southern Rhodesian Assembly in 1948, in 1962, sensing waning white resolve against black freedom, he founded the hard-line Rhodesian Front. His style and policies, though isolationist (Africa had widely decolonized, Macmillan had already made his winds of change speech), impressed fellow settlers, who made him prime minister in 1964. In 1965, while Britain was demanding extended political rights for blacks, Smith, to a fanfare of Beethoven's Ninth Symphony, phraseology from America's independence manifesto, claims about Christian civilization and blacks not ruling for a thousand years, issued his infamous Unilateral Declaration of Independence. The resulting war killed more than thirty thousand people, the overwhelming majority black, and delayed independence until 1980. Smith cut ties with Britain and, with help from self-interested Western allies and (decreasingly) South Africa, managed to circumvent sanctions and embargos. Interminable attempts at compromise (talks on HMS *Fearless* and *Tiger*, the Pearce Commission, and so on) found Smith skillfully deflecting anything suggesting black rule. In 1978, however,

worn down by war, sanctions, and international pressure, he finally agreed to include blacks in government and grant full franchise. Following elections in 1979 he left office as prime minister and handed power to Robert Mugabe. Unlike many supporters, who swiftly left for South Africa, Europe, Canada, Australia, and New Zealand, Smith stayed on, keeping his parliamentary seat until 1987. The monumental suffering he had caused (the forgiveness victims showed him anticipated a similar response via post-apartheid South Africa's Truth and Reconciliation Commission) is the theme of much Zimbabwean writing. In his memoir *The Great Betrayal* (1997), Smith denied that UDI had made the guerilla war inevitable and blamed mainly apartheid South Africa, rather than Britain, for destroying his dream of an enduring white Rhodesia.

Further reading: Peter Joyce, *Anatomy of a Rebel—Smith of Rhodesia* (Harare, 1974); Lawrence Vambe, *From Rhodesia to Zimbabwe* (London, 1976); Matthew White, *Smith of Rhodesia* (Cape Town, 1978).

Smith, Wilbur (b. 1933). Zambian-born novelist. On the family's 25,000-acre cattle ranch, his father taught him to love guns and his mother books, especially the standard fare for British children at that time: Captain W. E. Johns's Biggles stories, Ryder Haggard, John Buchan, and Richmal Crompton. A prep-school English teacher encouraged his reading (an extraordinary seven books a week) and once gave him as a writing prize Somerset Maugham's *Introduction to Modern English Literature*. Undergraduate study at South Africa's Rhodes University preceded training in accountancy, whose dullness he countered by writing his first story on tax office stationery, sending it to *Argosy*, and receiving seventy pounds. Thus began a career of astonishing productivity—some thirty-one novels written between 1964 (*When the Lion Feeds*) and 2004 (*The Triumph of the Sun*) with sometimes two published a year. They have been translated into twenty-six foreign languages and nine have become films.

Smith divides his work into four categories: The Ballantyne novels, the Courtney Novels, the Egyptian novels, and the Stand-alone novels. Early works include *The Dark of the Sun* (1968), *Shout at the Devil* (1968), *Gold Mine* (1972), *The Diamond Hunters* (1973), *The Sunbird* (1974), *Eagle in the Sky* (1975), *Cry Wolf* (1976), and *The Eye of the Tiger* (1976). Later work includes *A Time to Die* (1990), *Elephant Song* (1992), *River God* (1993), *The Seventh Scroll* (1995), *Birds of Prey* (1997), *Monsoon* (1999), *Warlock* (2001), *Blue Horizon* (2003), and *The Triumph of the Sun* (2004). No other writer in English has so extensively mined personal experience to satisfy the global hunger for stories about Africa.

To understand Smith's work, one must recall the Central Africa he was born into: solidly colonial with scarcely a hint of change. Indeed, the settlers of his youth would probably have shared the conviction expressed in 1965 by Southern Rhodesia's Ian Smith when he said that Africans would not rule for a thousand years. The world of privilege and comfort white society had arranged for itself seemed impregnable. Its children went to all-white primary schools; proceeded to exclusive all-white secondary schools (like Southern Rhodesia's Peterhouse and South Africa's Michaelhouse); and then went on to all-white South African universities such as Rhodes, where white children from over the Limpopo enjoyed a guaranteed quota. The empire, with its assumptions about progress, superiority, and privilege, would rarely be questioned. Its power and glam-

our were admired, its rightness felt in the bones, its core benevolence merely self-evident. If empire involved hard work (beyond laboring, of course) it was also pregnant with opportunity, with adventure, with fun. Life with servants on vast coffee or tea estates, with views over game-filled plains to distant mountains, was slightly different from, say, life in a British two-bedroom terraced house in Bradford with neither indoor toilet nor bathroom. As for racial attitudes (vividly recalled in Kaunda's *Zambia Shall Be Free*), these, if not actually born in apartheid South Africa, drew sustenance from there and permeated all areas of governance, education, social and commercial life. It is unsurprising, therefore, that while Smith can appreciate the predatory instincts of those who created the colonial Rhodesias and Nyasaland, he should find British imperial Africa an inexhaustible mine of material for his fiction: its powerful figures like Kitchener and Gordon; its conquering armies, grand titles, clipped upper-class discourse that exuded decisiveness and superiority; its self-belief and cultural assurance; its awareness of itself as the largest empire the world had ever seen.

Smith's success is based on good storytelling (a skill inherited, he says from grandfather and mother). The novels are strong on landscape description, on plots embodying adventure, warfare, sex, romance, and violence, and built on careful research. His view of empire inevitably produces stereotyping. The British tend to be dashingly heroic, brimming with civilized understanding of the world and history, in a word very decent chaps; their enemies, on the whole, do not make a mirror image. There can also be an unsavory wallowing in the gory slaughter of men and animals. But character variety, torrential action, and good pace drive the narratives forward and maintain reader engagement.

SRANC. The Southern Rhodesian African National Congress. Inaugurated in 1934, this was a nationalist movement commonly referred to as the African Nationalist Congress. It drew inspiration from South Africa's African National Congress, which fought white domination and finally came to power under Mandela in 1994.

T

Tembo, Lyson (n.d.). Zambian poet. Born in the eastern region, educated there and overseas, he pursued an academic career before becoming a diplomat, representing Zambia as ambassador extraordinary and plenipotentiary in Uzbekistan, Japan, and, until 2004, Russia. As a writer, he is known for his collection *Poems*, which Neczam published in 1972.

Tembo's essentially lyrical verse is free of colonial or postcolonial protest. It enjoys paradox, has a romantic way with scenic and human beauty ("listen to the water / sing over the pebbles / watch the reeds / dance in the mirror"), and privileges subjects domestic and local: hence poems on his father, mother, grandmother, or the river Kapoche near his home. A favored symbol for the paradox of life is the rose that combines aesthetic beauty and thorns. Similarly, a poem called "Protest" captures skylarks singing merrily while we hear the "guffawing cacophony of / hyenas in the distance." "The Story" seems to recall a heart attack. Walking out on a boiling day when "the sun's tongue / seemed to have licked / the entire land," the speaker feels dizzy and describes a "black wall" rushing toward him and, apparently, subsequent cardiac surgery.

Perhaps Tembo will revisit verse after a busy public and academic life. As it is, he has reversed the hallowed tradition of professors retiring to work on their slim volume of verse by completing his slim volume before getting his chair.

Tizora, Spencer S. M. (b. ca. 1945). Zimbabwean novelist. Born in the Bulawayo area, after graduating from the University of Zimbabwe he taught for many years in secondary schools before assuming a position at a Bulawayo teachers' college. He is best known for his novel *Crossroads* (1985).

Crossroads is a profoundly moral book, set shortly after Zimbabwe's guerilla war and independence. It rejects euphoria over victory in order to explore the complexity of the recent past and unclear hopes for the future. Lives portrayed unveil the harrowing disruption—individual, social, marital, educational, psychological, geographical—warfare has inflicted on its victims, black and white, and the imperatives of survival amidst carnage that have caused widespread lostness. There are no heroes. Those who fall from grace as warfare bludgeons innocence into experience need understanding not blame. Hence, like Ngugi's fiction on internecine slaughter within Kenya's Mau Mau struggle, the text's reverse chronology constantly feeds past into present. Tizora will not be judgmental. His multiracial society needs truth, peace, and reconciliation. People's personal histories should create understanding and space for forgiveness.

Like a helpful teacher, Tizora sits beside his characters. They include Priscilla the nurse, students Maria and Peter, and David the teacher, all of whose normal life trajectories the war smashes; and those, too, like the sad white Betty, who, in a pioneering symbol for the new Zimbabwe, "adopts" the black child Patson.

Moral force and optimism grow not just from Tizora's natural human sympathy but also from the ethos and skills of his caring profession. *Crossroads* displays lesson-plan design. But if its neat architecture, mistaken identities, scattering of figures across the land, and tidying denouement resemble eighteenth-century fiction, it also enjoys Lawrentian strengths in the areas of passion, landscape, and education. Like much Central African fiction, *Crossroads* rarely strays far from school and college. It makes heartfelt pleas for education and for the kind of teacher who, as here, has "the air of being there together with his students so that his individual energies were there for everyone else."

Further reading: Rino Zhuwarara, *Introduction to Zimbabwean Literature in English* (Harare, 2001).

A Tragedy of Lives: Women in Prison in Zimbabwe (2003). This collection of thirty-three life stories, edited by Chiedza Musengezi and Irene Staunton and published with Canadian government help, reflects a drive, pursued by both editors and the Zimbabwe Women Writers organization, to increase women's voices within Zimbabwean literary debate. It is a sequel to Musengezi's co-edited *Women of Resilience: Women Writing Africa* and Staunton's *Mothers of the Revolution: The War Experiences of Thirty Zimbabwean Women*. Almost all of the texts are written by women well beyond the channels of conventional literary production.

Offenses vary (they range from domestic violence and murder to fraud, abortion, prostitution, drug trafficking, and shoplifting), as do backgrounds. But commonalities also emerge. An egregious sense of integrity arises from these first-person narratives— from their manifest candor, honesty, and lack of self-pitying sentimentality. They carry a sense of right and wrong and a care that other women should strive to avoid a similar fate. Backgrounds are largely scenes of appalling dysfunction. Overwhelmingly,

the women are underprivileged and under-educated, ignorant of legal rights, raised amid hand-to-mouth survival strategies and family devastation: parents dead, separated, divorced, impoverished, alcoholic, abusive, unemployed. For many, marriage—any marriage—is an escape from the poverty trap but whose new burdens under patriarchy simply bring further disaster. As Amy Tsanga says in her reflections on the texts, "As long as women continue to have the primary responsibility for bringing up children, the pressures brought to bear on them will continue to be enormous." These are not criminals, she says, but women caught in their gendered roles fighting circumstance literally to survive, to feed themselves and their children, and perhaps even their extended family. Or else they have reached the outer limit of their capacity to suffer violently abusive husbands. Clara from Goromonzi, jailed for aborting her baby, was raised in a one-parent family by a mother who regularly beat her. Mercy from Bulawayo was jailed for fraud. When her parents divorced, her father sold the house and left the family homeless, making Mercy responsible for rebuilding family security. Marina from Mbara tells a similar story. The father, whom she only recently identified as a doctor of philosophy living in South Africa, abandoned his family of four boys and four girls when Marina's mother was pregnant with her. His action wrecked the family. Problems of drink and violence began. To get school fees and help feed her brothers and sisters, Marina had to sell vegetables, beg at the houses of whites, and even forage in dustbins. In secondary school, believing that marriage would rescue her, she became pregnant to a man who denied paternity. Money from drug dealing became an irresistible temptation. Beti from Sanyati and Maria from Mozambique both murdered their husbands, driven to it by unbearable violence, in Maria's case being slashed on the arms and inner thighs with a razor blade.

These personal histories reveal the country's prisons as appalling, partly because of overcrowding (sometimes forty women to one cell), partly because they were built for men and thus totally inadequate for the toilet and sanitary requirements of women, especially when menstruating.

The editors and their supporting team of interviewers question the system and society that drive such women to break the law. Their efforts assume increasing urgency as underlying economic conditions worsen, with Zimbabwe's inflation rate rising above 1,200 percent by 2006. The only crumb of comfort to be drawn from this disturbing volume is that, unlike evidence from similar texts from Malawi, imprisonment here results from legal process and not from despotic whim that knows no law. Nor, despite evidence of harsh conditions and punishment, does there appear to be the truly medieval torture and human degradation common under Banda.

UANC. The United African National Congress. A political party formed in 1973 by Bishop Abel Muzorewa. The name suggests its ideological link with the African National Congress of South Africa, which ultimately brought that country to independence and Nelson Mandela to its presidency.

UDI. The Unilateral Declaration of Independence, announced by Rhodesian Prime Minister Ian Smith in November 1965, was the key event that precipitated the guerilla war of independence, called by Zimbabweans the Second Chimurenga (the first recalling the uprising against Rhodes and his men in the 1890s and featured in much modern writing). The guerilla war killed over 30,000, the overwhelming majority, as in Kenya's 1950s Mau Mau uprising, being black. With its entirely predictable consequences, on any assessment this was an act of extraordinary folly and irresponsibility. Its performance to the strains of Beethoven's Ninth Symphony, hollow echoes of the American Declaration of Independence, and a Nazi-style thousand-year prediction about white rule only emphasized its tragicomedy. With South Africa a solitary exception, colonial Africa was already history. Yet, absurdly, Smith and his Rhodesian Front thought they could resist the internal forces of nationalism, the rest of the continent, and the overwhelming opposition of the United Nations. Britain's Labour prime minister, Harold Wilson, responded by merely sending jet fighters to neighboring Zambia, kith-and-kin considerations convincing him that a frontal assault would be electorally risky. Sanctions, commissions, lengthy talks, and mediation began, sometimes in the Rhodesian capital, sometimes on British warships. Smith miscalculated on South Africa, which, determined itself to stay white-ruled, offered only limited and diminishing help, hoping a Rhodesian settlement would bolster its own position. Much Zimbabwean literature since 1965 reflects the pain and bloodshed flowing from UDI.

The Unsung Song: An Anthology of Malawian Writing in English (2001). Edited by Reuben Chirambo, Max J. Iphani, and Zondiwe Mbano, and issued by the University of Malawi's Chancellor College Publications, this landmark collection of prose and verse inscribes the work of over seventy writers. Of central importance is its attempt to answer a question long hovering over Central African literary debate: if Malawian writing after independence so emphatically defined itself in response to

President Banda's tyranny, whither its direction following his death? This echoes South African questions about the end of apartheid. The ANC's Albie Sachs crystallized debate there with his 1989 seminar paper "Preparing Ourselves for Freedom," in which he urged writers and artists to walk out into the fresh air of independence, reject the expression "culture as a weapon of struggle," and put an end to the art of "fists and spears." Njabulo Ndebele's 1994 essay collection on South African Literature and Culture, with its subtitle "Rediscovery of the Ordinary," gave the message powerful reinforcement. With a candor hitherto impossible, the editors' signposting volume points back into political darkness and forward into democratic light.

Yet this is a multipurpose text: part prescription for the nation, grounded on literature's humane values as alternative to a discredited political discourse; part prophetic recall to a social order anterior to Banda; and part project to locate a literary voice at the heart of national debate. The moral vision is clear; and to drive it home texts carry questions tailored to focus younger readers on key topics. Many among these were taboo under Banda: democracy, disillusionment, the environment, gender and patriarchy, free speech, censorship, greed, murder, promise betrayal, poverty, drug and alcohol abuse, sexual license.

Paradox gives the volume a flavor distinctly postmodern. It is both renaissance flourish and extended elegy, both libertarian celebration and lament over a new order already shadowed by economic ruin, environmental degradation, moral breakdown, and an AIDS pandemic of monstrous proportions.

Traditional continuities are achieved by including writers familiar during Banda's rule—Chimombo, Lipenga, Mnthali, Moto, Mphande, Mpina, Nazombe, and the editors themselves—though missing are poets like Chipasula, Kamlongera, and Banda. The overwhelming majority are new voices: Chawanangwa Banda, Jayne Banda, Guyce Bvalani, George Chatha, Lackson Chatha, Tobias Chidzalo, Irene Chipeta-Zimba, Sophie Jobe, Helen Kachala, Ndekhane Kalumba, Owen Kandeu, Herbert Kapota, Thomas Khumuwa, Esme Kusauka, Patrick Kwalimba, Matilda Luhanga, Lydia Maideni, Elizabeth Makhala-Nyamatcherenga, Julia Mambo, Christopher Matewere, Bridget Mhemedi, Rosemary Mkumba, Edward Moyo, Kenneth Mtambalika, Dorah Mwase, Sophie Nazambo, Charity Ndhlovu-Chinkono, Louis Ngwira, George Pungulani, King Rudi, Andrew Thawe, Chris Zenengeya, MacDonald Bamusi, N. Bisani, Cecilia Hasha, Peter Kalitera, Marvin Kambuwa, Masuzgo Mhango, Kwesi Msusa, Kondwani Mwangulube, Alfred Nkhoma, Patrick Nyirenda, Davie Nswea, Immanuel Bofomo, Greyson Bongwe, Amos Chauma, Austin Chiwindo-Chirwa, Benjamin Chunda, Albert Kalimbakatha, Andrew Kulemeka, Mercy Longwe, Ben Malunga, Levi Manda, John Matope, Duncan Mboma, Mike Mvona, Christopher Mwawa, Norah Ngoma, Dickson Phiri, Kingston Phiri, Linda Saidi, and Steve Sharra.

The seismic event beneath the project is Banda's death. This is best seen in Steve Chimombo's "Who Is Responsible," his response to a news item in 2000 headed "Kamuzu's Grave in Ruins." While a cowed people had built a "cenotaph of all cenotaphs" in Heroes Acre, where heavy security "paraded and brooded day and night," it now lies in ruins fast disappearing into the bush. All menacing security has gone. Banda and burial are already "once upon a time." Nightmare, in a sense, has become fairytale. No text here captures the interment of an era more starkly.

If the writing celebrates new freedoms—to experiment, protest, scorn deference, craft erotic or scatological discourse—it also includes freedom to reject the metaphoric mode of indirection that was both imposition and strength in Banda-period writing. Notable also are imaginative ways in which oral narratives are being updated for contemporary use—witness Cecilia Hasha's "The Mzungu of Mkandanda Village," Dickens Vuwa-Phiri's "Achitiyeni, the Nanny Bird," Dawson Mbowa's "Why the Dog Chases Cars," and Sambalikagwa Mvona's "The Deadly Spear." A writer like Zondiwe Mbano, an increasingly important voice in prose and verse, can slide effortlessly from surrealism to realism, switch from prose to verse, and operate at diverse psychological levels, as he does in "The Goat" and "Zabeta." He can also celebrate nature and landscape with the best, though usually under clouds of existential gloom. He has a penchant for the elegiac and crepuscular that allies him with Chimombo, La Guma, Armah, Soyinka, and Marechera. His poem "The Road to Emmaus" has its speaker (almost certainly Mbano himself) declare, "A shadow is close by me / On this wandering road / Yet darkness attracts me / As flames attract a moth."

But in the new dispensation AIDS scythes viciously through every age group; death seems commoner than birth and orphanhood increases as incomes decline; domestic and industrial relationships are challenged as children's rights take a new profile, bad parenting is pilloried with bad politics, and trades unions attack the abuses of capital. If despotism has gone, there is still poverty, disease, corruption, greed, prostitution, sexual license, and the hardening contours of a class society. This is the age seen in the work of Steve Chimombo ("A Party for the Dead" and "Back to Your Room"), Greyson Bongwe ("Razia, Mum's Good Girl"), Zeleza Manda's title story, Evance Hlekayo Moyo's "The Symposium," and Max Iphani's "Whispers." In Peter Kalitera's "Old Nsimbi's Shadow" the new era is marked by broken promises, unemployment, tear-gassed strikers, and the yawning gap between old and young, bourgeois comfort and working-class humiliation.

Without censorship and intimidation, writers can safely revisit Banda's years. Lipenga does this in a characteristically witty satire called "Tiger"; so does Amos Chauma in his "Suits and Jewels," which unveils the rebel-sniffing ways of Banda's Special Branch. Two especially harrowing texts are Steve Sharra's "Walls of Shame" and Andrew Kulemeka's "A Small Matter." The first fictionalizes the death in leg-irons of the distinguished Orton Chirwa. An early victim of Banda's wrath, he and his wife Vera, kidnapped in Zambia, were sentenced to death but given life imprisonment because of international pressure. Separately incarcerated, they were never to meet again in life. Vera could see her husband's corpse, but only briefly, and not alone. She is told "The Life President, in his mercy, has sympathetically considered your request to see the body of your dead husband before it is taken for burial. You are only permitted to view the body, not to attend the burial." Few documents better highlight Banda's delight in physical and mental cruelty, his pitilessness, spitefulness, and ruthlessness. Kulemeka's piece attempts a broader sweep via the lives of two impoverished teachers and powerful metaphoric description. Overflowing bus station latrines reflect the broad squalor of Banda-period life:

Thirty years before, on the eve of independence and before the scum had reached the thresholds, an overzealous party youth has pinned special edition pictures of the Founder in each of the filthy latrine huts; to remind users of the goodness of the Leader. Over the years, as heat, fermentation and more shit had made the latrines impossible to use, the only face to continuously witness the progress of decay in the filthy latrines had been the Founder's. He wears a bold fly-stained smile, pointing resolutely to a future rich with putrid smells and the mass of squirming white maggots forever feeding on old human faeces whose pestilential odour hangs over the bus station like the drizzle.

Drunk to ease their pain, they are overheard by Special Branch men as they disparage Banda. Days later, in the cold and rain of a gray morning, "twenty-two eyes mourned and cried for their father whom they would never see again." Closure comes under a full moon as River Shire crocodiles rise to receive the bound and wriggling bodies of both men.

As in Zimbabwean and Zambian writing, AIDS features prominently. For poet Christopher Matewere, it is a spear poised over the whole world. The "woman seeking money in the dark" does not see it and the "rich man wastes away in a posh ward / Nourished only by drips and penicillin." A John Matope prayer-poem laments that hoes now wear out, not with cultivating soil for life but in digging graves; hymns are learned in cemeteries; hospitals are not for healing people "But keeping them to die," and only "The coffin seller / Has a happy profit." Chimombo's bitter "Formula for Funerals" weaves AIDS into a backcloth of disasters:

The formula required is not
    mysterious:
A few famines, droughts and
    pestilences;
One or two *napolos* and HIV /
    AIDS . . .

His "Grave Mates" laments that burials and cemeteries, and not workaday socializing, now bring people together:

We meet again at the same
Graveyard, familiar grave-mates.
The mounds like tumours of grief
On the ground's face separate us.
Misty eyes moisten the dust storms
Raised by the shovels and hoes
Refilling the freshly dug hole.
Todays it is Tatha's turn
Yesterday we mourned Malizani's
    end.
His bougainvillea wreaths are still
    fresh
As if watered by frequent teardrops.
Last week it was Ndatsalapati.
His flowers are yet less shrunken
Than his brothers' and sisters' before
    him
Heads heavy with haunted thoughts
We retrace our steps, eyes locking
And gazing over the question:
When shall we meet again
In laughter, sorrow or in pain.

Joy over Banda's going is not universal. Khwesi Msusa's "Democracy" finds the new scene anarchic: "brother gives up brother / mothers cast their babies in latrines / while fathers rape their own daughters." As for freedom, how can one exercise it "on an empty stomach"? And who can enjoy new rights "while corruption and insecurity reign?" The poem ends bluntly: "Democracy / I hate you!"

Vambe, Lawrence (b. 1917). Zimbabwean autobiographer and journalist. He was born in Chisawasha. Jesuits educated him there and at Kutama, where contemporaries included Robert Mugabe and James Chikerema. He rejected priestly ordination, first for teaching, then, from 1946, for journalism, rising to be editor-in-chief of eight papers serving Central Africa. He also started *African Parade*, an early forum for black fiction. Espousing racial partnership, he was a diplomat for the Central African Federation until disillusion set in. International journalism apart, he is known for two remarkable autobiographies: *An Ill-Fated People: Zimbabwe Before and After Rhodes* (1972) and *From Rhodesia to Zimbabwe* (1976). With the work of Stanlake Samkange and Ndabaningi Sithole, these texts provide the most vivid nonfiction account of Zimbabwean colonial life. Exiled in the 1970s, Vambe is in exile again, living in Britain.

An Ill-Fated People maps an African tragedy. Vambe's account of the fate of his VaShawasha people upon Rhodes's advent unfolds like a Tenebrae service as the candles of tribal tradition are slowly snuffed out. Readers would find it hard to cite documents from nonsettler colonies (Nigeria, Ghana, Sierra Leone, Gambia) quite so harrowing. Doris Lessing's foreword claims that Britain could have prevented the disaster but did not. Anger, bitterness, and puzzlement never transcend the dominant elegiac tone of Vambe's requiem for his peace-loving people: hospitable, cheerful, welcoming, industrious, deeply moral. The instrument of their destruction—"selfish, rapacious and inward-looking"—is a system that fails Africans on "all fundamental questions such as land, justice, truth and human relationships." But he says the Ndebele King Lobengula, cheated by Rhodes, was also to blame: "Never in history have so many people and their country been sold for so little" (one hundred pounds a month, a cruising boat, and a thousand Martini-Henry rifles).

Seeking fairness as a counterstatement to colonial immorality, Vambe pursues landmark topics: the VaShawasha and their rural arcadia, fatally close, alas, to the new white capital, Salisbury; settler mendacity in claiming that the VaShawasha needed protection from the warlike Ndebele; the gulf between VaShawasha morality and white society iniquity. Christianity features centrally. Like Croesus flaunting his wealth and power, mission-hating Rhodes gave a Jesuit the VaShawashas' entire territory. Hence a long association with this religious order, sometimes fruitful (village schooling, material and artistic progress to match even Jesuit *reducciones* in Latin America), and sometimes painful (cruel discipline, cultural vertigo, and failure to prevent further white land seizure).

Vambe cites white response to the 1896 Shona rebellion (testicle crushing, sjambok whipping, and back roasting) as a milestone in VaShawasha decline. He recalls his grandfather's fate. The police first crushed his right hand with hammers. When this drew no confession of guilt, the hand was amputated. Gangrene erupting, amputation up to the elbow followed. Gangrene's return and entire arm amputation preceded the hapless man's collapse and death.

Born only twenty-seven years into white rule, Vambe enjoys unrivalled chronological reach and first-hand family evidence. His grandmother, a Cassandran chorus-of-one for the unfolding tragedy, witnessed the whites arriving in 1890, saw through them at once, and hated them with a passion: "Madzidza held the view that not only was the white man the lowest human creature. He was 'mad' and 'dangerous' as well. He was a congenital liar and a brazen thief." "We fed them, but they bit us afterwards," she said. She and Vambe's father had also laughed when Rhodes's Pioneers arrived, bedraggled and absurd with their stiff clockwork movements.

From Rhodesia to Zimbabwe continues the narrative. Emerging from his Catholic education intellectually secure and analytically skilled, Vambe writes intimately on key liberation leaders: Leopold Takawira, Herbert Chitepo, Joshua Nkomo, Robert Mugabe, George Nyandoro, Robert Chikerema, Josiah Chinamano, Charles Mzingeli, Ndabaningi Sithole; and on white leaders such as Sir Edgar Whitehead, Godfrey Huggins, Garfield Todd, Sir Roy Welensky, Ian Smith, Neil Wilson, and Howard Moffat.

He also captures the heady rush among his contemporaries for modern education. Their icon was Gold Coast's Dr. Aggrey, whose biography read "like a thriller." The Jesuits meanwhile are criticized for Cold War hysteria. One of them shamefully excommunicated the devoutly Catholic Charles Mzingeli, whose trade union constitution he ignorantly called Communist. Infantile obsession with Moscow fueled white oppression generally, leading Vambe to speak of "a country that hated Communism but practiced all the methods of repression and autocracy associated with Communist regimes."

Identifying land theft as colonialism's mortal sin, Vambe asserts: "Of the many injustices committed in my country in the name of western civilization this one is probably the most blatant and shameless." And with a sharp eye for British legal chicanery, he notes that prime minister Huggins was to use the infamous Land Apportionment Act "with consummate skill and give it the aura of an inviolate commandment." He mocks white claims to moral superiority over racist South Africa because every tool of local oppression bore a South African trademark, apartheid was fervently admired, and Rhodesia's urban ghettoes were obvious clones of Soweto and Marabastad.

The Land Apportionment Act's polite deceit reappeared in the ludicrously styled Industrial Conciliation Bill (1934). This drove Africans from apprenticeships and technical training as viciously as its predecessor had driven them from ancestral land. Vambe also comments bitterly on the com-plicity of British working-class immigrants, who, oppressed at home, unfeelingly obstructed African participation in the colony's growing prosperity. Further, to save Britain from Hitler, blacks donated cattle, money and grain, yet, on joining the Rhodesian African Rifles, were initially denied even boots to march in. Little wonder the rumor at the war's end that "badly injured black soldiers from all parts of British Africa were put on a separate boat, which was sent to the bottom of the Indian Ocean."

Despite Vambe's portrait of a mean-minded, insecure settler community, he praises when appropriate and can nurse optimism about change. He applauds Huggins ("a man of vision and a prisoner of white supremacy") for creating a system of simple rural clinics and dispensaries, run by African medical orderlies, which, by the end of World War II, had become "probably the most efficient free medical service for Africans in this continent." He also recalls lines of emaciated and barefoot foreign workers walking into Rhodesia from Mozambique and Nyasaland and walking out again as well-fed owners of shining new bicycles and all manner of household goods.

Vambe's later career assumed an all too familiar pattern. If exile features centrally in black South African writing, so it does in Rhodesia's. Once independent, Malawi also caught the fashion. Now, as writers leave (the late Yvonne Vera, Hove, and Vambe among others), postcolonial Zimbabwe is following suit. Among some 400,000 compatriots in Britain, Vambe is again in exile. The year 2004 saw him in London eulogizing the late Garfield Todd, mentor of Ndabaningi Sithole and the liberal prime minister detained by the Smith regime. Ironies abound. The Vambe who had once written of the "double noose of religious and economic enslavement" was warmly hymning a former missionary also entwined in the history of a country that ultimately had rejected them both. An ill-fated son of an ill-fated people.

Further Reading: Douglas Killam and Ruth Rowe, eds., *The Companion to African Literatures* (Oxford, 2000).

Vera, Yvonne (1965–2005). Zimbabwean novelist and short-story writer. Born in Bulawayo, educated at Luveve and Mzilikazi secondary schools, from 1982 to 1984 she trained as a teacher at Bulawayo's Hillside College. She taught in schools for two years before graduate study at York University, Canada, where she took a doctorate in 1995. She then became writer-in-residence and Director of Commonwealth Fiction at Ontario's Trent University. Back home she occasionally lectured at Selousi University before becoming Director of Zimbabwe's National Gallery in Bulawayo. However, returning to Canada as an exile, she died there of meningitis in 2005. Her rise had been meteoric. By the time of her death, her five novels, *Nehanda* (1993), *Without a Name* (1994), *Under the Tongue* (1996), *Butterfly Burning* (1998), and *Stone Virgins* (2002) had already seen translation into German, Spanish, Catalan, Italian, Swedish, Dutch, Finnish, and Norwegian. Her edited collection *Opening Spaces: An Anthology of Contemporary African Women's Writing* appeared in 1999. She won the Commonwealth Writers' Prize, the Zimbabwe Publishers' Literary Award (twice), and most recently the Tucholsky Award from the Swedish section of PEN. Her writing, says Liz Gunner, "takes Anglophone African fiction into the exploration of new and difficult novelistic terrain." Critics call her novels poetic fiction and certainly her mind and sensibility seem essentially poetic, producing such a continuous flow of metaphoric statement that one might wonder why she chose prose over verse as her medium. The late Léopold Sédar Senghor would probably have said the prose could be cut into lines and read as verse anyway.

Vera's first published work was the short-story collection *Why Don't You Carve Other Animals* (1992). Its fifteen woman-focused pieces, mainly reflecting the Second Chimurenga, stylistically anticipate the longer fiction that began with *Nehanda*. Their continuities are organic: tightly drawn stories yield to tightly drawn novels, both informed by poetry's compression and figurative language. Images of darkness, shadow, and mist, concretion fusing with abstraction, short paragraphs closing with epigrammatic statement—all this survives. But realistic stories make way for novels surrealist, symbolic, and nightmarish.

Continuing thematic concerns include existential solitude; fractured tradition and struggle that produce "exiled souls"; land as a classic site of contestation ("there was nothing for the exiled spirit to cling to but the grey impoverished soil"); gender issues like the endemic plight of abandoned wives rearing "fatherless" children; psychological investigation of self-fearing individuals and wartime women resisting marriage and maternity; empowerment, disempowerment, and the tragic complexities of a hijacked history ("There is no truth except the one that we allow. The natives cannot shape our history").

Vera's Africa, like Soyinka's, is not sunlit but shadowy: one must flee it to inner landscapes for comfort and sanity. The disarmingly subtle opening of "Independence Day" signals her craft. Historic junctures and dawning freedom resonate with irony:

"Move back! Move back!" the policeman shouted.
Today they were lining the main street in the city to see the Prince who had come from England to give their country back to them. At midnight.

The woman took shelter in the green space in her head and waited.

There are Soyinkan echoes (*A Dance of the Forests* especially) as "the woman," symbolic colonial victim, reappears at the midnight stroke being paid for sex by a fellow African determined "to celebrate Independence properly: with cold beer and a woman." Meanwhile, in ironic juxtaposition, the stadium crowd rejoices to learn that it can now expect "Jobs and more money. Land and education."

"The Shoemaker" is a darkness-at-noon narrative. A resolutely unmarried cobbler, while mending ladies' soles, "locks" himself into both shop and memory to survive daily recollection of his destroyed village. In "It is Hard to Live Alone," market women discuss the implications of the Liberation War for maternity, spousal abandonment, and anomie of epidemic proportions. ("There are no rules any more. . . . We only know our loss, our fear and our silence.") "Whose Baby Is It," like South African Oswald Mtshali's celebrated poem "An Abandoned Bundle," makes large points about people of legendary humanity reduced to discarding babies in dustbins.

Nehanda, achieving major aims with strategic economy, offers a revisionist account of Zimbabwe's entanglement with Europe and its first rebellion. She counters white written history with a blend of oral practice elements—dream vision, surrealism, symbolism. Past addresses present through spirit possession, oracle, and medium. Vera's method produces authenticity and prolific detail. She portrays a collective society living peacefully with itself, its ancestors, and environment, practicing democracy, gender equality (men here kneel to Nehanda), sanctifying land and language, and dispensing lofty courtesy and land to strangers. White response is all ignorance and blasphemy: Africans are chil-dren, of no interest, their culture a matter for scorn. Whites simply want gold and land (which can be bought and sold). They violate custom, drive people from ancestral land, impose hut tax and compulsory labor. They answer Nehanda's inspired uprising with a massacre of innocents, widespread village burning, and her execution. A memorable image captures this encounter: "We opened our arms and embraced a cactus bush, and it has brought the desert with it."

In a land perennially drought-threatened, Vera pictures colonial havoc in images of infertility and reduced light: dead roots, rocks, empty streams, dry river beds, carrion birds, shadow, mist, darkness. Structural dualism links Nehanda, Kaguvi, and Mashoko with Browning, Smith, and an unnamed missionary; black guardians of the land with white speculators; collective morality with individualist rapacity; vegetal life with gunmetal and gold; African traditional religion with the new Christianity; allegory and dream with harsh realism.

New birth requires sacrifice and hope rises even from the tragedy's climax. Nehanda prophesies white defeat but says that envying them could be suicidal. Perhaps addressing contemporary Zimbabwe, after the disappointment of the second, successful, Chimurenga, and perhaps also alluding to this exercise in historical recovery, Vera writes, "Hope for the nation is born out of the intensity of newly created memory." Casting her narrative verbs throughout in the present tense certainly emphasizes this.

Mazvita, the protagonist of *Without a Name*, has not heeded Nehanda's warning about envy. The year is 1977, during the Second Chimurenga, and, as a victim of rural rape by a soldier, she craves escape to the city, which, with warfare waning, promises new life, freedom, personal growth, and discovery of her true self. Freedom from poverty, physical and mental fear, and deep loneliness lies in forgetting and moving on.

Nothing must block her ambition—not the wise Nyenyedzi, who remains behind, and not even the baby she murders before returning its body to her now devastated village. When Nyenyedzi is speaking about land and its sacred status, violated by strangers who grow tobacco where "once we buried the dead," and how nobody can own it, he accuses Mazvita of wanting to possess things: "you want things to belong to you, just like the stranger."

Under the Tongue takes Vera (she would approve of the grammar) into the taboo area of incest, where young Zhizha is a victim of terrifying sexual abuse by her father. Oral literature rarely deals with such a delicate topic and then only with nuanced indirection. Modern boldness, arising perhaps from bush war brutalities (a sensed and occasionally mentioned backcloth), and AIDS, situates Vera's text among writing that is breaking down inhibitions. This literally unspeakable crime creates a silence that must be broken for recovery and new emotional life. Hence the title, drawn from Vera's aphoristic comment, "A word does not rot unless it is carried in the mouth for too long, under the tongue." Over and above the struggle for physical survival amid township squalor, there is the greater struggle for Zhizha's psychological and emotional survival. Because the horror must be verbalized, we hear an interior narrative of Proustian detail from her, speaking to herself, the reader, her grandmother, and her mother.

The parallel worlds (external physical and internal psychological) between which Vera moves require a blending of fantasy and realism and a style essentially poetic. Prose carrying crafted patterns of metaphor to channel the conflicting streams of degradation and hope (so densely poetic as to be at times impenetrable) offers imagery constantly blending concrete and abstract: "He felt the darkness descend over his arms,"

"He gathered death from a calabash," "A woman's cry is naked like birth," "A dream grows roots where silence lingers," "a word that she has retrieved from an anthill," "The house has swallowed death," "Her voice is filled with milk." Images of knives, rocks, night, darkness, and nightmare are balanced by those of water, butterflies, birds, sky, wind, rain, and sea to suggest the possibility of recovery. Paeans for Zimbabwe's women contain effusions of sublime lyricism. Men fare less well. While Zhizha's father is guilty of his unspeakable crime, her grandmother laments that her husband totally rejected their hydrocephalic baby and even blamed her for its birth.

Butterfly Burning is more orthodox and accessible. Reflecting Vera's historical aims, it reaches from April 1896, when seventeen Africans were hanged by Rhodes's men, to 1948 and the aftermath of World War II. It begins symbolically in water and ends in fire when Phephelaphi, the vibrantly lovely "butterfly" who dreams of fresh landscapes and new life, burns herself to death. Like Nyenyedzi in *Without a Name*, she seeks escape from the squalor of Bulawayo's Makokoba township—to become, perhaps, her country's first black nurse trainee. And, like Nyenyedzi, she won't let an objecting male, Fumbatha, or a baby, block her way—her harrowing self-abortion paralleling the earlier text's infanticide. Sketching a Rhodesian mirror image of South Africa's apartheid, the 1940s episodes show Makokoba's squalid life: grinding poverty in unsanitary slums, unemployment, passbook checks, nocturnal police sirens, and battered doors. Though Africans have died fighting for Britain in a world war, local whites still wonder if they can be allowed on the sidewalks.

Vera's descriptive powers are given full rein. The abortion and a hanging scene shock with painful detail. Township characters—Zandile the prostitute, Deliwe the shebeen keeper, Fumbatha the building worker—are compellingly drawn. Its authenticity having provoked the historian Terence Ranger to respond professionally to it, Vera warmly dedicates the book to him: "I could speak until tomorrow / Of a glorious friendship and faith."

The Stone Virgins, another Bulawayo text, brings Vera up to the early 1980s, its narrative informed by historical fact rather than dream. The nation's independent government now inflicts on its own Ndebele people a massacre whose full horrors only slowly emerge. Anticolonial struggle, with stupefying speed, has metamorphosed into a species of civil war. Professor Ranger credits Vera with the courage to boldly address this notorious chapter in the nation's postcolonial history. To emphasize now a chosen realism, Vera eschews imaginary landscapes for well-known Bulawayo street names and landmarks.

Thenjiwe and Nonceba, their parents dead, live in rural Kezi. The single village shop, Thandabantu Store, symbolizes community. Sibaso, an idealist guerilla and subject of a bush-war Kurtzian metamorphosis, erupts into their lives, beheading Thenjiwe and cutting off Nonceba's lips. Government soldiers then arrive, inflict random slaughter, destroy the store, and burn its owner to death. Kezi becomes "a naked cemetery," a symbol of the whole region's condition. Cephas Dube, a sane and kindly historian who had loved Thenjiwe but left her in Kezi, attends Nonceba's hospital bedside and persuades her, deeply traumatized, to leave Kezi for a new life in Bulawayo. Here, in a mutually healing relationship, they live together, though separately, as Nonceba's wounds slowly begin to heal. Significantly, the novel's closing page reveals that Cephas's work now focuses on a beehive hut monument to be installed at King Lobengula's nearby ancient kraal. It was here that the initial colonial encounter occurred, here where Rhodes and his men duped the hapless king.

Vera's hallmarks are everywhere in evidence: her love of paradox ("The water is so absent you can taste drops of it on your tongue"); her love of trees—the marula, the mphafa, the mopani, the flamboyant, the masere; flowers—the flame lily, rose, hibiscus, chrysanthemum. They make a life-affirming counterstatement to the human horrors inflicted on rural innocence in a rocky, semiarid landscape.

Vera's fictive achievement is so starkly original as to contribute weightily to an ongoing debate about the rise of the modern African novel, its strengths and weaknesses, and the directions in which it might move.

Further reading: Robert Muponde and Mandi Taruvinga, eds., *Sign and Taboo: Perspectives on the Poetic Fiction of Yvonne Vera* (Harare, 2002); Stephen Gray, "The Unsayable Word": *Under The Tongue* by Yvonne Vera," *The Mail and Guardian*, 24 March 1997; Eva Hunter, "Shaping the Truth of the Struggle: An Interview with Yvonne Vera," *Current Writing* 10, no. 1: 75–86, and "Zimbabwean Nationalism and Motherhood in Yvonne Vera's *Butterfly Burning*," *African Studies* 59, no. 2 (2000): 229–243; P. Ludicke, "Writing from Inside-out, Reading from the Outside-in: A Review of Yvonne Vera's *Nehanda* and *Without a Name*," *Contemporary African Fiction*, ed. D. Wright (Bayreuth, 1993), 67–73; Ish Mafundikwa, "Yvonne Vera," *Skyhost* 5, no. 3 (1997): 15–17; Ranka Primorac, "Crossing into Space-Time of Memory: Borderline Identities in Novels by Yvonne Vera," *Journal of Commonwealth Literature* 36, no. 2 (2001): 77–93; Mandivavarira Taruvinga, "*Butterfly Burning*: Novel of Great Imagination," *Independent Extra* (Harare), 5 February 1999; John Vekris, "Talking to Yvonne Vera," *Social Change* (Harare), August 1997; Clive Wake, "Review of *Nehanda*," *Wasafiri*

19: 75; Liz Gunner, "Yvonne Vera," *Encyclo-paedia of Post-Colonial Literatures in English*, ed. Eugene Benson and L. W. Connolly (London, 2005); Angus Calder, "The New Zimbabwe Writing and Chimurenga," *Wasafiri* 22: 35–42; L. Stone, "Yvonne Vera," *Contemporary Authors Online* Gale Group: www.galegroup.com/LitRC.

Wa Kabika, Lyamba (1955). Zambian poet. Born in the former Northern Rhodesia, he is best known for his anthology *Swimming in Floods of Tears*, written in 1983 with Zimbabwean poet Chenjerai Hove. Its date means that Wa Kabika brought to the collaboration some twenty years' experience of independence in neighboring Zambia with its painfully mixed record: selfless assistance, often unappreciated, to freedom movements in Rhodesia, Mozambique, Namibia, and South Africa; devastating poverty resulting from drought; shifting terms of trade and sincere political ineptitude, as captured in the fiction of Miti and Sinyangwe. Qualified to advise Zimbabweans waking to freedom, he becomes a shade didactic. The struggle must mean something: freedom must deliver real change. But "Voices of Protesting Tears" tells us that, for the new elites ("singing in your overloaded bellies / crying on your arab-oiled lips"), and not excluding writers, the masses

Are slogans
Are poems
Are blows
Are food
Are drinks

Strong on ancestral communality, he still feels located within its networks. There is no disconnection or existentialist soli-

tude as seen in, say, the Zimbabwean poet Kristina Rungano. Anticolonial anger and pan-African solidarity stir admiration for the protesting style of Senegal's David Diop, to whom he directly addresses a poem. His opening exhortation to freedom fighters in "From Exile with Love,"

You who cried loudly
Because of pepper in your eyes

captures Diop's apostrophizing habit. Whether admiration and echo mean full negritudist identification, however, is doubtful. Like politicians, writers might grow cynical about the poor; but not Wa Kabika, who insists on literature's duty to endlessly teach, heal, and transform. Mpalive-Hangson Msiska, in a fresh angle on intertextuality, notes that "Contributing to the Struggle That Still Goes On" is a poem addressing the "other poems in the collection and is a kind of farewell speech to them, bidding them serve as the poet intended them to":

I've sent you to lead the way
please show yourself nicely
in order to reap good results—
you the torch of better things to
    come

Such is colonialism's psychic damage, and Wa Kabika's natural empathy with the other, that, despite citizenship of an independent Zambia since the age of ten, he can still say, "I've never been free / nor will I ever be / for I am continuously chained." He differs in this from the poet Elfigio Muronda, who declared that, though a son of colonial Rhodesia, "my spirit was always free."

Wa Kabika can blend transforming optimism (sometimes ironically nuanced) and struggle's worth with a view Msiska describes as looking "upon life as saturated with death." Six moving tributes to a dead sister and a description of hospitals as an antechamber to the tomb show this.

Further reading: Mpalive-Hangson Msiska, "Lyamba Wa Kabika," in *Encyclopaedia of Post-Colonial Literatures in English*, ed. Eugene Benson and L. W. Connolly (London, 1994); Adrian Roscoe and Mpalive-Hangson Msiska, *The Quiet Chameleon: Modern Poetry from Central Africa* (London, 1992).

WENELA. The Witwatersrand Native Labour Association, a recruiting agency for migrant labor throughout Southern and Central Africa, with headquarters in Johannesburg. Its creation followed an agreement in 1897 between the Transvaal government and Mozambique's Portuguese authorities to supply workers for South Africa's booming mining industry. It had exclusive recruiting rights and opened offices in the then Southwest Africa (Namibia), Bechuanaland (Botswana), Southern Rhodesia (Zimbabwe), Northern Rhodesia (Zambia), Nyasaland (Malawi), Basutoland (Lesotho), Swaziland, and Mozambique. Recruits also came from Angola and Tanganyika. While men were drawn by the lure of an income, it was often a form of forced labor too (called *thangata* in Malawi, *chibaro* in Zimbabwe, and *shibalo* in Mozambique) since a colonial hut tax, imposed on all fit adults, had to be paid in cash. The system's human and domestic damage, its body blows to village and family life, cannot be overstated (men leaving wives and children, in many cases never to return) and became a motif in the literature of Central and Southern Africa. At independence, Angola, Tanzania, Zambia, and Zimbabwe withdrew their workers. Malawi left the scheme in 1974 when a plane crash in Francistown killed seventy of its workers, but rejoined in 1978, before finally withdrawing in 1987.

Further reading: Godfrey Kanyenze, "The African Migration Labour Situation in Southern Africa," paper presented at the ICFTU-AFRO Conference on Migrant Labour, Nairobi, 15–17 March 2004.

Whaley, Andrew (1958). Zimbabwean playwright. Born in Harare, he attended Sir John Kennedy Primary School in Kadoma and Prince Edward High School, Harare. After reading English at Britain's Bristol University, he began writing for stage, screen, and television. Despite a distinctly international career, his work has retained an African focus. He is the author of four plays: *Platform 5* (1987), *The Nyoka Tree* (1988), *Chef's Breakfast* (1989), and *The Rise and Shine of Comrade Fiasco* (1991). A biography, *Brenda Remembered*, appeared in 2004. Films in which he has been involved in various capacities include *King Solomon's Mines* (1985), *Mandela* (1987), *Cry Freedom* (1987), *A World Apart* (1988), *A Dry White Season* (1989), *The Power of One* (1992), and *A Far Off Place* (1993). Outspoken against injustice, his writing, with echoes of Absurdist Theatre, assumes a satiric mode; he joins a growing list of black compatriots like Marechera, Vera, and Hove in expressing gloom over Zimbabwe's postcolonial record. *Platform 5*, for example, highlights the government's clearing Harare of street children in 1986 to impress delegates to a conference of the Nonaligned Movement—a foreshadowing of the clearing of street vendors throughout the country in 2005 and impoverished illegal miners in 2006. *The Nyoka Tree* shows up the absurdity of race relations in colonial Rhodesia. *Chef's Breakfast* explores postcolonial disenchantment as the victors betray one another and shatter the dreams of independence. A similar theme informs *The Rise and Shine of Comrade Fiasco*, which won a prize at the Edinburgh Festival in 1990.

Further reading: Martin Banham, ed., *A History of Theatre in Africa* (Cambridge, 2004); Douglas Killam and Ruth Rowe, eds., *The Companion to African Literatures* (Oxford, 2000).

Writing Still: New Stories from Zimbabwe. This important 2003 publication illustrates a continuing commitment by its editor Irene Staunton and her Weaver Press to the growth of Zimbabwean writing. The title seems ambiguous. It could mean that Zimbabweans, despite obstacles known to readers, continue to write; less likely, it might mean that, due to contemporary traumas, also known to readers, authors are writing in a state of paralytic shock. Teasingly, it might even suggest that Weaver Press, distilling life in the new millennium, resembles a producer of powerful spirits in danger of official discovery! Titular puzzles aside, the book boldly affirms a literary integrity when Zimbabwean news seems reliably bleak.

The collection is important partly because its twenty-three stories *are* indeed new and provide a snapshot of Zimbabwe in the new millennium; also because its literary and editing standards are high, themes diverse, and authorship multiracial. While capturing the contemporary scene, it can also reach back to the seedbed of the bush war from which current events have grown. It is bold because Staunton dares to challenge officialdom with such wide exposure of chaos (ubiquitous queues, food and fuel shortages, corruption, rampant inflation, the botched land grab) and with coverage of taboo subjects like gay and lesbian life and the infamous massacres in Matabeleland. On the other hand, Ms. Staunton might see the regime as liberal enough to tolerate her boldness or secure enough to see literature in English (one recalls Kenyatta's fury at Ngugi wa Thiong'o's switch into Gikuyu) as too marginal for concern.

Staunton's introduction is succinct: "In the past century Zimbabwe has been scarred by racism, discrimination and war, uplifted by hope and self-determination, and discouraged by economic decline and political intolerance." The serious fiction of the 1980s and 1990s, she says, explored the effects of the country's freedom struggle, while this volume mainly represents the less copious work that reflects the last twenty years. Writers include the established and the aspirant: Pat Brickhill, Clement Chihota, Brian Chikwava, Julius Chingono, Shimmer Chinodya, Memory Chirere, Alexandra Fuller, Wonder Guchu, Annie Holmes, Derek Huggins, Alexander Kanengoni, Rory Kilalea, Nevanji Madanhire, Charles Mungoshi, Stanley Mupfudza, Chiedza Musengezi, Gugu Ndlovu, Mary Ndlovu, Vivienne Ndlovu, Stanley Nyamfukudza, Freedom Nyamubaya, Bill Saidi, Yvonne Vera, and Chris Wilson.

Writing Still and *Modern Stories from Malawi*, the latter edited by Sambalikagwa Mvona, both appeared in 2003. Comparison is instructive. While the Malawian texts are invariably brief, some narratives here (Shimmer Chinodya's "Queues," Rory Kilalea's "Mea Culpa," Charles Mungoshi's "The Sins of the Fathers") drift toward the long story. There is closer editorial attention, too, and wider female authorship. Though both countries have suffered painful histories (Malawi's colonial destitution and thirty years of Banda; Zimbabwe's heavier colonialism and the brutality of war), the Zimbabwean narratives scale higher tragic peaks and plumb deeper levels of human depravity and psychological nightmare.

As one finds in Zambian and Malawian writing, Staunton here identifies regret as a refrain. Its genesis lies in postcolonial political mismanagement, but also in the class division that has succeeded race division; alienation arising from village and cultural despoliation; bloody fratricide, AIDS and prostitution, street children, alcohol, marital discord, and bureaucratic gaucherie.

Texts sometimes capture a range of these. Brian Chikwava's "Seventh Street Alchemy" describes how poverty daily drives Harare's masses to leave their "hovels" for work at 5:00 a.m., ravaging "all etches of dignity that only a few years back stood resilient. Threadbare resignation is concealed underneath threadbare shirts . . . [but] the will to be dignified by underpants and socks remains intact." Government inflicts "incessant roguery." People endure "never-ending queues, just to have their dignity thrown out of rickety windows by sadistic officials." Fiso, an aging prostitute, seen often "in the common ritual of massaging her dementia," is in denial about AIDS: "like a lot of the city's inhabitants she has conjured that death is mere spin, nobody ever really dies." Attempts by Fiso to get exit documents for a better life in South Africa are byzantine absurdism.

Shimmer Chinodya's twenty-page "Queues" includes a detailed history of Zimbabwe since 1980 and its oxymoronic fruits of victory. Life is as bad as ever in a land once the region's breadbasket. Everything consequential features here, from the Matabeleland massacres and the steady slide to hunger, to the IMF and structural adjustment, ideological cynicism, and AIDS. A drunk quips, "Our case is beyond politics. We need some kind of supernatural intervention."

William Saidi's "The Winning Side" epitomizes the collection's literary quality and mosaic of paradoxical experience, causally joining past to present, village to city, old to young, poverty to wealth, dead to living, health to sickness, virtue to vice. Orphaned street child Tichaona seeks out rich Uncle Charles in Harare's smart Borrowdale suburb. Though Tambudzai, his lady street friend, predicts otherwise, Uncle Charles welcomes and feeds him, laments the recent death of Tichaona's parents (brother to his mother), and helpfully expounds his philosophy of expediency. On seeing his own parents shot by whites during the freedom struggle, he had decided always to side with the winners—hence, for instance, with Mugabe's victorious ZANU-PF at independence. Also, it seems, with the brutal Fifth Brigade when they slaughtered Tichaona's parents. Tichaona, meanwhile, is remembering his father being butchered with machetes and his tiny mother being dragged naked from her hut to be raped and murdered. Both of them were "driven by principles," Uncle Charles laments, coughing the while, before handing Tichaona conscience money and polite advice to go away. Like his principled parents, when Tichaona finds Tambudzai suffering a tubercular attack, he spends the money curing her. Because the TB, she hints, is AIDS-related, Tichaona begins linking this to her close knowledge of his relative's address and Uncle Charles's own hacking cough.

Following the confessional strain of her verse, Freedom Nyamubaya's "That Special Place" recalls the fratricidal atrocities of the Liberation War, in which, inter alia, she was raped by a camp security commander. But Alex Kanengoni's "The Ugly Reflection in the Mirror" is one of several texts pouring the waters of reconciliation. The black narrator stands in his bean field with Fleming, an old white settler who has helped him plant his crop. Like himself, he loves the land and knows it is the heart of colonialism, the heart of the people's identity, and "the heart of Zimbabwe's politics." Fleming shares his land with black farmers, acknowledges historic land-theft, and cannot understand why Britain's Tony Blair disowns this past so ignorantly. Identifying with land brings human identification. The surprised narrator even reflects, "My God, how like my late father he looks."

This centrality of crop growing, its shaping of life pattern, identity, worldview, and self-worth, also emerges in Memory Chirere's beautiful rural story "Maize," while Pat Brickhill's "Universal Remedy," inverting stereotype, emphasizes both the soil's wholesomeness and Africa as physician to Europe. Traumatized by spousal desertion ("my soul was almost mortally wounded and I needed someone to nurture me and show me the way to heal myself"), the white narrator employs the even more damaged Esilina Sibanda, a daughter of the soil with a "consuming need to plant and grow things" and a mystical way with human sympathy. Esi's ability to "cope with immense pain and loneliness" is inspirational. Often beaten by a mother who despised her passion for cultivation, abandoned at forty-two by a husband as barren and thrown out of the house, she had never remarried. But she teaches the narrator to reject bitterness. Horticulture is the answer to everything. Sister victims of male cruelty must "plant, grow, heal." Though Esi is not important enough to benefit from presidential land redistribution, work with the soil and prayerful Methodism will see her through.

Z

ZANLA. The Zimbabwe African National Liberation Army. During the struggle for freedom it was the military wing of ZANU, the Zimbabwe African National Union. Its often problematic relations with ZIPRA, the military wing of ZAPU, the Zimbabwe African People's Union, receive frequent comment in literature addressing the guerilla war.

ZANU. The Zimbabwe African National Union, a political party formed in 1963 after a split within its predecessor, the Zimbabwe African People's Union, ZAPU. Its members included most of the key figures in the liberation struggle, and at independence it took power as ZANU-PF, the Zimbabwe African National Union People's Front, under the leadership of Robert Mugabe.

ZAPU. The Zimbabwe African People's Union, a political party formed in 1961 following the banning of its predecessor, the NDP or National Democratic Party, whose members included such central liberation figures as Robert Mugabe, Michael Mawema, George Silundika, Ndabaningi Sithole, Herbert Chitepo, Enos Nkala, Leopold Takawira, Eddison Zvogbo, and Moton Malinga. A split within it in 1963 produced ZANU-PF, which took power at independence.

Zeleza, Paul Tiyambe (b. 1955). Malawian novelist, short-story writer, and historian. Born in Salisbury, Rhodesia, he holds a B.A. from the University of Malawi, an M. A. from the University of London, and a Ph.D. from Canada's Dalhousie University. A resourceful and single-minded undergraduate, he edited college journals and contributed to the university's Writers' Workshop. Before graduating, he published his collection *Night of Darkness and Other Stories* (1976), which carries evidence of his energy and ability to explore oral narrative.

Once overseas as a graduate student, Zeleza chose exile over life under Banda's tyranny. From 1979 to 1980 he taught at the University of Nairobi, where, compatriot writer David Rubadiri informs us, he reported on the upsurge of Malawian writing, despite censorship and oppression. After a spell in the Caribbean, and five years at Nairobi's Kenyatta University (1984–89), he became associate professor of history at Canada's Trent University and master of one of its colleges. As of this writing he works in the United States. His academic work includes *Imperialism and Labour* (1987), *Labour, Unionization and Women's*

Participation in Kenya (1988), and *A Modern Economic History of Africa* (1993), which won him the International Noma Award.

In 1992 Zeleza returned to creative writing with his first novel, *Smouldering Charcoal*. Reflecting his professional interest in economics, labor relations, and postcolonialism, the narrative focuses on events surrounding the first strike African workers dared to organize in their country. Discussing Zeleza's accounts of "a life of terror, an unimaginable one. Rape, hero-worshipping, tribalism, polarization, detention without trial, job insecurity, immorality, hypocrisy," the critic Alfred Msadala says that "there is no inhumanity mentioned in the book that would be considered as odd to a country such as Malawi which has one of the worst records of human rights abuses in this part of the world and all this was experienced from 1964 to 1993, the period under one-party rule and one leader." Helen Ross, who discerns echoes of Ngugi Wa Thiong'o's *Grain of Wheat* (especially motifs of "betrayal, resurrection and salvation"), sees the book marking a turning point in the portrayal of Malawian women and calls it "a true novel of exile . . . certainly the very best novel ever to have been written by a Malawian author."

Further reading: Alfred Msadala, "The Future Has Begun," *Destined for Great Things: Papers* (Blantyre, 1999); Adrian Roscoe, *Uhuru's Fire: African Literature East to South* (London, 1977); Adrian Roscoe, "Paul Zeleza," in *Encyclopaedia of Post-Colonial Literatures in English*, ed. Eugene Benson and L. W. Connolly (London: Routledge, 1994).

Zimunya, Musaemura (1949). Zimbabwean poet and short-story writer. He was born at Umtali in the Vumba Mountains area (he herded cattle here and its landscape features in much of his verse). He attended Chikore Secondary School, Goromonzi High School (compatriot writer Shimmer Chindya was also a pupil), and the University of Rhodesia. But a 1973 riot, involving also the writer Dambudzo Marechera, brought arrest and five months' imprisonment. He completed his B.A. at Britain's University of Kent, reading English and history, and later an M.A. Zimbabwe's independence in 1980 drew him home, and he has since taught at the university that once expelled him. He was inspired to write by the splendid schoolmaster-poet Toby Moyana, and in the 1960s began appearing in small magazines. Major publication started in Kizito Muchemwa's *Zimbabwean Poetry in English* (1978) and with a collection he edited with Mudereri Khadani, *And Now the Poets Speak* (1981). Further verse collections include *Zimbabwe Ruins* (1979), *Thought Tracks* (1982), *Kingfisher, Jikinya and Other Poems* (1982), *Country Dawns and City Lights* (1985), *Perfect Poise* (1993), and *Selected Poems* (1995). A short-story collection, *Nightshift*, was published in 1993 and his acclaimed critical volume, *Those Years of Drought and Hunger: The Birth of African Fiction in English in Zimbabwe*, in 1982.

A prolific writer, Zimunya told Flora Wild that, despite colonial Rhodesia's cultural isolation, the charismatic Moyana introduced him to T. S. Eliot, crucially to Negritude's Senghor and the Diops ("to inspire us in the struggle"), and then to Achebe, Armah, Okigbo, Okot p'Bitek, and Ngugi. Later came existentialism—Sartre, Camus, Mann, Gide. This sequence helps to illuminates the verse, as does his declaration to the new Zimbabwe that a national literature should tell "the full story of the community" in all its variety, from love matters to children and espionage. Immersion in Shona oral tradition, negritudist passion, a taste for modernist fluidity, and an embracing vision for postcolonial literature were the launch pad for an output diverse in range and form.

Critics admire the early work on identity, home area evocation, and his orchestration of the haunting silences of Great Zimbabwe, done with liturgical solemnity. But later work is also memorable. Nature poetry reaches beyond the Vumba Mountains. There is prison verse to parallel Mapanje's and Mnthali's in Malawi. *Country Dawns and City Lights* heaps disgust on human behavior (babies thrown into refuse bins, village girls poverty-driven into urban prostitution) and paints multiform township horror. But he counters postcolonial gloom with an urge to conquer preindependence pessimism and with the thought that freedom is never fully achieved but always to be striven for. Angry at a white myth that Africans cannot write love poetry (he says it flows abundantly in Shona texts), he sets out to counter it in *Kingfisher, Jikinya and Other Poems. Country Dawn and City Lights* sees him descending from initial romanticism to a balancing exercise in which a revisited rural life (notwithstanding its superstition, suspicion, sexual imperatives, and unneighborly rivalry—for example, calling each other "Swine-tooth" and "Stink-nose") still outclasses urban life with its lack of cultural depth and incapacity for epic grandeur.

Mpalive-Hangson Msiska suggests that, while Zimunya's achievement is certainly impressive, it reflects the familiar snags of African writers wanting to privilege tradition: "The problem facing Zimunya is one that confronts every cultural conservationist: can one formulate, beyond mere criticism of the present, a social vision based on the past that sufficiently takes on board the necessity of historical change?"

Further reading: Flora Veit-Wild, *Patterns of Poetry in Zimbabwe* (Gweru, 1988); Solomon M. Mutswairo, "The Poetry of Musaemura Zimunya" in *New Writing from Southern Africa*, ed. Emmanuel Ngara (London, 1996); "Musaemura Zimunya," in *The Companion to African Literature*, ed. Douglas Killam and Ruth Howe (Oxford, 2000); Mpalive-Hangson Msiska, "Musaemura Zimunya," in *Encyclopaedia of Post-Colonial Literatures in English*, ed. Eugene Benson and L. W. Connolly (London, 1994); Adrian Roscoe and Mpalive-Hangson Msiska, *The Quiet Chameleon: Modern Poetry from Central Africa* (London, 1992).

ZIPRA. The military wing of ZAPU, the Zimbabwe African People's Union, during the Liberation War.

Zulu, Hannelie H. J. (b. ca. 1964). Zambian fiction writer, publisher, and journalist. Her career is one of inspiring struggle and creative enterprise. She was born in Luanshya, her father a lawyer (Patrick Chitambi Zulu, who was murdered), and her mother a headmistress. Her mathematician stepfather, Wadula Jere-Njere, was an important mentor. After Chipata Day Secondary School, a four-year apprenticeship as a machine carpenter and supervisor, and investigations into her father's death, she moved to Denmark, privately studying, taking a four-year course in business and administration, and, admirably, setting up her own publishing house. She lectures in schools, business houses, and UN organizations, and writes for such newspapers as Denmark's *Politiken, Information, The Socialist*, and Zambia's *The Zambian Post, The Green Times*, and *The Watch Dog*. Her work includes *Malawi Okongola, Nomeon, The Little Bad Guy*, and *Negotiating Blood: An Alternative Study Book for the World Citizen* (2002).

Negotiating Blood examines the West's complicity in Africa's postcolonial plight. With Zambian experience raw on her nerves, the purview is wide, the posture passionate. The West, she argues, continues to ruin Africa, which is stagnating rather than underdeveloped. For slavery and colonialism we must now read financial helotry and neocolonialism. The aid game is either high-minded nonsense or cynical exploitation. Dysfunction blights every aspect of life, the key one psychological. Her prescription is simple: total debt relief and a clean break between the West and Africa. Only Africa can solve African problems.

Whatever the issue—dependency, gender, publishing, religion, globalization, leadership, literacy, religion, economic migration, education ("What is education when it helps dismantle one's own community?"), Zulu's address is robust and detailed. She attacks the World Bank and the IMF, whose Structural Adjustment Programs have wrought havoc. Their policies have killed free primary education and health care for impoverished populations, privatized national utilities and corporations (buyers invariably Western), and stripped, without reciprocation, tariff protection from local markets. Countless thousands are now school dropouts or receive no health care.

Obliged to grow cash crops instead of food, crushed by the AIDS pandemic, their health levels and life expectancy have plummeted. Scandalously, Malawi was forced to sell 100,000 tons of emergency grain. People have left their "good farms and gardens and have given up tilling the soil in order to sell second-hand clothes," so-called gifts from the West. A world "all about consuming and nothing else," hurling globalization on Africans who are overwhelmingly "small-scale farmers," stokes the fires of Zulu's anger. Zambia "has nothing left. Its capital city is now being compared to a raped woman. . . . Companies have closed and people are leaving the country. . . . The towns that once were filled up with books and bookshops are now empty." She attacks any linking of business and aid.

She says, "Business and help never walked hand in hand," and impugns Liv-

ingstone (no true missionary he) for believing they could. Leadership dysfunction is a symptom of colonial psychic damage. Hence Robert Mugabe roaming "like a wounded and bleeding animal his own streets trying to restore his wounded pride." Nor should we wonder why so many Africans are migrating "to look for their stolen jewellery" in the West.

Zulu fires off her broadsides. Tone and style are prophetic. "A country is developed by people not money. . . . The borrower is always a slave." Africans restarting without the West will be more fortunate than the Israelites leaving Egypt. "They have no deserts and mountains to cross or climb. Their deserts and mountains are psychological."

Zulu, Patrick Citambi (b. 1940). Zambian poet. Born in Chingola, he was educated at St. Francis' School, Msoro, and Chizongwe Secondary School. Leaving Chizongwe in 1960 (the entire student body was expelled for insubordination), he went to South Africa, Botswana, and Southern Rhodesia, where he worked as a railway fireman from 1961 to 1965. Back home, he reported for the Kabwe Mine Newspaper, but soon left to study journalism in India. Family problems in 1966 saw him training as a magistrate in Lusaka and obtaining a distinction in criminal law. While working as a magistrate in Luanshya, and as a legal assistant with the Lusaka city council, he was also beginning his writing career. He is best known for his verse collection *A Sheaf of Gold* (1971).

Zulu's verse rises from a humanism that is part traditional morality, part Christian ethic, and part the distinctive Zambian philosophy President Kaunda promulgated. His introduction (Africans should write as Africans about African themes, though not ignore non-African models) alludes to Shelley and Wordsworth and anticipates echoes in his poems from Milton, Shakespeare, Donne, Wyatt ("They flee from me who sometime did me seek"), and even from Ireland's "Where the Praties Grow." But these are whispered echoes that do not drown Zulu's own voice. He announces lyricism, but a created persona might mediate it—an old man lamenting new generation softness, a cripple pondering the perspective of the able-bodied, a forest swearing it provides everything needful for the local community, a mother lamenting firstborn pain. There is love poetry, nature poetry that paints rural beauty, a poetic restatement of Genesis, and childhood nostalgia. Zulu likes rhyme, which causes restriction, but free rhythm too, though his "Weep Not," with its Wyatt echoes, shows he can handle a strict pentameter, even while altering the pattern with a carryover into two lines, as in "They do me wrong who say I / Come no more." Despite subdued political protest ("New Birth" is mildly negritudist), the volume ends with abrupt tonal change. Anger erupts about colonial sins. A persona in a valedictory message warns his children that Christianity and university degrees are but the tools of impostors. The good days of old are over. Where he is going the road is full of thorns:

> And you cannot
> Follow
> But,
> If you find my
> Grave,
> Please plant no flowers.
> There is no peace here.

Notes

Chapter 1

1. N. A. M. Rodger, "Guns and Sails in English Colonization," in *The Oxford History of the British Empire* (Oxford: Oxford University Press, 1998), 1:97.

2. Anthony Pagden, "The Struggle for Legitimacy and the Image of Empire in the Atlantic to c.1700," ibid., 34–54.

3. Federico de Onís, ed., *Antología de Ensayos Españoles* (Boston: Houghton Mifflin, 1936), 178.

4. Pagden, "The Struggle for Legitimacy," 35–36.

5. Megan Vaughan, "Tricky Business," *London Review of Books*, 12 December 2005.

Chapter 2

1. P. E. H. Hair and Robin Law, "The English in Western Africa to 1700," in *The Oxford History of the British Empire* (Oxford: Oxford University Press, 1998), 1:241–263.

2. John C. Appleby, "War, Politics, and Colonization, 1558–1625," ibid., 55–78.

3. Nicholas Canny, "The Origins of Empire: An Introduction," ibid., 10.

4. Anthony Pagden, "The Struggle for Legitimacy and the Image of Empire in the Atlantic to c.1700," ibid., 35.

5. Canny, "Origins of Empire," ibid., 1–33.

6. Hair and Law, "The English in Western Africa," ibid., 241–263.

7. Ibid.

8. Megan Vaughan, "Tricky Business," *London Review of Books*, 12 December 2005.

9. Daniel Defoe, *The History and Remarkable Life of the Truly Honourable Col. Jacques Commonly Call'd Col. Jack*, ed. Samuel Holt Monk (London: Oxford University Press, 1965), 173–174.

Chapter 3

1. Anthony Pagden, "The Struggle for Legitimacy and the Image of Empire in the Atlantic to c.1700," in *The Oxford History of the British Empire* (Oxford: Oxford University Press, 1998), 1:34–54. The essentials of this discussion are based on Pagden's essay and on his *Lords of All the World: Ideologies of Empire in Spain, Britain and France c.1500–c.1800* (New Haven, Conn.: Yale University Press, 1995).

Chapter 4

1. P. E. H. Hair and Robin Law, "The English in Western Africa to 1700," in *The Oxford History of the British Empire* (Oxford: Oxford University Press, 1998), 1:241–263.

2. Christopher Saunders and Iain R. Smith, "Southern Africa, 1795–1910," in ibid., 3:597–623.

3. Jonathan Israel, "The Emerging Empire: The Continental Perspective, 1650–1713," in ibid., 1:423–444.

4. Saunders and Smith, "Southern Africa."

5. Thomas Pakenham, *The Scramble for Africa, 1876–1912* (London: Abacus, 1992), 385.

6. David Cannadine, *History in Our Time* (London: Penguin, 1998), 212.

7. Pakenham, *The Scramble for Africa*, 374.

8. Cannadine, *History in Our Time*, 212.

Chapter 5

1. Rob Mackenzie, *David Livingstone: The Truth Behind the Legend* (Chinhoyi, Zimbabwe: Fig Tree Publications, 1993), 47.

2. Ibid., 311.

3. Roland Oliver, *Sir Harry Johnston and the Scramble for Africa* (London: Chatto and Windus, 1957), 235–236.

4. Ibid., 235.

5. Ibid., 181.

6. Ibid.

7. George Shepperson and Thomas Price, *Independent African: John Chilembwe and the Nyasaland Rising of 1915* (Edinburgh: Edinburgh University Press, 1958).

Chapter 7

1. Quoted by Claude Wauthier in *The Literature and Thought of Modern Africa* (London: Pall Mall, 1966), 103.

2. Terence Ranger, "History Has Its Ceiling: The Pressures of the Past in *The Stone Virgins*," in *Sign and Taboo: Perspectives on the Poetic Fiction of Yvonne Vera*, ed. Robert Muponde and Mandi Taruvinga (Harare, Zimbabwe: Weaver Press, 2002), 203–216.

3. Ibid., 214.

4. Dambudzo Marechera, *The House of Hunger* (London: Heinemann, 1978), 42.

5. Chenjerai Hove, *Palaver Finish* (Harare, Zimbabwe: Weaver Press, 2002), 85.

6. Felix Mnthali, *When Sunset Comes to Sapitwa* (Lusaka, Zambia: Neczam, 1980), 2.

7. George Shepperson, "Foreword" in D. D. Phiri, *Let Us Die for Africa: An African Perspective on the Life and Death of John Chilembwe of Nyasaland/Malawi* (Blantyre, Malawi: Central Africana, 1999), 5.

8. Rino Zhuwarara, *Introduction to Zimbabwean Literature in English* (Harare, Zimbabwe: College Press, 2001), 17.

9. Wm. Roger Louis, "Introduction," *Oxford History of the British Empire* (Oxford: Oxford University Press, 1999), 5:1–42.

10. Shepperson in Phiri, *Let Us Die For Africa*, v.

Chapter 8

1. Matthew Schoffeleers, ed., *Guardians of the Land: Essays on Central African Territorial Cults* (Gweru, Zimbabwe: Mambo Press, 1979).

2. David Kerr, *Drama, Media Entertainment and Popular Performance in South East Africa* (Bayreuth, Germany: Bayreuth University, 1998), 17.

3. Adrian Roscoe and Mpalive-Hangson Msiska, *The Quiet Chameleon: Modern Poetry from Central Africa* (London: Hans Zell, 1992), 3.

4. Flora Veit-Wild, *Patterns of Poetry in Zimbabwe* (Gweru, Zimbabwe: Mambo Press, 1988), 62.

5. Rino Zhuwarara, *Introduction to Zimbabwean Literature in English* (Harare, Zimbabwe: College Press, 2001), 18.

6. Ibid., 23.

Chapter 9

1. Rino Zhuwarara, *Introduction to Zimbabwean Literature in English* (Harare, Zimbabwe: College Press, 2001), 11–18.

2. Flora Veit-Wild, *Patterns of Poetry in Zimbabwe* (Gweru, Zimbabwe: Mambo Press, 1988), 127.

3. Jack Mapanje, *Of Chameleons and Gods* (London: Heinemann, 1981), 2.

4. Veit-Wild, *Patterns of Poetry in Zimbabwe*, 35.

5. Mudereri Kadhani and Musaemura Zimunya, *And Now the Poets Speak* (Gweru, Zimbabwe: Mambo Press, 1981), xiv.

6. Ibid.

Chapter 10

1. George Kahari, *Plots and Characters in Shona Fiction 1956–1984: A Handbook* (Gweru, Zimbabwe: Mambo Press, 1990), 1–4.

2. Adrian Roscoe and Mpalive-Hangson Msiska, *The Quiet Chameleon: Modern Poetry from Central Africa* (London: Hans Zell, 1992), 2–3.

3. Es'kia Mphahlele, *Down Second Avenue* (London: Faber and Faber, 1959), xxi.

Chapter 11

1. Quoted in Liz Gunner, ed., *Politics and Performance: Theatre, Poetry and Song in South Africa* (Johannesburg, South Africa: Witwatersrand University Press, 1994), 25.

2. David Kerr, *Dance, Media Entertainment and Popular Theatre in South East Africa* (Bayreuth, Germany: Bayreuth University, 1998), 19–32.

3. David Kerr, *African Popular Theatre* (Oxford: James Currey, 1995), 211–213.

4. Ibid., 142.

5. Ibid., 147.

Bibliography

Primary Sources

Aipira, Hoffmann. *Reflections and Sunsets*. Zomba, Malawi: Kachere, 2004.

Armstrong, Peter. *The Capital of Nowhere*. London: Pan, 2003.

——. *Operation Zambezi: The Raid Into Zambia*. Harare, Zimbabwe: Welston Press, 1979.

——. *Tobacco Spiced with Ginger*. Harare, Zimbabwe: Welston Press, 1987.

Ballinger, W. A. *The Big Steal*. London: Five Star, 1964.

——. *The Carrion Eaters*. London: Michael Joseph, 1971.

——. *Drums of the Dark Gods*. London: Mayflower Dell, 1966.

——. *Epitaph to Treason*. London: Fleetway, 1960.

——. *The Last Tiger*. London: Sexton Blake Library, 1963.

——. *There and Back Again*. London: New English Library, 1979.

——. *The Voyageurs*. London: New English Library, 1978.

——. *The Witches of Notting Hill*. London: Mayflower Dell, 1965.

Banana, Canaan Sodindo. *The Church in the Struggle for Zimbabwe*. Gweru, Zimbabwe: Mambo Press, 1996.

——. *The Gospel According to the Ghetto*. Gweru, Zimbabwe: Mambo Press, 1980.

——. *The Politics of Repression and Resistance Face to Face with Combat Theology*. Gweru, Zimbabwe: Mambo Press, 1996.

Banda, Joseph Alexander K. *Calling Dr. Kalulu*. Limbe, Malawi: Popular Publications, 1993.

Banda, Mordecai. *The Year of the Ice Age*. Zomba, Malawi: Lydia Publications, 2004.

Banda, Tito. *Sekani's Solution*. Limbe, Malawi: Popular Publications, 1979.

Barlow, C. H. *Of Feathers and Dead Leaves*. Harare, Zimbabwe: SAPES, 1989.

Bhebe, Ngwabi. *Benjamin Burombo: African Politics in Zimbabwe, 1947–1958*. Harare, Zimbabwe: College Press, 1989.

——. *Christianity and Traditional Religion in Western Zimbabwe, 1859–1923*. London: Longman, 1979.

——. *Simon Vengayi Muzenda and the Struggle for and Liberation of Zimbabwe*. Gweru, Zimbabwe: Mambo Press, 2004.

——. *The Struggle for Liberation in Zimbabwe*. Gweru, Zimbabwe: Mambo Press, 2004.

——. *The Zapu and Zanu Guerilla Warfare and the Evangelical Lutheran Church in Zimbabwe*. Gweru, Zimbabwe: Mambo Press, 1996.

Bhebe, Ngwabi, and Terence Ranger. *Soldiers in Zimbabwe's Liberation Army*. Oxford: James Currey, 1995.

——, eds. *Society in Zimbabwe's Liberation War*. London: James Currey and Heinemann, 1995.

Borer, Mary Cathcart. *Distant Hills*. London: Isaac Pitman, 1951.

Borrell, D. E. *A Patch of Sky*. Harare, Zimbabwe: Rhodesian Poetry Society, 1978.

Brettell, Noel. *Bronze Frieze*. Oxford: Oxford University Press, 1950.

——. *Season and Pretext*. Harare, Zimbabwe: Poetry Society of Zimbabwe, Mopani Poets' Series, 1977.

Burgess, Alan. *The Devil's Mode*. London: Vintage, 1990.

——. *The Lovely Sergeant*. London: Companion Book Club, 1964.

——. *The Small Woman*. London: Pan, 1961.

——. *The Word for Love*. London: Companion Book Club, 1968

Burton, Lloyd. *The Yellow Mountain*. Harare, Zimbabwe: Regal Publishers, 1978.

Bvuma, Thomas Sukutai. *Every Stone That Turns*. Harare, Zimbabwe: College Press, 1999.

Calder, Angus, and Jack Mapanje, eds. *Summer Fires: New Poetry of Africa*. London: Heinemann, 1983.

Carney, Daniel. *Macau*. London: Pan, 1986.

——. *Square Circle*. London: Corgi, 1982.

——. *Under a Raging Sky*. London: Corgi, 1985.

——. *The Whispering Death*. Harare, Zimbabwe: College Press, 1969.

Chaparadza, L. W. "My Skin May Be Black." *African Parade*, February 1957, 25.

Chappell, Mollie. *Cat with No Fiddle*. London: Collins, 1954.

——. *The Fortunes of Frick*. London: Collins, 1959.

——. *The House on the Kopje*. London: Collins, 1954.

——. *Kit and the Mystery Man*. London: Collins, 1958.

——. *Rhodesian Adventure*. London: The Children's Press, 1950.

——. *Valley of Lilacs*. London: Collins, 1972.

Chennells, Anthony, et al., eds. *Arthur Shearly Cripps: A Selection of His Prose and Poetry*. Gweru, Zimbabwe: Mambo Press, 1976.

Chihota, Clement. *Before the Next Song and Other Poems*. Gweru, Zimbabwe: Mambo Press, 1999.

Chihota, Clement, and Robert Muponde, eds. *No More Plastic Balls and Other Stories*. Harare, Zimbabwe: College Press, 2000.

Chilala, Cheel F. K., ed. *Death of a Tramp: An Anthology of Short Stories*. Lusaka, Zambia: Zambia Educational Publishing House, 1996.

Chima, Richard. *The Loneliness of a Drunkard*. Lusaka, Zambia: Neczam, 1973.

Chimedza, Albert, and Hopewell Seyaseya. *Counterpoint*. Harare, Zimbabwe: College Press, 1984.

Chimombo, Moira, ed. *Relationships*. Blantyre, Malawi: Christian Literature Association in Malawi, 1993.

Chimombo, Steve. *The Basket Girl*. Limbe, Malawi: Popular Publications, 1990.

——. *The Bird Boy's Song*. Zomba, Malawi: Wasi Publications, 2002.

——. *Breaking the Beadstrings*. Zomba, Malawi: WASI, 1995.

——. *The Caves of Nazimbuli*. Limbe, Malawi: Popular Publications, 1994.

——. *Child of Clay*. Limbe, Malawi: Popular Publications, 1993.

——. *Epic of the Forest Creatures*. Zomba, Malawi: WASI, 2005.

——. *The Harvests*. Limbe, Malawi: Popular Publications, 1978.

——. *The Hyena Wears Darkness*. Zomba, Malawi: WASI, 2006.

——. *The Locusts*. Limbe, Malawi: Popular Publications, 1978.

——. *Napolo and the Python*. London: Heinemann, 1994.

——. *Napolo Poems*. Zomba, Malawi: Manchichi, 1987.

——. *Operation Kalulu*. Limbe, Malawi: Popular Publications, 1984.

——. *The Rainmaker*. Limbe, Malawi: Popular Publications, 1978.

——. *Sister, Sister!* Zomba, Malawi: WASI Publications, 1983.

——. *The 'Vipya' Poem*. Zomba, Malawi: WASI, 1996.

——. *Wachiona Ndani?* Blantyre, Malawi: Dzuka Publications, 1983.

——. *The Wrath of Napolo*. Zomba, Malawi: WASI Publications, 2000.

Chimsoro, Samuel. *Nothing Is Impossible*. Harare, Zimbabwe: Longman Zimbabwe, 1983.

——. *Smoke and Flames*. Gweru, Zimbabwe: Mambo Press, 1978.

Chinodya, Shimmer. *Can We Talk and Other Stories*. Harare, Zimbabwe: Baobab Books, 1998.

——. *Child of War*. Harare, Zimbabwe: College Press, 1985.

——. *Dew in the Morning*. Gweru, Zimbabwe: Mambo Press, 1992.

——. *Farai's Girls*. Harare, Zimbabwe: College Press, 1984.

——. *Harvest of Thorns*. Harare, Zimbabwe: Baobab Books, 1989.

——. *Tale of Tamari*. Harare, Zimbabwe: Weaver Press, 2004.

Chipamaunga, Edmund. *Chains of Freedom*. Gweru, Zimbabwe: Mambo Press, 1998.

——. *A Fighter for Freedom*. Gweru, Zimbabwe: Mambo Press, 1983.

Chipasula, Frank. *Nightwatcher, Nightsong*. Peterborough, N.H.: Paul Green, 1986.

——. *O Earth, Wait for Me*. Johannesburg: Ravan Press, 1984.

——. *Visions and Reflections*. Lusaka, Zambia: Neczam, 1972.

——, ed. *When My Brothers Come Home: Poems from Central and Southern Africa*. Middletown, Conn.: Wesleyan University Press, 1985.

——. *Whispers in the Wings*. Oxford: Heinemann, 1991.

Chipasula, Frank, and Stella Chipasula, eds. *The Heinemann Book of African Women's Poetry*. Oxford: Heinemann, 1995.

Chipembere, Henry Blasius Masauko. *Hero of the Nation: Chipembere of Malawi, an Autobiography*. Edited by Robert I. Rotberg. Zomba, Malawi: Kachere Series, 2001.

Chirambo, R., M. J. Iphani, and Z. Mbano. *The Unsung Song: An Anthology of Malawian Writing in English*. Zomba, Malawi: Chancellor College Publications, 2001.

Chiume, W. Kanyama. *The African Deluge*. Nairobi: Kenya Literature Bureau, 1978.

——. *Kwacha: An Autobiography*. Nairobi: East African Publishing House, 1975.

——. *Nyasaland Speaks: An Appeal to the British People*. London: Union of Democratic Control, 1959.

Collin-Smith, Joyce. *Call No Man Master*. Sandy, England: Authors Online, 2004.

——. *Jeremy Craven*. Boston: Houghton Mifflin, 1959.

——. *Locusts and Wild Honey*. London: James Barrie, 1953.

——. *The Scorpion on the Stone*. London: James Barrie, 1954.

——. *A Wreath of Chains*. London: W. H. Allen, 1960.

Dangarembga, Tsitsi. *Nervous Conditions*. London: Women's Press, 1988.

Davis, John Gordon. *Cape of Storms*. London: Corgi Books, 1977.

——. *Fear No Evil*. London: Michael Joseph, 1977.

——. *Hold My Hand, I'm Dying*. London: Michael Joseph, 1967.

——. *The Land God Made in Anger*. London: Collins, 1990.

——. *Leviathan*. London: Pan, 1978.

———. *Seize the Reckless Wind.* Glasgow: Fontana, 1993.

———. *Talk to Me Tenderly, Tell Me Lies.* Glasgow: Fontana, 1993.

———. *Taller Than Trees.* London: Corgi, 1976

Dawson, D., ed. *Revival: An Anthology of African Poetry.* Harare, Zimbabwe: College Press, 1989.

Dibb, Emily. *The Bite.* London: Robert Hale, 1978.

———. *Conundrum Tree.* London: Modus, 1989.

———. *Spotted Soldiers.* Salisbury, Rhodesia: Leo Publications, 1978.

Diki, Basil. *The Tribe of Graves.* Harare, Zimbabwe: College Press, 2000.

Early, Robert. *Powers and Dominations.* Boston: Houghton Mifflin, 1975.

———. *A Time of Madness.* London: Star Books, 1978.

———. *Weavers and War: A True Story.* London: Routledge and Kegan Paul, 1984.

Erlwanger, Beatrice Bwalya. *Tales from Kasama.* Lusaka, Zambia: Multimedia Publications, 2000.

Fenton, Elizabeth. *Barrier to Love.* London: Robert Hale, 1959.

———. *Rhodesian Rhapsody.* London: Robert Hale, 1958.

———. *The Smoke That Thunders.* London: John Dennis, 1952.

———. *Song of India.* London: Robert Hale, 1956.

———. *Wild Cataracts.* London: John Dennis, 1952.

Fielding, Ann Mary. *Ashanti Blood.* London: Heinemann, 1952.

———. *The Mayfair Squatters.* London: Heinemann, 1945.

———. *The Noxious Weed.* London: Heinemann, 1951.

Finn, Betty, ed. *Poetry in Rhodesia: 75 Years.* Harare, Zimbabwe: College Press, 1968.

Finn, Hugh. *The Sunbathers and Other Poems.* Salisbury, Rhodesia: Poetry Society of Rhodesia, 1977.

Gibbs, James, ed. *Nine Malawian Plays.* Limbe, Malawi: Popular Publications, 1976.

Gibbs, Peter. *Avalanche in Central Africa.* London: Arthur Baker, 1961.

———. *Crimean Blunder.* London: Frederick Muller, 1960.

———. *Death of the Last Republic.* London: Frederick Muller, 1957.

———. *A Flag for the Matabele: A Story of Empire-Building in Africa.* London: Frederick Muller, 1955.

———. *The History of the British South Africa Police.* Salisbury, Rhodesia: BSAP and Kingston's, 1974.

———. *Landlocked Island: A Commentary on Southern Rhodesia.* London: Philpott and Collins, 1947.

———. *Stronger Than Armies.* London: Frederick Muller, 1953.

———. *The True Book About Cecil Rhodes.* London: Frederick Muller, 1956.

Gingell, Boughton. *The Queen's Prayer and Other Poems.* Harare, Zimbabwe: Longman, 1977.

Hanson, Benjamin. *Just Feelings.* Harare, Zimbabwe: Longman Zimbabwe, 1988.

Hartmann, Michael. *Game for Vultures.* London: Macmillan, 1976.

———. *Horses of Vengeance.* London: Knight Paperbacks, 2003.

———. *The Phoenix Pact.* London: Knight Paperbacks, 1989.

———. *Tigers of Deceit.* London: Knight Paperbacks, 2000.

Herold, A. *Harlequin.* Lusaka, Zambia: First Time Publishing, 1981.

Himuyanga-Phiri, Tsitsi V. *The Legacy*. Harare, Zimbabwe: Zimbabwe Publishing House, 1992.

Hove, Chenjerai. *Ancestors*. Harare, Zimbabwe: College Press, 1994.

———. *Blind Moon*. Harare, Zimbabwe: Weaver Press, 2003.

———. *Bones*. Harare, Zimbabwe: Baobab Books, 1988.

———. *Guardians of the Soil*. Harare, Zimbabwe: Baobab Books, 1997.

———. *Palaver Finish*. Harare, Zimbabwe: Weaver Press, 2002.

———. *Rainbows in the Dust*. Harare, Zimbabwe: Baobab Books, 1997.

———. *Red Hills of Home*. Gweru, Zimbabwe: Mambo Press, 1985.

———. *Shadows*. Harare, Zimbabwe: Baobab Books, 1991.

———. *Shebeen Tales*. London: Serif, 1997.

———. *Up in Arms*. Gweru, Zimbabwe: Mambo Press, 1985.

Hove, Chenjerai, and Lyamba wa Kabika. *Swimming in Floods of Tears*. Gweru, Zimbabwe: Mambo Press, 1983.

Imenda, Sitwala. *The Blairing Kofi Bush War of Iraq: Who Was Insane?* Victoria, B.C.: Trafford Publishing, 2004.

———. *Mind Over Matter*. Lusaka, Zambia: Mipal Printers, 2004.

———. *My Grandfather's God*. Lusaka, Zambia: Mipal Printers, 2004.

———. *Unmarried Wife*. Nairobi: Spear Books, 1994.

Imenda, Sitwala, and Lydia Nakutoma Inambao. *Dancing Mice and Other African Folktales*. Lusaka, Zambia: Mipal Printers, 2004.

Kachingwe, Aubrey. *No Easy Task*. London: Heinemann, 1996.

Kadhani, Mudereri. *Quarantine Rhythms*. London: Palladio Press, 1976.

Kala, Violet. *Waste Not Your Tears*. Harare, Zimbabwe: Baobab Books, 1994.

Kalonde, Ken. *Progress After Referendum*. Lilongwe, Malawi: Sunrise Publications, 1996.

———. *Smiles Round Africa*. Lilongwe, Malawi: Sunrise Publications, 1997.

Kamkondo, Dede. *Children of the Lake*. Limbe, Malawi: Popular Publications, 1987.

———. *For the Living*. Blantyre, Malawi: Dzuka Publishing, 1989.

———. *Sivo and the Cruel Thief*. Limbe, Malawi: Popular Publications, 1989.

———. *Truth Will Out*. Oxford: Macmillan Education, 1986.

Kanengoni, Alexander. *Echoing Silences*. Harare, Zimbabwe: Baobab Books, 1997.

———. *Effortless Tears*. Harare, Zimbabwe: Baobab Books, 1993.

———. *Vicious Circle*. Oxford: Macmillan Education, 1983.

Kangende, Kenneth. *Night Whispers*. Lusaka, Zambia: Minter, 2000.

Kasoma, Godfrey Kabwe. *Black Mamba Two*. In *African Plays for Playing*, ed. Michael Etherton. London: Heinemann, 1976.

Katiyo, Wilson. *A Son of the Soil*. Harlow: Longman, 1976.

Kaunda, Kenneth. *Black Government*. Nairobi: EAPH, 1966.

———. *Dominion Status for Central Africa?* London: Movement for Colonial Freedom, 1963.

———. *Humanism in Zambia and a Guide to its Implementation*. Lusaka, Zambia: Neczam, 1971.

———. *A Humanist in Africa*. London: Longman, 1966.

———. *Kaunda on Violence*. London: Collins, 1980.

———. *Letters to My Children*. London: Longman, 1974.

———. *Zambia Shall Be Free*. London: Heinemann, 1980.

Kayange, George. *Gone for a Walk*. Limbe, Malawi: Popular Publications, 2002.

Kayira, B. M. C. *Tremors of the Jungle*. Cape Town: Kwela Books, 1996.

Kayira, Legson. *The Civil Servant*. London: Longman, 1972.

———. *The Detainee*. London: Heinemann, 1974.

———. *I Will Try*. London: Longman, 1966.

———. *Jingala*. London: Longman, 1969.

———. *The Looming Shadow*. London: Longman, 1968.

Khadani, M. *Quarantine Rhythms*. Aberdeen, Scotland: Palladio Press, 1976.

Leavis, Ronald. *Hippodile*. London: Pan, 1964.

———. *A Voice in Every Wind*. London: Frederick Muller, 1955.

Lessing, Doris. *The Black Madonna*. London: Panther, 1978.

———. *Briefing for a Descent Into Hell*. London: Triad Books, 1973.

———. *The Diaries of Jane Somers*. London: Penguin, 1985.

———. *Ecclesiastes*. London: Canongate Books, 1998.

———. *The Fifth Child*. London: Grafton, 1993.

———. *Five*. London: Panther, 1977.

———. *Four Gated City*. London: Grafton, 1972.

———. *The Golden Notebook*. London: Grafton, 1972.

———. *The Good Terrorist*. London: Grafton, 1986.

———. *A Habit of Loving*. London: Penguin, 1960.

———. *In Pursuit of the English*. London: Granada, 1980.

———. *Landlocked*. London: Collins, 1969.

———. *A Man and Two Women*. London: Panther, 1984.

———. *Martha Quest*. London: Panther, 1973.

———. *Memories of a Survivor*. London: Picador, 1974.

———. *A Proper Marriage*. London: Panther, 1972.

———. *A Ripple from the Storm*. London: Grafton, 1969.

———. *The Sirian Experiments*. London: Grafton, 1984.

———. *The Story of a Non-Marrying Man and Other Stories*. London: Penguin, 1975.

———. *The Summer Before the Dark*. London, Penguin, 1975.

———. *The Winds Blow Away Our Words*. London: Picador, 1987.

———. *Winter in July*. London: Panther, 1974.

Lipenga, Ken, *Waiting for a Turn*. Limbe, Malawi: Popular Publications, 1981.

Lwanda, John Lloyd Chipembere. *The Second Harvest*. Glasgow: Dudu Nsomba Publications, 1994.

———. *Black Thoughts from the Diaspora*. Glasgow: Dudu Nsomba Publications, 1994.

MacArthur, Wilson. *Death at Slack Water*. London: Ward Lock, 1962.

———. *The Desert Watches*. London: Rupert Hart-Davis, 1954.

———. *East India Adventure*. London: Collins, 1946.

———. *The River Windrush*. London: Cassell, 1946.

———. *The Road from Chilanga*. London: Jarrold, 1957.

———. *Simba Bwana*. London: Arrow, 1958.

———. *The Valley of Hidden Gold*. London: Collins, 1962.

———. *Zambezi Adventure*. London: Collins, 1960.

Mackinnon, Clark. *Lost Hyena*. London: Mystery Book Guild, 1962.

Madanhire, Nevanji. *Goatsmell*. Harare, Zimbabwe: Anvil Press, 1992.

——. *If the Wind Blew*. Harare, Zimbabwe: Anvil Press, 1996.

Mahoso, Tafataona. *Footprints About the Bantustan*. Harare, Zimbabwe: Nehanda Publishers, 1989.

Maja-Pearce, Adewale, ed. *The Heinemann Book of African Poetry*. Oxford: Heinemann, 1990.

Makhalisa, Barbara. *The Underdog and Other Stories*. Gweru, Zimbabwe: Mambo Press, 1984.

Mapanje, Jack. *The Chattering Wagtails of Mikuyu Prison*. London: Heinemann, 1993.

——, ed. *Gathering Seaweed: African Prison Writing*. Oxford: Heinemann, 2002.

——. *The Last of the Sweet Bananas*. Highgreen: Bloodaxe Books, 2004.

——. *Of Chameleons and Gods*. London: Heinemann, 1981.

——. *Skipping Without Ropes*. Highgreen: Bloodaxe Books, 1998.

Mapanje, Jack, and Landeg White, eds. *Oral Poetry from Africa*. London: Longman, 1983.

Maraire, Nozipo. *Zenzele: A Letter for My Daughter*. London: Weidenfeld and Nicolson, 1996.

Marechera, Dambudzo. *The Black Insider*. Edited by Flora Veit-Wild. Harare, Zimbabwe: Baobab Books, 1990.

——. *Black Sunlight*. London: Heinemann, 1980.

——. *Cemetery of Mind*. Edited by Flora Veit-Wild. Harare, Zimbabwe: Baobab Books, 1992.

——. *The House of Hunger*. London: Heinemann, 1978.

——. *Mindblast*. Harare, Zimbabwe: College Press, 1984.

——. *Scrapiron Blues*. Edited by Flora Veit-Wild. Harare, Zimbabwe: Baobab Books, 1994.

Masauli, S.E. *My Life & My Aeroplanes*. Blantyre, Malawi: Self-published, n.d.

Masiye, Andreya. *Before Dawn*. Lusaka, Zambia: Neczam, 1971.

——. *The Lands of Kazembe*. Lusaka, Zambia: Neczam, 1973.

——. *Singing for Freedom*. Lusaka, Zambia: Longman, 1977.

Mbikusita-Lewanika, Akanshambatwa. *For the Seeds in Our Blood*. London: Inser, 1981.

McLoughlin, T. O. *Kurima*. Gweru, Zimbabwe: 1985.

——, ed. *New Writing in Rhodesia*. Gweru, Zimbabwe: Mambo Press, 1976.

Mitchley, H. *Poems of the Zambian Bush*. Self-published, n.d.

Miti, Lazarus. *The Father*. Lusaka, Zambia: Kenneth Kaunda Foundation, 1989.

——. *The Prodigal Husband*. Cape Town: Kwela, 1999.

Mnthali, Felix. *When Sunset Comes to Sapitwa*. Lusaka, Zambia: Neczam, 1980.

——. *Yoranivyoto*. Glasgow: Dudu Nsomba Publications, 1998.

Moetsabi, Titus. *Fated Changes*. Harare, Zimbabwe: Africa Community Communications, 1999.

Moore-King, Bruce. *White Man Black War*. London: Penguin, 1989.

Moyana, Tafirenyika T. *Education, Liberation and the Creative Act*. Harare, Zimbabwe: Zimbabwe Publishing House, 1988.

Mpasu, Sam. *Nobody's Friend*. Harare, Zimbabwe: African Publishing Group, 1995.

——. *Political Prisoner 3/75*. Harare, Zimbabwe: African Publishing Group, 1995.

Mphande, Lupenga. *Crackle at Midnight*. Ibadan, Nigeria: Heinemann Educational Books, 1998.

Mphande, Lupenga, and James Ng'ombe, eds. *Namaluzi: Ten Stories from Malawi*. Blantyre, Malawi: Dzuka Publications, 1984.

Mpina, Edison. *Freedom Avenue*. Limbe, Malawi: Popular Publications, 1991.

——. *The Low Road to Death*. Limbe, Malawi: Popular Publications, 1991.

——. *Malawi Poetry Today: A Telephone Conversation with Paul Engle*. Blantyre, Malawi: Hetherwick Press, 1986.

——. *Raw Pieces*. Blantyre, Malawi: Hetherwick Press, 1986.

Mpofu, Stephen. *Shadows on the Horizon*. Harare, Zimbabwe: Zimbabwe Publishing House, 1984.

Msadala, Alfred. *Reminiscence*. Blantyre, Malawi: Acin, 1996.

——. *We Lost Track of Ausi*. Blantyre, Malawi: Acin, 2000.

Msora, Bertha. *I Will Wait*. Harare, Zimbabwe: Zimbabwe Publishing House, 1984.

Muchemwa, Kizito, ed. *Zimbabwean Poetry in English*. Gweru, Zimbabwe: Mambo Press, 1978.

Mufuka, Kenneth. *Matters of Conscience: The Killers of the Dream*. Gweru, Zimbabwe: Mambo Press, 1999.

Mujajati, George. *The Rain of My Blood*. Gweru, Zimbabwe: Mambo Press, 1991.

——. *Victory*. Harare, Zimbabwe: College Press, 1993.

Mukuti, L., ed. *Breakfast of Sjamboks (from Mozambique)*. Harare, Zimbabwe: Zimbabwe Publishing, 1987.

Mulaisho, Dominic. *The Smoke That Thunders*. London: Heinemann, 1979.

——. *The Tongue of the Dumb*. London: Heinemann, 1971.

Mulenga, Luke, Chileshe. *Zambia I Love*. Stockholm, Forfatteres Bokmaskin, 1982.

Mulikita, Fwanyanga M. *A Point of No Return*. London: Macmillan, 1968.

——. *Shaka Zulu*. London: Longman, 1971.

Muluzi, Bakili. *Mau Anga: The Voice of a Democrat*. Johannesburg, South Africa: Skotaville Media, 2002.

Mumba, Norah. *A Song in the Night: A Personal Account of Widowhood in Zambia*. Lusaka, Zambia: Multimedia Publications, 1992.

Mumba, Norah, and Monde Sifuniso, eds. *The Heart of a Woman: Short Stories from Zambia*. Lusaka, Zambia: Zambia Women Writers Association, 1997.

Munatamba, Parnwell, ed. *My Battery*. Lusaka, Zambia: Neczam, 1982.

Mungazi, Dickson, A. *Humba Kumba Goes to School*. Harare, Zimbabwe: Sapes Books, 2002.

Mungoshi, Charles. *Coming of the Dry Season*. Nairobi: Oxford University Press, 1972.

——. *The Milkman Doesn't Only Deliver Milk*. Harare, Zimbabwe: Poetry Society of Zimbabwe, 1981.

——. *The Setting Sun and the Rolling World*. London: Heinemann, 1987.

——. *Some Kinds of Wounds and Other Stories*. Gweru, Zimbabwe: Mambo Press, 1980.

——. *Waiting for the Rain*. London: Heinemann, 1975.

——. *Walking Still*. Harare, Zimbabwe: Baobab Books, 1997.

Mungoshi, David. *Broken Dream and Other Stories*. Gweru, Zimbabwe: Mambo Press, 1987.

——. *Stains on the Wall*. Gweru, Zimbabwe: Mambo Press, 1992.

Muronda, Elfigio. *Echoes of My African Mind*. Harare, Zimbabwe: College Press, 1982.

Musengezi, Chiedza, and Irene Staunton, eds. *A Tragedy of Lives: Women in Prison in Zimbabwe*. Harare, Zimbabwe: Weaver Press, 2003.

Musengezi, H. G. *The Honourable MP.* Gweru, Zimbabwe: Mambo Press, 1984.

Musinga, Victor Eleame. *The Tragedy of Mr No-Balance.* In *African Plays for Playing*, ed. Michael Etherton. London: Heinemann, 1976.

Mutswairo, Solomon. *Chaminuka: Prophet of Zimbabwe.* Washington, D.C.: Three Continents Press, 1983.

———. *Feso.* Washington, D.C.: Three Continents Press, 1974.

Muzorewa, Abel Tendekai. *Rise Up and Walk.* London: Evans Brothers, 1978.

Mvona, Sambalikagwa, ed. *Modern Stories from Malawi.* Blantyre, Malawi: Malawi Writers Union, 2003.

———. *The Special Document.* Blantyre, Malawi: Likhula Publications, 2002.

———. *The Sun at Njuli.* Blantyre, Malawi: Likhula Publications, 2001.

Mvona, Sambalikagwa, and Stewart Lane, eds. *The Trap: An Anthology of Short Stories and Poems by the Malawi Writers Union.* Blantyre, Malawi: Malawi Writers Union, 2001.

Nazombe, Anthony, ed. *The Haunting Wind: New Poetry from Malawi.* Blantyre, Malawi: Dzuka, 1990.

———. *Operations and Tears: A New Anthology of Malawian Poetry.* Zomba, Malawi: Kachere Series, 2004.

Ndhlala, Geoffrey, *The Southern Circle.* Harlow: Longman, 1984.

Ngara, Emmanuel, ed. *Coming Home: Poems of Africa.* Harare, Zimbabwe: Zimbabwe Publishing House, 1989.

———. *Songs from the Temple.* Gweru, Zimbabwe: Mambo Press, 1992.

Ng'ombe, James. *How Pig Got His Snout.* Nairobi: East African Educational Publishers, 1998.

———. *Sugarcane with Salt.* London: Longman, 1989.

Nyamfukudza, Stanley. *If God Was a Woman.* Harare, Zimbabwe: College Press, 1991.

Nyamubaya, Freedom T. *Dusk of Dawn.* Harare, Zimbabwe: College Press, 1995.

———. *On the Road Again.* Harare, Zimbabwe: Zimbabwe Publishing House, 1986.

Phiri, Desmond Dudwa. *The Chief's Bride.* London: Evans Brothers, 1948.

———. *Diniwe in Dreamland.* Blantyre, Malawi: College Publishing Company, 2001.

———. *From Nguni to Ngoni.* Limbe, Malawi: Popular Publications, 1982.

———. *History of Malawi from Earliest Times to the Year 1915.* Blantyre, Malawi: Christian Literature Association in Malawi, 2004.

———. *I See You: Life of Clements Kadalie.* Blantyre, Malawi: College Publishing Company, 2000.

———. *Let Us Die for Africa.* Blantyre, Malawi: Longman, 1976.

———. *Let Us Fight For Africa.* Zomba, Malawi: Kachere Series, 2007.

Phiri, Kingston Lapukeni, ed. *Malawi Writing Today: A PEN Anthology of Recent Writing in Malawi.* Blantyre, Malawi: PEN, 1999.

Phiri, Virginia. *Desperate.* Harare, Zimbabwe: Indaba Enterprises, 2002.

Pongweni, Alec J. C., ed. *Songs That Won the Liberation War.* Harare, Zimbabwe: College Press, 1982.

Rayner, William. *Big Mister.* London: Collins, 1974.

———. *The Bloody Affair at Riverside Drive.* London: Collins, 1972.

———. *The Conversation of Dragons.* London: Collins, 1979.

———. *The Day of Chaminuka.* London: Collins, 1976.

———. *Eating the Big Fish*. London: Collins, 1977.

———. *Great Lion of Bechuanaland: The Life and Times of Roger Price, Missionary*. London: Independent Press, 1957.

———. *Knaves of Swords*. London: Collins, 1980.

———. *The Last Days*. London: Michael Joseph, 1968.

———. *The Reapers*. London: Collins, 1961.

———. *The Tribe and Its Successor: Account of African Traditional Life and European Settlement in Southern Rhodesia*. London: Faber, 1962.

———. *Wheels of Fortune*. London: Collins, 1979.

Rothert-Sarvan, L. *Night Poems and Others*. Lusaka, Zambia: Multimedia Zambia, 1986.

Rungano, Kristina. *A Storm Is Brewing*. Harare, Zimbabwe: Zimbabwe Publishing House, 1984.

Sagonja, Roy. *Heroes Under Fire*. Lilongwe, Malawi: Rosa Publications, 2002.

———. *Night of Terror*. Lilongwe, Malawi: Rosa Publications, 2001.

Saidi, William. *The Old Bricks Lives*. Gweru, Zimbabwe: Mambo Press, 1988.

Samkange, Stanlake. *The Mourned One*. London: Heinemann, 1975.

———. *On Trial for My Country*. London: Heinemann, 1967.

———. *Origins of Rhodesia*. London: Heinemann, 1968.

Samuel, J. M. *I Remember*. Lusaka, Zambia: Neczam, 1972.

Samupindi, Charles. *Pawns*. Harare, Zimbabwe: Baobab Books, 1992.

Schoffeleers, Matthew, and Adrian Roscoe, eds. *Land of Fire: Oral Literature from Malawi*. Limbe, Malawi: Popular Publications, 1985.

Seyaseya, Hopewell, and Albert Chimedza. *Counterpoint*. Harare, Zimbabwe: College Press, 1984.

Shaw, Angus. *Kandaya*. Harare, Zimbabwe: Baobab Books, 1993.

Simoko, Patu. *Africa Is Made of Clay*. Lusaka, Zambia: Neczam, 1975.

Singano, Ellis, and Adrian Roscoe, eds. *Tales of Old Malawi*. Limbe, Malawi: Popular Publications, 1974.

Sinyangwe, Binwell. *A Cowrie of Hope*. Oxford: Heinemann, 2000.

———. *Quills of Desire*. Harare, Zimbabwe: Baobab Books, 1993.

Sinyinza, Friday. *True Love Is Scarce*. Kafue, Zambia: Lome Publications, 2001.

Sithole, Ndabaningi. *African Nationalism*. Cape Town: Oxford University Press, 1959.

———. *Letters from Salisbury Prison*. Nairobi: Transafrica Publishers, 1976.

———. *Obed Mutezo of Zimbabwe*. Nairobi: Oxford University Press, 1970.

———. *The Polygamist*. London: Hodder & Stoughton, 1973.

———. *Roots of a Revolution*. London: Oxford University Press, 1977.

Smith, Wilbur. *The Angels Weep*. London: Pan Macmillan, 1982.

———. *Birds of Prey*. London: Pan Macmillan, 1997.

———. *Blue Horizon*. London: Pan Macmillan, 2003.

———. *The Burning Shore*. London: Pan Macmillan, 1985.

———. *Cry Wolf*. London: Pan Macmillan, 1976.

———. *The Dark of the Sun*. London: Pan Macmillan, 1968.

———. *The Diamond Hunters*. London: Pan Macmillan, 1973.

———. *Eagle in the Sky*. London: Pan Macmillan, 1975.

———. *Elephant Song*. London: Pan Macmillan, 1992.

———. *The Eye of the Tiger*. London: Pan Macmillan, 1976.

———. *A Falcon Flies*. London: Pan Macmillan, 1980.

———. *Gold Mine*. London: Pan Macmillan, 1972.

———. *Golden Fox*. London: Pan Macmillan, 1990.

———. *Hungry as the Sea*. London: Pan Macmillan, 1978.

———. *The Leopard Hunts in Darkness*. London: Pan Macmillan, 1984.

———. *Monsoon*. London: Pan Macmillan, 1999.

———. *Power of the Sword*. London: Pan Macmillan, 1986.

———. *Rage*. London: Pan Macmillan, 1988.

———. *River God*. London: Pan Macmillan, 1993.

———. *The Seventh Scroll*. London: Pan Macmillan, 1995.

———. *Shout at the Devil*. London: Pan Macmillan, 1968.

———. *The Sunbird*. London: Pan Macmillan, 1974.

———. *A Time to Die*. London: Pan Macmillan, 1990.

———. *Triumph of the Sun*. London: Pan Macmillan, 2004.

———. *Warlock*. London: Pan Macmillan, 2001.

———. *When the Lion Feeds*. London: Pan Macmillan, 1964.

———. *Wild Justice*. London: Pan Macmillan, 1979.

Staunton, Irene, ed. *Writing Still: New Stories from Zimbabwe*. Harare, Zimbabwe: Weaver Press, 2003.

Stiff, Peter. *Covert War*. Johannesburg: Galago, 2000.

———. *Cry Zimbabwe: Independence Twenty Years On*. Johannesburg: Galago, 1982.

———. *The Road to Armageddon*. Johannesburg: Galago, 1980.

———. *The Rain Goddess*. Johannesburg: Galago, 2004.

———. *Tommy Goes Home*. Harare, Zimbabwe: Jacaranda Press, 1977.

Style, Colin. *Musical Law*. Harare, Zimbabwe: Poetry Society of Zimbabwe, 1981.

Style, Colin, and Olan Style, eds. *The Mambo Book of Zimbabwean Poetry in English*. Gweru, Zimbabwe: Mambo Press, 1986.

Tembo, L. *Poems*. Lusaka, Zambia: Neczam, 1972.

Tizora, S. S. M. *Crossroads*. Gweru, Zimbabwe: Mambo Press, 1985.

Udensi, Uwa. *Monkey on the Tree*. In *African Plays for Playing*, ed. Michael Etherton. London: Heinemann, 1976.

University of Malawi Writers Group. *Mau: Thirty-Nine Poems from Malawi*. Blantyre, Malawi: Hetherwick Press, 1971.

Vambe, Lawrence. *From Rhodesia to Zimbabwe*. London: Heinemann, 1976.

———. *An Ill-Fated People: Zimbabwe Before and After Rhodes*. London: Heinemann, 1972.

Vera, Yvonne. *Butterfly Burning*. Harare, Zimbabwe: Baobab Books, 1998.

———, ed. *The Heinemann Book of Contemporary African Women's Writing*. Oxford: Heinemann, 1999.

———. *Nehanda*. Harare, Zimbabwe: Baobab Books, 1993.

———. *The Stone Virgins*. Harare, Zimbabwe: Weaver Press, 2002.

———. *Under the Tongue*. Harare, Zimbabwe: Baobab Books, 1996.

———. *Why Don't You Carve Other Animals*. Harare, Zimbabwe: Baobab Books, 1994.

———. *Without a Name*. Harare, Zimbabwe: Baobab Books, 1994.

Vyas, C. L. *The Falls and Other Poems*. Lusaka, Zambia: Zambia Cultural Services, 1973.

Wa Kabika, Lyamba and Chenjerai Hove. *Swimming in Floods of Tears*. Gweru, Zimbabwe: Mambo Press, 1983.

Wilson, Merna. *Explosion*. London: Robert Hale, 1966.

——. *Turn the Tide Gently*. London: Robert Hale, 1967.

Zanji, Brian. *Stories from Zambia*. Lusaka, Zambia: H. Grant Publishing, 2000.

Zeleza, Tiyambe. *Night of Darkness and Other Stories*. Limbe, Malawi: Popular Publications, 1976.

——. *Smouldering Charcoal*. Oxford: Heinemann, 1992.

Zimunya, Musaemura, ed. *Birthright*. London: Longman, 1990.

——. *Country Dawns and City Lights*. Harare, Zimbabwe: Longman Zimbabwe, 1985.

——, ed. *The Fate of Vultures*. London: Heinemann, 1989.

——. *Kingfisher, Jikinya and Other Poems*. Harare, Zimbabwe: Longman Zimbabwe, 1982.

——. *Thought Tracks*. London: Longman, 1982.

——. *Zimbabwe Ruins*. Harare, Zimbabwe: Poetry Society of Zimbabwe, 1979.

Zimunya, Musaemura, and Mudereri Kadhani, eds. *And Now the Poets Speak*. Gweru, Zimbabwe: Mambo Press, 1981.

Zulu, Hannelie. *Negotiating Blood*. Borre, Denmark: Zulu Publications, 2002.

——. *Malawi Okongola*. Borre, Denmark: Zulu Publications, 2000.

——. *Nomeon*. Borre, Denmark: Zulu Publications, 2001.

Zulu, Patrick C. *A Sheaf of Gold*. Lusaka, Zambia: Unity Press, 1971.

Secondary Sources

Benson, Eugene, and L. W. Connolly, eds. *Encyclopaedia of Post-Colonial Literatures in English*, 2nd ed. London and New York: Routledge, 2005.

Bone, David S., ed. *Malawi's Muslims: Historical Perspectives*. Zomba, Malawi: Kachere Series, 2000.

Booth, Joseph. *Africa for the African*. Edited by Laura Perry. Blantyre, Malawi: Christian Literature Association in Malawi, 1996.

Brockway, Fenner. *The Colonial Revolution*. London: Hart-Davis MacGibbon, 1973.

Brown, Judith M., and Wm. Roger Louis, eds. *The Oxford History of the British Empire*. Vol. 4, *The Twentieth Century*. Oxford: Oxford University Press, 1999.

Canny, Nicholas, ed. *The Oxford History of the British Empire*. Vol. 1, *The Origins of Empire: British Overseas Enterprise to the Close of the Seventeenth Century*. Oxford: Oxford University Press, 1998.

Chakanza, J. C. *Voices of Preachers in Protest: The Ministry of Two Malawian Prophets: Elliot Kamwana and Wilfred Gudu*. Blantyre, Malawi: Christian Literature Association in Malawi, 1998.

——. *Wisdom of the People: 2000 Chinyanja Proverbs*. Blantyre, Malawi: Christian Literature Association in Malawi, 2000.

Chennells, Anthony. "Settler Myths and the Southern Rhodesian Novel." PhD dissertation, University of Zimbabwe, 1982.

Chennells, Anthony, and Flora Veit-Wild, eds. *Emerging Perspectives on Dambudzo Marechera*. Asmara, Eritrea: Africa World Press, 1999.

Chimombo, Steve. *A Guide to Malawi's Literature*. Zomba, Malawi: Manchichi, 1996.

——. *Malawian Oral Literature*. Zomba, Malawi: Centre for Social Research, University of Malawi, 1988.

Chimombo, Steve, and Moira Chimombo. *The Culture of Democracy: Language, Literature, the Arts and Politics in Malawi, 1992–1994.* Zomba, Malawi: WASI, 1996.

Chipanyula, Eunice Nihero. *Political Reporting Trends in Malawi: 1980s and 1990s.* Makwasa, Malawi: Malamulo Publishing House, 2003.

Chiwome, E. M. *A Critical History of Shona Poetry.* Harare, Zimbabwe: Juta Zimbabwe, 1996.

———. *A Social History of the Shona Novel.* Harare, Zimbabwe: Juta Zimbabwe, 1996.

Conroy, Anne C., Malcolm J. Blackie, Alan Whiteside, Justin C. Malewezi, and Jeffrey D. Sachs, eds. *Poverty, AIDS and Hunger: Breaking the Poverty Trap in Malawi.* Basingstoke: Palgrave Macmillan, 2006.

Disch, Robert, ed. *The Future of Literacy.* Englewood Cliffs, N.J.: Prentice-Hall, 1973.

Etherton, Michael. *The Development of African Theatre.* London: Hutchinson, 1982.

Fanon, Frantz. *Black Skin White Mask.* London: Paladin Press, 1970.

———. *A Dying Colonialism.* New York: Grove Press, 1959.

———. *Toward the African Revolution.* New York: Grove Press, 1964.

———. *The Wretched of the Earth.* New York: Grove Press, 1968.

Ferguson, Niall. *Empire: How Britain Made the Modern World.* London: Penguin, 2004.

Findlay, Victoria. "Zambian Theatre and the Direction It Has Taken Since Independence." MA thesis, University of Zambia, 1987.

Freire, Paolo, and Ira Shor. *Pedagogy of the Oppressed.* London: Penguin, 1972.

Gaidzanwa, Rudo. *Images of Women in Zimbabwean Literature.* Harare, Zimbabwe: College Press, 1985.

Gerard, Albert. *African Language Literatures: An Introduction to the Literary History of Sub-Saharan Africa.* Harlow: Longman, 1981.

Gibbs, James. *A Handbook for African Writers.* Oxford: Hans Zell. 1986.

Gibbs, Patience. "Drama and Theatre in Malawi: A Study of Their Development and Direction." MA thesis, University of Malawi, 1979.

Goodwin, K. L. *Understanding African Poetry.* London: Heinemann, 1982.

Goody, Jack. *The Power of the Written Tradition.* Washington, D.C.: Smithsonian Institution Press, 2000.

Hodza, A. A., and G. Fortune. *Shona Praise Poetry.* Oxford: Oxford University Press, 1972.

Human Rights Watch. *Where Silence Rules: The Suppression of Dissent in Malawi.* New York: HRW, 1990.

Immink, Bado, Samson Lembani, and Martin Ott, eds. *From Freedom to Empowerment: Ten Years of Democratisation in Malawi.* Blantyre, Malawi: Forum for Dialogue and Peace and Konrad Adenauer Foundation, 2003.

Joffe, Selby. "Political Culture and Communication in Malawi: The Hortatory Regime of Kamuzu Banda." PhD dissertation, University of Boston, 1973.

Joyce, Peter. *Anatomy of a Rebel: Smith of Rhodesia.* Salisbury, Rhodesia: Graham, 1974.

Kahari, George. *The Imaginative Writings of Paul Chidyausiku.* Gweru, Zimbabwe: Mambo Press, 1978.

———. *The Novels of Patrick Chakaipa.* Salisbury: Longman, 1972.

———. *Plots and Character in Shona Fiction.* Gweru, Zimbabwe: Mambo Press, 1990.

———. *The Rise of the Shona Novel.* Gweru, Zimbabwe: Mambo Press, 1990.

———. *The Search for a Zimbabwean Identity*. Gweru, Zimbabwe: Mambo Press, 1980.

Kalaluka, L. *Kuomboka*. Lusaka, Zambia: Neczam, 1979.

Kamlongera, Christopher. *Theatre for Development*. Bonn: ZED, 1989.

Kandeke, Timothy, K. *Principles of Zambian Humanism*. Lusaka, Zambia: Neczam, 1977.

Katz, Elihu, and George Wedell, eds. *Broadcasting in the Third World: Promises and Performances*. London: Macmillan, 1977.

Kerr, David. *African Popular Theatre*. London: James Currey, 1995.

———. *Dance, Media Entertainment and Popular Theatre in South East Africa*. Bayreuth: Bayreuth University, 1998.

Killam, G. D., ed. *The Writing of East and Central Africa*. London: Heinemann, 1984.

Killam, G. D., and Ruth Rowe, eds. *The Companion to African Literatures*. Oxford and Bloomington: James Currey and Indiana University Press, 2000.

King, M., and E. King. *The Great Rift: Africa Surgery Aids Aid*. Cambridge: Arco Books, 2000.

Kotei, S. I. A. *The Book Today in Africa*. Paris: UNESCO, 1981.

Kroger, E. W., ed. *African Literature in Rhodesia*. Gweru, Zimbabwe: Mambo Press, 1966.

Legum, Colin, ed. *Zambia: Independence and Beyond*. London: Nelson, 1966.

Linden, Ian, and Jane Linden. *Catholics, Peasants, and Chewa Resistance in Nyasaland, 1899–1939*. London: Longman, 1974.

Lindfors, Bernth. *Kulankulu: Interviews with Writers from Malawi and Lesotho*. Bayreuth: Bayreuth University, 1989.

Lwanda, John L. *Kamuzu Banda of Malawi: A Study in Promise, Power and Paralysis*. Glasgow: Dudu Nsomba Publications, 1993.

———. *Politics, Culture, and Medicine in Malawi*. Zomba, Malawi: Kachere, 2005.

———. *Promises, Power, Politics and Poverty: Democratic Transition in Malawi, 1961–1994*. Glasgow: Dudu Nsoma Publications, 1996.

MacPherson, Fergus. *Kenneth Kaunda of Zambia: The Times and the Man*. Lusaka, Zambia: Oxford University Press, 1974.

Manda, Mtafu A. Z. *The State and Labour in Malawi*. Glasgow: Dudu Nsomba Publications, 2000.

Mangochi-Mbewe, M. V., and S. Made. *100 Years of Chichewa in Writing: 1875–1975*. Zomba, Malawi: University of Malawi, 1976.

Marshall, P. J., ed. *The Oxford History of the British Empire*. Vol. 2, *The Eighteenth Century*. Oxford: Oxford University Press, 1999.

McCracken, John. *Politics and Christianity in Malawi, 1875–1940: The Impact of the Livingstonia Mission in the Northern Province*. Cambridge: Cambridge University Press, 1977.

McIntosh, Hamish. *Robert Laws: Servant of Africa*. Carberry, Scotland: Handsel Press, 1993.

McLoughlin, T. O. *New Writing in Rhodesia*. Gweru, Zimbabwe: Mambo, 1976.

McLoughlin, T. O., and F. R. Mhonyera. *Insights: Criticism of Zimbabwean and Other Poetry*. Gweru, Zimbabwe: Mambo Press, 1984.

Mgawi, K. J. *Tracing the Footsteps of Dr. Hastings Banda*. Blantyre, Malawi: Dzuka Publications, 2005.

Mkamanga, Emily. *Suffering in Silence: Malawi Women's 30 Year Dance with Dr Banda*. Glasgow: Dudu Nsomba Publications, 2000.

Mkandawire, Austin C. *Living My Destiny: A Medical and Historical Narrative*. Glasgow: Dudu Nsomba Publications, 1998.

———. *Yuraia Chatonda Chirwa: The Faithful Servant*. Glasgow: Dudu Nsomba Publications, 2003.

Mkandawire, Thandika, ed. *African Intellectuals: Rethinking Politics, Language, Gender and Development*. London: Zed Books, 2005.

Moto, Francis. *Trends in Malawian Literature*. Zomba, Malawi: Chancellor College Publications, 2001.

Msadala, Alfred. *Destined for Great Things*. Blantyre, Malawi: Acin, 1999.

———. *One, Steve Chimombo*. Blantyre, Malawi: Acin, 1996.

———. *Reminiscence*. Blantyre, Malawi: Acin, 1996.

Mtshali, Vulindlela. *Rhodesia: Background to Conflict*. London: Leslie Frewen, 1968.

Muponde, Robert, and Mandi Taruvinga, eds. *Perspectives on the Poetic Fiction of Yvonne Vera*. Harare, Zimbabwe: Weaver Press, 2003.

Musengezi, Chiedza, and Irene Staunton, eds. *A Tragedy of Lives: Women in Prison in Zimbabwe*. Harare, Zimbabwe: Weaver Press, 2003.

Mwansa, Dickson, ed. *Zambian Performing Arts: Current Issues, Policies and Directions*. Lusaka: Centre for Continuing Education, University of Zambia, 1984.

Mwanza, A. M., ed. *The Structural Adjustment Programme in Zambia: Lessons from Experience*. Harare, Zimbabwe: SAPES Books, 1992.

Mwase, George Simeon. *Strike a Blow and Die: A Narrative of Race Relations in Colonial Africa*. London: Heinemann, 1975.

Ndlovu, M. "The Influence of Folktales and Other Factors on the Early Narratives in Ndebele." MPhil thesis, University of Zimbabwe, 1994.

Ngara, Arthur. *Art and Ideology in the African Novel*. London: Heinemann, 1985.

———. *Ideology and Form in African Poetry*. London: James Currey, 1990.

———, ed. *New Writing from Southern Africa*. Harare, Zimbabwe: Baobab Books, 1996.

———. *Stylistic Criticism and the African Novel*. London: Heinemann, 1982.

———. *Teaching Literature in Africa*. Harare, Zimbabwe: Zimbabwe Publishing House, 1984.

Ngara, Arthur, and Anne Morrison, eds. *Literature, Language and the Nation*. Harare, Zimbabwe: Baobab Books, 1989.

Nkabinde, Themba. "Ndebele Modern Poetry: Characteristics and Development." MPhil thesis, University of Zimbabwe, 1990.

Nkomo, Joshua. *The Story of My Life*. London: Methuen, 1984.

Oliver, Roland. *Sir Harry Johnston and the Scramble for Africa*. London: Chatto & Windus, 1957.

Olson, David R. *The World on Paper: The Conceptual and Cognitive Implications of Writing and Reading*. Cambridge: Cambridge University Press, 1994.

Ó Máille, Pádraig. *Living Dangerously*. Glasgow: Dudu Nsomba Publications, 1996.

Ong, Walter, J. *Orality and Literacy: The Technologizing of the Word*. London: Methuen, 1982.

Pakenham, Thomas. *The Scramble for Africa, 1876–1912*. London: Weidenfeld and Nicolson, 1991.

Pichanik, J., and Anthony Chennells, eds. *Rhodesian Literature in English: A Bibliography (1890–1974/75)*. Gweru, Zimbabwe: Mambo Press, 1977.

Plumbe, Wilfred J. *Cry of the Fish Eagle*. Glasgow: Dudu Nsomba Publications, 1997.

Porter, Andrew, ed. *The Oxford History of the British Empire*. Vol. 3, *The Nineteenth Century*. Oxford: Oxford University Press, 1999.

Rafael, B. R. *A Short History of Malawi*. Limbe, Malawi: Popular Publications, 1980.

Ranger, Terence O. *Revolt in Southern Rhodesia, 1896–97: A Study in African Resistance*. Evanston, Ill.: Northwestern University Press, 1967.

Roscoe, Adrian. *Uhuru's Fire: African Literature East to South*. London: Cambridge University Press, 1988.

Roscoe, Adrian, and Mpaliwe-Hangson Msiska. *The Quiet Chameleon: Modern Poetry from Central Africa*. London: Hans Zell, 1992.

Rotberg, Robert I. *The Rise of Nationalism in Central Africa: The Making of Malawi and Zambia*. Cambridge, Mass.: Harvard University Press, 1965.

Ryan, James R. *Picturing Empire: Photography and the Visualization of the British Empire*. London: Reaktion Books, 1997.

Schoffeleers, Matthew, ed. *Guardians of the Land: Essays on Central African Territorial Cults*. Gweru, Zimbabwe: Mambo Press, 1979.

Shepperson, George, and Thomas Price. *Independent African: John Chilembwe and the Nyasaland Rising of 1915*. Blantyre, Malawi: Christian Literature Association in Malawi, 2000.

Smith, Angela. *East African Writing in English*. London: Macmillan, 1989.

Snelson, Peter. *To Independence and Beyond*. London: I. B. Tauris, 1993.

Soko, Boston. *Nchimi Chikanga: The Battle Against Witchcraft in Malawi*. Blantyre, Malawi: Christian Literature Association in Malawi, 2002.

Staunton, Irene, ed. *Mothers of the Revolution*. Harare, Zimbabwe: Baobab, 1990.

Thiong'o, Ngugi wa. *Decolonising the Mind: The Politics of Language in African Literature*. London: Heinemann, 1986.

Vaughan, Megan. *Curing Their Ills: Colonial Power and African Illness*. Oxford: Blackwell, 1991.

Veit-Wild, Flora. *Dambudzo Marechera: 1952–1987*. Harare, Zimbabwe: Baobab Books, 1988.

———. *Dambudzo Marechera: A Source Book on His Life and Work*. Harare: University of Zimbabwe Publications, 1993.

———. *Patterns of Poetry in Zimbabwe*. Gweru, Zimbabwe: Mambo Press, 1988.

———. *Teachers, Preachers, Non-Believers: A Social History of Zimbabwean Literature*. Harare, Zimbabwe: Baobab Books, 1992.

White, Landeg. *Magomero: Portrait of an African Village*. Cambridge: Cambridge University Press, 1987.

Wilkinson, Jane. *Talking with African Writers*. London: James Currey, 1992.

Willey, Ann, and Jeanette Treiber, eds. *Emerging Perspectives on Tsitsi Dangarembga: Negotiating the Postcolonial*. Trenton: Africa World Press, 2002.

Williams, Judy, and John Williams, eds. *Our Future, Our Choice*. Blantyre, Malawi: Society of Malawi, 2006.

Winks, Robin W., ed. *The Oxford History of the British Empire*. Vol. 5, *Historiography*. Oxford: Oxford University Press, 1999.

Zhuwarara, Rino. *Introduction to Zimbabwean Literature in English*. Harare, Zimbabwe: College Press, 2001.

Zimunya, Musaemura. *Those Years of Drought and Hunger.* Gweru, Zimbabwe: Mambo Press, 1982.

Zinyemba, Ranga. *Zimbabwean Drama: A Study of Shona and English Plays.* Gweru, Zimbabwe: Mambo Press, 1986.

Index